Never a Dull Moment

Never a Dull Moment
The Ramblings of a Soldier and Sportsman

Ian Vaughan-Arbuckle

Copyright Ian Vaughan-Arbuckle © 2012
Produced in association with

www.wordsbydesign.co.uk

ISBN: 978-1-909075-06-1 (casebound)
ISBN: 978-1-909075-08-5 (paperback)

Cover photograph: Russell, New Zealand,
by the author.

Printed and bound in Great Britain by
Marston Book Services Limited, Didcot

The right of Ian Vaughan-Arbuckle to be identified as the Author of this Work has been asserted by him in accordance with the Copyright, Designs and Patents Act 1988.

All rights reserved. No part of this publication may be reproduced, stored in a retrieval system, or transmitted, in any form or by any means, electronic, mechanical, photocopying, recording or otherwise, without the prior permission of the publisher or a license permitting restricted copying.
In the UK such licenses are issued by the Copyright Licensing Agency, 90 Tottenham Court Road, London W1P 9HE.

The Author

Contents

Preface		ix
Prologue		1
1	The Early Years	5
2	What's in a Name?	33
3	Humble Beginnings	65
4	The End of a Name	91
5	First Appointment	121
6	West Germany – The Cold War	133
7	Back to School – Face of the Army	149
8	Colony in Conflict – Hong Kong	155
9	Mid-Career Posts	169
10	Sporting Memories	183
11	NATO's Fragile Flank – Turkey	221
12	Command within the Territorial Army	235
13	Falklands Aftermath	255
14	Out of Uniform	271
15	Travel – India, Pakistan and Nepal	281
16	An Invitation from the Secret Intelligence Service	319
17	Travel – Tigers, New Zealand, Yemen and China	331
18	Family Matters	351
Epilogue		363
Glossary		367
Timeline		369

Preface

This book, privately produced, records the findings of forty or so years' research into my ancestors and chronicles my personal memories. The book celebrates the memory of my parents, the blessing of my daughters Vivian, Juliet and Claire, the joy of my grandchildren Hugo, Megan, Ollie, Alec, Theo, Tom and Emily, and the love of Angelika and Lynn.

I believe that everyone, whatever their calling or standing, has a story to tell. I have always said that it was my intention to record my life not for any personal glorification, but rather to ensure that my family know from whence they came. It has always been a regret of mine that I did not talk to my father about his life. To have done so would have certainly given me a greater understanding of him, my mother and my grandparents. Perhaps he did not know as much as I have been able to glean and was embarrassed to admit as much.

I have been moved by what I have discovered during my journey towards recording this family history and telling my own story. By anyone's standard, we have an interesting and varied story to tell. From success, to real wealth, to barely making ends meet, family feuds, from position to personal tragedy, through adventure and military service, the Vaughan-Arbuckles have experienced the full range of human emotions and experience.

How true is this story? As true as I could make it is the answer. I have not kept a diary but I have gathered a collection of articles, notes and other material over the years, and I have used these extensively as an aid to writing this book. For matters of indisputable fact, I have relied upon Internet sources, without which I would have struggled for dates and other minutiae. The rest is based on my long-term memory which, unlike my short-term recall, remains surprisingly good!

The approach of my 75th birthday seemed as good a time as any to commit to paper my memories and thoughts. Suddenly life looked finite, I have reached and gone beyond threescore years and ten; although I remain reasonably fit, that fleshy flange that rides above my trouser belt is a permanent reminder of advancing years; I have some time on my hands and, most importantly, now is as good a time as any to panic! To have left the project any longer might have been to tempt providence!

Finally, I would like to thank those who have encouraged me in the writing of this book. They include my family, my partner Lynn, who has had to put up with long periods when I did little else than sit at my desk drafting and researching, and others who have helped me in this huge undertaking.

I am particularly grateful to Tony Gray at WORDS BY DESIGN for his encouragement, advice and unfailing support during the three years of this project. Quite simply, without him, there would have been no book.

Island View
Langton Matravers
Dorset

December 2012

Prologue

There was a loud bang as the VC10 aircraft swerved from side to side down the runway and onto the grass verge. "Front tyre blown," said the pilot, an Aussie on loan to the RAF, as he wrestled with the aircraft before bringing it safely to a standstill. I had been invited onto the flight deck by the navigator, after being introduced to him by an RAF friend before we left the UK. It was 1983 and I was on a flight from RAF Brize Norton to Ascension Island on the first 'leg' of an 8,000-mile journey to the Falkland Islands to take up my appointment as commanding officer of the logistic battalion. It was a sunny day as the airport emergency services at Dakar, Senegal, made their way to the stricken aircraft. After the aircraft had been recovered to a remote part of the airfield, we spent the next two hours, while the tyre was changed and the airframe checked for damage, sitting next to a monsoon drain with a couple of Senegalese armed guards for company. The reason for this singular lack of hospitality was, apparently, due to the bilateral agreement entered into with Senegal which allowed RAF flights to land and refuel provided there was no overt support of British service personnel.

RAF VC10

| Never a Dull Moment

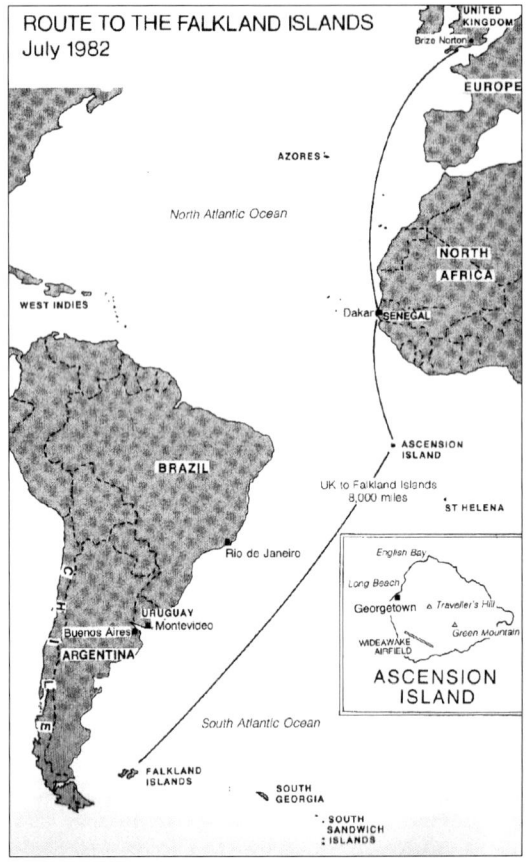
Route to the Falkland Islands

Grateful to be back on board, we flew the second part to Ascension without further incident. Ascension Island, about the size of the Isle of Wight, is a piece of volcanic rock in the middle of the South Atlantic administered by the Foreign Office. It has no indigenous population but at that time was 'home' to around 1,000 mostly expatriates employed mainly in support of British interests. Expecting to fly down to the Falklands by C130 Hercules aircraft the following day, I was informed that I would instead be going by sea, leaving in two days. 'Typical RAF,' I thought, as I made myself as comfortable as possible in the primitive canvas transit passenger hanger. Wherever the whine and roar of jets and helicopters is to be heard, an aroma of kerosene will be present: Wideawake airfield was no different. With little or no sleep that night, due to the constant noise generated by a crowded and overworked military airfield, I decided that the only thing to do was to get away from it all. This I did by walking up and around Green Mountain (859 metres), which dominates the entire island. From this green, lush and cool vantage point I spent a pleasant few hours admiring the stunning views, marvelling at the variety of vegetation and with an iridescent green lizard for company.

"It's too dangerous for the helicopter to land so you will have to abseil onto the deck," explained the young RAF NCO who arranged us into 'sticks' for the short flight to the *MV Norland*, which would take us to the Falkland Islands. Safely aboard, after a hair-raising landing onto

| 2 |

the deck of the violently pitching vessel, I settled into my cabin which was to be home for the next 13 days. And what a 13 days they turned out to be! Being by design a flat-bottomed North Sea ferry, the *Norland*, provided little respite from a raging South Atlantic storm. Night and day we seemed to pitch and roll our way south, the only company being an albatross which stayed with us for days, feeding on the scraps from our kitchens, so it was a great relief when we sighted land for the first time. Dropping anchor in the natural harbour of Stanley and being able to identify the Cathedral and the peaks of Tumbledown and Mount Kent, where fierce fighting had taken place not long before, was a thrill. As I boarded the landing craft for the short journey from ship to shore, I thought, 'No more exercises; at long last, this is the real thing.'

The arrival briefing started with the announcement that we were now in an operational zone, we would carry weapons at all times, and that alcohol would be limited to two cans of beer a week; cue audible groan from most in the audience! It was then a short journey to the headquarters of the Falkland Islands Logistic Battalion (FILOG), where I

MV Norland *anchored off the Falklands*

had a chat with my predecessor, who would be flying out later that day, before meeting other key members of the unit of which I was to take command. The next day, I was given a tour around my 'parish'. My abiding memory, as I travelled around in a captured Argentinian Mercedes 'Jeep', is of men wrapped up in green parkas against a bitter wind, going about their work, invariably in deep mud and harsh working conditions. But the unrivalled sense of humour of the British soldier, for which they are well-known, shone through during a long day of meeting people and being told about the roles they performed. I was left under no illusion that the next six months would be both extremely busy and yet immensely rewarding: a real challenge.

1: THE EARLY YEARS

Failure is the doorstep of success – Anon

It was in the early hours of 16th February 1938 that Dodo (Doreen) Vaughan-Arbuckle (née Chevers) gave birth to an underweight baby boy in the maternity wing of the Military Hospital, Abbassia, Cairo, after an extremely difficult labour which threatened the life of both mother and baby. The baby's father, Hector Vaughan-Arbuckle, was 31 and a Captain serving with 66 Company RASC (Royal Army Service Corps). Of course, I am merely quoting what my mother told me and from my birth certificate. I was christened into the Roman Catholic Church, my mother being Irish and a staunch Catholic, a few weeks later. My mother's problems giving birth were caused when she contracted diphtheria some weeks before giving birth. Diphtheria is a highly contagious, life-threatening illness of the upper respiratory tract. Small wonder, therefore that, throughout my life, I have suffered from upper respiratory infections. After years of problems it wasn't until I was in my mid-twenties that my tonsils were eventually removed during a not altogether straightforward time spent in hospital; more of that later. My mother's anxiety as her confinement approached is illustrated by the letter she wrote to her brother-in-law Tom Sutherland (shown overleaf).

I remember nothing of my time in Egypt, although I have since been back in an unsuccessful attempt to find the church where I was baptised. It was a garrison church located inside the barracks in Abbassia Garrison, Cairo, where my father worked. Once I was old enough and my mother fit enough to travel, with war threatened, we returned to the UK. Quite where we went I'm not sure, but it must have been somewhere near my maternal grandmother, Marguerite (known by all as Mater), who lived in a house named Pondtail Lodge, in Fleet. I know this as I remember visiting her there in the war years (1939-45). I recall her as a kindly, wizened old lady with fuzzy hair.

> 12 Sharia Pasteur.
> Heliopolis
> Jan 22nd
>
> My darling Tom,
>
> This is just a wee note to tell you that Bobby (sorry Kathleen!) arrived yesterday, it was a great surprise for us both as we didn't expect her till tomo today. She's looking terribly well I think, & in great form. Tom, it's grand having her here with me, & I can't thank you enough for letting her come, I'm sure you must be missing her terribly - I think it was very sweet of you, & Hector & I appreciate it more than I can tell you. I was feeling terribly nervous about the whole thing, but now that Bobby is here, it makes all the difference, & I don't mind half so much. Of course it is rather trying waiting but I hope it won't be for very much longer.
>
> I have no news of interest to give you so will close now.
>
> Tons of love & kisses
>
> from Dodo

Marguerite was formerly married to Charles Ashby-Pritt, a Cotton Factor (commission merchant) from Leamington Spa who died in India. She then married my grandfather, Bertram (Bertie) Vaughan-Arbuckle, who died 22nd April 1920, with whom she had two sons, my father and his younger brother Keith. Bertram was a Captain in The Royal Scots (1st Foot) before retiring to become head of the munitions factory at St Helens and Dagenham at various times. Both my paternal grandparents are buried together at St Mary's Church, Cold Ash, near Newbury.

Once my father had gone off to war, my mother joined the Auxiliary Service as a driver at, I think, RAF Farnborough. We shared a house in the Fleet area with my godmother Meg Watson, who had a daughter Anne (known as Fanny) and twin boys Robert and John.

Father and mother holding me

With my mother and grandmother about 1939

Robert Watson, me (sitting) and Anne Watson in 1943

Robert Watson (Junior) was to command The Royal Scots and to retire from the Army as a Colonel; I never met him. My godfather Robert Watson committed suicide, I believe, because of the dishonour he felt, as an officer, after failing to jump during parachute training. My godmother subsequently married Sandy Giles in 1953, who was knighted for his work in the Colonial Service after steering Lesotho to independence. After my father died, Meg Giles got in touch and we corresponded intermittently.

My father always told me that my godfather had made financial provision for me in his Will but I never got the money. What I did get, however, was an oil painting of two sailing boats which my father had 'liberated' from a house as the 8th Army made its way through Tripoli and which he had given to Meg Giles. She gave me the painting not long before she died which, at the time of writing, is in Rose Cottage.

But back to Fleet: the house we lived in was large with a detached garage, converted into a playroom for us children, protected by sandbags around the windows. We had a nanny to look after us while our mothers went out to work. From time to time, if the weather was nice, the nanny used to take us into the garden to play. This is what we were doing one day when a plane flew low over the house. I remember waving to the pilot and was excited to see the plane turn and come back towards us. As the plane approached at low level there was a 'rat-tat, tat' followed instantaneously by spurts of dirt flying around me, prompting the nanny to swoop me up and carry me back into the garage. She was not amused, neither was my mother, when she learnt that it was a German fighter that had fired upon us. I remember little else of this time apart from my mother making me sit at the table until I had finished every scrap of fat on my plate and had drunk every last drop of hot milk, skin and all. I hated both with a vengeance at the time and have never since been able to face fat or the smell of hot milk.

The next memory I have is of living in a house very near the sea, which I now know to be at Seaton Sluice, Northumberland. It was late 1943. My father had returned to the UK from Europe and was commanding 165 Infantry Brigade Company RASC (9th Armoured Division with its famous Panda sign) preparing to take part in the D Day Landings on 6th June 1944. The 9th Armoured Division was commanded at the time by Major-General Brian Horrocks, who was later to be knighted and rise to the rank of Lieutenant-General. My father's unit was equipped with DUWKs (popularly pronounced 'duck'), six-wheel drive amphibious vehicles that were designed for transporting goods and troops over land and water for approaching and crossing beaches in amphibious operations. I remember being fascinated watching these vehicles 'swimming' in the bay, loaded with fully-armed soldiers. The whole area was 'awash' with vehicles and soldiers as they practised drills for the invasion of Europe. This was my first encounter with the American GI who, I very soon discovered, had chewing gum they were often prepared to give to children. I honed the phrase 'Got any gum, chum?' which I used to best advantage, much to my mother's embarrassment. Quite where we were when the war ended on 8th May 1945 I'm not sure. At that time my father was serving with 55th (West Lancashire) Infantry Division, in the UK.

My next vivid memory was travelling on a boat, for what seemed an eternity but was actually only 18 days, bound for India. My father was already there. We stopped briefly at Port Said where I remember being mesmerised by the 'Gully-Gully' man who kept producing small live chicks from all over his body. I also recall an incident when a woman dropped her baby when leaning over the ship's handrails. The upset this caused was apparent to me even at that age. The ship was brought to a standstill and the baby recovered, still alive, when a shoal of porpoises was spotted playing with something. My mother always said this was as close to a miracle as one would ever be likely to witness. I think we were on board the *Monarch of Bermuda* (20,000 tons), which was going all the way to Australia. It was October 1945 when we disembarked in Bombay. Looking out of the hotel window one evening, I saw chickens having their throats cut and being thrown, still alive and flapping, into a tub of water. The water was red with blood, and seeing death for the first time upset me greatly. I never told my mother about this.

As will become clear, India has a very special place in my heart. Despite its myriad shortcomings, I love the sights, smells and sounds of India. Early in the morning it was the pigeons cooing, then the pye-dogs barking and the large black crows cawing. They would be joined by the *dhobi wallah* slapping his washing on stone slabs, with a splat, in an attempt, usually successful, to get the clothes white, if a little frayed and with the odd button missing. Days begin early in India and soon these familiar sounds would increase to include the voices of vendors selling their wares: '*Dood, gurum dood*' (milk, hot milk), '*Gurum pani*' (hot water) '*Narangi kayler*' (oranges, bananas), the call to prayer at the

With my parents and friend in India,
Mother kneeling and Father next to me

mosque and, loudest of all, the continuous honking of car horns and the ringing of rickshaw bells.

During the two or so years we spent in India, my father was seconded to the Indian Army and spent time in the cantonments at Landi Kotal and Nowshera. Both places are now part of Pakistan whereas, before Partition in 1947, they were in India. Landi Kotal is the main access to, and the highest point on, the Khyber Pass. The Khyber Pass features large in the history of British India as an important strategic military post which had to be defended from attack on more than one occasion, particularly in 1897 when the Afridis attacked British positions held by the Khyber Rifles. The Khyber still retains its strategic importance in the 21st century as a natural conduit between Pakistan and Afghanistan. Elsewhere in my story is an article I wrote resulting from a trip I made into the area in 2000. My father must only have spent a short time stationed in Landi Kotal as I have no personal memories, only recalling him talk of the place.

On the other hand, I remember our time in Nowshera, where my father commanded an Indian Army motor transport training centre. Nowshera is in the North West Frontier Province and lies on the Grand Trunk Road 27 miles east of Peshawar. It remains today a major cantonment housing two Pakistan Army training schools. We had a bungalow some distance from the barracks which stood at the apex of two long drives surrounded by dense undergrowth. Our nearest British neighbours were about ten miles away. There was no British school so I had a private Indian tutor to teach me instead. Life was, perforce, somewhat lonely, particularly as I was an only child. On the other hand, I made friends with our servants' children who lived in huts elsewhere in the grounds, I learnt how to speak some Hindustani, and for the rest of my life have had no difficulty in getting on with people no matter what their background. My enduring love of *dal baht* and *chapattis* began at this time. So fond did I become of Indian food that I would often lurk around the servants' quarters at meal times in the hope of being invited to eat with a family. I was, and still am, fascinated by the pots and pans used in India. Light, shiny metal receptacles, kept immaculately clean by using a mixture of earth and water, adorned every hut, some used to fetch and store water, others for cooking. It seemed to be a matter of pride amongst the women as to whose pots were the cleanest. I much preferred these to the heavy English metal pots used in our house!

Of the 3,000 species of snakes in the world, about 270 are found in India and, to my certain knowledge, we had three of the deadliest living within our grounds. My parents had warned me of the dangers posed by snakes but the first time I came across one I had forgotten their warning. One day I was playing outside the front veranda when I saw what I thought was a large worm and started poking it with a stick. When the bearer saw me, he yanked me out of the way and proceeded to beat the 'worm' until it no longer moved. Later that evening my father explained that I had been playing with the highly venomous common krait, one of the 'big four' in India. My next encounter, thankfully from a distance, was with the cobra, a

King cobras

large, powerful, fast and agile snake that, when roused, extends its neck into a hood. It has mesmeric eyes and a lightning-fast strike. A cobra bite is almost always fatal. An average size cobra is around five feet in length. Once seen, there's no mistaking or forgetting a cobra!

One day when playing with my friends near their huts our attention was drawn to some excited chatter. On investigation there was a large cobra, in all its glory, being harassed by a mongoose. The famous Rudyard Kipling tale of *Rikki Tikki Tavi*, which tells the story of a valiant young mongoose that defends its adopted English family against an aggressive cobra, has always reminded me of this incident. While all this was going on, one of the servants struck and killed the cobra with a machete to the great relief of all. I had a second close encounter with a cobra when walking with a friend, Richard Hutchings, in the New Territories of Hong Kong, the tale of which I will tell later. One evening my father, who quite often would walk down the drive after being dropped off by his driver, came into the house ashen-faced saying he had nearly stepped on a huge python. After collecting his automatic sub-machine gun, which he kept in the house, and taking the cook and bearer with him, went to look for the snake. Unsuccessful, they returned to the house. From that day onwards, I was banned from venturing into the undergrowth. Despite other encounters, related elsewhere, I have remained respectful of and yet fascinated by snakes.

My father had a pet rhesus monkey, caught by one of the servants as it played with others in the grounds. The monkey became so tame that it used to lie on my father's bare chest in the evening as he relaxed with his first gin and tonic and a cigarette. The monkey 'lived' in the outside pantry tied by a lead to its collar. There was great sadness when one morning the monkey was found dead, hanged by its lead which had got tangled up in the rafters. The constant chatter of the monkeys, while they cavorted in the tree-tops, was another sound of India I shall never forget.

During the unbearable heat and humidity of the summer we used to retreat, for a few weeks, to the one of the towns in the foothills of the Himalaya. I particularly remember Nainital and Ranikhet. Ranikhet was established as the Headquarters of the Kumaon Regiment, probably the finest regiment in the Indian Army, by the British in 1869 and it is still there. I have since been back to visit the area and have included a full description of the town elsewhere in the book. My parents' favourite holiday destination was, without doubt, Nainital with its clean, crisp, warm climate and full social life. Built around Naini Lake, which is surrounded by forested hills, the town still maintains a boat club and race track. From any of the hill-tops there are breathtaking views of the Himalayas. Later in the book I have described Nainital in some detail.

The lake at Nainital

There are two things that I particularly recall about holidaying in Nainital. The first was the day-long car journey from the plains. Winding roads, with hairpin bends, and a sheer drop of thousands of feet waiting for a careless driver was a terrifying experience. I was also learning to ride at that time. One day, under the supervision of a *syce* (horseman), I went out for a ride around the paths in Nainital. Into the ride, the trees somehow came alive with screaming, chattering monkeys. All of a sudden, a big male jumped down from the branches and landed just in front of my horse which immediately reared up, threw me off and bolted. At this point I was surrounded by what seemed to be a large group of monkeys who became aggressive. With a deafening screech, which only an excited monkey can make, one of them lunged at and bit me on the arm. Others followed and I was bitten a few times. Eventually, the syce came to my aid, drove the monkeys away and we returned home with me on the back of his horse. My mother was hysterical and immediately took me to the hospital where I started on a course of 25 anti-rabies injections into my stomach wall. It wasn't until I was required to ride as a young officer that I got back onto a horse. There was another incident concerning the danger of rabies, again on one of our trips. Our small dog, which I think was a dachshund, started to foam at the mouth. Seeing this, father immediately shot the dog, causing both my mother and I great sadness. Going to a hill station provided my father with an opportunity of painting water-colours. I remember particularly him explaining that the mountain he was painting was the highest in the world. It's a shame that I do not have an example of my father's work for there is little doubt that he was a talented water-colourist.

Quite what my mother did during the day when my father was at work I'm not sure as I have little recollection of her being a particular influence in my life. I can 'see' her issuing instructions to the bearer, cook, gardener and *chowkidar* (caretaker) and occasionally getting fussed if someone important was coming to dinner. It was, I believe, around this time that my parents' drinking and smoking habits developed into a problem which would stay with them for the rest of their lives. They would start drinking every night as soon as my father came in from work. I particularly remember Gordon's Gin being a favourite 'tipple' of theirs. The green gin bottle would always be on the table, with ice, lemon and angostura bitters available to mix whatever they fancied. They were also heavy smokers, particularly my father, who would always have a tin of fifty Players Full Strength open. I used to love opening a new tin for him by inserting the point into the tin-foil lid and screwing it around to release the intoxicating smell of fresh tobacco.

From time to time I was allowed to accompany my father to the barracks. The sight of smartly dressed soldiers wearing highly polished belts and boots, colourful *pugree* headdress, carrying a rifle on guard at the main gate to the barracks, springing to attention and saluting as my father approached made me very proud. Bugle calls, whitewashed stones, brushed pathways, lorries lined up bumper to bumper gleaming and soldiers marching around made a lasting impression. That's almost certainly why I love reading about former times in India, in books like *Bugles and a Tiger* by John Masters, and returning to an 'India' where life hasn't changed much in the intervening years.

Hong Kong Island circa 1950

Then, out of the blue, my father was posted to Hong Kong, for what reason he never told me but I have always surmised that it was something to do with the anticipated problems arising from the partitioning of India. We left Madras (now Chennai) by sea bound for Hong Kong, on 10th July 1947. Little was I to know that my association with Hong Kong was to last for many years, through school to a posting in the Army and beyond. I remember little of the journey by sea to Hong Kong except that it lasted about ten days. In the normal way, my father was allocated a married quarter in, I think, Bowen Road on Hong Kong Island. It must have been summer as I remember it being hot and sticky, unlike India which had dry heat. It wasn't long before I first experienced prickly heat or, to give it is medical name, Miliaria, a *skin disease* marked by small and extremely itchy *rashes*.

I was enrolled in The Peak School and kitted out with several pairs of green flannel shorts and short-sleeved green shirts, onto which was sewn the school badge. I used to travel to school on the Peak Tram, a funicular railway which runs from Central District to Victoria Peak over a distance of 1.4 kilometres and a height difference of just over 400 metres. The gradient varies considerably throughout the ascent which,

The Peak Tram 1950

until I got used to it, I found scary. The tram still operates today, although it is now more a tourist attraction rather than the working facility which I first knew.

Hong Kong was the complete antithesis to my humdrum life in India. Day and night there was always something going on. It seemed to me that Hong Kong never slept. People scurried hither and thither going about their business like worker ants. The Chinese dressed differently and wore conical rattan hats; women wore black and tied their hair back in a bun, and men either pulled rickshaws or walked around balancing baskets, suspended at either end of bamboo, across their shoulder filled with all manner of goods; at least, that is initially how I saw it. I recall my first ride in a rickshaw as a strange sensation. The coolie lowered the shafts to the ground; one stepped between them and sat on a padded seat. At this moment the seat was sloping forwards and down. The coolie then picked up the shafts, having the effect of throwing one into the back of the seat, then set off walking to begin with before breaking into a trot. Most coolies were sallow-faced, grossly underweight and likely opium addicts, whose life span was very short. They have not been seen in Hong Kong for some years. I never really took to the Chinese people. Compared with the Indians, I found them dour and humourless and their language impossible to pick up.

Rickshaw coolies 1950

Hong Kong harbour was a place of endless fascination. As well as the 'coming and goings' of passenger liners and the world-renowned Star Ferry, three types of vessels predominated. The smallest was the sampan. Constructed of wood, they were propelled by a single oar at the stern and most had an arch canvas awning beneath which whole families lived. Sampans were used to ferry small loads and for fishing. The next was the walla-wallas; small motorboats that operated around

A Star ferry

the harbour as water taxis. Lastly and by far the most famous was the Chinese junk. These could and often were huge vessels made of teak, some as long as eighty feet. Used for all types of haulage work as well as deep-sea fishing, whole families and their livestock lived on board.

Due to the heavy rains, Hong Kong Island was criss-crossed with deep *nullahs* (storm drains) to carry surplus water away to the harbour. These nullahs became a special place for me where I would play for hours, usually on my own. Actually, it was most exciting when I was on my own. It was as though I was on a great adventure exploring these channels, particularly as my parents had no idea where I was. It was at this time that I developed my lifelong passion for collecting which began with matchbox tops. Being a convenient dumping ground which got washed away from time to time, the nullah was a great source of all manner of rubbish including matchboxes. I also began to find white balloons with a teat on the end. You can imagine my mother's anguish when she found me blowing up what I subsequently learnt was a used condom!

Me and my scooter in Hong Kong

After about a year, I 'graduated' to King George V School, Kowloon. To get there, I had to use the Star Ferry. The Star Ferry is world-famous for its efficient, no-frills service. Over 400 times a day the green double-ended, diesel ferries ply between Hong Kong Island and Kowloon, and have been doing so since 1868. Only the severest typhoon or tropical storm stops the service. The fares have been kept low by government subsidy ever since a proposed increase in fares prompted rioting in 1966. The ferries, all with the word Star in their name, are manned by skilled sailors who move the ferries into the wharf with a practised ease. No tickets are issued in return for the fare and the seats are reversible to face the right direction. I loved my journey to school which gave me a sense of freedom and independence. I became an avid watcher of people and a bubblegum addict.

After the war KGV reopened in the summer of 1946. The Principal was Mr Ferguson. At the first assembly held in September 1946 the Japanese flag of the Rising Sun could still be seen painted at the back of the stage in the hall. The sports field looked like a vegetable garden and there were only 79 students. In 1947 children of all nationalities were permitted to attend the school. On Speech Day 1948 it was announced that the school would be called King George V School. King George had been king in 1935 when the Foundation Stone of the school was laid. I remember little of my short time at the school, although it is certain that Jalu Schroff, under whose captaincy I played for Hong Kong at cricket, was a student at the same time. He was later to become Head Boy for two successive years.

Perhaps through playing in nullahs, I developed a seriously septic thumb which eventually had to be lanced under general anaesthetic at the British Military Hospital: thereafter I developed a dislike of hospitals particularly the *ubiquitous* smell of ether. Before I knew it, we were on our way back to the UK at which point my father left the Army on 12th December 1948. For what reason and under what circumstances I never really found out. I suspect that it may have had something to do with his drinking. To begin with, we lived with my aunt and uncle, Tom and Bobby Sutherland, in Walton-on-Thames within walking distance of the station from which Tom used to commute daily to London. From my point of view I was delighted to be living with Colin, my cousin, who was slightly younger but a great friend in those days. We played together, 'scrumped' apples from next door, made a den in the rhododendron bushes and even staged a boxing match for our parents. Colin recalls our time at 'Golfwood':

> *At the back of the house were rather large woods, which swept round to the right and linked in to other gardens, most of which were orchards. Ian's father nobly played the part of the SAS colonel, sending raiding parties into 'enemy' territory while positioning his HQ on a shooting stick near a large oak The raiding parties consisted of Ian and I plus the odd neighbour's son (from the other side of the house). He loved being included, & never realised that he was always given the most dangerous tasks, e.g. climbing under barbed wire, or*

relieving a cherry tree of half its crop in full view of the owner's wife. We, the seasoned veterans, majored on apples until our

mothers got fed up making apple pie & started asking questions about the seemingly never-ending supply. Occasionally there was hot pursuit, but the 'colonel' seemed to have a sixth sense, and always moved HQ sufficiently far from enemy lines' Judging by this photo, Colin may well have a point (I'm the one saluting!).

Me in 'command' of cousin Colin Sutherland

After some months, my father had a five-bedroom, detached house, 'Bryan', with a large garden, built in West Grove, between Walton and Hersham. His idea was that my mother would do Bed and Breakfast and he would breed rabbits for sale to local butchers. In those days of rationing, which included meat, his idea may have been sound but the execution of his plan was less well considered. Rows of hutches were built at the bottom of the garden but, like any animal, rabbits need feeding and cleaning daily. After a time my father's enthusiasm waned and the task of cleaning the cages and the collection of dandelions for feed was left to me. Eventually, the opportunity of finding enough free food petered out and food had to be purchased. Then, one animal caught Myxomatosis and very soon all the rabbits died or were put out of their misery. Talking of which, it was during this period that my father taught me how to kill a rabbit humanely by breaking its neck with a karate-style chop, a skill that I was later able to use during my Army service.

'Bryan', West Grove, Hersham 2010

I visited the house, which is now 17 West Grove, in 2010. Whereas the house stood alone in extensive grounds, surrounded by woodland, the whole of West

| 18 |

The Early Years

Grove is now built up. But the long white house that stood opposite, where I remember carol-singing with my father, is still there and now bears a plaque recording that it had been the home of Edgar J Hoover, President of the USA, in 1902. I met the current owner of 'our' house who kindly invited me to see the garden of which I have fond memories. During our chat, he told me that he had bought '17' for £900,000 only eight months earlier, a far cry from the £3,000 it cost my father to build!

My father found it difficult to find employment locally but I remember him working as a storeman for an ironmonger's shop in Weybridge. This didn't last long and arguments between my parents grew louder and more frequent, invariably fuelled by alcohol. After a time my father got a job in Peterborough, working for Perkins Diesel Engines, which he held until finally retiring. Meanwhile, my mother, a very sociable person, was doing reasonably well taking in paying guests.

I went to St Martin's Preparatory School, Hersham, where I played for the school team at football. Undoubtedly one of my proudest moments was being awarded my colours during school assembly. Being a holder of colours was signified by wearing the school cap with a tassel, my pride and joy. One day when cycling home, I stopped to buy some sweets when I was surrounded by some local boys making fun of my cap. The incident finished up with them tearing the tassel off the cap and roughing me up a bit. This was the first time I had encountered loutish behaviour and had no idea of how to handle the situation. I rode home in tears and after being consoled by my mother and prompted by my father, resolved that from then on I would stick up for myself in any similar situation.

Sometimes after leaving school, I would stop with other boys on the way home to play football on the green in Hersham. It was here that I became infatuated with Linda Lark, the daughter of the local garage owner, who used to hang around the green. After unsuccessfully trying to kiss her one day, her father came round to complain to my parents about my behaviour – so that was the end of my first affair! Most of my friends had a football but I didn't. One day, I saw a ten-shilling note lying around, so I took it and bought myself a new T-football, the best money could buy at the time. This is not something of which I am proud but it does illustrate, I suppose, just how keen I was to have a football of my own. That ball was my prized possession. I played with it most days and, after use, cleaned it lovingly with 'Dubbin' to preserve the leather. My parents never knew that I had purloined ten shillings.

Whenever I could, I watched Walton & Hersham FC, at their Stompond Lane ground, who played in the Athenian League. On the eve of the 1948-49 season FA Cup Final Wolverhampton Wanderers visited Stompond Lane before playing Leicester City at Wembley. I was thrilled to get the autograph of Bert Williams, at the time England's goalkeeper and a hero of mine, Billy Wright, who won a record 105 caps for England, ninety of them as captain, and other members of the Wolves team. I was delighted when they won the cup by beating Leicester 3-1, although it was considered a poor final. I also saw and got the autograph of Bill Nankeville, who won the AAA mile title four times between 1948 and 1952, win an invitation mile at Stompond Lane, still home to Walton AC, at the height of his prowess. He also represented GB in the 1948 Olympic Games held in London, known as 'The Austerity Games', because the country had no money at the end of the war.

One of our near neighbours in West Grove was a family called Andrews who lived in The Old Meuse which had what, I thought at the time, was a long driveway. The Old Meuse was still there when I went back to West Grove in 2010. Disappointingly, the house was run down and the grounds overgrown and neglected. I remember playing with and being 'bossed' by their daughter Julie who I now know was nearly three years older than me. I was invited to attend one of her birthday parties and remember feeling somewhat 'out of my depth' at what was a very grand affair. Julie looked stunning in a white, frilly dress with her long hair hanging well into the middle of her back. There was a large piano in the lounge, and at one point, accompanied by her father, she sang one or two songs. I was captivated. Readers may by now have guessed that the person to whom I am referring is no less than the world-famous actress, singer and author Dame Julie Andrews, of *My Fair Lady* and *Mary Poppins* fame – to name but two of her many musical successes.

In 1948 I attended the cinema for the first time to see *Scott of the Antarctic*, starring John Mills, a film about Captain Scott's ill-fated expedition to the South Pole in 1910. The film emphasised the heroic character of Scott and his men rather than the mistakes he made, and left with me a lasting impression of adventure and heroic deeds, and is probably responsible, at least in part, for my abiding interest in travel and those lucky enough to be able to 'taste' real adventure.

Eventually, my mother and I left Walton and moved to Peterborough to be with my father. As he worked on the eastern outskirts of the town for Perkins Diesel, we lived in a rented house between Eye and Thorney on what is now the busy A47 trunk road. The imposing house is still there. I had an attic room and was happy

The Early Years |

roaming around the fields on my own, adding to my extensive collection of bird's eggs. I remember well the thrill of finding a Cuckoo's egg in a Hedge Sparrow's nest and proudly showing my father the egg once I had carefully hard-boiled it rather than by making a hole in either end blowing the yolk out, a process that could easily end up with the egg in pieces! My egg collection won First Prize at the school Arts Exhibition, the only prize I ever won at King's School!

After taking and, I assume, passing the Common Entrance exam and successfully negotiating an interview with the headmaster, I started at The King's School, Peterborough, in 1949, initially as a boarder while my parents sorted themselves out. Founded in 1541 by Henry VIII as a cathedral school, King's School retained its independent grammar school status until 1975 when it became comprehensive and co-educational. The King's School has maintained its outstanding record of academic and sporting success over the years and still appears regularly in the list of the Top 100 schools.

The King's School, Peterborough

Life in the boarding house (Madeley House, Park Road), known as the 'Pig', was challenging for someone who had never been away from his parents. But once I settled down, I really enjoyed the comradeship and team spirit which prevailed amongst the boarders of School House. I slept in a dormitory of about twelve. One of the favourite games at the time was 'Truth, Dare or Promise', which we invariably played after dark. Dare was obligatory for new boys, who were initially challenged to climb out of the window, drop down onto the ground from the veranda and then run round the mulberry tree. My first and only 'mulberry tree' dash was a disaster! On returning I found the window closed and, thinking that the others had locked me out on purpose, banged on the window with a plea to let me in. I realised my predicament when a torch light was shone in my face and the voice, I recognised as the housemaster, Mr Parker (aka Nosey), enquired "Who's out there?" My subsequent visit to his room and interrogation resulted in three strokes with his gym shoe. Despite my whimpering I was welcomed back into the dormitory as something of a hero!

Meals in the 'Pig' were taken in the dining room with boys seated at a long table and with either the matron or the housemaster at the head of the table. Matron was a kindly person but during the winter, particularly in the morning, invariably had a 'dew drop' on the end of her nose. Watching which bowl received the dew drop resulted in that particular bowl of porridge being passed around the table until it could go no further! But, so far as I can recall, I never ended up with the contaminated porridge in front of me! One of the main pastimes played by the boarders was cycle speedway using bikes, stripped down to all but the bare essentials of wheels and a rear brake. Competition was fierce and crashes often occurred with boys requiring treatment for cuts and grazes. There were no safety helmets in those days.

I was a poor scholar amongst some very bright boys, although I had plenty of spirit, seemed popular and was good at sport. By the time I arrived at King's School, I was already about a year behind my peers in my studies, a gap that I never really recovered. This was almost certainly due to the time I spent in India being 'taught' by an Indian tutor. As I have already said, mathematics was my weakest subject and has been throughout my life. I did particularly well at cricket and athletics and was always selected for school teams. Although high-spirited and game for a lark, I managed to steer clear of serious trouble at school apart from one particular incident. Along with my best mate, Martin 'Ginner' Gray, we occasionally used the cricket score hut to have a few drags of a cigarette during the lunch break. On one such occasion we were caught in the act by a school prefect who reported us, resulting in a visit to the headmaster's study. For some reason Ginner got away with seeing the headmaster whereas I was caned after being threatened with expulsion!

When I first went to King's School, the headmaster was Mr Harry Hornsby, a fine man who knew every boy by name and ran the school with firmness within a balanced 'diet' of academics and sport. In 1951 he went to New Zealand to be headmaster of Christ's College, Canterbury, the oldest and arguably the most prestigious school in New Zealand. He was replaced by Mr Cecil Harrison, a rather weak and ineffectual man compared with his predecessor. The teachers had among their ranks some real characters: Mr Robinson (Robbie), who obviously liked a 'fag' and a pint and whose gown was always covered in chalk dust, and who taught maths; Mr Pybus (Bean Pole), a tall man who walked as though he was fighting to remain upright on board ship, was a mountaineer whose subject was geography. To emphasise a point or administer a rebuke, he would place his outstretched fingertips on your head and then allow the heel of his hand to crash into your forehead; Mr Larrett (Daddy) was the deputy HM; Mr Bainbridge who ran the junior cricket teams and taught maths; Mr Barker, who taught woodwork or art. The Head Boy, Michael (Mick) Allison, and another prefect, Peter Kingston, were the school icons. Allison was a magnificent games player, who went to Cambridge and then into, I believe, teaching while Kingston was commissioned into the Parachute Regiment and was subsequently awarded the Military Cross for bravery. Both played for England Schoolboys at rugby and Allison joined Bedford RFC.

The County School for Girls, whose uniform was chocolate brown, provided a ready supply of girl friends for the boys of King's School. A particular favourite at the time was Anthea Beals for whom I held a candle without ever being able to attract her attention. Alas! like many famous grammar schools, The County School ceased to exist in 1982. School friendships rarely sustain in later life although in my case I have managed to stay in touch with 'Ginner' Gray, who followed me into the Army. A very good sportsman, Ginner excelled at rugby and went on to captain the Army Canoe Team. After leaving the Army, Ginner settled in Germany and started what was to become a successful business to do with installing clean-air systems for operating theatres. Then in the early 1990s things started to go wrong. His business folded and he was declared bankrupt; he lost his three sons, two to suicide and a third resulting from a traffic accident; his house burnt down and he had no insurance cover; he was viciously attacked and robbed in Berlin; he was involved in a serious traffic accident resulting in injuries from which he nearly died and then, to cap it all, his wife Irena was diagnosed with breast cancer! An extraordinary catalogue of misfortune the veracity of which would be hard to believe were it not true.

Another Old Petriburgian with whom I re-established contact later in life was Barry Kay. After a glittering academic career at Edinburgh and Cambridge Universities and the Harvard Medical School, Barry went on to become one of the most distinguished clinical scientists in the UK and was recognised as a world-leading expert in the field of allergy and asthma. He became Professor Emeritus and Senior Research Investigator at Imperial College London and Honorary Consultant Physician at both The Royal Brompton Hospital and The London Clinic. A quiet, unassuming man whom I remember from schooldays as just another boarder, Barry, admits that it wasn't until he developed an interest in chemistry that he decided to knuckle down to some serious work from which he has never looked back. Even though I did not make the most of my time at King's, there is no doubt that the

| Never a Dull Moment

THE KING'S SCHOOL. PETERBOROUGH. 1951

Me 4th from right, Ginner 8th and Barry 9th – all in back row

The Early Years

Me, Barry and Ginner October 2011

school played an important part in my development. That I went to such a fine school, during the 'Golden Age' of Grammar Schools, with their best traditions for academic excellence and sporting prowess, provided me with principles of self-discipline, good manners and a respect for others, that have stood me in good stead throughout my life. I may not have made the best of my time academically but that KSP taught me the important lessons of life there is no doubt. Competition and the spirit of 'play up and play the game' was the essence of grammar school life.

It was during this period that I earned money for the first time. One summer holiday I went plum-picking in Evesham with a party from school. It was during this working holiday that I smoked my first cigarette and went with another boy to climb the clock-tower of the local church after dark. The following year, during the summer, I worked on a local farm, helping with the harvest, mainly stooking (stacking) sheaves of harvested corn so that they were self-supporting, to provide an open space between each pair of sheaves. This enabled the wind and sun to get into the middle of the stooks to dry and further ripen them. Once ready, the sheaves would be loaded using a pitchfork onto a horse and cart and taken off for threshing. Stooking was hard and sometimes painful work since thistles and nettles were invariably within the sheaves ready to play havoc on forearms and sides as they were picked up and carried under each arm. But it was healthy work and great fun working in the open air – and the money wasn't bad either! Horse-drawn milk wagons delivered milk to the door as I was growing up in the early 1950s.

I got a Saturday job helping the milkman on his round in Peterborough. My job was to ride on the step at the back of the wagon and, when we reached a house, to jump off, collect the empty milk bottles or container, bring them to the wagon where the milkman, using a ladle, would fill them up from a milk churn and I would then return the full ones to the doorstep. Horse dung was deposited on the street to be cleaned every few days or collected by a keen gardener. It was also my job to give the horse its nosebag of food about midway through the round, which would last from early in the morning until mid-afternoon. For this, I was paid the princely sum of, I think, three shillings. After being on the waiting-list for months, I eventually got a newspaper round, consisting of around thirty houses. By this time I was smoking as often as I could afford to buy a packet of five Woodbines, the cheapest on the market. The paper shop was about a mile from home and was run by a 'Scrooge-like' man who wore wool mittens and a scarf throughout the year and was never without a 'fag' in the corner of his mouth, the ash from which eventually dropped off, usually onto the papers he was sorting. I along with other boys turned up at around 6.30 to collect our papers which were carried around in a canvas bag draped over the shoulder. The round took me about an hour to complete on foot as I had no bicycle at the time. This gave me just about enough time to have a bowl of porridge before going to school. For this I think I earned around ten shillings per week.

My recollection of life was of formality and good manners. Men mostly wore hats, doffed them to women and walked on the outside of pavements. My mother would never leave the house without wearing a hat and gloves or without lipstick etc.; such was convention at the time. There was an unwritten no-swearing rule in front of women. Children were to be seen and not heard. Social class was determined by accent and dress. Derogatory references to Jews, 'niggers' and jokes about the Irish were commonplace and acceptable. Britain was a land with a sense of history and pride emanating from victory in the war and the Empire. Britain was a deeply conservative country. Only white faces to be seen. At the time there were no supermarkets, only corner shops – all run by Brits, no motorways, no teabags – only loose tea leaves, proper bread cut with a knife, no microwaves, no ready-made meals, no duvets – only blankets, pubs on every street corner, very few houses, and not ours, with TVs, but every High Street had at least one cinema, no hoodies, no washing machines. Abortion, homosexuality and suicide were illegal, capital punishment legal. Austins and Fords, no foreign cars, no seat-belts, motor cycles with sidecars. Bakelite wirelesses and gramophones. No computers or mobile phones. Listened to *Dick Barton Special Agent*. Milk of Magnesia, Vick's Vapour Rub, Aspirin, Enos Salts and Germolene in the medicine cabinet. Meat rationed, butter rationed, lard rationed, sugar rationed, tea rationed, cheese rationed, jam rationed, soap rationed, sweets rationed, clothes rationed – all controlled by ration books. Rationing, introduced at the outset of war, finally ended in 1954 just as I was to enter the Army. Since then, the majority of people have known nothing but growing affluence and a range of choice unthinkable in the early 1950s. My mother would spend more than an hour queuing every day. Oranges, which had begun to appear in the shops, required far too many coupons for most people to be able to afford them. The weekly food allowance for the average adult male was one egg, thirteen ounces of meat, six ounces of butter or margarine, an ounce of cooking fat, eight ounces of sugar, and two pints of milk. It is small wonder therefore that one seldom saw an overweight person on the streets. A far cry from the obese society Britain is spawning today! The 1950s was not all doom and gloom either. The Coronation of Elizabeth II, the conquest of Everest and, in May 1954, Roger Bannister breaking the four-minute mile, spring to mind.

Manners were an important part of my upbringing. Both my parents were 'sticklers' for correct behaviour. I remember, particularly: no elbows on the table; don't speak with your mouth full; hold you knife, fork and spoon correctly; don't slouch over your food; sit up with shoulders back; always say 'please', 'thank you' and 'excuse me'; blow your nose pointing away from the table; don't fart in public; it's rude to stare; don't wipe your nose on your sleeve; hold the door open for ladies; offer your seat to an old person; and raise your cap when greeting someone your know.

After leaving the house near Eye, we moved into rented accommodation in Stanley Road next to the Stanley Recreation Ground, within which was the Peterborough Cricket Club ground, and within easy walking distance to King's School. Our landlady was a kindly old woman, with whiskers on her chin, who always smelt of drink. I liked living near the recreation ground where I spent most of my time kicking, throwing or hitting a ball. During the season I operated the scoreboard at the cricket ground which got me free entrance and a cup of tea. I remember the thrill of seeing Frank Tyson, one of the fastest bowlers ever, play for Northamptonshire against Glamorgan at the ground. His run-up nearly reached the boundary! In his first over there was a mighty crack as the ball thumped into the diminutive opening batsman who went down pole-axed! The game was suspended for some minutes before one of the players emerged from the crowd carrying a bat which he took to the pavilion steps to hammer out the dent in the batsman's protective box! He had no need to have gone to the trouble as the batsman was out, clean bowled, next ball.

After about a year, we moved into the bottom flat of 61 New Road, on the opposite side of the recreation ground. It was from here that I got my paper round. The house was well placed, being within easy distance of the town centre, close to the three cinemas and still within walking distance of school. I had my own room, we shared a bathroom with upstairs, and we had an outside toilet in which my mother had placed a paraffin stove in the winter to prevent the pipes freezing. I remember the slippery, slightly abrasive, San Izal loo paper which used to hang by a piece of string by the toilet; no soft tissues in those days!

It was during this time that I developed a problem in both my knees, usually after playing football, to the extent that I often lay crying in my bed – so severe was the pain. Despite the advice of the family doctor, I continued to play as much sport as I could. Not surprisingly, my knees got worse and worse to the point where I could hardly walk without pain. After a visit to a specialist, who diagnosed chronic inflammation of the cartilage, both my legs were encased in plaster from ankle to hip for six months, so that I walked with stiff legs. This had certain advantages, one being that I could play cricket without wearing any protective pads when batting. On the other hand, one incident very nearly ended in disaster when I was pushed from behind and fell crashing to land in a heap at the bottom of the stairs at school, requiring a trip to the hospital to check all was well. The culprit came off far worse than me after a particularly painful trip to see the headmaster! After the orthopaedic cast was removed, my legs were naturally very weak and required extra support. This was provided by a thick Elastoplast adhesive bandage, which was not only very uncomfortable but extremely painful when the time came to remove it. The mistake I made was to opt to take it off myself rather than let the hospital do the job. After some days lying in the bath with a pair of scissors cutting small strips away, my mother did the job one evening. As she ripped the plaster away from the skin, taking with it all the hairs, the pain was something I had never previously experienced and would not wish to do so again. After a year of being immobilised, my legs were obviously pretty weak, but it didn't take too long for me to start playing sport again, but it did result in the definition of my leg muscles never fully re-forming.

Going to the pictures (cinema) on Saturday morning was a 'must' – the treat of the week. Proudly wearing my 'ABC Minors' badge and sucking on a halfpenny gob-stopper that lasted for the whole performance, I longed for the film to never end. I lost count of the number of times the manager stopped the film and told us to behave, or else he'd cancel the film and send us off home. Of course, he never did. We were certainly in a world of fantasy during the show, and I always felt utterly miserable going out into the bright sunlight afterwards. The Saturday morning 'flick' and getting my copies of the *Eagle* and *Dandy* comics were the highlights of the week: there was nothing better in life at that time. But I did not only go to the cinema on Saturday morning. Whenever I wanted to see an 'A' (over 16) film, I would ask someone to 'take me in, please' – a tactic that invariably worked, sometimes with the adult, usually a woman, volunteering to pay for my ticket as well. In the austere and gloomy Fifties, the 'flicks' provided the only real alternative view of the world. It was during an afternoon at the cinema I had my first and only encounter with a 'dirty old man.' Engrossed in the film, I became aware of the man sitting next to me easing his mackintosh over my lap. Then I felt his hand creeping up my leg to alight on my private parts. I was smoking at the time and instinctively lifted up the coat and placed the lighted cigarette on the back of his hand. He moved away immediately without saying anything! I relayed the incident to my parents who seemed to be amused by what I had done. I knew what the New York skyline looked like long before I sI knew what the New York skyline looked like long before I saw Big Ben and the Houses of Parliament. It was watching Debbie Reynolds that I fell in love for the first time; she was not like Marilyn Monroe.

This was love, not lust! Although I was not an avid reader, I did enjoy the *Just William* books written by Richmal Crompton and WE Johns' *Biggles*. *Just William* were tales of a rather scruffy, nonconformist boy, while *Biggles* featured stories of adventure. Perhaps those books had more than a passing influence on me at the time and in the choices I made in later life.

Girls also began to feature in my thoughts at around this time. As I have already said, the County Grammar School for Girls was the main source although my success rate with the girls was never great. As a teenager, gawky and somewhat shy of girls, I had an uncertain and tentative initiation into love and romance. My parents never talked to me about 'the facts of life' and the only time I ever got a glimpse of the female form was by looking at the 'saucy' drawings and photographs in the magazine *Health and Efficiency* usually dog-eared and well-used by the time I got hold of a copy.

I did have a couple of 'flings' which amounted to nothing other than a kiss. That was until I met a girl in the recreation ground who one evening guided my hand onto her breasts over her gabardine raincoat. The experience aroused me sufficiently to awaken a keener interest in the female form than otherwise had been the case! Then there was the daughter of the landlord of The Swan, a pub which my parents frequented, who in her bedroom one night after a round of heavy 'snogging' invited me to 'Show me yours and I will show you mine'. I readily accepted her offer but only if the act was carried out using a torchlight!

My new-found interest in the opposite sex made me more aware of my dress and appearance. The 'cool' image in those days was that of a 'Teddy Boy'. Teddy Boy clothing included a drape jacket, dark in colour, with a velvet trim collar and pocket flaps, and high-waist 'drainpipe' trousers, exposing the socks, so called because they were narrow from ankle to thigh. My outfit also included a high-necked loose-collared white shirt, a narrow 'Slim Jim' tie and a brocade waistcoat. My suit was tailor-made and paid for through weekly instalments. Quite how I managed to pay the instalments, I'm not sure but my mother would have helped me. Shoes were crêpe-soled and

Teddy Boy, but not me!

known as brothel creepers, so thick that they looked and felt like you were wearing a landing craft on each foot.

Thus attired, aged 16, acned, with long brilliantined hair, with a quiff at the front and the side swept back into a duck's arse, I used to walk through the streets of Peterborough, hoping I would catch the eye of some pretty girl – no such luck! The popular music of the day, which my mother listened to, included Perry Como, Al Martino, Guy Mitchell and Doris Day. My taste, at that time, centred on the new Be-Bop to which one nodded one's head to the beat of the music. But I also developed a 'taste' for jazz including Humphrey Lyttelton, Ronnie Scott, Chris Barber and Johnny Dankworth, whose concerts I attended later in life.

I remember little else of life at that time. My mother, who often worked, used to make me do the shopping for her, at the local corner shop, at David Gregg for groceries, Brown's for meat and, most importantly, an off-licence for booze and cigarettes. In all of these shops my mother had an account. Shops in those days were very different. The butcher had sawdust on the floor and he sold local meat, which he cut up in front of you, and vegetables. The local hardware shop, where you could purchase anything from a single nail to a lawn-mower, had its own distinctive smell, while my joy was the local sweet shop with tall glass jars full of all manner of delights including sherbet lemons and humbugs. I seldom went out with my parents but when I did it was invariably to a pub, where I would sit outside with a lemonade and a packet of crisps until my parents finished drinking, usually when the pub closed. I did enjoy going to the Perkins Diesel Social Club where I was allowed inside to play snooker or just watch the adults. My father was known and referred to as 'The Major', a sobriquet which I always thought was poking fun at him. I remember once when the National Anthem was played at the club, my father alone got to his feet and stood rigidly to attention. This was the sort of person he was – very much a royalist with old-fashioned values. In those days, an evening's entertainment at the cinema came to a formal end with everyone standing to the National Anthem except those who rushed out to avoid the convention.

The only holiday I can remember with my parents was to Skegness (aka Skeggy). The drive from Peterborough, with my mother at the wheel of a hired car (my father could not drive!), was a real ordeal with my parents arguing the whole time, mostly about which was the correct route! Sound familiar, doesn't it? We stayed in a guesthouse on the seafront. While my parents went their own way, I was left to my own devices and whiled away days playing by myself. I remember 'Skeggy' had sand-dunes, marram grass and lizards, and a beautiful seashore. The beach had clean and golden sand, a rose garden, a boating lake, an amusement park and donkey rides. I also recall going to a cricket match with my father and him explaining that I was watching one or two who had played for England in the past; one, I think, was Reg Simpson (Notts and England), an opening batsman.

Knowing that I was really making little progress at school, particularly after failing the Dartmouth entrance exam, I decided that the best thing I could do was to leave school and start to make my way in the world. After applying unsuccessfully – thank goodness – for a job as an apprentice photographer with Perkins Diesel, I decided to visit the Army Recruiting Office. This leads me conveniently into the next chapter of my life.

2: What's in a Name?

"What's that crest you have on your ring?" asked a fellow officer as we stood around the Officers' Mess bar, in Germany, late one night. He was referring to the crest on the signet ring my father had given me.

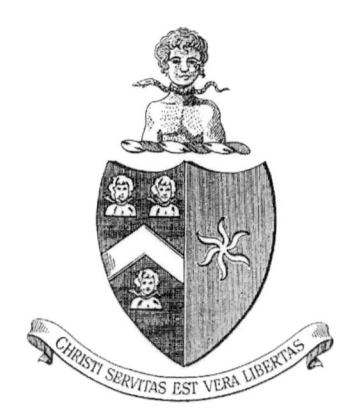

'Service to Christ is true Liberty'

Without any great conviction, I waffled that it was my family crest within which the Vaughan was represented by the boy with a serpent wound around his neck, and Arbuckle by a 'starfish', which I later identified, in armorial terms, as an *estoile*. He wanted to know more. "How did the two names get joined together in the first place?" he asked; "What does the motto mean?" and other probing questions. I was unable adequately to answer his questions for the only real background my father had given me was that the Arbuckle was Scottish and the Vaughan Welsh, which turned out to be complete nonsense! He knew nothing of the story leading to the joining of the two names by a hyphen. Feeling acutely embarrassed and not a little ignorant, I resolved there and then to find out the answers to these questions and more, if possible, regarding the background and history

| Never a Dull Moment

of the Vaughan-Arbuckle family. Little was I to know what an incredible 'journey' would result from this chance conversation. My research has put me in touch with people all over the world; it has prompted visits to India, Ireland and the USA as well as journeys all around the UK looking at houses and visiting graveyards and churches. The number of hours I have spent in libraries, reading books and manuscripts and, more recently, surfing the Internet, must run into many hundreds. What follows is a shortened narrative of what I have discovered during my research. I say 'shortened' as it would take a book of its own to write a comprehensive history about our family.

Even though I shall be starting the family story midway into the generations, I believe it would be useful if I were to address first the questions posed during that evening in 1961. The most important matter to establish is that we, the Vaughan-Arbuckles, are directly descended from William Vaughan (1620-1699) who is recorded in various documents as a 'Merchant Adventurer for Irish Lands' or, put another way, he was sent to Ireland as one of Oliver Cromwell's English settlers to keep the Protestant faith: more of him later. We then have to move forward five generations to Benjamin Hutcheson Vaughan (1790-1874) who took the name Arbuckle by Royal Warrant which was promulgated in The London Gazette Number 3665 dated 8th November 1843.

My research suggests that no such record is held in the College of Arms so it must be debatable whether the family have been entitled to use the name Arbuckle through the generations! At the outset, I decided to concentrate my research on the male line of the Vaughans. In the time available, to do otherwise would have been virtually impossible, although, whenever appropriate, I will refer to the female line, particularly in the modern era. The name Vaughan is of Welsh origin and is derived from the word Vychan, meaning 'little'. Despite my best efforts, including contacting various Vaughans throughout the world, I have failed to establish a link back beyond

> *Whitehall*, November 8, 1843.
>
> The Queen has been pleased to grant unto Benjamin-Hutcheson Vaughan, Esq. Major in the Army, and Captain in the Royal Regiment of Artillery, Her royal licence and authority, that he and his issue may take and use the surname of Arbuckle, in addition to and after that of Vaughan, in compliance with a request contained in the last will and testament of Sophia Arbuckle (commonly called Lady Sophia Arbuckle), widow and relict of James Arbuckle, of Maryvale, in the county of Down, Esq. as well as in order to testify his grateful and affectionate regard to their memory :
>
> And also to command, that the said royal concession and declaration be recorded in Her Majesty's College of Arms, otherwise to be void and of none effect.

William. It is interesting that the Vaughan family, of Courtfield, Ross-on-Wye, have exactly the same family crest although there is no link with us that I could establish. So, although I have discovered and researched many William Vaughans, 'our' William's antecedents remain a mystery, at least for the time being.

William Vaughan (1620-1698), being the first ancestor with a direct lineage to the Vaughan-Arbuckles, is the starting point of the family history. The first we know of him is when he is recorded as being a leading figure in Clonmel (Co Tipperary) after the siege of the town in April-May 1650 during the Cromwellian conquest of Ireland. Those sent to Ireland by Cromwell were in the main citizens of London, Puritan shopkeepers and tradesmen, who looked to advance the cause of Protestantism and to secure a good return for their money at the end of the war by investment in rebel land. In about 1659, William began the banking business which his descendents, the Rialls, continued for three generations. By 1666, religious sectarianism had become a serious problem with a move to re-establish Catholicism in the town. Described as a 'sturdy Cromwellian', William held out, along with others, against the trend and formed the first dissenting congregation in the town. This 'dissenting congregation' was a tight-knit community, as a result of which the Vaughan and Riall families became close friends and business partners. One of William's daughters, Elizabeth, married Phineas Riall, who owned the bank in Clonmel and was a leading member of the community. His remains rest in St Mary's Church. By 1670, William had opened a shop, with integral accommodation, in the High Street, four doors from the Main Guard which stayed open until he died. The Main Guard can be seen in this early drawing at the entrance to the walled city: William's house may therefore be assumed to have been in the block on the right hand side of the Main Guard

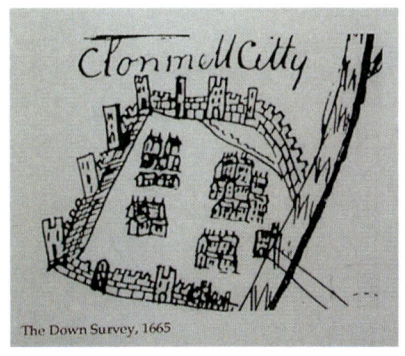

The Main Guard, Clonmel

William traded, principally, in wool purchased from all over South Tipperary, which he then shipped to the north coast of Somerset/Devon, a voyage of considerable danger in those days.

In 1668, William married Mary Colesary, the daughter of a fellow 'adventurer'. There were four children. In 1678, with the proceeds from his successful business interests, William achieved his ambition of becoming a landowner with the purchase of lands of Ballyvoher, Ballyvaughan (*Bally* means 'Land of'), Cleare, Ballyboe and Ballnaveene. The picture is of the farmhouse within Ballyvaughan, thought to be on the same site as the original building.

Ballyvaughan

At around the same time, William adopted the crest still used by the family, with the Latin motto meaning 'Service to Christ is True Liberty'. William was named in the Charter to Clonmel as an Alderman and *sectary* of the town. These details are taken from *The History of Clonmel* by the Rev William P. Burke (Harvey & Co 1907). Pages 340ff contains extracts from William's will, including the following: *'I give and bequeth to the poore English Protestants of the towne of Clonmell the sume of twenty pounds sterling* (at least £1,500 today) *to be putt out at interest for them by my executors and the interest thereof yearely to be distributed and given every New Yeares day to whom and to such*

What's in a Name?

English poore Protestants as my executors hereafter named shall think fit.' William died on 18th August 1698.

I have visited Clonmel on three occasions and each time felt a strong affinity with the town.

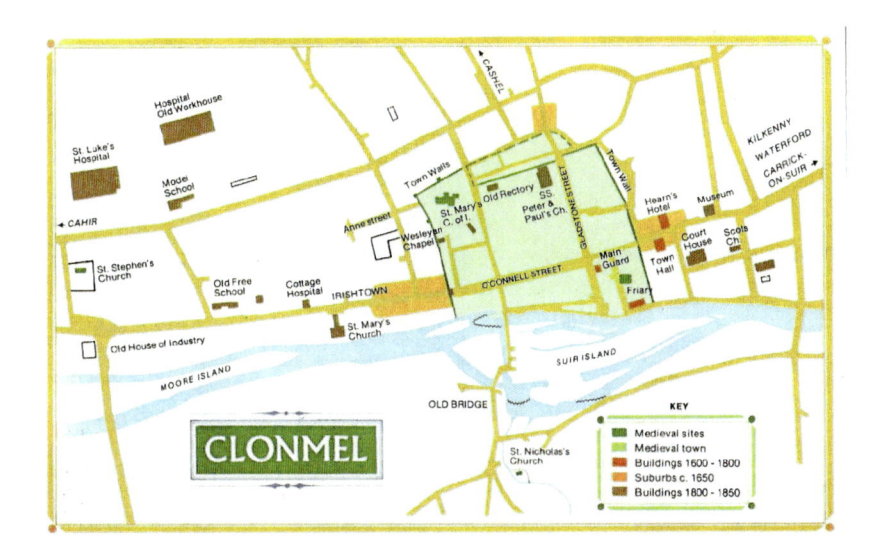

Set in the heart of Tipperary, in the Suir Valley, the area is stunningly beautiful. On the southern side of the river are the Waterford Hills, from the top of which there are some great views towards Slievenamon Mountain in the north and the splendid open country towards Cashel, where William farmed. The ancient bridge across the River Suir, the Main Guard and 800-year-old St Mary's Church are reminders of what the town was like when William and his four children lived there.

Benjamin[1]* **Vaughan (1679-1742)** was born on 28th April 1679 in Clonmel at about half-past four in the morning. He had three sisters, one older and two younger than himself. Being the only son, Benjamin inherited the majority of his father's goods, plate (silver), horses, corn, etc. with a value upward of £1,000 (£80,000 today) and the lands at Cullinagh. Benjamin married Anne Wolf in Dublin on 19th November 1700. No fewer than eight daughters and four sons were born to the couple which, according to other writings, "From this time he (Benjamin) was concerned with the weight of his purse rather than the cut of his cravat!"

---

* Due to the fact that there are seven ancestors with the name 'Benjamin', the numbers in the text relate to numbers on the family tree, in an attempt to ease identification and avoid confusion!

Benjamin was mainly a sheep farmer. In June 1699 he had in excess of 3,000 sheep but because wool was becoming unprofitable, Benjamin decided to 'spread-bet' his assets by buying woods and selling timber. In the long run, this turned out to be a wise move. After buying a house, Benjamin started to move his residence from Ballyboe (Clonmel) to Waterford. He bought a share in a ship and engaged in the fish trade. His oldest son, William, went to London in 1722 where he married Mrs Mary Bond two years later. Significantly, they had no children. As William was 'the apple of his father's eye', it is hardly surprising that Benjamin and Anne went to London 'to view their magnificent son' who had, by now, been made a Freeman of the City after being sworn in as a Ticket Broker. The journey home at the end of the visit took seven weeks.

Life for Benjamin and his family changed in 1738 when his son William, together with sixty others, was drowned on the Goodwin Sands during a voyage between Cork and Rotterdam. Then three years later, Anne's health began to fail. After rallying at least once, she died, of a *'nervious* (sic) *disorder and a decay of her spirits'*, in August 1741. In his diary, Benjamin wrote of his wife: *'She was one of ye Patientest persons that could be, taking everything she was Bid & Doing everything she was Desired & went off with out a Sigh or grown like a lamb. She resinged her soul to her God whom early in her youth she began to serve & soon entred into covenant with him at his Table never missing an Ordinaunce when she was able to goe to it, for when she lived in the country no weather would keep her from Church, she Proved her self to be one of the best Christian, wives, mothers neibour & nurse tenders to ye Sick & of Universall charity. None could take more pains or Care in ye Education of her children she having ten alive when she Dyed Espeshally as to their Eternal Happyness, the Last she allways took care to instill in all children that was under her care.'*

Benjamin himself died a year later of a broken heart. Family memorials speak of a sincere, tranquil and kindly person, of trials meekly borne and of prosperity graciously enjoyed.

Benjamin^2 Vaughan (1713-1786) came into the world on 23rd June 1713 in the family home in Ballyboe, Tipperary. For some reason, in all probability because the family did not wish to be classed as Irish, his birth was registered at St Dionis Church, London. The next we know of him is that he moved to London aged 15 where he was formally apprenticed to his older brother William, who was by then a Freeman of the City of London, in the profession of Ticket Broker. Benjamin's apprenticeship was to last seven years. Soon after successfully completing his apprenticeship, Benjamin married Hannah Halfhide (28), who was from a well-to-do London family, in St Benet, Paul's

Wharf, London, a church designed by Sir Christopher Wren which is today considered a 'particularly valuable example' of his work.

Benjamin is described as a *scrivener* (copyist, notary, broker, money-lender, drafter of documents) and a resident of the City of London. Clearly an eminent man of substance and reputation, Benjamin was eventually elected a Freeman of the Scriveners' Company, of which he became Master in 1769-70.

Benjamin and Hannah had seven children, two sons and five daughters, and lived most of their lives in Enfield, although they did return to Ireland on at least one occasion. The fact that Benjamin enjoyed a most prosperous and successful life is borne out by the fact that both he and Hannah had their portraits painted by Sir Francis Cotes, one of the pioneers of English pastel painting, and a founder-member of the Royal Academy, in 1768. The two life-size portraits are now the property of the Boston Museum of Fine Arts, having been sold to an American relative, probably by Charles Vaughan-Arbuckle in the early 1900s. Mrs Mary Vaughan Marvin subsequently gave the two pictures to the Museum in 1948. Today the portraits would be worth a small fortune. A smaller version of Benjamin's portrait is in my possession.

Benjamin and Hannah

Benjamin died in April 1786, aged 73. Hannah followed him just over a year later. Both are buried at St Mary's Church, Great Parndon, near Harlow, Essex, in a vault just outside the church, along with other family members, including their eldest son Benjamin,[5] and Sarah Vaughan their granddaughter.

American 'Cousins'

It was July 1992. We had made arrangements to visit George and Diana Vaughan Gibson, at The Vaughan Homestead, Hallowell, Maine, with whom I had been corresponding for many years, about our mutual family history. After looking around the village, we drove up to the vicinity of The Homestead and waited for the clock to tick around to midday, our agreed time of arrival. Passing through the imposing gates, I could see a figure standing by the large flagstaff located at the end of the winding drive. As he caught sight of the car, the man hoisted the Stars and Stripes with the Union Jack underneath. As I stopped the car, he gave an American-style military salute. I got out and shook hands with George Gibson, husband of the then owner of The Vaughan Homestead. After exchanging pleasantries, during which he remarked that our second perfect arrival was 'nothing more than I would have expected from a military man', we moved to the house where Diana was waiting on the veranda with a chilled bottle of champagne. The toast was to 'To William Vaughan and his descendants'. But what was the story behind the Vaughans making their way to New England (America)?

Diana and George at The Homestead

Samuel (1720-1802), Benjamin's (1713-1786) youngest son, spawned the highly successful American branch of the Vaughan family. In the mid-16th century, London bankers were buying lands in coastal New England and in the Caribbean for future development. Tea drinking was very much the 'in thing' for which sugar was an essential ingredient and a highly lucrative commodity. Samuel became apprentice to a successful merchant in 1736 and some time afterwards went to Jamaica. He sailed from London to Boston, there to await a coastal ship from northern New England following the coastline to Jamaica. During what turned out to be a long delay in Boston, he fell in love with Sarah Hallowell, the daughter of Benjamin Hallowell, the King's Naval Commissioner, and a much-liked and respected citizen of Boston. Samuel married Sarah in 1750. Shortly afterwards they went to Jamaica. After the birth of their first son, Benjamin[4] in 1751, the family returned to England where they remained until returning to America 22 years later. Samuel's entrepreneurial spirit must have been strong since he soon opened his own merchant banking firm in London as well as acquiring at least two sugar plantations, Vaughansfield (now a town not far from Montego Bay) and Flamstead, both close to each other in the north of Jamaica. Samuel was one of the first planters to introduce religion to his 'workers' (slaves) of which he had 333 split, principally, between Flamstead and Vaughansfield. It was during his time in Jamaica that Samuel became Clerk to the Supreme Court, an important and prestigious position. Papers from that time show that Samuel attempted some 'shady' business which brought him into legal conflict with the Duke of Grafton. The case was settled circa 1769 by which time Samuel had returned to London and was living in Mincing Lane: he had another residence in Essex. Overleaf is a letter from Samuel to the Duke of Grafton.

Samuel returned to America with his wife in 1773 where he remained until 1790. Wanting to see Washington's battlefields south of Princeton, Samuel made the trip on horseback going all the way to Fort Pitt from Philadelphia, some 300 miles. He kept a journal of this trip which is in the archives at Mount Vernon, where he twice stayed with George Washington. Samuel arranged for a marble mantelpiece from his London home to be delivered to George Washington's house, where to this day it resides in the large dining room.

The Vaughan Fireplace

He also commissioned a portrait of Washington by Gilbert Stuart, labelled 'The Vaughan Washington', which hangs in the U.S. National Gallery.

Being Unitarians, the Vaughans did not belong to the established Church of England. The word Unitarian first appeared in Britain in 1673. English law at the time prevented Unitarians, Quakers, Baptists, etc. from becoming officers in the Army or Navy, nor could they hold other important positions in society, e.g. as members of Parliament. They could not send their children to any of the public schools nor could they graduate fully from any university. No laws of prejudice existed in those days! Collectively they were known as the Dissenters. Unitarianism has always been a reform movement both in religion and in politics. Its opposition to the state church was not popular in Britain, nor was its support for the principles of the French Revolution. These affirmations led to renewed persecution in the late 1700s which disappeared with the arrival of the 19th century, the age of confidence

| Never a Dull Moment

My Lord Duke

    Mr Henry Newcome's strict Honor as well as his very sincere regard for your Grace, rendered him (in my Opinion) the properest person to entrust with a proposition that required the utmost Secrecy, but his delicacy preventing, I am (by the nature of it) precluded from every other method, but by immediate application to your Grace, in which am confirm'd by Mr Howell's applying again Yesterday to purchase a Resignation of the Patentee who is my friend

    The inclosed Affidavit will shew the proposal, which will be encreased if necessary, and would your Grace indulge me by perusing the Cases, I trust it would appear, that I have a pretention in preferance to any other

    I will take an opportunity of waiting upon your Grace, hoping the Honor of a Conference, otherwise to receive back the Affidavit in order to destroy the same

    I am
      Your Grace's
        most obedient and
        most humble Servant
        Sam Vaughan
        Mincing Lane 10th June 1769

His Grace the Duke of Grafton

and influence for Unitarianism with its strong belief in individual liberty. Responding to the need for self-help, a group of well-to-do Unitarians, including Samuel, felt that they must start an independent school for their sons. Samuel was one of the prime-movers

Warrington Academy

and fund-raisers in creating an academy for nonconformists at Warrington, Lancashire. Known as 'The cradle of Unitarianism', Warrington Academy opened in 1756.

Samuel's eldest son, Benjamin[4] (1751-1836), was one of the first to attend this 'school'.

Benjamin[4] and his younger brother **Charles (1759-1839)** came to Hallowell circa 1794 to make a permanent home for themselves and their children, which came to be known as The Vaughan Homestead. Along with others, they stand pre-eminent in the list of founders of Hallowell. The Homestead lies in the midst of a landscape of truly outstanding beauty just off Highway 95, not far from Augusta, the state capital of Maine. Beyond The Homestead there is a magnificent view of the distant hills with the Kennebec River winding its way gently past, below and beyond the house. Behind the house a powerful stream rushes headlong from ledge to ledge, underneath an old stone bridge (known as The Vaughan Bridge), through trees before cascading down a large waterfall. In former days, the stream powered the mill owned by the family. In the garden, below the summerhouse, a private graveyard provides a peaceful resting place for generations of the family. The Homestead itself is constructed of shiplap, surmounted with a roof constructed of slate and a number of chimney stacks built of brick. Each of the numerous windows has a shutter on either side. On the south side there is a large veranda which houses the imposing front door. Behind the house stand a number of outbuildings, one of which houses the antique family fire engine! Inside the house is constructed mainly of wood. Simple in design and entirely unpretentious, despite being close on 200 years old, the house has a 'nice' feel to it.

Over supper on our first night, when asked how many bedrooms there were, Diana thought for a moment before replying, 'Actually, I have no idea. Do you, George?' George did not, leaving us with the

| Never a Dull Moment

The Vaughan Homestead and grounds

impression that the house was enormous. What I did notice was that each of the rooms had a large fireplace. The furnishings of the house were mostly English, obviously brought over when the Vaughans first settled there. Family portraits hung everywhere and the crockery bore the Vaughan coat-of-arms. During the three days we spent at The Homestead, I felt entirely at ease. It was as though I belonged there.

By the time we visited, both George and Diana were in their eighties but with a young attitude to life. Diana, a direct descendant of Benjamin's, was suffering with advanced arthritis. Her remedy to keep the painful condition under control was to have a hot bath in the morning and a strong gin and vermouth in the evening! She was a great character with a wonderful sense of family history and an acute understanding of her responsibilities for maintaining The Homestead, as far as possible, in its original state. After our visit she sent me many papers and one or two portraits, which rightly belonged to the English line, and which had found their way to America. Sadly, Diana and George both passed away some years after our visit. But I shall never forget their kindness and generous hospitality. Diana was proud to be a Vaughan. So that the house and gardens would remain open to the public with their children running it, George and Diana made The Homestead a Foundation, a typically generous gesture by them.

Benjamin[4] **Vaughan (1751-1836)** was born on 19th April 1751 in Jamaica, during one of the visits by his parents to their estate on that island. Benjamin's parents Samuel and Sarah were keen to give their children a good education, while his mother paid great attention to her children's health, religion, morals and 'temper'. As we know, Benjamin attended Warrington Academy. During his time at Warrington, Benjamin developed a lifelong relationship with his tutor Joseph Priestley. Joseph Priestley, the renowned theologian, natural philosopher, chemist and political theorist, had joined the teaching staff in 1761. It was from this start that Benjamin was to become an eminent man in his own right. After leaving Warrington, young Benjamin went to Cambridge and onwards to study law at The Temple. His studies continued at Edinburgh, 1780-81, where he read medicine. Surprisingly, he never practiced either law or medicine professionally. He did, however, become the Member of Parliament for Calne, Wiltshire, before emigrating to America. In his maiden speech, 2nd April 1792, Benjamin described himself as: '... *connected with the West Indies by birth, profession and private fortune. He had not resorted to merchandise from motives of necessity, but from those of independence, a noble personage having offered to provide for him in a very simple manner. At an early period of life he had resisted this temptation and had resolved to improve his own fortune, free from the operations of political parties. With regard to his sentiments of freedom, he believed every person would be convinced that he had certainly imbibed principles of the most laudable nature, when he mentioned that he had been the pupil of Dr Priestley and had also studied with Mrs Barbould's father.*'

Benjamin went on to oppose the emancipation of negro slaves; as they were not ready for it and the planters would be ruined by it; he believed that there would be an end of civilisation in Jamaica. That the condition of the slaves might be improved, he did not deny. Two years later, in 1794, Benjamin came out in favour of the abolition of the slave trade.

That Benjamin never matriculated from Cambridge was due, as previously explained, to him being a Unitarian. Nonetheless, he did obtain an MD from Edinburgh.

Benjamin 1781-1836

In 1781, aged 30, Benjamin married Sarah, daughter of William Manning, a wealthy London merchant, after he had obtained his MD, a condition of him being allowed Sarah's hand in marriage. It is said that the two fathers settled a handsome fortune on the happy couple.

His father-in-law, William Manning, took Benjamin into partnership but the political arena held more fascination for him than the humdrum of trade. Mrs Vaughan is variously described as 'a very handsome, elegant and accomplished lady'. A portrait representing her in her advanced years shows a sweet-faced woman, wearing a cap and kerchief of flimsy lace. Sarah was a woman of many interests including the theatre, music, and painting. She sang and played the harpsichord. Benjamin and Sarah had seven children, three boys and four daughters.

One of the most influential men of the day was the second Earl of Shelbourne, William Petty Fitzmaurice, who was introduced to Benjamin by Joseph Priestley. Over time, Benjamin developed a close relationship with Shelbourne who often had him at dinner in London and the two of them to 'Bowood' for 'away' weekends. Before settling in Hallowell, Benjamin was involved in a number of high-profile events including the French Revolution, with which he was ardently sympathetic. In Paris he was imprisoned at the Carmelite Monastery but, probably due to the good offices of Robespierre, was released to Switzerland. A man of considerable influence and importance, Benjamin established himself with 'the great and the good' in America. During the period of the American Revolution, Benjamin engaged in propagandist activities for the Americans. In particular, he became a close friend of Benjamin Franklin, a founding father of the USA, and of Thomas Jefferson, principal author of the United States Declaration of Independence and third President of the United States who, after a visit by Benjamin to Monticello (Jefferson's residence just outside Charlottesville, Virginia), wrote to him in June 1819:

'... *I hope you effected your journey with health and pleasure, and found your family as well as the frigid sensations of a Polar climate can admit to its inhabitants. I have often wondered that any one should settle in a cold country while there is room for him in a warm one; and lamented that yourself and Dr Priestley should have been led into the snows of Maine and Northumberland rather than the genial climates of the South. In all situations however I sincerely wish to yourself and family health, happiness and prosperity and salute you with great friendship and respect.*'

Benjamin was an extraordinarily modest man with a genius for friendship. He knew and corresponded with most of the eminent liberal thinkers of his time. Such was his modesty that he rarely published anything under his own name. Consequently much of his work remains unidentified. Much has been written about Benjamin. One of the more important sources of further reading about this eminent Vaughan is *Benjamin Vaughan* by Mary Marvin Vaughan, privately published in 1979 (I have a copy). There is also a large piece

Vaughan·Arbuckle

The mists of Celtic twilight shroud the ancient name of Vaughan,
Hibernia knew its morning, and Cambria its dawn:
English was the seed that in New England took firm hold.

Vigorous was its growth in that New World as in the old.
A vital part played Benjamin[1] in peacemaking debates
Upon whose outcome was to flower the proud United States!
Grew with the land the vine of Vaughan with widely-branching shoots
Hallowell was its vineyard where anchored were its roots:
Americans true, Dissenters who though free men breathing-free
Never forgot "To serve the Lord is truly liberty."

As Lady Sophie Arbuckle in eighteen forty-three
Required a guardian for her name in perpetuity
Benjamin Vaughan was whom she chose to be its keeper true
United by a Warrant Royal and a handsome dowry too.
Contiguous with the English vine, which ever wider grew
Kept growing on that stem of Maine in generations new.
Longevity and fruitfulness proclaim the stalwart strain
Enhanced by lively local grafts which helped it grow amain:

Librarians at Harvard still guard Benjamin's bequest,
In Hallowell his homestead[2] still withstands time's wearing test:
No dynasty has better claim to history's Hall of Fame.
Enduring today~like the U.S.A.~the Vaughan·Arbuckle name!

1 BENJAMIN VAUGHAN (1755-1835) 2 HOMESTEAD 3 MOTTO

| Never a Dull Moment

on him in the *Dictionary of American Biography – Volume X*. I presented this parchment (opposite) to our American cousins (the Gibsons) in 1994 to mark the 200th anniversary of The Vaughan Homestead.

But back to the English-domiciled line of Vaughans, from which the Vaughan-Arbuckles are directly descended:

Benjamin[5] **Vaughan (1735-1828)** was baptised in London so he might be *'a free born Cittyson (citizen), his father being made of ye Scriveners' Company'*. Benjamin married Martha Carr in June 1762 aged 26. They had three sons:

George, born circa 1760 (see below).

Benjamin[6] **Kerr,** born Holborn, London, in 1763. He married Julia, daughter of Sir Thomas Stacey. Benjamin who was Rector of St Andrew's Church, Aveton Gifford in South Devon, for a remarkable 57 years, his entire ministry. The Rectory was a substantial building with fairly extensive grounds and it required a housekeeper, two maids and two groundsmen to attend to the property. The Rector was always dressed for outdoors in a black silk top hat, a dark morning suit with tails, and the inevitable starched shirt and collar. Benjamin was a very generous person known to help villagers with financial problems. He was also most supportive of the village school and he visited the sick on a regular basis The public were allowed to walk in The Rectory grounds on a Sunday and it was the habit of some families to visit a family grave in the churchyard and then to walk around the grounds of The Rectory. For his transport Benjamin maintained a horse and carriage.

Benjamin and Julia

Benjamin was awarded a DCL (Honorary Doctorate of Law). The degree is a higher doctorate usually awarded on the basis of exceptionally insightful and distinctive publications that contain significant and original contributions to the study of law or politics in general. They had one son who was dragged to death while riding a horse. Benjamin died in 1847 aged 84. Both he and his wife are buried at Aveton Gifford, Benjamin beneath the chancel. On the wall to the right of the altar, there is a marble plaque to Benjamin, his wife and his brother Edward, late Archdeacon of Madras.

St Andrew's, Aveton Gifford

| 48 |

Edward, born in 1776. He matriculated at St Peter's College, Cambridge, in 1790, graduated BA in 1794, and MA in 1798. In the following year he was appointed Chaplain, having obtained a Doctorate of Divinity. He arrived at Madras in March 1800 and for the next five years was Chaplain to various military parishes, before returning to St Mary's Church, Fort St George. In 1819 he was appointed second Archdeacon of Madras by the King in which appointment he remained for ten years. He married first, in 1816, Cecilia Collins, daughter of Major-General E Collins with whom he had two sons and one daughter. Edward became a freemason of Madras in 1833. After Cecilia's death he married Henrietta Clarke, widow of Colonel J Colebrooke, CB, with whom he had no children.

Edward retired to Devon from India to Devon and became Rector of St Mary's Church, Woodley (Woodleigh), now a listed building. At the time of the 1841 Census, Edward was shown to be living at Woolston House – described as a large mansion, with a well-wooded lawn of thirty acres. Edward died in 1849 of *'debility arising from obstructed bowels'*. He is buried at Aveton Gifford. During a holiday to south India in 2010, I visited St Mary's Church, Madras, which is now, sadly, in a very poor state of repair while retaining the aura of a building with so much history.

Edward

St Mary's Church, Fort St George, Madras

Christian Cemetery, Madras

I also went to the graveyard, located some way from the church under a flyover in one of the busiest parts of the city. Despite my best efforts, including a chat with the caretaker and his family, I was unable to locate Cecilia's grave within what is now a dilapidated collection of memorials largely hidden under scrub. Rather sad really, but then this part of India's past is no longer relevant or of interest in the modern world.

Little else is known about this branch of the family except that Benjamin is buried along with his parents at St Mary's Church, Great Parndon, having died on 10th April 1828, aged 92.

George Vaughan (1760-1804) is reputed to have lived in Lisburne (now Lisburn, Northern Ireland). He married Martha, daughter of Dr Francis Hutcheson, MD of Dublin, at Donaghadee on 24th January 1788. Francis Hutcheson (1694-1746), an eminent philosopher, was born in the parish of Saintfield, Co Down, Ireland. Both his father and grandfather were ministers of dissenting congregations in the north of Ireland. George and Martha had one son, Benjamin,[7] and a daughter, Martha, who married Rear-Admiral Samuel Leake. Little is known about George except that he was an Ensign (a junior commissioned officer) in the Horatio Militia. In 1798, Colonel Whitelock's Regiment of Foot in the West Indies was formally numbered as the 6th West India Regiment.

The following is an extract of a letter to Martha, his wife, that makes a number of references to his son, viz:

> *Tell Benjamin with my most affectionate love, that I desire he will write to me a very long letter, to give me a full and particular account of the manner in which he has been spending his time, how much he has improved since I left him, if he has attended to your directions; his books, his drawings and immediately to write me a very long letter, which you will send me, in his best writing, that I may be enabled to judge of his improvement in penmanship by ocular demonstration. I am sure he has been a very good boy, and tell him I hope I shall very soon see him, and reward him accordingly either at school or at Donagahdee in Ireland.'* In the same letter, George makes reference to his brother Edward (see above): *'Edward's nomination to his elegant appointment, what a transition from povety* (sic) *to affluence it is a good £1400* (over £100,000 today) *per annum with a noble house, and he has besides, a Palanquin* (covered seat carried by men) *carried by 6 Bearers kept for him, free of expense which is worth one hundred pounds a year more. I wished of all things to go out with him now, but it is not possible till something is found out after he gets to Madras. He will be as Lord Clive is and live in splendour and magnificence. I hope he promises most faithfully to make every enquiry for me on his arrival, and if it is in the bounds of probability to obtain any good thing for me, he will and he has*

promised to remember small darling, as he calls Miss Polly (George's daughter Martha). *Indeed I am convinced, if he does not marry, he will leave us all he acquires. He desires to be affectionately remembered to you and will, I think, sail in about a month ... I feel my affection for you stronger and stronger every day I live and only wish I had the means of proving it by more than words... I remain, ever and ever, your most truly affectionate husband.*
    Geo: Vaughan

Sophia, the fourth of six daughters to The 1st Earl of Roden, married James Arbuckle in 1798. They lived in Ballywilliam Cottage, Donaghadee, Ireland, where James was the Customs Collector. He signed a petition to the British Parliament in 1784 regarding affairs in Ireland and wrote reports to Lord Downshire regarding activities of the United Irishmen Rebellion in circa 1796 and again in 1798, when hostilities broke out in Donaghadee. The link between our family and Lady Sophia Arbuckle started when George Vaughan (1760-1804) met her at some time before 9th April 1799. We know this from a letter George wrote to his wife Martha (aka Polly), from Millman Street, London, dated 9th April 1799, in which he writes: *'I am quite enchanted with Lady Sophia and anxious for the honour of being introduced to her, she is a delightful creature. I am sure my heart warms to her, with the most gratified thanks for her kindness to you and my darlings... I by you will make my compliments and thanks acceptable to both her and Mr Arbuckle, as I, if I can be of the smallest service to either of them in London, they have but to command me ...'* Clearly, the friendship that ensued passed from father to son (Benjamin[7] 1790-1874) and, perhaps, became even stronger so that, when Lady Sophia died in 1825, she left him a large sum of money in return for Benjamin taking her name. Were it possible further to unravel this matter, it would surely make a fascinating story! The letter (I have the original) he wrote to Martha is an important family document for it speaks volumes of the relationship they had, his thinking on various matters and the way English was written in those days. We know that James Arbuckle died in October 1823, three years before Lady Sophia, and that both are buried in the graveyard at

George

Donaghadee. Donaghadee (meaning 'Daoi's church') is a small town in Co Down, Northern Ireland. It lies on the northeast coast of the Ards Peninsula, about 18 miles east of Belfast and about six miles south east of Bangor. It took Benjamin 17 years to accede to Sophia's wishes by taking her name.

There is another letter from George to Martha, written from the ship *William & Elizabeth* at sea Latitude 30, Longitude 58 (mid-Atlantic Ocean, NNE of West Indies) on 7th March 1800. The following is an extract of that letter:

> *My dearest love,*
> *I have been anxiously impatient for an opportunity of sending you this letter, and hoped to have found some homeward bound vessel at sea by it could have been conveyed to England. I have no doubt but that your impatience to hear from me is equal to mine of wishing to send it to you. No conveyance has offered itself – it must therefore wait till we have land, which is expected every day. The whole fleet are destined collectively to rendezvous at the island of Barbados from thence to be dispersed to separate places of destination, but I can go no further till I inquire how you and the darling pledges of my love are. I often wonder at myself how any circumstance on Earth could endure me to submit to be thus transported to an unknown region that's fit residence only of Cannibals and savages – My God – and when I think of what I have gone through, it tortures me, and almost makes me wild, but the Almighty has enabled me to do it, and I earnestly pray the result may be propitious to my wishes for all our sakes, and that the reward may be found adequate to the risque (sic) encountered. Words cannot express the distressing situation our fleet has been in since we put to sea; we have had one continual tempest for near a month. The fleet has at times separated, and hardly a ship has not been damaged, more or less, dismasted, others the sails torn all to pieces and two ships sunk and lost altogether. One of these was run down by an East Indian as close to our ship, went down and every soul perished. This ship was so near to us when she was struck that I could have thrown a biscuit on board from our vessel … we had to get out of the way of such mountainous seas I could have had no conception of. They were awfully majestic and grand, but to make a long story short we have had as bad a passage as ever was undertaken and it is exactly this day two months since I left Portsmouth and no appearance yet of any land of any kind. The greatest happiness I can receive in my*

absence will be in your giving me a good account of yourself and my darlings. You are also ever in my thoughts, and by the blessing of God, I hope we shall meet again, which is now all I desire, and I think if I could once again see you, I should be the happiest man alive, if I have not a shilling in the world before me so my separation from you and them ... I have already been resolving in my mind to return immediately to Ireland, by the very first ship homeward bound. I cannot be happy without you and what signifies leading a life of misery in any times whatsoever. I would rather have a bare subsistence with you and them than the collective wealth of the whole West Indian islands put together – so it is and ever will be ... I shall not forget the amiable Lady Sophia and send you and her the best ... I intend also to get for Mr Arbuckle the best collection of seeds I can ... I have so far written a composition of inherent nonsense ...'

These extracts are a fascinating insight into what sort of a man George was. There seems no doubt that he set sail for the West Indies to seek his fortune as so many did. But he survived only a further five years after writing this letter before dying of yellow fever in Surinam, South America while serving as an Ensign with the 6th West India Regiment in July 1804.

Benjamin[7] Hutcheson Vaughan-Arbuckle (1790-1874) was born on 23rd February 1790 in Lisburne, Ireland. His father, George, died when he was 14. As his father was a soldier serving overseas, it seems unlikely that he would have had any great influence on Benjamin. More likely, it would have been his mother, Martha, who did not remarry, who brought him up. As for his early education, nothing is recorded although Benjamin must have been bright otherwise he would not have passed the stiff entrance examinations for the military academy in Mathematics, English Language, Classics, French, History, Science and Drawing. As a Gentleman Cadet, the cost of his tuition fees, board, books and equipment would have been paid by his mother, although these might have been discounted because his father died during service in the Army.

Benjamin was admitted to the Royal Military Academy, Woolwich on 19th August 1805, having passed the entrance exam a year earlier. The RMA Woolwich (known as 'The Shop') was founded in 1741 to train Gentlemen Cadets for the Royal Artillery and Royal Engineers.

The period of instruction at Woolwich lasted a maximum of three years, after which time a Cadet would either have passed or would have been required to leave. Daily routine at the RMA was tough and demanding. A day in the life of a Cadet started at 6:15 am with drill,

| Never a Dull Moment

followed by an hour for breakfast at 7 am. An hour's riding or drill would have followed with a two-hour study period before lunch at 11:30 am. Lunch would routinely consist of bread, biscuits and butter and a pint of beer. A further two-hour session of study was followed by 'afternoon lunch', more study and then supper (in rooms), rounds at 10 pm and lights out at 10:30 pm.

It was customary for the Governor of the Academy (a serving Major-General) to write to the Commander-in-Chief, in those days HRH The Duke of Cambridge, on the success and conduct of each group of finishing cadets, certifying they were ready to take their commissions. Normally, such reports commended the good behaviour and example of this senior class, with a sword awarded to one student for good conduct (this tradition is still followed at the RMA with the sword being awarded to the Best Cadet). Benjamin passed out after a year and was commissioned into the Royal Artillery, as a Second Lieutenant on 4th October 1806. When a Major, Benjamin assumed the name Arbuckle in accordance with the wishes of Lady Sophia Arbuckle (died 1825) by Royal Warrant in 1843. In return for taking her name, Benjamin stood to inherit £3,000, worth a staggering £350,000 today.

Royal Military Academy, Woolwich

As a First Lieutenant, Royal Artillery, Benjamin saw service in France and the Netherlands, including the Battle of Waterloo and the capture of Paris in 1815, under Field-Marshal His Grace The Duke of Wellington, for which he was awarded the Waterloo Medal. Benjamin was also involved in the second of three Burmese Wars fought over six months in 1852, which resulted in the British annexation of Lower Burma. Benjamin made steady progress and, as this copy parchment (opposite) signed by George IV, shows, he was promoted Captain on 29th August 1826. By 1852 Benjamin had reached the rank of Lieutenant-Colonel and was almost certainly commanding a regiment. For this campaign he was awarded the Burmese Medal with clasp for Pegu. Now a Colonel, Benjamin served in the Crimea War and was involved in the Siege of Sevastopol, in which artillery played a huge and important part. He was awarded the Crimea Medal with clasp for Sevastopol and the Turkish Medal, having been on the staff of Omar Pasha's Army. Omar Pasha was a Serb convert to Islam. He also saw

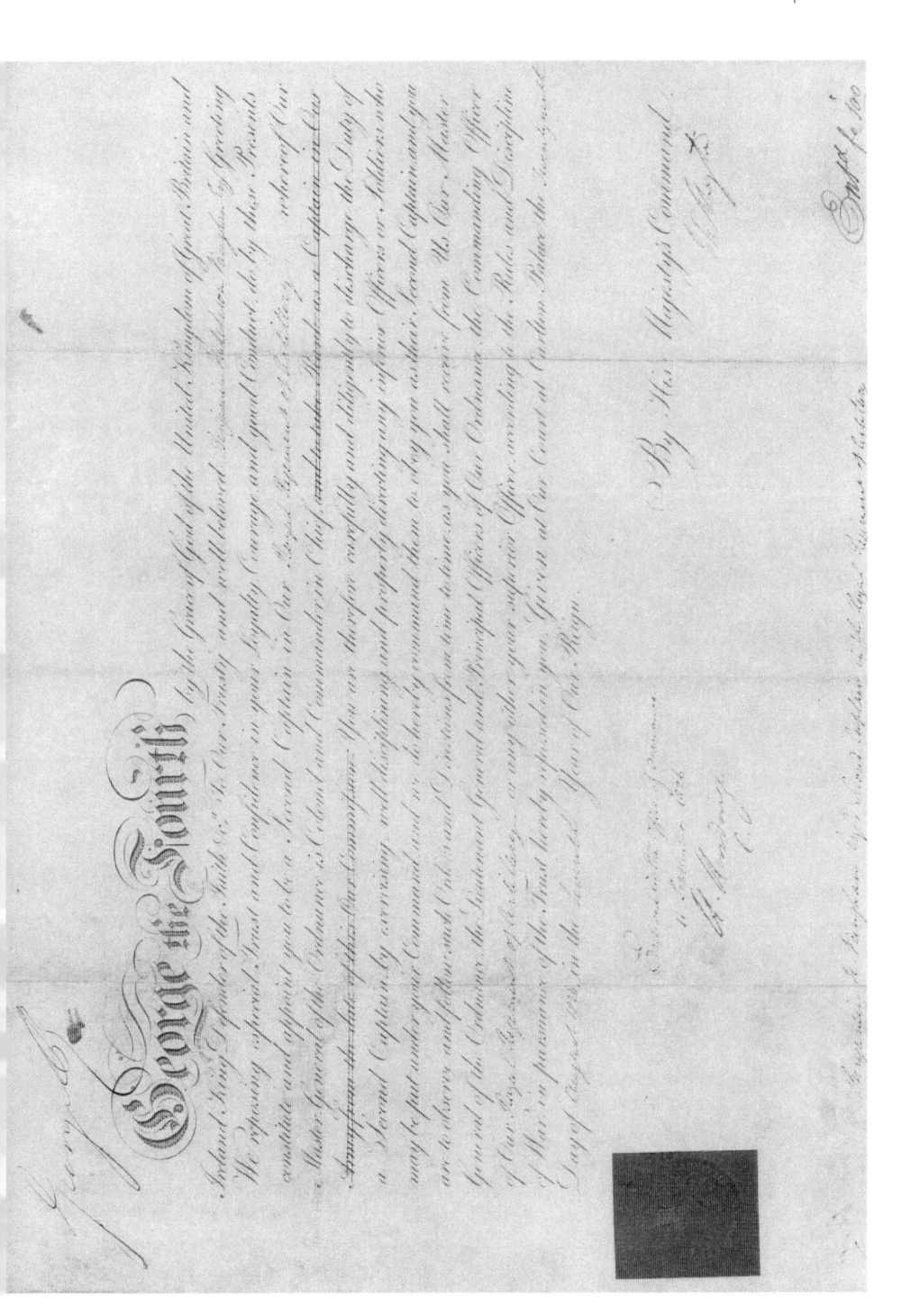

George the Fourth by the Grace of God of the United Kingdom of Great Britain and Ireland, King, Defender of the Faith &c &c To Our Trusty and well beloved _____ _____ Greeting

We reposing especial Trust and Confidence in your Loyalty Courage and good Conduct do by these Presents constitute and appoint you to be a Second Captain in Our Royal Regiment of Artillery _____ whereof Our Master General of the Ordnance is Colonel and Commander in Chief, and to take Rank as a Captain in Our Army from the date of this Our Commission. You are therefore carefully and diligently to discharge the Duty of a Second Captain by exercising well disciplining and properly directing any inferior Officers or Soldiers who may be put under your Command and we hereby command them to obey you as their Second Captain and you are to observe and follow such Orders and Directions from time to time as you shall receive from Us Our Master General of the Ordnance the Lieutenant General and Principal Officers of the Ordnance the Commanding Officer of Our Royal Regiment of Artillery or any other your superior Officer according to the Rules and Discipline of War in pursuance of the Trust hereby reposed in you. Given at Our Court at Carlton House the _____ day of August 1826, in the seventh Year of Our Reign.

By His Majesty's Command

service overseas in Malta, Ceylon and Jamaica. Benjamin was promoted Major-General in October 1856 and Lieutenant-General on 24th August 1866. He retired on full pay on 7th May 1867, age 77, at the end of a distinguished career. He was appointed JP on retirement from the Army. Like many soldiers, at the end of his service, he settled in the area near his regimental depot, in his case at Little Heath, Old Charlton, described as a suburb of the metropolis, and pleasantly situated, about one mile and a half from Blackheath, Woolwich, and Greenwich. The population of Charlton in 1851 was 4,818.

St Saviour's Church, Southwark

Benjamin

In 1830, at the age of 40, Benjamin married Mary Elizabeth McCutcheon, who lived in Woolwich, at St Saviour's Church, Southwark.

Benjamin and Mary had eleven children, seven boys and four girls. None of the girls ever married, while five of the boys followed their father into the Army, and a sixth died aged two. It was this Benjamin who was the first in a long-line of men in the family joining the Army. Starting with him, no less than six generations of Vaughan-Arbuckles have all had at least one officer in the Army, the latest being my own daughter Claire.

It has been impossible to identify positively the names of Benjamin's sons from the photographs opposite, although the first on the left in the top row is likely to be a young Benjamin[8] (born 1839) as he is wearing the uniform of an officer in the Royal Horse Artillery. The bottom photograph is almost certainly Charles (born 1831), about

What's in a Name?

Five of Benjamin's sons – all officers in the Army

whom we shall learn more later as he had a major part to play in the family history. Benjamin seems to have been a man of high moral principles judging by the fact that he gave evidence against his son, Edward, at the Central Criminal Court, London on Monday 16th April 1868. Edward (37 at the time), by now his eldest son, was charged with 'Unlawfully obtaining by false pretences 18s 6d from Frederick Marmaduke Marsden and £3 from Thomas Wittaker, with intent to defraud'. The court proceedings show that Edward presented cheques to be drawn on his father's account, knowing that he did not have his father's authority for doing so. The following is a record of the evidence in the case:

> Benjamin Hutchinson Vaughan-Arbuckle: *I am a Lieutenant-General in Her Majesty's service and live at Little Heath, Charlton. The prisoner is my son. He was formerly in the West India Regiment. I never gave him authority to draw on Messrs Cox & Co* (at the time I joined the Army, Cox & Kings were still the Army Banking Agents) *on my account. I have often told him not to do so on any account, and the last few years particularly. What I have said also applies to these cheques. I have one son in the Army, in India, in the 3rd Buffs – the prisoner drew on his account a short time ago.*
> Prisoner Question: *Have I not constantly for several years past, drawn on you with similar cheques to these?*
> Answer: *You have occasionally had permission. I allowed you money when you were in France. I did not allow you to draw on me when you were in Jamaica or in the Crimea or Montreal. Cox's have never paid without permission from me. You have*

> no money whatever in my hands. I expended £1,000 when you got a commission, in paying your debts. I tried to get you to go to Australia, but you would not go and I had nothing else to do but to bring your conduct forward. I have done it very reluctantly. Your debts amounted to £540 (£37,600 today). I have told you that I must get rid of you. You are my eldest son. You have nothing whatever to do with my property. Some clothes of yours were sent back to the tailors because we knew that the man would not be paid, and we advised him to take them back.
>
> Prosecuting Lawyer: *I believe you are supported by all your sons?*
>
> Answer: *Yes, I was obliged to lock up the plate* (silver). *Some of my clothes and plate was stolen and taken to the pawn shop. I am in my seventy-fifth year.*
>
> Prisoner Statement: *The prisoner, in his defence, stated that his father never brought him up in any profession until he was twenty-four years of age and that he had been accustomed to draw on his father for several years, and he had never made any objection.*
>
> Finding and Sentence: *Guilty. Five years' penal servitude* (imprisonment with compulsory labour).

What happened to Edward after he was released from prison is not known, but his father would have been 80 by then. By the time he died, Benjamin had been predeceased by five of his children. Of the remaining children, he left his sons Edmund, Charles, James and Benjamin[8] the sum of £3,000 (£216,000 at today's value) and his daughter Mary £2,000 (£144,000). He also left his son Edward £3,000 with the proviso that the money was to be used to clear his debts. His lands in Maryvale, Co Down, Ireland, were to be sold and split equally between his four sons, excluding Edward. He left his house in Little Heath, Charlton, and all its contents to his daughter Mary; she never married.

Benjamin died at Old Charlton on 11th October 1874 in his 85th year. He, along with his wife Mary and five of his children, are remembered by a monument (Plot 31) in the churchyard of St Luke's Church, near Woolwich, very close to where he lived.

Charles Vaughan (1831-1884) was born in 1831 in Woolwich. Following in his father's footsteps, he attended the RMA Woolwich and was commissioned into the Royal Artillery as a 2nd Lieutenant on 13th June 1851. Rising steadily through the ranks, seeing service with the Bengal (Indian) Artillery in the Burmese War (1852-53) and the

St. Luke's Church. *Old Charlton.*

Crimea, in which his father also fought, he ended his service in the rank of Major-General.

Charles married, first, Harriet Neild on 1st August 1857, at St John the Evangelist, Notting Hill, London, when he was 26. They had one child, Edith Annie, who is thought to have been born at sea in 1861, probably on the way to India. There is also something of a mystery surrounding Harriet's death although the likelihood is that she died in India where many expats fell victim to the climate and lack of hygiene or medical care. In 1865, Charles brought a claim for maintenance in respect of Edith Annie Vaughan-Arbuckle, against the trustees (Messrs John Hope Neild and Marcus Henry Johnson) of the Will of Sarah Kent, in The Chancery. Harriet's parents were Henry Isaac Neild and Sarah Kent. After Harriet's death, Charles decided to claim for maintenance for Edith Annie from his former mother-in-law's Will. Whether or not his case was successful is not known although, in absence of any documentation to the contrary, it seems likely that his claim was upheld. A copy of the Summons, dated 12th June 1865, is overleaf. Interestingly, Edith Annie married Philip

Charles VA

In Chancery 1865. A. 54

Filed 15 June 1865. In the Matter of Edith Annie Vaughan
Arbuckle an infant by Charles Vaughan
Arbuckle her next friend
Between Robert Plumbe and another
and Henry Isaac Neild and others
and Between Henry Palmer and others

Let all parties concerned attend at my Chambers No. 3
Stone Buildings Lincolns Inn in the County of
Middlesex on Monday the 19 day of June 1865
at 11 of the Clock in the fore noon on the
hearing of an application on the part of the said infant
that John Hope Neild and Marcus Henry Johnson the
surviving Trustees of the Will of Sarah Kent late of
Kensington Park Gardens in the County of Middlesex
who died on the 29th day of March 1857 may be at liberty
to pay to the said Charles Vaughan Arbuckle the father and
natural Guardian of the said above named infant Edith
Annie Vaughan Arbuckle the income of the one ninth share
to which the said infant is contingently entitled on her
attaining her age of 21 Years or marriage of and in the
residuary real and personal estate of the said Sarah Kent
deceased and to be applied by him in and towards the
maintenance and education of the said infant And that the
costs of the said infant and of the said Trustees as between
Solicitor and Client may be paid by the said Trustees out of
such income of the said one ninth share of the said infant the
same to be taxed —

Dated this 12th day of June 1865
Richard Torin Kindersley
Vice Chancellor

Summons was taken out by Robinson & Preston 35
Lincolns Inn Fields in the County of Middlesex Solicitors
for the said Infant.
To the within named
John H. Neild and Marcus Henry Johnson

Rickman in 1883, with whom she had a son, Philip Charles Rickman (1891-1982) who was well-known, respected and a successful painter of birds.

PHILIP RICKMAN 1891-1982

If his father had succeeded in dissuading Philip Rickman from turning to art for his livelihood, Britain would have lost one of the finest ever exponents of painting birds.

He began by chalking bantam cocks and farmyard ducks in his nursery and carried on painting during a solitary childhood at his home in Sussex, before his talent was encouraged at school. The disapproval of his father Commander Philip Howard Rickman did nothing to deter his teenage son from pursuing his chosen career. He went to Paris for two and a half years to study painting and his continuing fascination for birds took him to the aviaries and caged ponds of the Jardin des Plantes, where he was able to sketch at his leisure.

On returning to England his skills were developed further by instruction from George Lodge at Thurloe Square, London. Lodge instilled in Rickman that same passion for accuracy for which he himself was renowned. The Lodge connection was to remain strong. In later life the two sketched together when the mentor visited Rickman's home in Sussex.

Charles married his second wife Emma Jane Parker, daughter of Sir Henry Parker, Premier of New South Wales until 1857. He was knighted soon after returning to England, where he settled into Stawell House, Richmond.

In 1868, Henry Parker contested, unsuccessfully, the seat of Greenwich against William Gladstone, who became Prime Minister in 1892. On her father's death in 1881, Emma inherited Stawell House where she and Charles lived until it and all the contents were sold by auction on 18th June 1935. The house again changed hands a year later

| Never a Dull Moment

and was demolished in early 1937. On the original eleven-acre site, including a lake, there now stands Courtlands, a development consisting of a number of residential facilities. Courtlands is on the corner of Queens Road and Sheen Road, Richmond. The only original feature that remains today is the porter's rest. The area around the lake, surrounded by mature trees and lawns, is little changed from the time of Stawell House. The Tulip tree in this area is registered as a Champion Tree because it has the largest single girth in Greater London. Charles and Emma had two children, Lionel, who died unmarried aged 52 while living at Stawell House, and Grace, who married Randolph Hine-Haycock.

ICHMOND AND TWICKENHAM TIMES—SATURDAY, MARCH

ANOTHER DOOMED RICHMOND LANDMARK.

Stawell House stands at the corner of Queen's-road and Sheen-road in thickly-imbered grounds behind walls which will disappear and allow of a needed road widening at a busy corner. It was the residence of Major Vaughan Arbuckle, and on his death came into the market. The balustrading seen in the picture came from old London Bridge. The estate is to be developed, but the lay out will provide for blocks of flats set well back, and as a paddock in Sheen-r. 1 is to be turned into a garden, and many of the trees are to be retained, the aspect of the corner, both from Sheen-road and from the common in Queen's-road, should be a considerable improvement on the present walled enclosure. The plans were rejected by the Richmond Council at its last meeting for certain modifications.

What's in a Name?

On 30th December 1990 I was watching the TV programme Antiques Roadshow when my attention was alerted to an item regarding a set of crockery worth an absolute fortune. Described by the expert as 'enchanting', he dated the plate as c 1760, made in China. The middle-aged woman showing the set, when asked about the crest, explained that she had inherited the crockery from her father and that it had originally come as a result of him having married into the Vaughan-Arbuckle family. During a close-up, the realisation dawned on me that it was the Vaughan crest (a boy's head with a snake entwined about the neck) which was being displayed. The woman, who turned out to be from the Hine-Haycock family, said that she had about fifty pieces of the set. The expert valued each dinner plate (see below) at between £400-500 each, and estimated the whole set to be worth in the region of £50,000! On further enquiry, the BBC rightly said they would not give me the name and address of the woman but would pass any letter I might like to write to her. I did write but never heard anything back! Hardly surprising when the value of the crockery ran into many thousands of pounds – not that I wanted anything from her: all I wanted was information about how her family came into owning the crockery. From its date, it is reasonably certain that it was ordered by Benjamin[2] (1713-1786).

A Vaughan plate seen on the Antiques Roadshow

There is more than ample evidence of the amount of time, effort and money which Charles put in to trace the family history before William (1620), all to no avail. All his papers were returned to me by Diane and George Gibson, and if I needed any additional motivation, to continue my research into our family, Charles's work certainly provided it.

Charles died on 16th April 1884 and his wife Emma on 9th November 1934. The 1891 Census shows Emma living at Stawell House, with Lionel (21) and Grace (12), her children. She had six servants working for her: a butler, a housekeeper, three housemaids and a page-boy. Stawell House was ultimately sold for £34,400 (worth £7 million in 2011) on 14th July 1936.

3: Humble Beginnings

I was 15 and my parents were becoming exasperated by my lack of progress at school. My father, who was reasonably tolerant when it came to school reports, blew his top when my grading and written assessment for Games & PT was less than favourable. "I can accept most things, Ian, but a report which says that you are idle in games is totally unacceptable," my father reacted in exasperation. That I had upset my father, knowing what a talented sportsman he had been, really shook me. Looking back, I suppose this was the catalyst which started me thinking about what I was going to do with myself. Although I was in the Sea Cadets and interested in a career in the Royal Navy, aged 13 I had tried twice to pass the entrance exam for the Royal Naval College, Dartmouth, only to fail miserably in mathematics, always my Achilles heel. I could write, I knew a lot about geography, I had an interest in science, and history was a passion, but maths – forget it. A period of two years in India, in theory being tutored by a well-meaning Indian, but in reality playing cricket in the garden, meant that I had become a more than useful cricketer, but mathematically all I could manage was simple arithmetic: basically, I was innumerate! So my options were going to be limited. I wanted an active, open-air life: something with a challenge and which, if possible, included travel.

It wasn't long before the realisation dawned on me that a life in the Army was, in all probability, my best option even though my father had always told me being a soldier had many drawbacks. The Army recruiting office was located on Park Street, Peterborough, next to the doctor's surgery, so I knew exactly where it was. My heart raced as I rang the bell. After what seemed an eternity, the door was opened by a huge man in uniform, sporting a handlebar moustache. His jacket was festooned with medals and badges. I particularly noticed the three 'gold' stripes surmounted by crossed flags on his upper arm and the red sash that ran from left to right across his body. He was a formidable and impressive sight. "Yes, lad, what can I do for you?" he said looking down at me, or should I say, through me! He was even scarier than Mr Bainbridge, my maths teacher, and that was saying something. "I would like to join the Army," I replied, probably without much conviction.

We went into an office, much like any other office except that the walls were decorated, I remember, with posters of soldiers, tanks, guns and vehicles. 'Join the Army and see the world' was one poster that particularly caught my attention. I don't remember much about the 'chat' we had, apart from a few of his questions: "Why is it that you want to leave school before you take your School Certificate? What part of the Army do you want to join? Do your parents know that you want to enlist?" It was his final question that worried me as I had not told my parents anything of my plan to join the Army. After a few simple written tests, the recruiting sergeant said that he would have to call round to make sure my parents were in agreement with me joining up. My mother was in when I got home. With trepidation, I explained my plans and said the recruiting sergeant would be calling round that evening. She burst into tears. When my father got home, I could hear my parents talking about what I had done. I remember nothing of the detail apart from my father saying, "If that's what he really wants to do, let him do it. It will either break him or make a man of him."

I was in my room when the door bell rang. I knew it was the sergeant. He and my father went into the sitting room where I could hear them talking between themselves. My mother joined them before I was called into the room. To my relief, my father seemed to be in a good frame of mind. Was I serious about joining? Had I really made up my mind? Did I know that, once I had enlisted, there was no going back? The life was going to be tough, much tougher than anything I had yet done. He would not buy me out if I didn't like it. After downing another drink, the sergeant took his leave with a knowing smile in my direction.

Some days later a letter arrived from the recruiting office addressed to my parents. This invited me to make a second visit to the recruiting office which would include a medical. As I was still considered a minor, with the letter was enclosed a parental consent form which my mother made a great deal of fuss about before signing. After the medical, which I passed without problems, I took another batch of tests, this time a little more searching. The three tests were marked and the results discussed with me on the spot. I had not gained sufficient marks to qualify for officer training: no surprise there. I had, however, quite a lot of choice. I could enter one of the Army Apprentice Colleges, where I would learn a trade; I could opt for one of the Boys' training units; or I could go directly into an infantry regiment as a boy drummer. My father had advised me not to go into the infantry, but

Humble Beginnings |

join some part of the Army where I would be taught a trade which would be useful in later life. After I had read various pamphlets, the Royal Army Service Corps (RASC), in which my father had ended up, seemed the best bet, so I opted to join the Boys' Company RASC, at Buller Barracks, Aldershot, a place which was very familiar to my father. The next intake would be sometime in early May, about a month later.

It was 10th May 1954 and I was three months past my 16th birthday when I left home to make my appointment at the regional recruiting office in Northampton. Here I was to take the Oath of Allegiance, receive the Queen's Shilling and enlist. It was raining as I walked the mile or so to Peterborough station, with tears streaming down my face. The formalities of joining the Army, sealed with a handshake and 'Good luck' from the recruiting officer, did not take long. Armed with a rail warrant and other paperwork, proving I was a soldier, I proudly made my way, via London, to Aldershot. It was a nervous bunch of adolescent boys who left the train at Aldershot each carrying a suitcase. At the exit to the station, someone was shouting 'Anyone for Buller Barracks follow me.' Along with half a dozen others, I hauled myself up and over the tailgate into the back of the Army truck, something which was to become second nature over time. It was around lunchtime when we got to Buller (named after General Sir Redvers Buller of Boer War fame) Barracks.

After we had sampled army food for the first time, the next few hours were something of a blur as we were moved from building to building, collecting various items of bedding and uniform under the direction of a fierce Corporal who kept reminding us that 'You are in the Army now!' Oh yes, and by this time, I had been allocated an Army number: 22976359. Almost everywhere we went we had to recite our number and name (and in that order). My name invariably prompted some sarcastic comment or other. "Vaughan-Harbuckle! Where d'yer get a handle like that?" or "Posh bugger, eh?" were some of the favoured comments. It was as though I was being singled out for special attention. Then, out of the blue, I was taken to the Company HQ and ushered into an office where, to my complete surprise, I saw my father sitting alongside someone I got to know as the commanding officer. "Don't worry, Hector, old boy, the lad will be fine," said the major. After a few minutes general chit-chat, my father stood up, shook hands, wished me good luck and left. I had no idea he was coming. Even though he had obviously done so with the best of intentions, I never really forgave my father for visiting as this did me no favours in the eyes of my contemporaries, who drew the conclusion, wrongly, that I was some sort of special case. By the end of our first day we had been marched to the regimental barbers and subjected to our first 'short back and sides'. The haircut was hideous and I looked like a convict, but then so did everyone else.

Back in the barrack room, word had already filtered around that I was an officer's son – not a good thing, for thereafter I was invariably singled out for 'special' unwanted attention. The first such occasion was the following day at tea (the evening meal) when I was 'invited' by a boy NCO (non-commissioned officer) to get him a second helping. I was turned away by the cook who recognised me as already having had a meal. This upset the NCO who said he would 'see me later'. I had an uncomfortable feeling that this meant trouble and so it did. In front of the entire barrack room of 31 other recruits I was given a good hiding. Because I was considered different and 'posh', I was picked on for some time until one day, under threat of being sorted if I was no good, I attended a trial for the football team. I played well and was immediately picked for the team. As time progressed, proving that I was good at most sports ensured I was accepted as 'one of the lads' and left alone. Others were not so lucky.

I don't remember many of the boys who joined up in the same intake, apart from one named Blatch, a fragile-looking lad who came from a West Country, Christian family. Intelligent, quietly spoken, conscientious and hard-working, he and I seemed to be better educated and on the same wavelength. We became friendly. On the first night, in front of a full barrack room, Blatch knelt by the side of his bed to say his prayers. Despite the ridicule that came his way, he never once flinched from his convictions. Eventually the others got used to him praying and left him alone. His was a display of moral courage that I have never forgotten. Blatch, who was not really cut out for soldiering, 'bought himself out' for the required £20, leaving the way clear for me to receive the Best Recruit medal for the intake. By the end of term, the intake of 64 boys, who had started basic training 16 weeks earlier, had reduced by about a third for various reasons. The training was tough and uncompromising. The daily programme started with reveille bugle call at 6 am, followed by breakfast and morning muster parade at 7.30. Formal training consisted of a mix of drill, weapon training, physical training, education, fieldcraft, live weapon-firing and an assortment of other lectures. Tea would be at 5.30 pm. The five hours between tea and lights out were called Interior Economy. This was the period for cleaning personal kit and preparing the barrack room for inspection the following morning. But it was not all about kit cleaning.

I remember, particularly, a camp in the Isle of Wight, a part of England with which I was to become very familiar. Leaving Aldershot

Humble Beginnings |

by train, having marched the two miles to the railway station, 300 or so boy soldiers in Field Service Marching Order (full kit), carrying a Lee Enfield .303 rifle, must have been quite a sight. I was very proud to be a part of it. At Portsmouth, we caught a special ferry to Ryde and then a special train to Sandown. Another two-or-so-mile march brought us to a tented camp at Yaverland where we spent much of the next two weeks getting fit, shooting rifles and other weapons, for a lot of us the first time we had done so, and many days map reading our way around the island. The climax was a cross-country run up to a monument on the top of Culver Cliffs and back. I thoroughly enjoyed the experience of living outdoors and was proud to wear my uniform to walk out in the evenings, having passed inspection at the gate. It was during a Saturday night out that I met a Swedish girl who was working in the town. She was blonde, curvaceous and tanned and quite the loveliest girl I had ever seen. It was 'love', or possible 'lust', at first sight and the feeling seemed mutual. A kiss and cuddle on the beach after the dance was the climax to a wonderful evening but I never saw or heard from her again!

My father and his brother Keith, who must have been home on leave from India, where he was a tea planter, visited and took me out for a meal. I remember well (Uncle) Keith, of whom I became very fond, asking me loads of questions designed, I suspect, to make sure I was happy. He encouraged me to work hard, get my O Levels and then apply for a commission, something which was a long way from my mind at the time!

The task of keeping one's personal kit clean and uniforms pressed was all-consuming. The rough uncomfortable worsted tunic, woollen khaki shirt, webbing gaiters and belt, unyielding boots and peaked hat with a leather chinstrap, had to be prepared for parade each day. The issue boots made of stout leather uppers, thick soles with steel heel plates and studded throughout the sole, had to be polished to get a mirror-like surface on them. This could only be achieved by burning the pimples off the leather with a heated spoon or iron followed by hours of polishing with a mixture of heated Kiwi or Cherry Blossom boot polish and spit. This was known as 'bulling'. Webbing, of which there was plenty, had to be blancoed, brasses polished back and front, uniforms pressed so that creases were knife-edged, best achieved using a piece of brown paper, and socks darned – yes, darned – using a wooden 'mushroom'. Then there was the weekly inspection when every item of personal kit, down to needle and cotton, had to be displayed in accordance with a standard layout.

Lockers had to be open, and the barrack room, washroom and toilets immaculate in presentation. Woe betide anyone whose kit did

| Never a Dull Moment

Standard kit layout. Note polished wooden floor & bare walls.

not reach the required standard! Punishment could range from the layout being thrown all over the room or out of the window, to show parade where an item had to be produced to the satisfaction of the duty NCO or, in extreme cases, being charged and awarded 'jankers', a routine of three inspections each day for a period of up to fourteen days. At the time I found it difficult to understand why so much emphasis was placed on 'bulling' kit. However, as I progressed in the Army and became responsible for others, the rationale became clear. Many, left to their own habits, would not have maintained the standards of personal hygiene and cleanliness required when living in a barrack room environment. It also provided an important opportunity for those in positions of authority to maintain regular contact with their subordinates by having to keep a formal register of checks (like a monthly check of feet) and inspections. The only respite from the constant pressure was on Sundays when the regime was relaxed. But there was still a Church Parade once a month when the entire unit marched to church behind the band. During an early talk from the padre, he let it be known that anyone would be welcome to attend the social gathering held each Sunday after Evensong. I duly went along and was pleasantly surprised to find that girls went too. I became a regular churchgoer! I started to smoke regularly and used to buy packets of five Woodbines, the cheapest cigarette on the market.

When times were hard, I rolled my own cigarettes using Golden Virginia tobacco and Rizla cigarette papers.

Bullying was endemic in the unit. The boy NCOs, equivalent to prefects at school, were the worst culprits and it was far worse than the 'fagging' system prevalent in a lot of the top public schools. In my unit, 'fagging' consisted of cleaning the NCOs' kit, bringing a meal from the cookhouse (strictly against rules) and in some cases granting sexual favours. One of the worst incidents of bullying I witnessed was of a boy being put in a steel locker and a newspaper set alight in the space left by a drawer. On another occasion a boy's genitals were blackened with shoe polish. The regimental bath, for those deemed to be unclean, consisted of being scrubbed with a bristle brush in a cold bath, after which most emerged bleeding from grazes. I managed to avoid being picked on by refusing the first time I was asked to do something for a boy NCO. This resulted in another hiding but after that I was generally left alone. I joined up with a group of boys from all parts of the UK, from all backgrounds, with different levels of education and even some with criminal records. They were a rough, tough lot, but most were decent lads. It seemed that sport, particularly football, was a common denominator. Being a supporter of Manchester United gave me considerable 'street cred' and meant I had an ally in our Boy Corporal, named John Thomas (true!), a tough 'nut' from Manchester who also supported the Reds (Manchester United). JT also played for the unit football team and, until he was thrown out for fighting, we became good friends. The Head Boy, who had the title Boy Sergeant-Major, held a position of great power and influence in the unit. I remember well an occasion when, in the absence of a permanent staff instructor, he took one of our drill lessons. One lad, who had difficulty in telling the difference between his left and right – a serious deficiency in the Army – was taking a real 'bollocking' when I noticed a trickle of liquid running down the parade ground. The poor lad had wet himself, such was the terror inflicted upon him by the Boy Sergeant-Major!

As we were paid ten shillings (£10 in today's money) one week and five shillings the next, money was tight! This led to there being money-lending syndicates in the unit. The rate of interest was 100% so that if you borrowed one week you paid back double the next week. If the debt was carried over to the next week, the debt, including the previous interest, was doubled and so on. I knew of boys who owed so much by the end of term that they were obliged to hand over all their savings at the end of term so that they went home on leave with nothing. Searches of barrack rooms were carried out regularly by the permanent staff, usually after a theft was reported. But a visit by the military police – 'Red Caps' – was unusual. So when the whole unit

| Never a Dull Moment

was once confined to barracks and subjected to a search by the RMP, something serious was afoot. The search took all day and resulted in the arrest of four boys and a corporal of the permanent staff. They had been visiting other units in Aldershot at night and stealing money and valuables from soldiers as they lay asleep. Subsequently known as the 'Artful Dodger Gang' – after the pickpocket 'team' in Charles Dickens' book *Oliver Twist* – they were subsequently sentenced to various terms of imprisonment.

The general situation was of such concern that, in 1955, a report was commissioned into 'The Organisation and Administration of Boys' Units in the Army' which came to be known as the Miller Report after its author Lieutenant-General Sir Euan Miller. Among the more important recommendations in the report was that boys' units be conducted more as schools than military establishments, and that more care be taken in the selection of the permanent staff. Most importantly, the title 'Junior Leader' was to replace, with immediate effect, 'Boy' for both individuals and units. As I was to find out later in my career, this title change was to have an important impact on how these establishments were perceived by parents and the educational establishment. One of the recommendations of the report was for each boy's unit to have a WRVS (Women's Royal Voluntary Service) individual to provide female counselling, a library and a quiet room. Miss Ena Blazier, a petite, pleasant woman of about 30, duly arrived. She made an instant impact by starting a relationship with one of the officers!

Despite the down side, I generally enjoyed my time as a boy soldier. I could take the harsh discipline and found the physical side of life to my liking. I represented the unit at football, basketball, cricket and cross-country running. I beat all-comers at throwing the cricket ball on Sports Day, including a young officer, Richard Hutchings, who was to become a lifelong friend. To this day, he still cannot believe I could have thrown further than him! My prowess at sport resulted in me being awarded the coveted Sportsman of the

Outstanding Sportsman 1955

Year prize in 1955: a very proud moment and I still have the trophy to prove it.

I particularly enjoyed the four-week Outward Bound Course in Towyn, Mid-Wales, during which we were taught and tested through various activities including canoeing, rock-climbing, fell-walking including map reading, assault course work, potholing and a daily run. All this was designed to build character and flesh out leadership qualities. The final test was a three-day survival exercise over mountainous country in small groups of three or four. I must have done well for soon after the course I was promoted to Boy Sergeant to become 'Head Boy' of my platoon of 60 boys. During my last year, I was invited to appear before a unit selection board to judge whether I had sufficient qualities to suggest that I could be a credible candidate for officer training. I don't recall too much about the interview except that I found some of the questions a bit 'deep'. It therefore came as no surprise when I was told that I had not passed. I don't recall any great disappointment in failing, which must mean that I agreed with the board's conclusion that I was generally immature!

The permanent staff were a mixed bunch. Corporal Atkinson, who was in charge of the section of my intake, was a formidable and yet fair man. His tales of the war in North Africa, Italy and Germany, given credence by his chest of medals, always demanded our full attention as did his instructions! Trumpet-Major (a rank which has long disappeared) Botley was my platoon sergeant. A kindly, fair-minded man, he had enormous experience of life and soldiering and always had time for an encouraging chat as I made steady progress in the unit. He was also in charge of the football team and made sure his 'boys' were looked after and given extra time to prepare for important games. Under his coaching we went on to win the Army Challenge Cup for boys' units in, I think, 1955; I do remember scoring two goals in the final. I don't really remember my platoon officer except that he was a Scottish lawyer doing his National Service. During the latter part of boy's service, I took part as an extra in the highly acclaimed film *Tunes of Glory* starring Alec Guinness and John Mills (both of whom were later knighted). The 1960 film is a 'dark psychological drama' centering on events in a Scottish Highland regiment in the period following the Second World War.

In the middle of 1956, I recall there being a significant influx of soldiers into Aldershot, including Buller Barracks. They made an immediate impression as most had long hair and ill-fitting uniforms. After a period of febrile activity, these men seemed to spend ages hanging around the NAAFI canteen or wandering aimlessly around the barracks. Then suddenly they were gone as though a magic wand

Private I V-A

had been waved. Subsequently, all became clear when it transpired that they were Z Reservists who had been called up to reinforce the regulars who were on stand-by to take part in the Suez Campaign. The majority of British Army soldiers whose terms of engagement, including conscripts, had a reserve liability after they had finished their 'full-time' service 'with the Colours' were transferred to the Z Reserve. The Z Reserve could be mobilised if there was a threat to national security and after an Order in Council had been passed. In July 1956, General Abdul Nasser, of Egypt, seized control of the Suez Canal. In November of that year a combined force of British, French and Israeli ships, aircraft and troops recaptured the canal, but pressure from the USA and the Soviet Union compelled the Allies to make a humiliating retreat, leaving the canal in Egypt's hands.

Leaving junior leader training at the end of two years was something of an anti-climax. There was no ceremony, just a change of uniform into battledress from the tunic which identified junior leaders. Those of us who had held junior rank now reverted to the rank of private.

I had learnt how to drive and passed my driving test on 15-hundredweight truck as a way of getting a driving licence rather than any long-term ambition to be a driver. So, it was with a feeling of some trepidation that, along with a handful of other ex-junior leaders and apprentices, I reported to Willems Barracks, Aldershot, to commence clerical training. I remember very little of the few months I spent learning about office procedures and being taught how to type. Suffice it to say that I passed the various tests and left clerical training as a fully qualified clerk, able to type at thirty words per minute, without being at all sure that was what I wanted to do. Somewhere along the way, I recall attending yet another selection board to see whether I was suitable to attend a non-commissioned officers' course. Out of the blue, just before I was due to be posted to my first adult unit as a clerk, I was told that I would be going on the next course at the Junior NCOs'

Humble Beginnings |

School at Golden Hill Fort (recently converted into luxury flats), Freshwater in the Isle of Wight. To attend this course it was necessary to be an NCO, so it was with some pride that I took my uniforms to the tailors to have a single chevron (stripe) sewn on to denote that I was now an acting, unpaid lance-corporal. Well, we all have to start somewhere! The hard and demanding course lasted 16 weeks and was a true test of leadership qualities. As I look back, I think it was this time which made me realise that to get on in life it would be necessary to apply myself by working hard. The instruction and general management on this course was as high as I ever experienced in my army career. Although the youngest and by far the least experienced, I think I finished up around sixth in the order of merit and left the school as a substantive Corporal. I was also chosen to command the Passing Out Parade, a very proud occasion. Every two years, the Royal Army Service Corps held a rally at the Albert Hall in London where, in front of the Colonel-in-Chief, various military displays and trooping of the British Legion banners, like the current Royal British Legion Festival of Remembrance, took place. In 1957 I was a member of the Guard of Honour for the Duke of Gloucester, furnished by the Junior NCOs' School, as part of the Rally for that year. I particularly remember spending most of the day practising marching down the steep steps into the arena to make sure nobody tripped and took the guard with

I'm third from the left

them! I can't remember what he said to me, but I do recall the Duke asking me a question. It was many years later when, as a Major, I was responsible for organising the same rally. The saying 'What goes round, comes round' seems apposite!

To my surprise, I was posted back to the Junior Leaders' unit I had left barely a year before, as an instructor. By this time the unit had relocated to Bordon, Hampshire. I remember little of this phase of my career apart from one incident involving another member of staff. I was on duty when a boy told me he had been approached by a cook to meet him in the toilets that evening. I instructed the boy to go ahead and I would be there to intervene should it be necessary. I was hiding in the toilets when I heard what were obviously inappropriate sounds coming from a cubicle. Sure enough both had their trousers down when I broke in. I placed the cook in close arrest. The next morning he appeared in front of the commanding officer on a charge of indecency. After I had given evidence, to my surprise the charge was dismissed, as the CO explained, because I had aided and abetted the crime by telling the boy to agree to meet the cook! The word 'entrapment' comes to mind. The ramifications of what I had done were explained by the CO: an embarrassing mistake which I was never to forget.

I played football and cricket for local teams which brought me into contact with civilians of my own age for the first time since I joined the Army. My working life was humdrum so I was glad when, one day, I was sent for by the commanding officer who said he had been asked whether or not he thought I was suitable to be posted as personal assistant to the military adviser in Karachi, Pakistan. I remember the tenor of his questions giving me the distinct impression that he had doubts about whether, given my lack of experience, I was ready for such a special job. After all, I was only 20 and had little experience of life or the Army. I think the fact that I had lived in India probably swung the decision in my favour. A formal posting order followed, which showed that I was to travel by ship to Pakistan. I was overjoyed and not a little excited at the prospect of this 'special' posting. After passing the medical, having my 'jabs' (inoculations) and being issued with a set of tropical uniforms, I boarded *RMS Cilicia* on 28th June 1958 to travel the 6,000 miles, via Port Said and Aden, to Karachi.

It was a very nervous young man who was shown to his cabin. I was relieved to see a 'Vaughan-Arbuckle Mr IM' shown in the passenger list and not 'Acting Corporal', particularly as there were a number of officers listed. To my delight, a number of 'Misses' would be on board during the voyage. I remember very little about the three weeks on board, except that a lot of time was spent eating, drinking, playing cards and sunbathing. I suppose that since I had already travelled this route twice with my parents, it did not hold the same excitement as if I were a first-timer. However, I do recall watching land creep into view over the horizon as we approached Port Said, the jostle of small (bum) boats selling things, bringing the 'Gully-Gully' men conjuring with live chicks and ping-pong balls and the smell of the flotsam and jetsam floating on the water. My constant companions during the voyage were a couple of junior civil servants who would also be working in the UK High Commission. I remember what I thought to be their sophistication and worldliness being somewhat daunting as I came to the realisation that I was sadly lacking in those areas.

On 13th July 1958, we moved very slowly into Karachi harbour to tie up alongside one of the many berths for large ships. It was extremely hot as I searched the quay for anyone who might be there to meet me. There was no-one in uniform, so, it was a complete surprise when, after a tap on my shoulder, a young sun-tanned man, carrying a black leather briefcase and wearing an open-necked sports shirt and casual trousers, introduced himself as Sergeant Gerry Dakin. I thought he looked far too young to be a sergeant as he drove me, in the office Land Rover, through the chaotic streets of Karachi, talking non-stop about the job and life in Pakistan. We would be working together in the same office and I was relieved that he seemed a decent, friendly guy, if perhaps a little intense.

"Our house, known as 'The Chummery', is a couple of miles out of town just off the airport road," Gerry explained as he wove his way through crowded streets at what I thought was breakneck speed in the office Land Rover. Liberal use of the horn, which would not have been tolerated in the UK, and abrupt use of the brakes, ensured that we avoided sundry cyclists on their rickety old bikes. The Chummery, off the Drigh Road, was part of a small complex of flats, surrounded by a wall, with a pretty garden in the centre of the complex. We were met by the Bearer, who was wearing a long, white frock coat, a coloured cummerbund and a *pugree* headdress. Well over six feet, upright, with a handlebar moustache, I thought Shaffi was an impressive figure as he showed me to my room on the first floor. "Get yourself together and I will see you for dinner at 7 pm sharp. Once we have eaten, we might

Shaffi

just go to Speedbird House for a jar or two," said Gerry as he left me to unpack and reflect on my new situation. I remember having to shake myself to ensure that I was not dreaming.

At dinner, I met the other two who would be my companions in The Chummery: RAF Sergeant John Giles, who was PA to the Air Adviser, and Roger Austin, a junior civil servant. On first acquaintance, both seemed pleasant although, because he was somewhat older and not at all sporty, John kept himself to himself whereas I and the other two became almost inseparable. Life in The Chummery was good. We ate together and took it in turns to maintain the housekeeping account, keep an eye on the building and garden, supervise the food, agree the menu and, the most popular job of all, arrange our social programme. After dinner on that first night, we did visit Speedbird House, run by BOAC for their crews and passengers. The attraction of Speedbird House, which required a special pass acquired by Gerry, was twofold: English beer and a good selection of air hostesses. Both were expensive and beyond our means except for, perhaps, a monthly visit!

I soon settled into my job as personal assistant to Major WHA (Bill) Becke, of the Worcester & Sherwood Foresters, very much of the 'old school' who set and demanded the highest standards of etiquette, manners and efficiency. With a black patch over his left eye, to hide the loss of his eye during a fire-fight in Italy, for which he was awarded the DSO, 'The Major' was a popular and respected figure within the High Commission and outside with the other military attachés. Subsequently, Bill Becke was promoted to Lieutenant-Colonel and posted to Indonesia where in 1962, in the face of an attack on the British Embassy, he made the front pages in the UK for guarding the strong-room, at pistol point, when it was threatened by communist insurgents. For this act he was awarded the CMG. Bill Becke was to play a major part in my future. Gerry, meanwhile, reported directly to Brigadier Alistair Tuck, late of the 10th Hussars, the Military Adviser. As a team we got on extremely well. Not only were we responsible for providing clerical support to our officers, our duties also included clearing their diplomatic consignments through the port authorities, sending out invitations for their official parties, sometimes being present at those parties to keep our eyes and ears open for information, arranging tour programmes and, perhaps most interestingly, typing classified tour reports on the Pakistan Army and related subjects, which went back to London.

I was woken, early on the morning of 8th October 1958, by a worried Gerry Dakin who told me that there had been a takeover by the Pakistan Army. In the morning we were to wear uniform to work

Humble Beginnings |

Outside the High Commission with Gerry Dakin

and make sure that other staff on the bus were protected from any trouble on the way in to the High Commission. I remember getting up to look for my uniform and iron it, since I had worn it only rarely since arriving in Pakistan. On the three-mile journey into the centre of town, the streets were almost deserted apart from the presence of armed soldiers on almost every street corner. It was a surreal and somewhat worrying drive. On our arrival, we found the High Commission guarded by a detachment of armed soldiers while a sense of urgency prevailed inside the building. In brief, what had happened was that the Army, under General Mohammad Ayub Khan, had declared Martial Law throughout the country in a bloodless coup d'état, with the connivance and co-operation of the outgoing President, retired Major-General Iskander Mirza.

In a statement to the nation, the deposed President explained that for two years he had been watching a ruthless struggle for power, corruption, and shameful exploitation of the people. He

8th October 1958, UK High Commission, Karachi

referred to the continuing food crisis, organised smuggling and black-marketing, and to the disgraceful scenes in the Provincial Assembly of East Pakistan. He considered the existing political parties to be selfish and unscrupulous, and could not be relied upon to participate in fair elections. For these reasons, and to avert a bloody revolution, he had decided to place the country under Martial Law. Simultaneously, General Ayub Khan released his own statement proclaiming Martial Law, but significantly making no mention of the delegation of power to him by the President. The view in the High Commission was that Martial Law had been imposed by the Army, not ceded to them. That the coup was bloodlessly and efficiently imposed supports the view that it had been planned and executed over time by the Chiefs of Staff. Within a week, under the threat of severe action, prices of staple foodstuffs had fallen by 50%, and a number of high-profile arrests had been made. The new military government, with reforming zeal, introduced regulations requiring a greater sense of civic responsibility, in particular a general regard for cleanliness, hygiene and civic well-being. Anyone found guilty of molesting women was liable to five years' hard labour, begging was prohibited on pain of six months in jail and a whipping, while throwing refuse on the streets was made punishable. Almost overnight, the deliberately and hideously twisted bodies of children placed on the streets by parents with a begging bowl in front of them disappeared. No longer were the dying to be seen lying unattended on the streets of Karachi just waiting to be thrown into the back of a truck which plied the streets daily to collect the dead.

Brigadier Tuck knew General Ayub Khan well. Having almost unfettered access to him, the brigadier was able to submit highly regarded reports to London. I remember well one incident in his dealings with London which infuriated Alistair Tuck. During a visit to the President, who was a very keen sportsman, the General asked whether it would be possible for the British Army to provide a boxing instructor from the Army Physical Training Corps, for whom he had the highest regard from his student days at the Royal Military Academy, Sandhurst, to train the Pakistan Army team for the forthcoming Asian Games. The reply from the War Office (now MOD) was that they would be willing to do so if Pakistan paid his salary, the expense of his travel, and his board and lodging in Pakistan! Despite his efforts to get this ruling overturned, the War Office would not budge, leaving the Brigadier with the unenviable and embarrassing task of telling the President that we could not meet his request! This decision, particularly when the USA was pouring millions of dollars into Pakistan, made absolutely no sense. The damage it did on a personal level between Alistair Tuck and the President was immense.

The USA was delighted to oblige!

The news that I had been chosen as a replacement for the Queen's Messenger, who had not arrived from the UK, to take the diplomatic bag from Karachi (Pakistan) to Delhi (India), came as a complete surprise. The white canvass mailbag on which was painted in black 'Her Britannic Majesty's Diplomatic Service' was locked to my wrist before I left the High Commission until it was unlocked at the British Embassy in Delhi. I was taken to and met by a dedicated diplomatic car at the steps of the aircraft, a twin-engine Dakota used extensively in the Second World War, on which I was allocated a special seat to myself. The flight, the first I had ever taken, couldn't have been a worse introduction. Flying over the Sind desert we hit huge pockets of air, on a regular basis during the two hour flight, when the aircraft would drop like a stone and then shudder violently as it re-entered normal air. Frankly, I was terrified and it took many years for me to conquer a fear of flying based on this flight. On arrival in Delhi, I discovered why the 'Dip Bag' was so heavy. Apparently, the bag contained a leg of beef going from Karachi to Delhi and a leg of pork on the way back bound for the Ambassador, in addition to classified material!

Life both at and outside work was good. I was enjoying myself and the freedom which responsibility gave me. I could get on with my life without being supervised, within reason I could make mistakes without penalty, and my character was developing as I became more mature. For the first time in my life, I started taking a close interest in the opposite sex. In the days before gyms and health studios, the easiest way to keep a semblance of fitness was to go for a run, which I did about three times a week, wearing my army boots. One of my favourite routes took me past an enormous house surrounded by a six-foot whitewashed wall with an armed guard on the gate, obviously owned by an important person. Once or twice I had seen a beautiful Pakistani girl sitting on the balcony. She was there again one evening as I approached. I don't know what made me do it but as I grew level with where she was sitting, I waved. To my astonishment, the girl returned my wave. For the next couple of weeks I always ran past her house where my wave was always reciprocated. But how was I ever going to make real contact with her? Then one day something landed in front of me. It was a note saying she would be at the cinema on a given date and could I meet her? Next day she was on the balcony and I gave her the thumbs-up. We duly met after she was dropped by the family driver, held hands throughout the film and made tentative arrangements to meet again at the cinema. She was stunning and the others were amazed to hear that I had 'pulled' a Pakistani girl as they were normally heavily chaperoned. A few nights later, as we were having supper, Shaffi came in with a very worried look on his face. He said there was a *chowkidar* in the kitchen who wanted to see me. Sure enough, standing in the kitchen was this tall man, with a beard, holding a rifle with a dagger in his cummerbund, fixing me with his staring, blue eyes. Through Shaffi, he explained in an authoritative voice that he had been sent by his master to warn me not to see his daughter again. To do so would require him to return and, to demonstrate what would happen if I did not comply, he drew his hand across his throat. I never did run past that particular house again or try to make contact with a Muslim woman!!

The High Commission did have a number of expatriate young women working in various departments. One with a larger number of eligible ladies than anywhere else was the cypher room. So it was to my advantage to deliver and collect classified telegrams on a regular basis. Eventually I got to know Kaye Hunt, an ex-WREN, who was ten years my senior. She taught me a lot about life and was a great source of encouragement for me to better myself. She also gave me my first lesson in jealousy. A previous boyfriend in the RAF used to pilot occasional flights into Karachi and invite Kaye out. This really upset me to the extent that I used to wait in hiding for her to come home. Looking back, this was immature but when you are in love for the first time, logic goes out of the window! Anyhow, we stayed together until I left Karachi about a year later.

Kaye and me 1961 on my Francis Barnett

In the meantime, with Kaye we made a memorable trip into Afghanistan, via Hyderabad, the Sukkur Barrage and the Bolan Pass to Kandahar, a journey of well over 1,000 miles in her Morris 1000 convertible, staying in government rest houses on the way. I remember Kaye finding a large snake in the shower at one stopover which resulted in not much sleep that night even though the offending reptile was removed by the *chowkidar*. Wherever we stopped a large crowd gathered and, even in the remotest places, someone seemed to appear from nowhere. Occupied, in the main, by a 'terrifying' mix of Pathan and Baluchi tribesmen, this tribal territory is a potentially dangerous passage for unwary travellers. The Pathans are possibly the most ferocious, independent and warlike race ever, a fact that can be amply borne out by the successive armies to have been put to flight by them. Their aquiline noses, piercing blue eyes, long hair and black beards make them impossible to ignore. To do so is foolhardy in the extreme. So it was with some alarm in a remote area that we suddenly became aware of three tribesmen, carrying ancient rifles, looking at us from a distance of about twenty yards. Inviting them to join us for some food defused a palpable tension so that we were able to go on our way with smiles and handshakes all round. But it could so easily have ended in tears.

I particularly enjoyed the short time we spent in Quetta looking around the town, which occupies a vital and strategic position. The city remains a stronghold of the Pakistan Army and was formerly home to the British Army Staff College. The Pakistan Army is intensely proud of its links with the British Army. Our guide showed us around the bungalow occupied by one Colonel Bernard Law Montgomery (latterly Field-Marshal of World War II fame) who had been the chief instructor from 1934 to 1937, which is now a small museum containing military memorabilia. Quetta, situated on the fault line from the Himalaya, suffered a catastrophic earthquake in 1935 when 35,000 people died and every building in the town was razed. To reach Quetta from Sibi, it is necessary to pass through the famous Bolan Pass, which evoked thoughts of derring-do by British forces as they fought their way through the pass at the cost of great physical hardship and loss of life.

Travelling the 85 kilometres on the rough road through steep gorges and blazing heat, it was easy to

Entry to the Bolan Pass

Pakistan

understand the hardship endured by those who built the road and rail links in previous centuries, and those who have fought and still continue to fight over this barren and desolate area.

After an uneventful journey into Afghanistan, we were turned back at Kandahar by the police with a message from the High Commission that we were required back in Karachi! With all kinds of negative thoughts going through our minds, we drove home in around 48 hours to be informed by the security staff that, given the sensitivity of her job, Kaye should not have entered Afghanistan! This trip gave me a real sense of adventure and a deep-seated desire, that has remained with me to this day, to return to this part of the world.

Life in Karachi was less exciting. I played football for the High Commission and cricket for a local team. With some pride, I was chosen to represent the High Commissioner at the opening ceremony of the National Coaching & Training Scheme for Cricket at the National Stadium, Karachi, in June 1959. In those days Pakistan was a minor player on the world cricket scene. I remember well the Minister for Sport introducing Hanif Mohammad and Alimuddin, the former being one of the greatest batsmen ever to have played the game, to a tumultuous round of applause. Soon after I arrived it was clear that to make the most of life I would need my own 'wheels', so I bought a green Francis Barnett 125 motor cycle.

Riding around the town was trouble-free until one day on the way home I had an accident. I was approaching a *dudh-wallah* (milkman) riding his bike, with churns hanging off every spare space, when he suddenly got into a wobble. In an attempt to avoid hitting him, I went into a broadside but my back wheel just clipped his bike. He went flying and I careered, under my motor cycle, to the other side of the road. I picked myself up, covered with blood from grazes all down one side of my body. The road was awash with milk and the milkman was understandably bewailing his loss. A crowd quickly gathered and I was soon surrounded. Everyone was talking and it became obvious that the milkman was after compensation. Then a policeman, carrying a *lathi* (wooden staff), pushed his way through the crowd and was harangued by the milkman, who by his gesticulations was obviously blaming me for what happened. At that point, a well-dressed young man stepped forward and in perfect English offered his help. Yes, he had seen what happened. Could he please explain this to the policeman? Unwisely, as it turned out, the milkman continued to wail. After a short dialogue with the witness, the policeman raised his *lathi* and hit the milkman over his collar-bone. He fell to the ground out cold. Helping me to pick up my motor cycle and clear the crowd, the policeman waved me on my way without taking any details whatsoever. This was my introduction to summary justice in Pakistan.

I had been instructed by the Brigadier to book a number of passages to England by sea for the visiting British Army Mountaineering Expedition which had successfully conquered Rakaposhi, a 25,550-foot mountain in the Karakoram Range of Pakistan. During the course of some other routine business and out of the blue, the Brigadier told me to book an extra passage. On enquiring who it was for, the Brigadier replied 'You'. He was sending me home to attend the Regular Commissions Board. This came as a real shock since going for a commission was the last thing on my mind at the time. I was thoroughly enjoying life as a bachelor in Karachi and had no desire to cut short my three-year tour. Explaining my feelings to the Brigadier brought an immediate response. "The matter is not for discussion," he replied. So I left Karachi as a passenger on *MV Circassia* in October 1959, stopping at Aden and Port Said on the way home to Liverpool. The journey was uneventful once I had recovered from saying a tearful goodbye to Kaye. During the voyage I made friends with George Chapman, a captain in the Gloucestershire Regiment, who had been on the expedition to Rakaposhi, so it was hardly surprising when, during a visit to the pyramids, he persuaded me to join him in climbing up the outside of one of them! Socialising with an officer throughout the voyage helped me to get an idea of what selection process I would have to negotiate if I were to be successful in my quest to become an officer.

The stop in Aden enabled me to have a look around what was to become one of the 'hot spots' of the Empire four or so years later, when an insurgency against British rule began with a grenade attack by the communist National Liberation Front (NLF) against the British High Commission, killing one and injuring fifty. At the height of the troubles, the Argyll and Sutherland Highlanders, commanded by Colin (Mad Mitch) Mitchell, were sent to the British Protectorate as part of the peacekeeping force. Early in their tour, 22 British soldiers, including several Argylls, were killed in the Crater District and some others were held hostage. Mitchell, though not in command of Crater, urged an immediate rescue attempt but this was refused by the commanding general. Then about a week later, Mitchell led his soldiers into Crater with bagpipes and drums playing, wearing their distinctive glengarry headdress and recaptured the district from the terrorists. This brave action did not find favour with the general who ordered Mitchell to relax his firm military grip, with the result that terrorism immediately increased. Unhappily, Mitchell's differences with the general continued so that his outstanding leadership was never officially recognised. Mitchell retired prematurely and, as well as fighting a successful campaign to 'Save the Argylls', wrote his memoirs *Having Been a Soldier*. Many years later, I spent a fascinating afternoon with Sue, Colin Mitchell's widow, talking about her husband who was a hero of mine, who had died a few years earlier.

After a couple of weeks' leave, I reported to the Depot Battalion RASC, Bordon. I was there for about a month before I received instructions to report to the War Office Selection Board (WOSB), known to one and all as a 'Wasbee'. Daily tasks were allocated each morning on a muster parade. After being assigned to tasks such as coal fatigues and cookhouse duties, I complained that this was hardly appropriate preparation for officer training. This resulted in me working directly for the Company Sergeant-Major, sharing an office with him as his clerk. Watching him deal with all manner of problems and listening to his sage advice was invaluable and taught me lessons of man-management I have never forgotten.

It was a very nervous young man who made his way to the WOSB, held at Barton Stacey near Andover. We were divided into groups of five and were from all manner of backgrounds. The majority seemed to be from public schools and I was certainly the only regular soldier in my group. Allocated individual numbers displayed on bibs, to be worn at all times, it was clear that we were under constant scrutiny except when in bed! During the next three, highly intensive days we were submitted to a number of tests. At the top of the list was the individual assignment known as 'the situation', whereby the group would be confronted by five challenges with each man taking his turn as leader. My task involved me getting my group across a 'gorge' using a piece of rope, an oil drum and a plank. I remember getting into a real 'pickle' halfway across but still managed to complete the task within the time. There was also the individual assault course consisting of ten obstacles, as many of which as possible had to be successfully completed in three minutes. I foundered at the high wall after successfully negotiating around seven of the obstacles, finishing up with a blooded face after slipping and bashing my nose into the wall.

Then there were the written tests of intellect and logic including writing an essay, a battery of intelligence tests, and forming a written plan of action from a scenario involving escaping from an island guarded by insurgents. There were discussion groups and interviews: one of the more difficult questions, in my case, was 'Why do you want to be an officer?' – a question which contained a number of pitfalls for the unwary. We were required to give a ten-minute lecturette. The subject I chose was the Muslim festival of *Muhurram*, the first month of the Islamic calendar, when mainstream Shia Muslims stop eating during daylight hours and beat themselves in memory of an Imam of Shiism who was killed on the tenth day of the month.

Selection ended with each candidate marching into a room and reciting their full name and service details – presumably to ensure the Board had the right person when arriving at a decision – and then being asked a couple of questions by the senior board member while the others noted the candidate's reaction. Individual results were delivered when the squad NCO lined up the group and handed each person a piece of paper with their name on it. The paper declared Pass, Fail or Deferred (meaning come back in six months). Much relieved at being selected, I spent the journey back to Bordon wondering what officer training would be like. No more than 70% of those who appeared at WOSB passed the Board. It was an intense and tightly compressed examination of both practical and theoretical skills, and it was meant to be.

Although I had been selected, I was disappointed to discover that, because of my age (and background), I was to undergo training for a short-service commission rather than a regular commission at RMA Sandhurst where I would have followed my father. Fairly soon, I was off to Mons Officer Cadet School, Aldershot, where the most rigorous standards of turnout and bearing were applied. Mons was a very intense ten weeks of written and practical challenges, where being a team player was an integral part of searching for personal success and showing leadership qualities. The assault course, the tactical exercises – of which there were many, mostly leading a group through some kind of situation requiring an appreciation and orders – and all the other tests and exams were character-building and character-questioning. I remember in particular three individuals. The first was my platoon officer, Captain Jeremy Warner-Johnson, an infantryman. He was a cut above any other junior officer I had met. Suave, dashing, intelligent and understanding, he was my first, and perhaps the best, role model I ever had. The second was Sergeant Croft, my platoon sergeant, again an infantryman, from the north, with a habit of marching alongside your shoulder and delivering, in a considered voice, the most damning observations. The third was Regimental Sergeant-Major Lynch, Irish Guards, a huge man with a fearsome voice whose mere presence struck fear into the hearts of cadets and instructors alike. I remember well the talk he gave us on our initial parade, on the need for discipline, enthusiasm, hard work and some other virtues of the Army by which he set much store. He finished his talk by saying, "You'll call me 'Sir' and I'll call you 'Sir'. The difference is you will mean it!"

There was another occasion when the whole unit was preparing for a passing out parade of the senior division. The RSM was taking the parade when he suddenly caught sight of a cadet wearing leather gloves. "That cadet in the centre rank take your gloves off, sir." No-one moved. "Take your gloves off, sir!" Still no movement. At this point the RSM, clearly very annoyed, whipped his pace stick under his arm and moved forward with great determination towards the cadet in question. As he drew nearer he saw the enormity of his mistake. The cadet in question was an Indian!! One day, towards the end of our time at Mons, we were drilling in the presence of RSM Lynch, who could spot a badly timed about turn, a misaligned foot or a poor rifle movement from hundreds of yards. Suddenly he bellowed, "Sergeant Croft, you have an idle cadet in the second rank: take his name!" To my utter surprise and consternation, Croft replied, "Got him, Sir, Cadet Vaughan-Arbuckle on report!" This was a travesty and only occurred because, unusually, he had my name in his mind whereas normally with such a 'handle' few remembered it, let alone being able to articulate it.

Next morning, I appeared along with a dozen or so in front of the regimental adjutant named Captain Tollemache, a languid guardsman who just seemed to strut around in his riding breeches and shiny boots, carrying a cane, and looking important. When he got to me, my name and a charge of idleness on the square was read out. How did I plead? "Not guilty," I replied. This brought an immediate response from RSM

Lynch who said that he had personally witnessed my appalling lack of effort. Fixing me with eyes which strongly suggested that he had had a good night out, the adjutant awarded me 'seven days' restriction of privileges for the offence, and a further seven days for wasting my time'. I was shattered. Restriction of privileges (or *jankers*) involved parading morning, noon and night in various forms of dress and, in between, carrying out other menial tasks. I managed to negotiate the fourteen days without further mishap and went on to complete successfully that phase of cadet training.

The second 16-week phase of officer training, for those cadets destined for the RASC, was back in Buller Barracks where I had begun my army life. Coincidentally, I found myself living in the same barrack block as I had done some five years before, although the rooms were now much smaller and the communal facilities much improved. Life in Officer Cadet Company was less frenetic but that was to be expected since any weakness in a cadet would have been identified and dealt with at Mons, where the failure rate was pretty high. I found the training fairly straightforward and had little difficulty in passing the various written and practical tests, but it still came as a surprise and honour when I was chosen to be the Senior Under Officer (Best Cadet) of my course. But an incident, about a week before we were due to be commissioned, very nearly scuppered my career.

One Saturday night, four of us decided to gatecrash a Young Conservative dance in a local hotel. All was going well until one of our group took a fancy to a girl. Unbeknown to him, she was with her boyfriend who started a fight in the toilet. Before we knew it, others had joined in and all four of us got involved in a brawl. Someone must

Passing Out Parade 1st April 1960

have called the police, for very quickly the military police were on the scene and we were arrested. The civilians got away scot-free! We were allowed to go after making statements but the next morning found ourselves parading in front of the commanding officer. As I was SUO, he took the line that I should have intervened and calmed things down. Despite my protestations that we were the victims, he threatened us all with being kicked off the course. Fortunately, the Sergeant-Major, a great guy called Jack Genever, believed our story and persuaded the 'boss' to let us off with a reprimand. Anyhow, it was a very proud moment when, as the Best Cadet and Parade Commander, I received the coveted Stick of Honour at my Passing Out Parade.

4: The End of a Name

Moving into the 19th century of our direct line of descendants, we start with my great-grandfather.

Benjamin[8] Vaughan-Arbuckle (1839-1924). Benjamin, his parent's penultimate child, was born on 10th September 1839 at Charlton. Latterly, he was educated privately at the Reverend J Fraser's, Peckham and the Reverend WH Pritchett's, Old Charlton, who gave him the following references, in support of his application to be admitted for service with the East India Company as a cadet for commissioning into the Bengal Artillery:

> *'I have much pleasure in certifying that Master Arbuckle was a resident pupil in my establishment for nearly a year and a half preceding Midsummer 1855 and that he conducted himself while with me as a Gentleman in every respect. I have every reason to consider him a youth of good character and excellent talent. He has my sincere wishes for his prosperity and happiness both as to time and Eternity.'* John Fraser, 10th April 1858.

> *'I beg to certify that Mr B Vaughan-Arbuckle has been my pupil since August 1857, and that during this period I have been entirely satisfied with his character and general conduct.'* WH Pritchett MA, 9th April 1858.

Benjamin's nominator for RMA Sandhurst, for entry to the Bengal Artillery, was Sir Frederick Currie, who had a distinguished career in the British East India Company and the Indian Civil Service. His posts included Foreign Secretary to the Government of India, Member of the Supreme Council of India, and Chairman of the East India Company. Benjamin duly joined the East India Company on 23rd June 1858, aged 19.

He arrived in Calcutta on 27th August 1858 and was appointed to No 3 Company, 6th Battalion Bengal Artillery, Peshawar. Two years

| Never a Dull Moment

later, he saw action during the Wuzeeree Expedition for which he was awarded the medal and clasp.

Truncated extract from the *Melbourne Argus*, April 1860:

> *Expedition against the Wuzeerees*
> (Waziris – native to Waziristan, now an agency of Pakistan)

> *The official despatches leave no doubt as to the decisive character of the victory gained by Major Honner over the Waghers* (Hindu caste). *His success must not be estimated only by the number of enemies slain or taken prisoner. The chief value is the moral effect it will have throughout the whole of the district in which the Waghers had so long braved our arms with impunity. Rumour had, as usual, exaggerated the fact that this robber tribe, through the mismanagement and misconduct of some of the European troops. It was even at one time incredibly reported that these wild and daring Waghers had cut their way through H.M.'s 28th regiment. To those who know what wretched creatures the Waghers really are, such a story seems*

ludicrous enough, and, disgraceful as an explanation is, we imagine that, when all the facts of the case are disclosed, it will be found that the men of the 28th were not beaten by the Waghers in fair fight, but that they were drunk and had forgotten to attend to their picket lines. But, as this was not known, people set the ill success of the Okhamundel expedition to the credit of the superior bravery of our barbarian foes, and the bubble of Wagher's reputation was blown to vast divisions.

'*Major Honner, with the troops under command, defeated The Waghers in a fort on what was deemed an inaccessible peak of the hill of Abhpoora. Here they gathered themselves together, with their wives and children, to make a glorious ending of the campaign. Their numbers were variously estimated from 1,000 to 2,000. They were wronged in calculating that they could hold their own in this position, where, as artillery would not be brought into action, the advantages of fighting would be all on their side, against any force the British might send to capture their stronghold. But British officers have never been unsuccessful as in storming inaccessible positions. It is just the sort of work requiring the sense of daring, almost reckless, gallantry which suits their eager disposition. Major Honner's plain duty, as commander of the expedition, was forthwith to subdue the rebellious Waghers driving them out of the stronghold. He had 1,058 men, besides a small gun train. Instead of hurling these in a barrage against the face of the breastworks, which the Waghers had armed in front of the fort, the commander divided his troops into seven parties of 200 men each. These were so disposed at the base of the hill in a wide circle – the right of the attack being 30 miles distant from the extreme left – as to bar every way out against the Waghers. The principle of the plan was the same as that of the old Highland one, in which the gillies commenced beating from all quarters at a great distance toward one another, and then gradually converging towards a common centre, enclosed the game with impenetrable toils.*

'*The chief and most active share in the attack was taken by the detachments under Major Honner, Captain Hill, and Lieutenant Lewis: all bore their parts well, and, from the officers down to the men who dragged the guns up – all worked most zealously and courageously to carry out the plan of their leader. Our loss was big in proportion to that of the enemy; we had 12 men killed and 44 officers and men wounded, while the Waghers are estimated to have lost only 25. The rebels attempted to*

> *execute again the same plan which they had pursued so successfully previously. As soon as they found they could no longer avoid a hand-to-hand combat, they tried to fly with their wives and children to another place of refuge. But this time their retreat was cut off by Captain Walker, who captured in all 639 of the tribe and have also taken a good many prisoners. The tribe may now be said to be broken up. The whole affair is one of the most brilliant results in the history of the Bombay army.*

Benjamin also qualified for the India Medal and clasp for operations on the North West Frontier for service during April 1860, and was present at the forcing of the Burrarah Pass and the destruction of Makeem. During the Afghan War, 1879-80, he was employed on Commissariat duty for which he was duly awarded the campaign medal.

This article gives a flavour of what it was like during the campaign on the North-West Frontier of India:

> *The people of the country, always with matchlocks across their shoulders, pursued their agricultural avocations. It speaks volumes for the state of the country, when men at the plough are armed to the teeth and ready for a fight. One of the first things that happened after my arrival in the Peshawur cantonments, was to have a shot fired at me when going home from dinner with friends. This was a solemn warning. The shot was fired not thirty yards from the place where I was dining. It was pitch dark and the man who fired it, no doubt a Khyberee, was not to be found. At this period of our history, it was not safe to dine by candle light in camp, as the lights attracted the fire of the enemy. The hill robbers sneaked about the ravines, which intersect the country, and take a pot shot at any object, apparently for the*

> sake of mischief. On one occasion a shot was fired at me when riding along the road, and a bullet whizzed past my ear, an unmistakable sound, that no one can doubt about, who has heard it. The two native troopers, riding behind me, were called upon to ride off the track, with me in pursuit of the enemy, who at once dropped into a ravine, beyond the reach of horsemen. One of the troopers said, 'They were only firing at a bird.' I replied, 'You scoundrel, I see no bird.' The fact was that the troopers did not much like the look of the sort of gentleman that he had upon us, and as the better part of valour is discretion, and as nothing was to be gained by shooting nigger, even if we succeeded in doing so, it was the worst of policy, they thought, to incur an additional risk by going in pursuit.
>
> Extracted from *Nine Years on the North West Frontier of India 1854-1863* by Lieutenant General Sir Sydney Cotton KCB.

Benjamin remained in India until he sailed home on board *St Lawrence*, around the Cape, arriving in England nearly three months later, on 27th April 1863. Obviously, India took a toll on his health as he spent the next 15 months on sick leave before reporting to Woolwich. After attending the Long (Gunnery) Course, on which he obtained a First Class Certificate, he went back to India where he remained, on and off, throughout his career. During the period 1887-1892 he saw service in Malta and Aden. By 1888 he had reached the rank of Lieutenant-Colonel commanding the Royal Artillery, Western Region from the Imperial Hotel, Sliema.

The Malta Directory of 1888 describes life there as follows:

> *During 1888 the Officers of the Malta Garrison and Royal Navy would find themselves face to face with pretty young females rather than a foreign foe, and handle a bat or racquet more often than a firearm. Invitations to society events were especially sought after since several members of the Royal family were present in Malta. The Duke and Duchess of Edinburgh, the Princesses Marie, Victoria Melita, and Alexandra of Edinburgh. The Princess Louise, and the Prince Louis and Princess of Battenberg. Without doubt the most prestigious gathering of the year was the Carnival Fancy Dress Ball held on Monday 13th February by Governor and Lady Simmons at the Palace to which over 900 guests were invited.*
>
> *Just over two weeks later The Medical Staff gave a Grand Ball at the Malta Union Club which was then housed in the*

| Never a Dull Moment

Benjamin

Auberge de Provence in Strada Reale. Again the Royal guests attended together with over 550 others, and spent a very enjoyable evening.

The Malta Garrison that year included two Scottish Regiments, the Black Watch and the Gordon Highlanders, so in March the Highland Games were held at Marsa, when men from both regiments competed in traditional Scottish sports. Private Paton of the Gordon Highlanders took 1st place at Tossing the Caber, and Private Cairns of the Black Watch was the champion Sword Dancer. The English Regiments held their own Regimental Games.

Another important Royal occasion took place in HM Dockyard on 20th March, when the young Princess Melita launched a gun-boat named HMS Melita. In front of a large crowd of officials and public onlookers, she smashed a bottle of champagne over the bows in the traditional manner. The Reverend G Sutton then read the prayers used at the launching of a ship, after which the young Princess cut the cord holding the Dogshore with a chisel and mallet, and the new vessel slid slowly towards the water.

During the summer months, the Eighth Annual Malta Rifle Meeting lasted for several days, and challenge Cricket Matches were played by Army as well as Naval teams. Even in November the weather was still favourable for a Lawn Tennis Tournament to be held and for Cricket Matches to continue.

After his time in Malta, Benjamin was moved to Aden in 1892, where, as a Lieutenant-Colonel, he commanded the Royal Artillery. This was his last active posting as he retired on 1st September 1893, aged 54.

During one of his periods in England, Benjamin married Judith Emily Preston Delpratt on 20th October 1872 in Paddington. She was born in 1845 in St Helier, Jersey. They had three children, a boy and two girls.

Benjamin died on 24th April 1924, while residing St Brelade's Bay Hotel, Jersey, aged 85. My father told me that Benjamin, his grandfather, lived for many years in an annexe of the hotel.

St Brelade's Bay Hotel, Jersey

He was predeceased by his son Bertram by four years. As provided by his Will, Benjamin left the majority his estate to his wife Judith who, in turn, left most of her belongings to her two daughters Sibyl and Effie.

Bertram Vaughan-Arbuckle (1873-1920). My grandfather was born on 30th December 1873 in a married quarter in Dover. At the time of the 1891 Census he was a boarding scholar at Portsmouth Grammar School, of which the boarding house was, and still is, located in St Edward's Road. He was a lifelong supporter of Portsmouth FC and, according to my father, used to go regularly to Fratton Park to watch Pompey, in those days a 'top' club playing in the Football League 1st Division.

Bertram joined the Militia (today's Territorial Army) and was appointed Second Lieutenant with the Haddington Artillery (Southern Region) on 7th April 1893. On 29th May 1895, he was accepted to fill a vacancy in The Royal Scots (Lothian Regiment), the premier regiment in the British Army, in the rank of 2nd Lieutenant. On transfer to the infantry, he attended and passed a Musketry Course at Hythe and a Signalling Course at Aldershot, both in 1897. He was promoted Captain in 1900. His records show that he spoke French and that he spent from December 1898 to January 1906 in India. It was during his time as Adjutant of the Poona Rifles that he met

Portsmouth Grammar School

and married Margaret Bianca Selina Ashby-Pritt (née Turner), widow of Walter C Ashby-Pritt, a Cotton Factor (commission merchant) of Leamington Spa who died in India, on 11th July 1905 in Poona.

Bertram and 'Peg'

After returning to England in January 1906, Bertram resigned his commission two years later in June 1908. During his time in India, he was known as an accomplished linguist and author of a standard work on Urdu grammar, used extensively by those being posted to India. Why he left the Army cannot be substantiated but it does seem that money problems led to his resignation.

In a letter to me dated 4th April 1986, Meg Giles (my godmother) wrote,

> *The only thing I've heard about your grandfather was that he was, like your father, the most charming and delightful person, but alas money melted like snow in his hands and he finally had to send in his papers.* (Presumably meaning that he was forced to resign due to money problems. This might account for the fact that my father never really spoke to me about him.) *The other thing was that your grandmother adored him and said he was the most wonderful person to be married to. His maxim was that you should tell your wife at least once a day that you love her and pay her unexpected compliments. The other bit of family gossip was that your great-grandmother Vaughan-Arbuckle wore a wig. She had two, one for weekdays and one for Sundays. An*

aunt who was apparently visiting them in Jersey, where they were living, couldn't make out, until she found out about the wigs, why your great-grandmother looked different on Sundays!

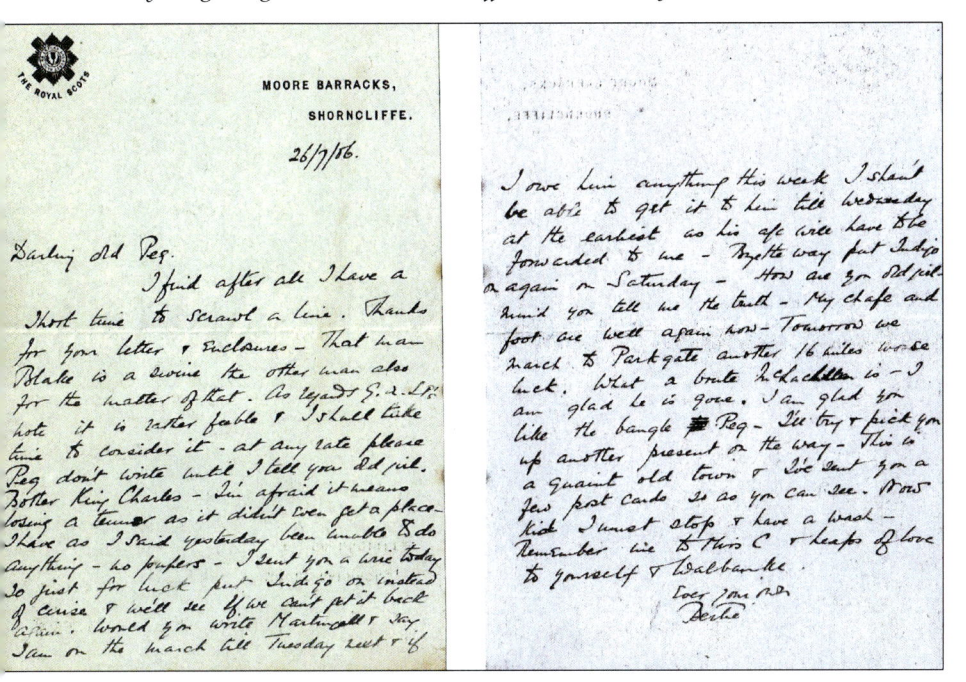

The letter shown above from Bertram (aka Bertie) to my grandmother (aka Peg) in July 1906, when he was stationed in Shorncliffe, is revealing in a couple of aspects. He obviously enjoyed gambling on horses and clearly got into debt doing so. This is borne out by his reference to 'King Charles' and 'Indigo'. His reference to Walbanke in the final line is interesting as it wasn't until the following year that my grandmother gave birth to my father.

On leaving the Army, Bertram joined the Ministry of Munitions for which he worked in Lancashire, Berkshire and Somerset. Encouraged by Lloyd George, Lord Northcliffe published an article in May 1915 that blamed Kitchener and the War Office for the shortage of shells. The so-called 'Shell Scandal' helped to knock the Liberal Government from power and on 25th May 1915 a new coalition government was set up in its place. Within this government Lloyd George was given control over a newly-created Ministry of Munitions department. It is recorded that he did some 'most useful work' during the Great War. Bertram's last job was as director of the munitions factory, Barking. It was when my grandparents lived in a house called Kurrymore in

Thatcham that Bertram fell gravely ill and died of peritonitis and an abscess of his appendix in hospital on 23rd April 1920. He was buried at St Mary's Church, Cold Ash. Together with his two sons, Hector (my father) and Keith, others who attended his funeral included his stepson Walbanke Ashby-Pritt. In conversation about him, my aunt, Betty Vaughan-Arbuckle, Keith's wife, remembers others describing Bertram as 'a fine man, with a twinkle in his eye, who enjoyed life and was very popular'.

Walbanke was a flying ace in the First World War. He gained his fame during a five-month period, 4th July to 14th November 1917, while flying Sopwith Pups with No 66 Squadron. During this period he became an ace and earned the Military Cross. The citation is dated 24th August 1917. He is officially credited with five kills; but there is evidence of a possible sixth victory.

Military Cross Citation:

For conspicuous gallantry and devotion to duty in attacking a hostile aerodrome with exceptional dash and determination. Having reached his objective and dropped bombs from a very low altitude, he then attacked and destroyed two hostile machines almost as soon as they had left the ground. A machine gun then opened upon him from the aerodrome, which he immediately attacked. Both on his outward and homeward journey he was under very heavy machine gun and anti-aircraft fire. On another occasion he attacked a motor-car, and shot one of the occupants from about 50 feet, afterwards attacking infantry on the march and inflicting severe casualties upon them. He has at all times shown constant gallantry and fine offensive spirit.

It is necessary to put Walbanke's award of the MC into context. At that time, the planes were made of wood and wire struts, covered with Irish linen and dope, all of which were horribly flammable. Although parachutes were being developed, they were not given to pilots, because it was felt that the

Walbanke Ashby-Pritt

temptation to jump rather than stay and fight would be too great. As a result of attrition rates, pilots were in short supply. Such was the demand that more and more men arrived with insufficient training and paid the ultimate price: all told, nearly 9,500 died. The motto of the Royal Flying Corps, which the RAF continues to use and is on Walbanke's grave headstone, was *Per ardua ad astra* (Through adversity to the stars).

On 15th February 1918 Walbanke was injured while flying a 44 Squadron Sopwith Camel; he had an engine failure at 500 feet over Hainault Farm, Essex. His post-war flying career is sketchy and appears to be without merit. On 19th April 1920 he was granted a Short-Service Commission by the RAF in the rank of Lieutenant. During August 1920, he failed the RAF Flight Instructor Course at the Central Flying School. Accompanying note states, 'Did not take exams, absent sick, CFS cat B, graded unsuitable as instructor at present.' He resigned his commission on 12th August 1920 and was denied permission to retain his rank because of 'unsatisfactory dealings with cheques'.

Walbanke married in 1925. There is no record of any children and his wife was still referred to as Mrs Pritt until her death in 1965. Records indicate Walbanke was a commercial artist and poultry farmer until his untimely death on 27th January 1928 at the age of 31 in an automobile accident near Bagby in North Yorkshire. A local paper reported his death in this cutting.

Walbanke is buried in All Saints' Church, Great Thirkleby, North Yorkshire (four miles south-east of Thirsk) where I had his grave refurbished in 2012. Surrounded by fields, with part of the churchyard a sanctuary for wildlife, it provides a tranquil resting place.

FATAL MOTOR ACCIDENT NEAR BAGBY.

VICTIM WELL KNOWN IN YORK.

27th January 1928

EX-OFFICER PINNED BENEATH OVERTURNED CAR.

Mr. Walbanke Ashby Pritt, who was well-known in York, was killed in a motoring accident between Bagby and Thirkleby last night.

Mr. Pritt, accompanied by his wife, was returning to his home, Pond House, Thirkleby Park, near Thirsk, about 11.30 p.m., from a whist drive and dance at Bagby, and driving down the hill to York-road he failed to negotiate a left-hand turn. The car ran into the bank on the right side of the road, rebounded to the other side, and turned over. The steering wheel was forced into Mr. Pritt's chest, and broke a rib, which penetrated his heart. When extricated he was dead.

THE LATE MR. W. A. PRITT.

Mrs. Pritt, who received bruises, was taken to Thirsk Hospital. She is reported to be progressing as well as can be expected.

Mr. Pritt, who had been engaged in poultry farming during the last few years, was educated at St. Peter's School, York, and formerly resided with an aunt in The Avenue, Clifton. He was 29 years of age in October last. Mrs. Pritt was a Miss Evans, whose parents formerly resided in Grosvenor terrace, York.

Mr. Pritt was a son of the late Mr. Walter C. Ashby Pritt, of Wallasey, Cheshire. In November, 1916, after taking his pilot's certificate, he entered the Royal Flying Corps Cadet Unit, received his commission in March of the following year, and his "wings" in June. He joined his squadron at the front in July, 1917, and was awarded the Military Cross six weeks later for meritorious service.

It is on record that on his first flight alone over the German lines early one morning, he killed one of the German officers whom he engaged in a pistol fight in the air, afterwards killing six or seven infantrymen amongst a party whom he saw on the road as he was returning in his 'plane.

| Never a Dull Moment

All Saints' Church, and (right) with my mother and grandmother, aged about 4

I remember my paternal grandmother, Mater (or Peggy) as she was known throughout the family, as a rather wizened old lady with 'fuzzy' hair who used to sit me on her lap in the garden of her bungalow, Pondtail Lodge, Fleet, and tell me stories.

A kindly, gentle woman, softly spoken, she had a definite air of authority about her. I remember she had a dachshund dog that was utterly spoilt. She died on 20th February 1950 age 78 and was buried alongside Bertram at St Mary's Church, Cold Ash. Knowing they were buried there, I visited the cemetery and, finding the grave in a poor state of repair, I had it refurbished. Out of the blue, I had to attend another funeral at St Mary's and was able to pay my respects to my grandparents; I was pleased to note that theirs is a shining 'light' among the graves.

My grandparents' grave

| 102 |

Hector Barnard Vaughan-Arbuckle (1907-1977). My father was born on 27th July 1907 at home at Colney Lodge, Folkestone-next-Sandgate, Kent. He attended Ardingly College for one term only, aged 13 (1920), when his mother was living in Ripley, Surrey. The school entry register shows 'fees not paid'. Whether he left because of the fees or for another reason is not clear. Perhaps this is why my father never spoke of his time at Ardingly. He then went to Bedford Modern School, where he was described as an average student and a fine all-round athlete who represented the school at rugby, boxing, cricket and athletics.

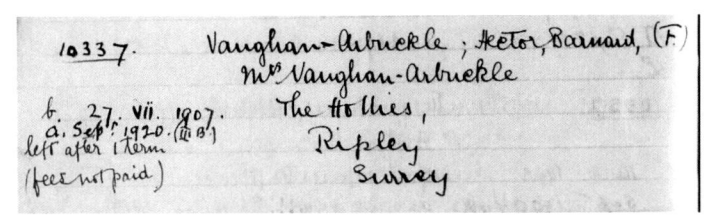

Ardingly College Entry Register 1920

It was difficult to get my father to talk about his sporting achievements but that he played for Bedfordshire County Cricket Club in 1930-33, as a batsman, is well documented. He also played for Bedford Rugby Football Club. He was in the Combined Cadet Corps at school. He enlisted into the Bedfordshire and Hertfordshire Regiment on 14th March 1927, aged 19, and was allocated the Army number 5946627. At the time of his enlistment, my father was living with his mother and brother, Keith, at 50 Clapham Road, Bedford, conveniently very close to Bedford Modern School. After basic training, he was posted to 2nd Battalion, at that time serving in England, where he remained before entering the Royal Military Academy, Sandhurst, in February 1930. He represented the RMA at cricket and rugby.

His record shows that he was a Lance-Corporal on entry to the RMA and that, on passing out, he was 120th in the Order of Merit (about halfway). He was commissioned on 26th August 1931 into The King's Own Royal Regiment for service with 2nd Battalion in the UK. A year later he was transferred to the 1st Battalion for service in Egypt.

Regimental life suited him and soon became a leading light on the sports field captaining the rugby team to triumph in the 1932 Army Cup.

In a letter to me, after my father's death, Pip Powell wrote: *'Hector was my closest friend in Egypt. His friendship was never more generously given than at the time of my Courts-Martial. By a million-to-one chance we got together again for a few hectic hours during the war, when I was on my*

| Never a Dull Moment

RMA Cricket team 1930 – Father second from left in front row

way up the line in Holland. It was typical of him that he gave me his leather jerkin, which he thought would be of more use to me than to him. It was!!'

In a subsequent letter, Pip Powell sent me a few photographs of life in Egypt with the King's Own, one of which is overleaf, in which he said, *'Your father introduced me, after my debacle, to his mother near Pangbourne* (actually, she lived at Cold Ash): *only a man like him would have had the decency to make such a generous gesture to a disgraced fellow officer.'* Quite why and for what Pip Powell was courts-martialled, I have not been able to discover.

As a subaltern, my father was popular and well thought of. Regimental life in Egypt was good within what was essentially a garrison existence of routine duties and exercises, sport and plenty of social life. I suspect that it was this rather superficial lifestyle which was to set him off on a path which would eventually lead to his self-destruction all those years later. Apparently, the very attractive and flirtatious wife of his company commander took a 'shine' to my father who eventually succumbed to her advances. When the affair came to light, my father was immediately banished to the desert on detachment with the machine gun platoon while his future was considered. In those days, to have an affair with another officer's wife was about the worst crime that could be committed, let alone with a superior's wife! On his return to barracks some weeks later, he was told that he was being sent back to the UK to face disciplinary proceedings. After

Father's record of entry to Sandhurst

King's Own Regiment rugby team 1932 – Father holding the ball with friend 'Pip' Powell on his right

landing in the UK in late December 1934, he faced a Board of Officers, convened by the War Office, to consider his future. In their findings the Board gave him two options: either to resign his commission and leave the Army or to transfer to the Royal Army Service Corps. Not wishing to resign, my father decided to transfer. He attended, on probation, a RASC Junior Officers' Course which he passed. He was confirmed in the rank of Lieutenant and posted to 6 Company RASC in March 1934. Three years later he was posted to Palestine for service with 14 Company RASC. After a year, in late 1937, he was posted to Egypt on promotion to Captain. In 1937, the British military were busy controlling Aliyah Bet, the name given to 'illegal' Jewish immigration into British-controlled Palestine, for which he received the General Service Medal (Palestine).

Quite where and in what circumstances my father met my mother, Mary Madeline Sophie Frances Chevers (aka Dodo), I am not sure. At the time, my mother (aged 21) was living with her parents at Jacobean House, Capel-le-Ferne, Kent.

Jacobean House, Capel-le-Ferne

After a short relationship they married at Our Lady Help of Christians and St Aloysius Church, Folkestone on 13th March 1937. After marrying, my parents took a house at 34 Surrey Road, Bournemouth. My mother came from an old-established Irish Catholic family, Chevers of Killyan, Co Galway. She was the second-youngest daughter of ten children to John Joseph Chevers, late of the Connaught

Rangers, and Frederica Sophia (née Owen-Lewis). At the end of 1935, the Irish Government informed the family that the lands and house of Killyan, along with very many other notable houses in Ireland, were to be acquired compulsorily for division among former tenants. So the family, with very little time to react, decamped to take up residence in Jacobean House. They had been unable to take with them many of their personal possessions. The remainder were auctioned in Ireland. The family were victims of the nationalist policies of the Irish Free State Government under their leader Eamon de Valera. My birth is covered elsewhere. My mother was typically Irish. She was superstitious; she read the tea leaves; she never walked under a ladder; the number 13 was bad luck while the number 7 was a good omen, and she was an avid reader of horoscopes! Without being a regular churchgoer, she was strongly Roman Catholic. As an example, fish was always on the menu on Fridays. She was a very kind and compassionate woman, with a sunny nature and a great sense of humour. As can be seen in photographs, she was a beautiful woman with pitch-black hair.

Parents' wedding day 31st March 1937, Folkestone

On the outbreak of war, my father returned to the UK, was promoted to acting Major in 6th Anti-Aircraft Brigade as officer in charge of RASC personnel. During 1940 he served with the British Expeditionary Force. After returning to the UK for a few months, he went to the Middle East where he commanded a Water Tank Company and a general Transport Company, both of which took part in the Eighth Army campaign in North Africa. From there he followed the 'classic' war route through Italy and into Germany before returning to

| Never a Dull Moment

Officers of 165 Infantry Brigade Company RASC – Father centre front row

the UK in May 1944, where he commanded 165 Infantry Brigade Company based in Seaton Sluice, Northumberland.

My father seldom talked about his experiences during the war but he did tell me about one particular engagement. This concerned a fire-fight with a German unit in North Africa which resulted in a number of deaths on both sides. In the aftermath, my father came across a seriously wounded German who, sensing he was going to die, asked my father to contact his wife after the war. He gave my father a photograph of himself with his wife's address on the back. My father duly wrote and had an acknowledgement from the widow thanking him for describing her husband's honourable death. My father had a great deal of respect for the German soldier, although the same could not be said of the Italians who, based on his experience of fighting against them, he thought were cowards. The following piece provides a flavour of the sort of everyday skirmish which took place in the desert:

> *First came one troop of 25-pounders, another troop protected the tail. Flank guards were the anti-tank gunners armed with the suicidal pop-gun, the 2-pounder mounted on a lorry chassis. Soft stuff; lorried infantry, command vehicles, supply trucks and ambulances, was in the centre. Way out in front, one on each flank, was a Bren carrier. Our army marched on its petrol tanks. I had gone down to the wagon lines for a mug of tea.*

Drinking, I chatted with the sergeant about the Yorkshire dales and ales as we both came from the finest county in England. Nearby were a dozen or so of the lads. Some way away a German gunner finished adjusting his sights and, at the command 'Feuer' flicked the firing lever ... "See you later, Sergeant," I said and started to walk away. Then came a short sudden scream above my head, and I hit the deck about half a second after the shell did. All the sirens of all the raided cities of England buzzed in my head, and I did not hear the groans of the wounded. Next I was aware for a moment of that sudden surging exhilaration that is part of the feeling that according to the rules you should be dead, but are not. Then I heard the groans of a man who was dying. I bandaged him ... the dressings nearly fell into the hole in his stomach. I remember that minutes afterwards I noticed dozens of flies around me, and saw that my shirt, my thighs and my arms up to the elbows were covered with drying blood. Extract from *For You the War is Over*, Gordon Horner.1948.

During the campaign through Italy, Allied troops often found themselves occupying houses vacated by fleeing members of the population. It was during a stay in such accommodation that my father 'liberated' (his word) an oil painting of sailing boats which, at the time of writing, is still hanging in Rose Cottage.

At the end of the war my father found himself back in the UK as a temporary major, a rank which he had held throughout the war. In October 1945 we accompanied him to India. Landing in Bombay he was initially posted to the RASC Depot, Kalyan. After the first of a number of periods in hospital, I suspect related to what had by now had developed into a serious alcohol problem, he spent time in Nowshera and Bareilly. I have described our time in India elsewhere; suffice it to say that our two years there had a profound and lasting impression on me and my subsequent life. We left India in August 1947 for Hong Kong, where my father was to take up a Captain's appointment in the Supply Depot. By this time, it seems clear that his drink problem had developed into a very serious medical condition. I say this because his record shows that he had two more spells in hospital before being returned to the UK after only a year in post. There seems little doubt that he had been 'advised' to resign his commission before leaving Hong Kong for that is exactly what he did, on 12th December 1948. He retired as Captain, although he always referred to himself as Major: he was 41. Being relatively young and with wartime experience, had he been fit, my father could have

Father's medals
L to R: 1939-45 Star; Africa Star 8th Army; France and Germany Star; Defence Medal; War Medal 1939-45; General Service Medal Palestine

anticipated another 14 or so years in the Army. It was a tragedy that his problem with alcohol not only cut short his career in the Army but also continued to blight his (and my mother's) life to the end of their lives.

It was not until I started researching material for this book that I came across a few of my father's personal papers. Among these were handwritten notes he had used as an aide memoire when relating his story at meetings of Alcoholic Anonymous (AA). These clearly reveal that his heavy drinking started when, in 1944 during the Normandy campaign, he was drinking copious quantities of Calvados (apple brandy). After he was posted to India, my father notes that he made a good start as Commandant of a Reinforcement Camp, Kalyan, but that his heavy drinking resulted in a rapid deterioration in his performance and, ultimately, led to his arrest (presumably for drunkenness or an offence related to drink). His subsequent resignation from the Army has already been covered. Using his gratuity, my father built the house, 'Bryan', in Walton-on-Thames from where my mother ran a B & B business. He had no job and this led to what he describes as a 'very serious drink problem'. Problems linked to his drinking included 'pretending to faint', 'stealing', 'Xmas carol-singing to get money' and 'hiding in fields to avoid detection'. Around this time, ie 1948-49, he entered a private nursing home for treatment. This treatment did no good for, not long afterwards, my father was 'certified' in a local magistrate's court and committed to St Bernard's Hospice, Southall, where he spent six weeks undergoing treatment for alcoholism.

Returning home to Walton, he had managed to stay 'teetotal' (abstained from alcohol) for a month before there was a dramatic relapse, resulting in my father attempting suicide by over-dosing on Lithium Bromide. Once more he entered, voluntarily, a private hospital to undergo eight weeks' treatment. Being ostracised, he had no contact with the family during this time. My mother, probably at her wit's end, had sought a formal separation from my father and 'Bryan' had to be sold. After applying unsuccessfully for a number of jobs, my father eventually found labourer's work on a government farm in Huntingdonshire, where he remained until October 1949.

Knowing that there was a good chance of finding more permanent work in Peterborough, my father moved there and got a job as a storeman with Perkins Diesel Ltd. After a couple of months he was promoted for employment as a stores section leader. Life was good. He worked overtime on Saturdays and Sundays to build up some savings before persuading my mother to join him; it was May 1950. For the first year or so, I boarded at King's School, probably to give my parents breathing space to sort out their marriage. My mother got a job as manageress at the Bedford Hotel. Both my parents were earning decent money; the downside was that this led to an enhanced social life and a consequent increase in their drinking. It did not take long for my mother to lose her job and for my father to start drinking heavily again. Around this time, my father notes, 'I had severe spells of melancholia which lasted for six months.' In an attempt to alleviate the depression, my parents had a holiday at Wells, including some 'very heavy drinking'. After returning home, my father again tried to end his life, this time by taking Seconal (a barbiturate). 'I woke up in Peterborough Memorial Hospital, where I was being drip-fed. After about ten days, I volunteered to go to Rauceby Hospital for Mental Disorders, where I spent twelve weeks in a private room, being treated with Lagactol (used to treat various problems such as severe depression or behavioural disturbances),' he recalled.

In the meantime my mother got herself a job, with a car, as a travelling salesperson. After three months off sick, my father was welcomed back to work and he was 'off the booze'. Somewhat predictably, both my parents started drinking heavily again until, in 1961, my mother attempted to take her own life. I knew nothing about this as I was stationed in Hong Kong; my father never told me what had happened. There followed, according to my father, two years' happiness. Late in 1962, my father, by his own admission, was again drinking heavily; as a result, my mother again left him but only for a week. On her return, my father agreed to 'go on the wagon' (to abstain from alcohol). All was well for a time until withdrawal symptoms caused him acute anxiety, prompting a further six weeks in Rauceby Hospital.

Spells of drinking continued until, in 1964, my father was referred to St Bartholomew's Hospital where, after an IQ and other tests, he was graded a 50% disability case. According to my father's notes, my mother was arrested in 1964, without any further detail being available – a shocking revelation. Three years later, in 1967, my father was given the choice of retiring voluntarily, or being forced to retire, from Perkins; he chose the former. He was 60. My parents moved to Tunbridge Wells into accommodation provided by the Officers' Association. By the time I returned from Hong Kong in 1971, my father was a 100% disability case. At the time, his notes state, 'We are both going downhill.' On 21st December 1971, during the time when I was attached to the Mersey Docks & Harbour Board, Liverpool, as part of a year-long professional transportation course, I got a call telling me my mother was very seriously ill. Returning to Tunbridge Wells the same day, I was met with the news that my mother had died a couple of hours earlier. She was 56. Identifying my mother in the morgue, I was shocked to see that her skin was totally yellow. I now understand that this was to be expected as she died of 'Cirrhosis and hepatic failure'; in other words, liver failure caused by alcoholism: a tragic waste of life. My mother had a quiet funeral in the chapel of the local convent, attended by one of the Sisters of Mercy who taught her and other daughters of the Chevers family.

Not long after my mother's death, my father came to stay at the house we had rented, in Farnham, for the year while I was on the course. I confronted my father and asked him not to drink in front of the children. All seemed well until I discovered that he was drinking secretly after we had gone to bed. He denied doing so. Then, one day, Angelika telephoned me at work to say that she could not rouse my father. I told her to call a doctor. She did and the doctor arranged for his immediate admittance to Farnham Hospital suffering from a serious overdose of Tuinal (barbiturate). My father remained in intensive care for some days before regaining consciousness. As soon as he was out of danger, I let him know, in no uncertain terms, how angry and disappointed I was. I said that until he gave up alcohol altogether, I wanted nothing to do with him, and I meant it.

Having seen my parents succumb to temptations and horrors leading to chronic alcoholism, I want to say a few words about this progressive and fatal disease. Contrary to popular opinion, it is an illness. An alcoholic is a chronically sick person. Not a bad or weak individual, a sick person. As hard as it was to watch my parents on the road to self-destruction, I'm sure that they were not deliberately drinking themselves to death. Rather, they were obeying the compulsion to drink. They were doing what came naturally. In other words, alleviating their symptoms or, put another way, treating the disease. To an alcoholic, to drink is to be well. It's their normal state. Not to drink is to be ill, very ill. Small wonder, therefore, that the temptation to imbibe is overwhelming. Some, like my father, are able to rationalise, with the help of others, what is happening to them; others who are not, like my mother, will keep on drinking because they have to. She did not necessarily want to – she had to and ultimately alcohol killed her.

Later, my father moved to Brighton and was living in a private hotel. He had joined Alcoholic Anonymous (AA) and was acting as one of their counsellors. I used to visit him in Brighton, with the girls, on a fairly regular basis and we exchanged telephone calls most Sunday evenings. During a visit to our house in Haslemere, the first we owned, I found a copy of *Men Only* in my father's room a sure indication, if ever there was one, that the old 'fella' really was regaining his zest for life! One autumn Sunday evening, the telephone rang in our house; it was my father. After the usual pleasantries, he suddenly announced, "Ian, old boy, I have some important news. I'm getting married again and wondered whether you would be my best man?" Completely taken aback by this news, I think I enquired about the lady concerned and was told they had met through AA. She was one of his mentoring contacts. Her name was Trudie (Gertrude) Lynch; she was an Irish Catholic. No surprise there, given that my mother was also from the same background. Over the next few months we travelled to Brighton to meet and get to know Trudie, a good-looking woman with a sharp sense of humour and Irish from tip to toe! They were duly married in St Mary Magdalen's RC Church, Brighton on 4th January 1975 and afterwards held a small reception at which I acted as my father's best man. In my short speech, I naturally alluded to the unusual circumstances of a son acting as his father's best man.

Shortly afterwards I was posted to Germany and consequently saw a lot less of my father and his new bride. Being reasonably close their school, my father and Trudie sometimes made arrangements to see the girls. My father seemed

My father and Trudie on their wedding day

happy with his 'new' life living in Rottingdean, even though he had more than his fair share of upper bronchial tract infections, which invariably laid him low.

Then on 12th December 1977 I was told, during a regimental hockey match, that my father was very seriously ill in the Royal Sussex County Hospital, Brighton. A car was waiting to take me to Hannover airport to catch a plane to London where another car was on stand-by to drive me straight to Brighton. In such circumstances the Army are magnificent in their support: nothing is too much trouble. Angelika got the same treatment in Hong Kong when her mother was VSI (Very Seriously Ill) and she had to fly back to Germany with three small children.

On arrival at the hospital some hours later, I was ushered into a room. Instinctively, I knew my father had 'gone' – a fact confirmed by a doctor some minutes later. He told me that my father had died a few hours earlier of broncho-pneumonia and chronic bronchitis, caused by a lifetime of heavy smoking (my deduction). My overriding memory of seeing my father in the morgue was how peaceful he looked. I gave him a kiss, said my farewells and went to his flat to see Trudie. Although upset, she seemed very much in control of her emotions, accusing me of 'abandoning my father by going off to Germany at his time of need'. This infuriated me and confirmed that she knew nothing about life in the Army. From that moment our relationship was never the same. My father's cremation was a very small affair, conducted by a military padre and attended by a small congregation including Keith, his brother, my cousin Duncan (Keith's son) and Charles Morrell, an old friend of my father's from his days in the King's Own. My father's ashes were subsequently buried, next to my mother's, in the crematorium's garden of remembrance, Tunbridge Wells.

About six months later, I received a call in Germany from Charles Morrell informing me ('as a matter of courtesy') that he and Trudie intended to get married. They did so in 1978. Sometime later, Trudie and Charles bought a house in Downham Market, close to where we lived in Norfolk, so we saw something of them. Then, out of the blue, it came to light that Trudie had been caught shoplifting. In a subsequent court appearance, she received a three-month suspended sentence. Being of the 'old school', Charles was devastated to discover that Trudie was a thief. From then he seemed to go 'downhill' rapidly from the shame of it all. He died shortly afterwards in 1985. After Charles died, Trudie moved back to Ireland as Mrs Morrell, and we never heard from her again! So ended a sad phase in our family history.

Keith Hutcheson Vaughan-Arbuckle (1909-1989). My father's younger brother was born in Lambeth. He attended, first, Bedford School and then Bedford Modern School where my father went, but I am not sure why he changed schools. After finishing his education, he joined Brooke Bond Tea and was posted to India as a trainee plantation manager. It was at a dance in Cochin, Kerala, South India, in 1935 that he met and proposed to Betty Juliette Beaumont, who was visiting her brother. Unsure, Betty returned to England to consider the proposal. A year or so later, she returned and married Keith in Cochin. Soon after the outbreak of war, Keith decided to join the Army, a decision that was not supported by his employers. Brooke Bond issued him with an ultimatum that if he did go to war, they would not re-employ him. Keith went ahead and was commissioned into the famous Jat Regiment (Indian Army) in October 1940. After a period on the front line in Burma, Keith worked his way up the ranks so that when the war ended he had reached the rank of acting Lieutenant-Colonel; at the time, he was serving with HQ 39 Indian Infantry Division. After the war, Keith got a job with Pierce Leslie Company (Tea Merchants), Cochin, as the general manager of their Chembra Peak Estate, near Coimbatore. Keith told me as the struggle for communist superiority grew stronger in Kerala, so did his workers' attitude harden towards him as the British manager. On a few occasions he was assaulted by workers as he travelled around the estate on horseback. After a few successful years managing Chembra Peak Estate, Keith was moved to Pierce Leslie Company HQ in Coimbatore, responsible for all company estates in India and East Africa. He remained in this appointment until he retired and returned to the UK in the 1960s.

In 2010, during a six-week tour of south India with Lynn, we visited the estate. In seeking permission to visit, the Indian manager explained that the general manager's bungalow, which Keith and Betty occupied, was now such a valuable asset he lived in a much smaller house at the bottom of the estate. Such was the attractiveness of the old bungalow, he could charge the film industry and others vast sums of money for its use. For example, he had recently charged a Bollywood film director 20, 000 Indian Rupees (£250) a day to hire the bungalow – a fortune in India! We spent a delightful couple of hours looking around. Overleaf are a few photographs taken during our visit.

On his return from India, Keith ran a small herd of fattening calves in Devon before retiring completely and settling in Suffolk. Tragically, he contracted Parkinson's disease and finished his later life living in Nayland. Keith was always very kind. As I have already recalled, I remember Keith visiting me at camp in the 1950s when he was on leave from India and encouraging me to work hard and get on in the Army.

| Never a Dull Moment

Chembra Peak Estate

He actually offered to initiate a transfer for me from the RASC to a Gurkha regiment which, in hindsight, might well have been an excellent move. It was obviously a proud moment for him when I got my commission and latterly captained the Army at cricket. I know this because he wrote to me at the time.

Keith and Betty had two sons – Duncan, born 26th March 1938 in Ootacamund, south India, and Anthony, born 30th November 1943 in the Military Hospital, Lahore (now Pakistan).

Duncan was educated at Wellington College, Crowthorne, where he played cricket and hockey for the school. Entering RMA Sandhurst

Betty and Keith at Anthony's house in Nayland circa 1984

in 1956, Duncan was commissioned a year later into the 8th King's Royal Irish Hussars, shortly afterwards to become the Queen's Royal Irish Hussars. He subsequently saw service in Borneo and Germany, where he was a member of the Army bobsleigh team. A good cricketer, Duncan represented his school, Wellington College, and the British Army of the Rhine, and was a member of the famous I Zingari cricket club. He left the Army in 1968 as a Captain to work as a broker with Lloyds before branching out on his own in the wine trade. After many years' toil, Duncan brought his idea of a London Wine Museum, located in Southwark opposite St Paul's Cathedral, to fruition. Initially, the facility enjoyed considerable success but, as profits declined, the emphasis changed from a museum to a retail outlet and was renamed Vinopolis. Soon afterwards, Duncan relinquished control and left the business (see article overleaf).

Duncan married Victoria (Vicky) Banbury in a society wedding in London on 23rd February 1962. They had two daughters Louise (b January 1963) and Desdemona (b April 1965) who, in 1994, married Jonathan Freeman. They have a son and two daughters, while Louise remains single and is a very successful reflexology therapist practising mainly in France.

Anthony followed his older brother into Wellington College, where he was a prefect and a triple colour. I actually played cricket against Anthony for the RASC when he was captain of Wellington; neither of us did particularly well that day, I remember! Also a good scholar, Anthony was therefore greatly disappointed when he failed to get a place at Oxford for which he had been strongly recommended by the school. Not really knowing what to do, Anthony was guided into the

Dark glass: Duncan Vaughan-Arbuckle would like to welcome more visitors — Charlie Bibby

Vinopolis plans £5m float

By Astrid Wendlandt

The company operating Vinopolis, the £20m wine theme park near the Thames in Southwark, is planning a Stock Market flotation this year to raise £5m, after disappointing attendances.

Wineworld London will use the new funds to pay back some of its £3m debt to Allied Irish Bank and put its wine accessories and museum online.

Duncan Vaughan-Arbuckle, Vinopolis founder and president, said the company has had to borrow more money than planned because of number of visitors has been lower than expected.

"We have had difficulty forecasting our number of visitors," he said.

Since the opening of Vinopolis last July, Wineworld has raised an extra £4.2m from private investors and is looking for another £2m to cover costs and repay debt.

"We are in the midst of negotiations with potential and existing private investors," said Mr Vaughan-Arbuckle.

This amount would come on top of the £5m it is hoping to tap on the London Stock Market.

Wineworld expects a £3m loss in its first year, but hopes to break even by 2001, said Mr Vaughan-Arbuckle.

The main risk for large leisure attractions such as Vinopolis is the unpredictability of attendances.

Disneyland Paris in France faced significant losses during its first years of operation because visitors fell below forecasts, while the Millennium Dome at Greenwich has asked for a loan to cover costs while numbers build up.

Before its opening, Vinopolis was hoping to attract 500,000 people a year. In its six months of operation, only 120,000 visitors have gone through its turnstiles.

Vinopolis, or city of wine, includes a multi-media museum with wine tasting sessions, restaurants, shops, private party rooms and an art gallery.

Of the £6m total sales this year, only £1m will come from visitors' wallets, the rest will come from private parties, retail and restaurant operations. Annual sales are expected to reach £16m within five years, said Roger Wood, Wineworld's finance director.

The company has not advertised since last September but said it will resume putting up posters around London in March.

Wineworld is majority owned by private businessmen, including Sandy Anderson, the former Porterbrook leasing millionaire, now chairman of Honeycombe Leisure, a pubs business quoted on Aim. Mr Anderson holds a 29 per cent stake in Wineworld.

Mr Wood said the company could issue more than £5m of shares if some of its principal shareholders wanted to sell shares in the initial public offering.

Mr Vaughan-Arbuckle said he discovered the "sacred tipple" while working as a lieutenant for the British army in northern Germany in the 1960s.

"I was patrolling the east-west border and drinking wine to keep warm," he said.

British South Africa Police (BSAP), Rhodesia, by his father. The BSAP was responsible for maintaining law and order in the vast territories between the Limpopo and Zambesi Rivers and the Bechuanaland Protectorate on the West and Portuguese East Africa on the East. These territories became Southern Rhodesia (now Zimbabwe), named after Cecil Rhodes who was the driving force behind the BSAP. From commencement in 1889 until disbandment in 1980, the BSAP steadily evolved from a para-military organisation, the first line of defence of Rhodesia, to a modern police force. The basic training was a year-long, tough and uncompromising course, of which a large part was equitation as much of the patrolling was carried out on horseback. Anthony told me that he didn't much care for the life and took the first realistic opportunity to return to the UK after his marriage broke up. He had married Beverley van Rijnbek, a Boer by extraction, in 1968. They had a son, Jeremy, in 1969. After Anthony had divorced his mother and remarried, Jeremy changed his name to Holly, that of his stepfather. Anthony found it difficult to settle into a job in the UK and held a number of jobs, none of which were particularly successful. He did, however, find love again and married Margaret (Mags), only child of Sir Arthur Eliott, 12th Chief of Stobs, in March 1974, with whom he had a son, Benjamin (Ben) (b 1978) and daughter Kate (b 1981).

Left to right: Juliet, Vivian, Ben, Kate, Mags, Anthony, Claire, Angelika

Tragically, Anthony contracted Hepatitis and, not recognising the seriousness of his symptoms, only sought medical help after it was too late. He died in Addenbrooke's Hospital, Cambridge, after an unsuccessful liver transplant operation in March 1986. History repeated itself when, after this father's death, Ben too decided to change his name to Eliott, principally so that he would inherit his mother's title of Clan Chief of the Eliotts.

This means that, on the death of Duncan and myself, there will be no male line carrying the name Vaughan-Arbuckle. Effectively, therefore, the family name will cease to exist from that moment. It will be end of a name, even though some of my grandchildren retain

| Never a Dull Moment

Betty's Grandchildren:
Left to right: Louise, Kate, Jeremy, Desdemona and Ben

Vaughan as a forename. There was a time when I asked Vivian, Juliet and Claire whether they would like to change the surname to Vaughan, our original family name, by dropping Arbuckle which, after all, was added many generations later in perpetuity of someone who means nothing to us. They did not wish to change. As the author of *McCarthy's Bar*, Pete McCarthy wrote in dedicating his book: *'To the magnificently-monikored Ian Vaughan-Arbuckle.'* He had a point.

5. First Appointment

After commissioning leave, I reported, feeling rather self-conscious in my brand-new uniform wearing the insignia of a 2nd Lieutenant, to Buller Barracks, Aldershot, on 2nd April 1960, to take up my first appointment as an officer. My first preference had been for the Trucial Oman Scouts but this had not found favour with the appointments board, so I landed up in the same barracks where I started my career – in 1 Training Battalion, Royal Army Service Corps. I was told that there had been a request for me to be posted to the training establishment (probably because I was good at sport – my words)! My job was to turn civilians into soldiers, during an intensive eight weeks' basic training, capable of taking their place in a working unit.

This task started on Day One with the recruits being taught how to wear and clean their uniform, how to make a bed neatly and what standard of personal hygiene was required. Each intake of 48 was broken down in three sections of 16 recruits. A section was looked after by a Corporal and had their own barrack room. I was in overall charge of the welfare and training of the intake with a Sergeant to assist me. The training syllabus included drill, weapon training on the .303 Lee Enfield rifle, the light machine gun, the Mills hand-grenade and rocket launcher, map reading, first aid, physical training, basic military law and fieldcraft. It was the latter which was my immediate concern. The recruits were introduced to living in the field with a 36-hour exercise which required them to cook for themselves, make a bivouac and find their way from one place to another. Towards the end of their course, I took them to the Isle of Wight for 72 hours where they were tested on the skills they had been taught. The basic scenario I devised was that a murderer had escaped from Parkhurst jail and the police had asked the military to help recapture the prisoner. The look of terror on the faces of most of the recruits as I briefed them was proof enough that they genuinely believed the task was real. They were taken by lorry to Gosport to be transported by either a landing craft or hovercraft to a beach on the Isle of Wight. After what was usually a wet landing, the recruits had to sweep through the countryside towards Newport, looking for the criminal, played by a member of staff, who was known to be dressed in certain clothes. By the time they landed the light was fading. The recruits were required to rendezvous with me at a prearranged point by midnight. They were armed, had blank ammunition and carried their own kit weighing around 25 kilos. Only rarely was the 'criminal' apprehended. The remainder of the exercise was spent in various activities including initiative tests, canoeing, climbing and map reading. The weekend ended with a few beers. Getting the recruits away from barracks was by far the best form of training. Providing them with the challenge, excitement and sense of achievement that most of them joined the Army for was a fitting climax to their basic training and an experience few would forget. I know this from meeting former recruits later who almost always referred to their Isle of Wight experience. My immediate boss was entirely supportive of my approach although even in those days one or two senior officers who visited spoke of their concern at recruits jumping off a landing craft into the sea! My strongly held view, which I applied throughout my military career, was that for training to be meaningful and effective, it had to contain an element of risk. I thoroughly enjoyed this important and worthwhile job although, looking back, I would have much preferred to have gained the experience of serving in the Oman.

One of my early memories was being saluted by a squad of soldiers from the Parachute Regiment wearing their distinctive red berets. As they passed, the NCO in charge gave the command 'eyes left', and as convention decreed, I returned the compliment with a salute. In doing so, I realised that it was my maternal cousin Sean in charge of the marchers. It was one of those quirks of fate moments to which I was unable to react. The next time I heard news of him, he had risen to the rank of warrant officer, no mean achievement in an elite infantry regiment. It was my father who advised Sean to enter the Army when, for the umpteenth time, he found himself in trouble – on this occasion for putting a girl 'in the family way'. The rights and wrongs of what he did are open to question but in the 1950s, with the social stigma associated with abortion and no support available for unmarried mothers, Sean took what he saw as the only way out for him. Whether the baby was ever born, I'm not aware, because my contact with him has been confined to no more than a handful of meetings during the ensuing fifty or so years.

Life as an officer was a complete revelation. Socially, it was 'all go': regimental dinner nights, cocktail parties, casual parties, unlimited sport and routine of life in an Officers' Mess was brilliant. I was single and having a whale of a time! The daily routine would go something like this:

First Appointment

- Woken by Charlie at around 6.15 am with a cup of tea. Charlie was my batman, a personal servant to me and one other officer. His duties were quite simply to 'look after me'. He cleaned and tidied my room, polished my shoes, ironed my uniforms, which he laid out depending on what I needed for the day, he looked after my civilian clothes and, for a few extra 'bob' (shillings), would clean my car. An old soldier, he had seen service during the First World War and was a fund of stories. Not afraid to speak his mind, he kept me out of trouble. For example, I well remember him rebuking me when he discovered I had had a woman in my room. Over time we built a strong relationship and he became a good friend and trusted adviser; I learnt a lot from him.
- Before breakfast I would attend muster parade during which I would inspect my soldiers and get the 'once over' myself from the sergeant-major, a man by the name of Cliff Morgan whose sheer presence demanded respect. I well remember him once 'eyeing me up and down' and then 'inviting' me to see him in his office later that morning. On arrival, I was offered a cup of tea and we spent the first few minutes chatting generally. Then, without warning, he asked, "Did you shave this morning, sir?" to which I replied rather indignantly, "Of course, why do you ask?" "Because of the stubble on you top lip," he replied. I explained that I was growing a moustache. "If I were you, sir, I wouldn't bother," he said without a smile. I never did!
- Returning to the mess, with a good appetite, I would normally devour a full English breakfast, including cereal, toast and sundry cups of tea, all served by mess waiters in their smart white jackets and black trousers. Casual chat at breakfast was frowned upon as the more senior usually had their head in a paper. The daily running of the mess was left in the capable hands of the mess manager, who in my time was Mr Cattell. I use the title Mr advisedly since all junior officers never did anything else. If one ever stepped out of line in the mess, including being late for a meal, Mr Cattell usually pointed out the errors of your ways, which left you in no doubt where you had gone wrong. Like any senior member of staff in a good hotel, he wore a white shirt and silver tie, dark jacket and waistcoat, with a gold pocket-watch chain and fob dangling for all to see, grey trousers and highly polished black brogue shoes. He was a formidable man with a heart of gold behind a gruff exterior. He had our respect. I remember returning to the mess late after a night out, starving hungry. In the kitchen I found a

loaf of bread and some butter in the fridge. I toasted some slices over an electric fire in one of the small ante-rooms. Next morning at breakfast, Mr Cattell castigated me not for taking the bread but for not covering my tracks!
- The remainder of the morning would be spent teaching, interviewing or inspecting my soldiers. In those days, regular inspections of the body, including feet, were normal as a significant minority of the recruits had poor personal hygiene habits. Living as they did in large barrack rooms (dormitories) sleeping up to as many as 24 men, a high standard of hygiene was important. It was known for 'smelly' soldiers to be subjected to a regimental bath by their colleagues. This consisted of a cold bath and a scrubbing with carbolic (disinfectant) soap. Such 'punishment' was not condoned but it was effective!
- After a three-course lunch, sometimes preceded by a drink in the bar if there was a special occasion and a quick snooze in the ante-room, it was either sport or back to work. Work usually finished at around 5 pm. Then it was back to the mess for afternoon tea, self-service style, read the papers and a chat before going for a run, a game of squash or some other form of recreation. We changed into a dark suit and tie for dinner every night except Wednesday and Sunday when casual attire was permitted. This meant a sports jacket and tie: no jeans or sportswear of any kind was allowed. Most assembled in the bar for an aperitif before dining together. After a three-course meal it was a game of snooker, table tennis or out for a drink at a local pub with a car load of chums. In those days there were no 'drink and drive' restrictions. My car – an Austin 7 – would only carry four at a squeeze so I was rarely called upon to drive.

There must have been in excess of twenty junior officers living in the Royal Army Service Corps Headquarters Mess which guaranteed an active social life, good companionship and a wide range of experiences and skills. The Mess building was set on a bank overlooking the cricket ground, known as 'God's Acre' in recognition of its hallowed turf. Mr 'Jacko' Jackman had been the groundsman for as long as anyone could remember. Woe betide anyone who walked anywhere near the square, whatever their rank! When I was first introduced to Jacko, he was very quick to tell me that I would do well if I could emulate my father! Although unqualified and unashamedly biased at times, particularly whenever the Brigadier was involved, Jacko's verdicts were always accepted (with a smile) by visiting teams. One of his favourite turns of phrase when rejecting an appeal for LBW was 'No, I'm not' which often perplexed an opposition bowler.

But back to the Mess. The public rooms were in the centre on the ground floor. The imposing main entrance, leading into the lobby, was flanked by two cast-iron cannons, relics of the Crimean War. On the right was a large ante-room furnished with leather settees and armchairs, a large table for magazines and newspapers with small coffee tables spread around the room. On the opposite side of the lobby was the magnificent oak-panelled dining room, around which hung oil paintings of generals throughout the ages. Their beady eyes seemed to be watching every move. The dining room was furnished with three highly polished mahogany tables, an oval-shaped 'top table' and two oblong tables, each seating around thirty. At the far end of the room was a raised platform used by the regimental band at formal dinners, dances and special lunches. The Medal Room, which as the name suggests, housed one of the finest medal collections in the UK, was used for smaller functions. The bar, served by a hatch, was very small. There was also a games room housing a full-size snooker table with a raised leather bench along one side for spectators. There was also a Ladies Room, reflecting the fact that ladies were not allowed in the public (or private) rooms. A lady guest had to be signed in and out, although this rule was often broken! I well remember returning late one night and hearing in hushed terms "Shh, someone is coming." Freezing so as to not reveal my presence, the unmistakable sound of high heels was coming my way. At the last moment I stepped off the carpeted stairs to come face-to-face with my friend Harold (Riley) and a very attractive young woman. I think I blurted out 'Good evening' or, given the circumstances, some other inadequate greeting as they passed. The matter was never again spoken of.

My best friend in those days was Paul Honeyman. He had completed his National Service with the Devon and Dorset Regiment before transferring to the RASC after deciding to become a regular. We first got to know each other on the Junior Officer's Course before finding ourselves as fellow recruit platoon commanders. Artistic, erudite and a talented thespian, I always thought that Paul had missed his vocation. So, it was no real surprise to me that he left the Army about five years later to work initially for Tyne-Tees Television and subsequently for Anglia TV, as a producer. It was as a result of my introduction that Paul met and married Wendy (née Cattle) with whom he had two sons. Tragically, Paul died of cancer in his early forties but I kept in touch with Wendy over the years as she is godmother to Vivian. It was Paul who persuaded me, against my better judgement, to join the amateur dramatic society; if nothing else, it was a way of meeting girls. Such was my ineptitude that my one and only bit part was as the arresting officer in the final scene of *Dial M for Murder*. As a way of meeting girls, it was far more successful!

As was often the case, an invitation arrived in the Mess for 'Three officers' to attend a party given by the nurses of, I think, Guildford Hospital. Paul and I plus another colleague volunteered for this arduous duty! On the way to the party, we stopped off at a pub where we decided to be pilots of 111 Squadron (The Black Arrows) RAF display team in which we taking part at the Farnborough Air Display. Forerunners to the Red Arrows, the Black Arrows were the RAF's display team flying Hawker Hunters. On arrival we introduced ourselves as pilots from the famous display team and the word quickly spread. Being the good-looking, charismatic guy he was, Paul quickly established himself with the prettiest girl in the room. Jealous of his success, we decided to deflate his ego by getting the band leader to announce him, by name, as the youngest leader in the history of the Black Arrows and that it was his birthday! His face was a picture of embarrassment when all joined in singing him Happy Birthday. He immediately left the dance floor, on his own, and headed for the bar. Soon afterwards, I noticed that he was engaged in what was obviously a serious conversation with a military type. I headed that way and to my horror discovered that the person to whom he was talking was an RAF officer. We beat a hasty retreat although quite often continued to be something we weren't when going to such parties. Infantile perhaps, but great fun nevertheless.

Sport was a large and important part of regimental life with competition going down to company level. I spent a good deal of my spare time training so I kept myself in good shape. I've always been plagued by upper-respiratory tract infections which, at that time, were the bane of my life. I suffered at least two serious bouts of tonsillitis each winter, sometimes resulting in me spending days in bed. Flying in the face of medical advice, my mother had always refused to let me have my tonsils out. After one particularly nasty infection, the medical officer arranged for me to go into the Cambridge Military Hospital to have my tonsils removed. Entering the Officers' Medical Ward, a day before my operation, I quickly got to know Captain David Gilbert-Smith, Duke of Wellington's Regiment, who at that time was serving with the Special Air Service. He occupied the next bed and was in hospital for treatment for acute acne. David won a Military Cross for his bravery and leadership during the Battle of the Hook in Korea, and for his 'coolness and daring over many months while leading a number of fighting patrols. On several occasions he had ventured right into the enemy's positions with only one man in support.' A passionate all-round sportsman, David was capped for Scotland against England at rugby in 1952. After leaving the Army in 1975, David founded the Leadership Trust, to enhance and influence leadership, and develop leaders in all aspects of society, which under his management became a multi-million pound enterprise and is still successful today. David married three times. He died in 2003, aged 71.

I had my operation the next afternoon. By the following day, I had recovered sufficiently to get up and walk about. It was a Thursday, the day when the Officers' Club, Aldershot, always had a dance in the evening. 'GS', as he was known, had itchy feet and persuaded me to take him to the dance. I was not at all sure this was a good idea so soon after my operation, but I eventually agreed. The plan was that, after lights out, we would stuff pillows down our beds, leave the hospital by the conservatory door at the end of the ward and drive to the club in his car. The first part of the plan worked well. By the time we got to the club, the place was humming. Knowing the local scene, I was able to introduce GS to a number of girls. After a couple of pints, he busied himself on the dance floor while I chatted in the bar. Eventually, I succumbed to the temptation of having a dance. I soon began to feel distinctly queasy. Excusing myself I went into the toilet and collapsed. GS was eventually located and declared that I looked 'terrible.' He took me straight back to hospital. Not long afterwards, I started bleeding from my mouth. I remember little else until I woke up the following morning, feeling awful, with my bed covered by an oxygen tent. A number of people were staring in at me. After examining me, the surgeon said my operation had been a complete success and he did not understand why I had had a massive haemorrhage: had I been prancing around the ward, he asked? My eye caught GS grinning at me from his bed!

This episode delayed my discharge from hospital by more than a week, during which time GS and I got to know each other very well. The problem was that GS felt trapped in hospital as his treatment consisted only of a few injections each day. He was a fit, active and frustrated man who wanted to get out. GS was always making asides to the nurses and had been warned, by the ward sister, a Major, nicknamed 'Black Bess', more than once to behave himself. One morning as a pretty nurse passed by, GS pinched her bottom. Not long afterwards Black Bess appeared, gave GS an almighty dressing down and ordered him to conduct the hospital pay parade the following day. This entailed finding around 150 soldiers spread throughout the hospital and paying them their dues. Not an easy job as every single soldier had to be found and paid. GS was away all day. The punishment certainly curbed his ardour for the remainder of his time in hospital. I was due to take the Lieutenant to Captain Promotion exam and felt pretty shaky on infantry tactics. GS spent a great deal of time tutoring me on the principles of attack, defence and withdrawal using our beds, with pillows to simulate ground and other objects to denote obstacles. With this help I passed the exam.

Life was certainly busy. Between recruit courses, we had two weeks to recharge our batteries, take leave and prepare for the next intake. It was 'full on' during a course. Apart from being in overall charge, I was required to conduct all field training, which I have already described, teach certain subjects, carry out routine inspections, appear in court to represent my soldiers if necessary, write reports, interview each recruit at the beginning, middle and end of the course and, in safety terms probably most importantly, conduct live firing of weapons. The majority of soldiers, when first firing weapons, are nervous and unsure. Handling a weapon loaded with live ammunition can be a hazardous business. To become fully qualified to run live-firing ranges, I attended a month-long course at the School of Infantry – in those days located at Hythe, Kent. This was, without doubt, the best course I attended in the Army. Staffed by outstanding instructors, specially selected from throughout the Army, by the end of the course there was nothing I did not know about the weapons we covered. It was not long before my knowledge was put to the test. During the throwing of live grenades, one failed to explode. After waiting the requisite time, it was my job to locate the unexploded weapon then go forward and destroy it. Leaving the safety of the trench, I made my way into the impact area of loose shingle and approached the grenade acutely aware that any movement could cause the grenade to explode. My next job was to pack explosive around the grenade, insert a detonator, light the fuse, turn away and walk carefully back to the safety of the trench. To my relief the grenade exploded and we finished the live throwing without any further incidents. Not until I noticed my hand shaking did I realise how nervous I had been!

As a junior officer, I was required to attend ongoing training which took place at various times during the working week. One of the mandatory subjects was equitation. This meant being at the stables by 6.30 am, dressed in riding gear, to be allocated a horse by the NCO in charge of the stables. After a painful lesson, I was never late again! Turning up late one morning, I was allocated a horse called 'Buller' and told to saddle it up. Struggling to get the girth harness tightened as the horse inflated its stomach, the NCO told me to hold the harness in one hand and with the other punch the horse's stomach so that, when the horse breathed out, pull the harness tight. As I did so the horse bit my arse! The pain was excruciating! Actually, I never really took to riding army-style which was based on the principle of falling off until you figured out how to remain mounted!

First Appointment

I don't remember his name, but one of my recruits had gone AWOL (Absent Without Leave), a not altogether unusual occurrence, particularly in the early stages of training when recruits were in the process of settling into life in the Army. One day, I was informed that the soldier had been arrested while in the process of burgling a house. I was required to attend his hearing at Leeds Crown Court to speak on his behalf. My first appearance in court was a daunting prospect. I stayed the night in an hotel near the court in the centre of Leeds. Next morning I made my way to the court to find people scurrying around looking busy. I had been told that the defending lawyer would seek me out. "Are you Lieutenant Vaughan-Arbuckle?" asked a middle-aged man wearing a wig and gown. "Thank you for coming. I will need you to speak on 'X's' behalf as he intends pleading guilty to the charge. What you have to say will have a direct bearing on the sentence he receives," the lawyer explained. With that, he scurried off saying, "I'll see you in court."

The court room was large and imposing. The judge was sitting on a throne-like seat with other officials in front and on either side of him. My eyes alighted on a fearsome-looking man with a ruddy face, wearing a military style uniform. The case got under way and the court accepted the guilty plea. It was then up to the defending barrister to make his plea in mitigation. After a short introduction, I was suddenly aware of my name being mentioned: "Call Lieutenant Vaughan-Arbuckle." I got up and made my way to the witness box from the gallery feeling extremely nervous and self-conscious. After taking the oath, the barrister said, "Please tell the court you name, rank, unit and your association with the accused." My mind went blank and I felt the eyes of the whole court on me; I was in a state of blind panic. After what seemed like an eternity I spluttered an answer explaining that I did not know the accused well as he had gone AWOL soon after starting his basic training. "Would the Army be prepared to take him back in view of his conviction?" asked the judge. No-one had briefed me on this point so what was I to do? Factors raced through my head. Surely, it would not be right to take someone back who had been convicted of a serious crime, I reasoned? I glanced toward the man in uniform who seemed to scowl. I took this as a sign that the Army would discharge the soldier as 'services no longer being required' and said so. The man in uniform nodded his approval. 'X' was given a prison sentence and I made my way back to Aldershot, where to my relief I was told that I had done the right thing.

Regimental life was expensive. By the time I had paid my mess bill, kept my car on the road and met other sundry expenses, I had little or no money left by the end of the month. I was banking with Lloyds

Bank, Cox & Kings Branch, London, who were one of a few official banking agents for the Army. They had come to talk during officer cadet training and seemed to offer the financial security and support required by impecunious junior officers. They had assured their audience that, knowing the severe consequences involved, they would never bounce an officer's cheque. Within my first year of commissioned service, it was clear I would need an overdraft facility to keep me out of trouble. On returning to the mess one afternoon, I was met by Mr Cattell who said he had taken a call from my bank manager who wanted to speak to me urgently. Returning his call, Mr Cox (coincidentally of the same name as the bank) said he had something he wanted to discuss with me and that the matter was urgent. Could I come to London during the week? Having a shrewd idea that it was because I was overdrawn by a few 'quid' I said I was very busy and would be grateful if the meeting could be delayed until the following week. "No, that is not an option," he replied. Furthermore, if I insisted in delaying the meeting, he would have to speak to my commanding officer.

Two days later, dressed in a dark suit, stiff-collared white shirt, regimental tie and wearing the *de rigueur* bowler hat, I duly arrived at the bank located in a fine Georgian building at the bottom of Pall Mall. I was expected! Treated like a naughty boy, Mr Cox kept me waiting for fully ten minutes, presumably to ensure that I pondered my fate before our meeting. After greeting me with the utmost courtesy and thanking me profusely for keeping the appointment, we spent a few minutes, over a cup of tea served from a 'silver' service, in small talk. That over, we got down to business. Mr Cox explained that it had come to his attention that I was overdrawn by a few pounds without the bank's agreement. This was a serious matter and one which he could not allow to continue. The bank would always support me, within reason, but it was totally unacceptable for me to be overdrawn without the bank's agreement. If I did so again, he would have to report the matter to my CO. Did I have any questions? He then offered me an immediate overdraft facility of, I think, £5 (£90 today) before thanking me again for coming and terminating the interview. I had been there, in total, for no more than twenty minutes! Tail between my legs, I returned to Aldershot by train and never again went overdrawn without first getting the bank's authority!

After about eighteen months' commissioned service, my commanding officer said that he had recommended me for a Regular Commission. This recommendation would have to be confirmed by the Regular Commissions Board (RCB). Leighton Park, Westbury, which has been home to the RCB for the past fifty years. Every boy or girl, man or woman, who wishes to become an officer in the Army is assessed and accepted or assessed and rejected by the RCB. This assessment has become a model for other countries, and industry has aped a few of its principles.

On arrival, we were broken into groups of eight and each given a unique number on a tabard which we wore throughout.

I am number 15

We were to be judged on our own merits and not against other candidates: there were no quotas to be filled. If you were good enough you passed. We debated a range of subjects designed to display powers of verbal expression and reasoning. Each candidate was required to give a five-minute lecturette. Although I cannot remember the subject I chose, I would not have fallen into the trap of talking about work! There were written tests to assess innate intelligence; two one-and-a-half hour essays to be written; tests to gauge physical fitness, practical ability and planning capacity. There were also, I think, three one-on-one interviews conducted by an officer, the last with a brigadier. Lastly, there was the planning exercise which involved rescuing captives from a remote island. You had one and a half hours to write out a solution and then, in discussion, arrive at a corporate solution. From what I can recall, a number of my ideas found favour and were adopted for the group plan. On the last night there was a formal dinner, supposedly not part of selection although not many believed this! I returned to Aldershot having no real idea how I had fared. There was then a horrible 36 hours before notification, by letter, of the result. I was still in bed after 'a few beers' the night before when Paul came into my room clutching the official envelope. Opening it with trembling hands, it took a few moments to sink in that I had passed. I do not remember much of the remainder of that weekend! But I could now look forward to the long-term security of a career to the age of 55 of a regular officer.

After about eighteen months in Aldershot, I received notification of my next appointment. This was to be in a lieutenant's appointment in 119 Heavy Transport Company RASC, Bielefeld, West Germany, in support of NATO (North Atlantic Treaty Organisation), even though I had asked for an loan appointment with a foreign army like the Trucial Oman Scouts.

6. West Germany – The Cold War

It was 2nd February 1962. Clutching my travel instructions, I made my way to Heathrow in uniform to board an afternoon military flight to Hannover. It was with a *frisson* of excitement at the prospect of a new challenge in a foreign country that I made my way through German Immigration and Customs, the officials dressed in their green uniforms, Germanic-style peaked hats and, to my surprise, armed with a pistol, into the Arrivals concourse. Looking around, I saw a Corporal holding a card bearing my name. "Vaughan-Arbuckle?" he asked quizzically. "That's right," I replied, thinking that he had neither saluted nor welcomed me. "Follow me" – and, with that, he set off through the concourse without offering to help me with my luggage; very odd and without doubt impolite, I thought; not a good first impression of my new unit. We made our way to the vehicle, an Austin Champ, which was open on all sides. The driver made no move to get out of the vehicle. The Corporal beckoned me to the back of the vehicle with my luggage. We set off and soon entered the autobahn network (the nationally co-ordinated motorway system in Germany on which there is no speed limit) in the direction of Düsseldorf. Travelling at over 70 mph, cars were passing us as if we were not there. I was wearing a military mackintosh which gave me very little protection from the freezing conditions and strong wind. I had to remove my hat otherwise I would never have seen it again. The driver and Corporal, on the other hand, were snug in their heavy-duty clothing in the front of the vehicle with extra warmth provided by a heater.

Few words, if any, passed between us for the next hour as we sped south. Leaving the autobahn at the exit for Bielefeld, it was not long before what was clearly a former barracks of the *Wehrmacht* (the German Army in World War II) came into view, with its huge and imposing four-storey accommodation blocks.

The gates opened, the sentry saluted and we drove over the cobbled roads until, a couple of minutes later, we pulled up outside a building signed Officers' Mess. There we were met by a smiling young man wearing civilian clothes who introduced himself saying, "I expect you

| Never a Dull Moment

Typical German barrack block

would like a drink?" Actually, all I wanted to do was to warm up. The bar was full. I was given a brandy, introduced to everyone, given more brandy and the rest of the evening was a complete blur. Next morning, feeling distinctly fragile, I made my way to breakfast. The waiter, a buxom German woman, took my order and then asked whether I would like 'a hair of the dog'. The look on my face must have told its own story, for those present thought it hugely amusing! I then caught sight of the 'driver' and 'corporal' who had picked me up the night before sitting at the table wearing Lieutenant's badges of rank. Both introduced themselves and explained that it was normal for newly arrived junior officers to be treated in a similar fashion. I made no comment for to do so would have been futile. Quite what they thought of my reaction the previous night I'm not sure as it was never subsequently discussed, at least not with me!

Since the end of the Second World War in 1945 and up to the time in question, Britain's major military contribution to world peace had been focused on the forces stationed in BAOR (British Army of the Rhine). In 1947, Germany was divided in to West and East, the former occupied by the Allies, and further divided into zones controlled by the forces of Britain, France and the United States, and the East occupied by the USSR.

The peacetime development of tactics, techniques and new equipment stemmed from the tactical requirements of BAOR, which was under operational command of NATO. NATO was conceived in April 1949 to oppose the forces of the Eastern Block, led by the USSR. It was against this background that I joined 9 Company RASC, whose

West Germany – The Cold War

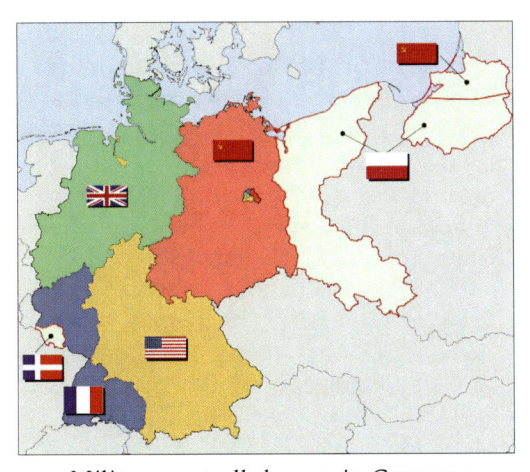

Military controlled zones in Germany

role was to transport elements of the Honest John rocket from depots to their designated war locations. This required me to have Top Secret security clearance approved by the USA, since the Honest John battlefield missile system was controlled by the U.S. My platoon consisted of 22 10-ton AEC lorries, each manned by two drivers which, together with supporting staff and equipment, meant I had a total of over 60 personnel under my direct command. At least half of those were soldiers forming the last intake of National Servicemen coming towards the end of their two years' compulsory service. Within the regular element, my two senior NCOs (Sergeant 'Smudger' Smith and Sergeant Whitlock) had seen wartime service.

After formally taking command of my platoon, I decided that the best way of getting to know them, and to test their state of readiness to fulfil our role in war, was to take them out of barracks on an extended exercise. My company commander agreed and allowed me to be away for up to 28 days, providing I could always be reached in case of emergency. Together with 'Smudger' we concocted an exercise which involved driving many thousands of kilometres around West Germany, including parts of the American Zone. A military exercise, sometimes referred to as a war game, is the employment of military resources in training for military operations, often testing plans without actual combat. It was a very excited and proud young officer who left at the head of his convoy to test his ability in command. In those days it was possible to clear land, buildings and other facilities privately owned for use by the Army. The process took about a month. Generally, German landowners, farmers and others were keen to agree to 'host' the British Army on their property as this enabled swaps of food to take place e.g. freshly slaughtered meat for tinned rations and coffee, which were still not readily available in Germany. The farmers welcomed damage to their fields and crops caused by manœuvring vehicles as compensation was generous; many claims for damage were exaggerated!

The exercise, which involved map reading and surviving throughout the length and breadth of the British and American Zones of West Germany, started in the north, where I experienced my first encounter with German aristocracy. We had settled into a location deep in a forest and were having a meal when a small *Unimog* (4-wheel drive vehicle) arrived escorted by one of our sentries. Out got a huge German wearing all-green clothing and carrying a hunting rifle. *"Forstmeister*" (Forest Warden)," Smudger said immediately on catching sight of the man. "Better go and introduce yourself and offer him a brandy," he continued. In haltering German I did just that and we were soon sitting around the fire exchanging pleasantries after he had examined our authorisation papers. In exchange for a bottle of not very good brandy, we got a freshly shot deer which the *Forstmeister* produced from his vehicle. Once he knew we intended staying for a couple of days, he insisted that I call on the landowner who lived about ten miles away.

Arriving at the front of the imposing front door of the *schloss* (what we would call a stately home), I rang the front door bell. Eventually, the door was opened by a man wearing a servant's uniform. I asked to speak with Herr Von 'Flensburg' (in German personal names, Von is a preposition which usually denotes some sort of nobility). *"Einen moment,"* the servant replied; he obviously had no trouble in picking me for what I was! After a couple of minutes, a middle-age man appeared, immaculately dressed and wearing a black patch over one eye. I saluted and introduced myself to which he responded with a click of the heels and a half-bow. I explained why I had called and what we were doing. In perfect English, he apologised for not being able to invite me in as he was just on the way out, but he would be pleased to invite me for supper that evening: "Shall we say 7 pm?" I agreed and went back to rejoin my platoon.

Returning that evening, armed with a bottle of Scotch, I was welcomed by the same servant and shown into a huge oak-panelled room. Mounted heads of animals adorned the walls along with what I took to be family portraits. To my astonishment, Von 'Flensburg' arrived wearing the uniform of a Colonel in the *Wehrmacht* and displaying a full chest of medals and the Knight's Cross of the Iron Cross (recognised for extreme battlefield bravery or successful leadership) around his neck. We sat down to eat in what I can only describe as a baronial hall, each at the end of a highly polished oak table. Displayed on the walls were more mounted heads of animals the family had shot, including deer and boar. The meal of venison, shot by him some days before, was served by the man who had met me at the door. We drank liberal quantities of red wine so that by the end of the meal I was feeling very relaxed! My host told me that he had mainly fought the British – an admission which, I was to discover, was rare. When talking to Brits about the war, most German ex-soldiers had fought on the Eastern Front against the Russians! After the meal, we adjourned to the lounge for coffee. Excusing himself, my guest left me – to return some moments later to the unmistakable strains of a bagpipe, which he was playing. I have little recollection of the remainder of the evening except that it was snowing as my driver took me back to our location. It was an incredible evening and an experience I have never forgotten.

There were two other incidents I remember vividly from that first foray into command. The first was when, not knowing the meaning of *Sackgasse*, I led my convoy of 22 vehicles up a cul de sac. I shall never forget the uncomplimentary language and V-sign gestures of my soldiers as they struggled to back their vehicles for some distance up the narrow lane to the open road: it was utter chaos! The second incident occurred when we were in the American Zone in southern Germany. It had been a long day when I spotted what was obviously a large American Army base. I decided to chance my arm. I went forward to the brightly lit sentry room which controlled both 'in' and 'out' traffic. Control was vested in two soldiers, each wearing highly polished chrome helmets and wearing MP (Military Police) armbands. They were armed with sub-machine guns. I could sense the understandable suspicion as I approached from the shadows wearing my camouflage smock and beret. I introduced myself to the first MP who promptly referred me to his colleague. I explained the situation and asked whether it might be possible for me and my driver to be billeted for the night or whether they might be able to offer any other facilities like a bath and a meal. I repeated myself at least twice. It was as though I was speaking a foreign language. In frustration, I asked if it would be possible to speak to the duty officer. At least this brought a reaction: "Wait a minute," at which point he disappeared into the sentry room, leaving the door ajar so I could hear what was being said. "This is Dumbrowski on Gate One, sir. I got some guy here who wants to speak to you. He's from some foreign army, I think. OK, sir," and with that he passed me the phone. After explaining what I was about, the officer agreed to come down and meet me.

While I was waiting, still outside, I watched a car drive up to the sentry post to re-enter the barracks. It stopped and a large black man offered his ID to the guard. As he did so, he spotted me and said to the MP in a loud voice, "Hey, man – you look as though you have some problems." "Sure thing, but I can handle it," replied Dumbrowski (and that was his real name!). The duty officer duly arrived and was most helpful. He fixed us up with a bed for the night in the top room of a barrack block and arranged for us to go to the mess hall for breakfast. Waking in the morning, I was conscious of some soldiers peering around the door. They had obviously heard there were some strangers around. "Do come in," I said. They did and we started a conversation. One asked where we were from. Replying 'Bielefeld', this obviously meant nothing so I expanded by explaining it was halfway between Hannover in the north and Düsseldorf in the south. "Gee man, all the way from Blighty!" exclaimed one. I thought it futile to explain further!

Soon after returning to Bielefeld, I was told that National Service was to be extended for around 10,000 men due to a manpower shortage in the Army. I was given a list of my soldiers who were to be retained and told to inform them. In discussion on how best to deal with what was almost certainly going to be a contentious and highly unpopular decision, Smudger said that the best approach would be to advance pay parade, to give them the news and then open the bar. Slightly against my better judgment, I proposed this to my company commander who, to my surprise, thought it an excellent idea. The plan was duly executed with mixed results. To their credit, most accepted the inevitable and I remember only one wanting to appeal against the decision. The down side was the cost to me in drinks that afternoon, while the lads drowned their sorrows, and a sore head.

To retain those national servicemen turned out to be a wise decision as a real crisis, which threatened the peace of the world, was looming. In 1962, at the height of the Cold War, the Soviet Union was desperately behind the United States in the arms race. Soviet missiles were only powerful enough to be launched against Europe whereas U.S. missiles were capable of striking the entire Soviet Union. In late April 1962, Soviet Premier Nikita Khrushchev conceived the idea of placing intermediate-range missiles in Cuba. A deployment in Cuba would double the Soviet strategic arsenal and provide a real deterrent to a potential U.S. attack against the Soviet Union.

The Cuban President, Fidel Castro, approved of Khrushchev's plan to place missiles on the island. For the United States, the crisis began on 15th October 1962 when reconnaissance photographs revealed Soviet missile sites under construction in Cuba. President Kennedy imposed a naval quarantine around Cuba to prevent the arrival of more Soviet offensive weapons on the island. On 22nd October, he proclaimed that any nuclear missile launched from Cuba would be regarded as an attack on the United States by the Soviet Union and demanded that the Soviets remove all their offensive weapons from the island. Three days later, Kennedy raised military readiness to the highest level. It was at this point that all NATO forces in Europe were deployed, fully armed, to their war locations. We remained in our war location for about a week, refining plans and procedures so that if war was declared, we would be ready. The tension around our location was tangible. Soldiers could be heard discussing the possible consequences of nuclear war. It was a scary time. Thankfully, tensions began to ease in late October when Khrushchev announced that he would dismantle the installations and return the missiles to the Soviet Union. The Cuban Missile Crisis was the closest the world ever came to nuclear war. Later in life, I was discover that SIS (Secret Intelligence Service or MI6) had played a significant part in persuading Kennedy that if he called Khrushchev's bluff, the Soviet leader would back down. This was based on intelligence provided by the debriefing of Soviet spy Oleg Penkovsky principally by one SIS officer whom I knew. Penkovsky was later believed to have been executed as a spy.

John Fitzgerald Kennedy, President of the USA, was assassinated on 22nd November 1963 as his motorcade drove through Dallas, Texas. Most people will remember where they were at the time when they heard this shocking news. I was at an inter-unit boxing match when the news broke, and can recall the sense of loss of probably the most powerful man in the world to an assassin's bullet.

Orderly officer duty came round about once a month. The duty lasted 24 hours and consisted of a number of random checks including calibrating the amount of petrol held in storage tanks, checking a percentage of arms and ammunition, and carrying out a cash check on at least one unit account. In addition, the duty required you to attend all meals to take any complaints and to visit each soldier held in the unit guardroom, either on remand or completing a sentence. You had the authority to initiate a fire practice to make sure the fire picket knew their duties. You were responsible for inspecting the incoming guard and to turn them out at least once during the night. The guard were issued with live ammunition. The orderly officer slept and ate his meals in a special room which was equipped with a dedicated telephone. You were allowed to sleep but seldom got the chance to do so.

During my first orderly officer duty, I was called to the guardroom where a soldier under arrest was banging his head against the cell walls and injuring himself. The guard had tried to restrain him but had failed. To begin with, I tried to reason with him from outside the cell but this had no effect whatsoever. So, together with a couple of guards, I entered the cell. The prisoner's face and clothes were covered in blood, he was screaming and his eyes were staring as though he were in a trance. It took three guards to restrain him while I telephoned the medical officer to ask whether it would be alright to handcuff him to the bedstead so that he could no longer do himself harm. The medical

| Never a Dull Moment

officer knew the man and said that restraining him would, almost certainly, put an end to his antics. He was right for, as we put his first hand in cuffs, he shook himself as though he was coming around from a fit and asked "What's going on?" He caused no further trouble.

During another duty, while walking around the barracks with the duty sergeant, we came across a soldier lying in the gutter with vomit all around him. He was obviously drunk. After trying unsuccessfully to arouse him, I took his pulse only to find that he had none. He was dead! The post mortem put the cause of death down to asphyxiation caused by choking on his vomit. I had no sleep that night and spent the majority of next day writing my report.

Extra orderly officer duties were used as a punishment for junior officers who had committed a minor breach of discipline or had failed in their normal duties. 'Extras' were usually awarded by the adjutant (a senior captain who was the commanding officer's personal staff officer). I fell foul of the system when I failed to see that all my soldiers had eaten after returning to barracks at the end of two weeks away. In fact, I had seen all but a couple of them through but that was not acceptable. I should have ensured that they had *all* had a meal. For that I was given 14 days' extra orderly officer duties, carried out on alternate days: in other words, my life was disrupted for a month. I never made the same mistake again!

Honest John

It was not long after I arrived that I was involved in a joint exercise with the Americans to test the procedures for the deployment of the Honest John rocket system.

The MGR-1 Honest John missile, to give it its correct title, was the first nuclear-capable surface-to-surface rocket in the U.S. arsenal. It was first introduced in 1953 as a battlefield weapon made up of three component parts: a warhead, a rocket motor and a fin. These components had to be delivered by standard trucks until a chassis-mounted launcher system was introduced in the mid-1960s. The weapon had a range of around 30 miles. Being an American system, command and control was vested in a special U.S. Army headquarters. Deployment of the missile in the field was subject to

West Germany – The Cold War

rigorous procedures. These included a policy that warheads had to be collected from an exclusively American-controlled area, known as the NASP (Nuclear Ammunition Supply Point), travel separately from the other components, and be escorted by armoured vehicles.

It was late at night, after we had been living in a forest for a couple of days, when I was woken and presented with a 'Flash' (highest priority) message. After decoding the contents, my orders were clear. I had to report to the NASP some 20 miles away with ten vehicles to collect, rendezvous with an armoured escort from the Life Guards and then deliver the weapons to a Royal Artillery regiment, whose location would be given to me at the NASP. We duly arrived at the NASP, located in the middle of a forest, surrounded by barbed wire, patrolled by a large number of GIs (American soldiers), with half a dozen command vehicles located in the centre. The scene was reminiscent of a circle of wagons fighting off Indians in a Wild West film. After having my credentials checked at least twice, I made my way up the steps into the command vehicle. The cigar smoke was overpowering. My orders were checked and stamped (everything was classified Top Secret) and I was passed to another desk. Seated here was an overweight black Sergeant whose job was to issue me with a release order for the warheads. I watched him laboriously fill out the form until he paused, turned to a colleague and asked, "Hey man, how do you spell secret – with an 's' or a 'c'?" He was referring to the first letter of the word: this was the man giving me the authority to collect a number of nuclear weapons! We duly delivered the weapons and, together with our Life Guard escort, returned to our location, where I retired to bed.

Later that day, a helicopter seemed to be taking an unusual interest in us. In those days, helicopters were few and far between and usually meant that a high-ranking officer was being flown around. 'Smudger' was rushing around making sure that our camouflage was in order, that the sentries were alert and that there was nothing which could attract criticism. To our collective anxiety, the 'chopper' landed, out got three officers who started heading in our direction. I went forward to meet them and soon recognised General Sir Charles Jones, Commander 1 (BR) Corps, the highest-ranking British field commander in Germany, a big man with a fearsome reputation. I saluted and gave him my name. "Are you in charge here?" I replied in the affirmative. "What on earth do you mean – allowing your soldiers to sunbathe? This kind of slack behaviour is disgraceful and unacceptable." This was a tricky situation since I was pretty sure that my lads were not culpable, but how to say so was the question! I can't really recall what I said but it brought an immediate response from the General who stomped off saying, "We'll see."

As we passed through my lines, it became clear that the culprits were our escort from Life Guards who were located next to us but in a separate area. Soon aware of approaching trouble, a few Life Guard soldiers stood up hurriedly, putting on their shirts and beating a hasty retreat. Seeing this, the General shouted, "You there, come here!" A couple of soldiers stopped. Pointing his finger at one hapless lad and without pausing, the General asked, "What unit is this? Who's in charge? Where's your personal weapon?" The now terrified soldier, realising his predicament, replied, "The Life Guards, sir, Mr Mackintosh, sir …" but before he could finish the General said, "Get him!" After a few minutes, the rather languid, laid-back Mr Mackintosh, Lieutenant of the Life Guards, appeared, looking as though he had just woken, approached the General, saluted in a rather casual way, and said, "Good afternoon, General." At this, the General flew into a diatribe of what he thought of the conduct of the unit and finished by saying, "And I shall be reporting this to your Commanding Officer" – as though this would put the fear of God up the young officer. "Very well, general" replied Mackintosh. What the General had not bargained for was that 2nd Lieutenant Mackintosh was a National Service officer and heir to the Mackintosh sweet empire (famous for *Quality Street* chocolates, a tin of which will be found in most homes at Christmas). The wrath of any senior officer was not going to threaten *his* future!

But it was by no means a case of 'all work …' I ran the regimental football team which was very successful. Together with 'Smudger', we were able to field a strong side to play in the Army league as well as having regular fixtures with local German teams. The latter did a lot to foster Anglo-German relations in Bielefeld. In my final year, the team got to the final of the Army Cup, only to be beaten by the 4/7th Dragoon Guards in a match which was decided in extra time by the odd goal, after we had led for most of the game. Smudger had made the fatal mistake of telling the team to defend the lead – rather than attack being employed as the best form of defence, a lesson I have never forgotten. I was also involved in most other sporting and social activities. We had an excellent group of young officers in the unit which guaranteed a lively social life. Initially, I managed to form a relationship with the Colonel's nanny but this came to an end when I found she was keener on an officer in another unit. Like at lot of others, I had a crush on the German girl who looked after British officers' accounts in the Commerzbank without ever being successful in getting a date with her. At the time, I owned a Willys (U.S. Army) Jeep, manufactured between 1941 and 1945, considered the iconic World War II vehicle. I bought mine, which I painted blue, from another officer for a 'song'. Wearing bowler hats, a group of us used regularly to drive into Bielefeld, hoping to attract the attention of German girls: we usually did but I cannot remember this ever leading to a date!

We also frequented a place called the *Gesellschafthaus* – a complex which consisted of a *Bier Keller*, a bowling alley, a night club and a very smart restaurant, owned by one family named Hülsewede. The small bar was run by one of the daughters, a very attractive young woman with blond hair. She had been pursued, without success, by many young British officers. Whenever there was an opportunity, I used to go to the *Bier Keller* in the hope of getting a date with Angelika. Fraternisation with Germans was still frowned upon in some quarters, particularly in German society. Eventually, my perseverance paid off and she agreed to come out with me. Language was something of a problem as my German was almost non-existent while her English was not much better but somehow that didn't seem to matter. As they say, 'Love is blind.' Our courtship was intense, frantic and not without problems. I remember being set upon and beaten up outside the bar by a group of German youths, while my lifestyle at the time was unbelievable. Most days, at the end of work, I would have tea and then retire to bed before getting-up at around 10 pm. I would then have a shave and drive the two miles into town and stay in the bar to around 1.30 am after the bar closed. We would then spend the next few hours at her place or she would come back to my room. Never once did I miss the 7.30 morning working parade. Such a full-on lifestyle was bound to catch up sooner or later as it did with me when I went down with Shingles (a viral disease characterised by a painful skin rash with blisters in a limited area on one side of the body) after six months.

Much to the surprise of many, we got engaged and set a date about three months later to get married. My Colonel, from whom I was required to get formal permission to marry, was against my plans and wrote to my father, essentially saying Angelika was not right for me. To his credit, my father replied that this was a family matter and he would make up his own mind after meeting her. At the end of our visit, my parents both gave their blessing to our marriage. We celebrated with a wonderfully happy engagement party at which my new Colonel enjoyed himself so much that he formed enduring relationships with a number of Germans. All was well as the big day approached.

A Willys Jeep

| Never a Dull Moment

Angelika had a brother, Peter, and two sisters, Margrit and Ingrid. Her father, Reinhold, a larger-than-life character who led life to the full, was a well-known and popular man in Bielefeld. A measure of his popularity was that some 2,000 people attended his funeral. Although we were unable to converse other than in the most rudimentary terms, I liked Reinhold once I had established that he no longer 'owned' Angelika. Peter spoke good English and I always got on well with him, football being a matter of mutual interest and rivalry. Peter took over running the family business when his father died.

It was a Friday 7th June 1963, the day I was to marry. My mother had been staying with a major in my unit after travelling to Germany by train. Unfortunately, my father was prevented from coming due to illness (or perhaps had he been concerned about his problem with alcohol?). The weather was good and a large crowd was expected to attend the church in the centre of town. My best man was Graham Pollock, with whom I had played a lot of cricket. Sadly, I lost touch with Graham once we left Germany, although I did hear that he too married a German. My guard of honour was made up of senior NCOs and warrant officers who would form an arch of lances as we left the church. Unfortunately, they had a minor accident on the way to the church. No-one was hurt but a couple of the lances were broken, which necessitated a re-jigging of the guard. As the ceremony was conducted in German, I understood nothing apart from responding with *Ja* to the standard question of 'Do you take …'

Greeted by Angelika's father and accompanied by Graham Pollock and Erica

West Germany – The Cold War

The post-wedding celebration was held in the *Gesellschafthaus*, starting with a reception, progressing to a formal wedding dinner and finishing with a dance. It started in the early afternoon and finished when we left at around 2 am. German tradition demands that the newly-married couple can leave only once the last guest departs.

My mother and I at the wedding dinner

The next day we drove to Playa de Aro on the Costa Brava, where I had booked a self-catering bungalow on the edge of the beach. Our journey was not without incident, however. Nearing Playa we went into a village to, I think, pick up the keys. It was pouring with rain. Stopping at a junction in a narrow street, I was horrified to see a bus reversing towards us. Not being able to reverse and despite blowing the horn, the bus continued to reverse until it collided with the front of our Renault Dauphine. The front of the car, which had the engine at the back, was crunched like a corrugated tin sheet. After much gesticulating and chatter, I managed to make it understood that I wanted to talk to a policeman. The bus driver and I walked some distance through flooded streets before spotting a sign indicating *La Policia*.

Entering the smoke-filled room, with four men in uniform sitting around a table playing cards, it proved difficult to make myself understood as none of them spoke any English. In desperation, I resorted to drawing a sketch which did the trick. Accompanied by one of the police, we went back to where the crash had occurred to find the vehicles in precisely the same place. After taking stock, the policeman beckoned me and the bus driver to follow him. We finished up in a shop where, thank goodness, the assistant spoke English. It was explained to me that the car would be repaired, free of charge. We left the car with them and were taken the five or so miles to Playa in a bus! A week later I was delighted to pick up the repaired car which showed no sign of ever being involved in an accident. All of this had been achieved in an open yard with few overt signs that the business was capable of such good work. The remainder of our honeymoon went well.

During my time in Bielefeld I had the opportunity to travel to Berlin on both the military train and by car; each was a real experience. Together with a couple of colleagues, we drove to Berlin through the Helmstedt-Berlin corridor. Paperwork had to be completed well in advance and approved before the trip. As the route involved going through East Germany, we were required to stop at the NATO border checkpoint followed by the Soviet checkpoint; at both points our paperwork was checked methodically and carefully. Any error would result in passage being denied. The distance to Berlin was 110 miles which had to be completed in a certain time. Too fast and you got a ticket, too slow and you were subject to rigorous investigation. Since NATO did not recognise the East German government, all dealings were with the Russians. No stopping was allowed, no photographs permitted, nor any deviation from the designated route, which essentially followed the autobahn to Berlin. The trip was interesting: Soviet and East German troop convoys on the road and the East German *Polizei* monitoring our progress. There were very few other vehicles on the road. It was like driving through a time warp and so radically different from West Germany.

During a subsequent visit to Berlin, I had the opportunity of visiting East Berlin. Passing through Checkpoint Charlie, it was a surreal experience being watched by East German Border Police taking photos of all transitees from their watch-tower control point.

I visited the Soviet war memorial in Treptower Park, guarded by the Russians, where I was surprised to

Checkpoint Charlie

West Germany – The Cold War |

see coachloads of Russian soldiers arriving to pay their respects. I was also impressed that, as I walked around in uniform, my rank was recognised and I was saluted by Russian soldiers. I doubt that the same could be said of British soldiers.

I took the opportunity of walking around Alexanderplatz, where I looked around the sparsely stocked shops and took the time to watch the East Germans going about their day. I have to say they looked a sombre, downtrodden lot in a drab part of the great city of Berlin. The contrast with West Berlin could not have been greater.

Russian War Memorial, Berlin

It was 1963 and I was travelling from Hannover to Berlin using the military train which plied daily, except Christmas Day, between the garrison in West Berlin and the Rhine Army in West Germany. The train had large Union Jacks on the side of its blue carriages. A trip on *The Berliner*, the only British Army train in service at the time, was a unique experience. The journey took us through the bright lights of the West to the dull grey of the East. At first glance, it could be any train except that the doors were sealed, with chains and wedges, from the inside. As the train pulled out of Marienborn into East Germany, watch-towers, high and unscalable wire mesh fences, tripwires and ploughed minefields appeared against the darkening sky. They belonged to the ugly death strip which divided East and West. The eerie reality of a divided Germany was there to be seen. While the document-checking ritual was performed, a Soviet soldier watched at each end of the train for any sign of movement. The purpose of the sealed doors and the guard became clear. If an East German tried to board the train, he would be arrested. At Potsdam the engine was

Military Train

| 147 |

uncoupled, searched for stowaways and then re-coupled. It was then on to Charlottenburg station in West Berlin. The locomotives were changed from West German to East German as the train transited East Germany, between Marienborn and Potsdam. The military train service ended in 1990.

After a year as a platoon commander, I was promoted to Captain and moved into the post of Operations & Training Officer, a job which involved the writing of operational plans, the clearance of land for use in training by the unit and, most satisfyingly, organising trade and military training. I did this job until February 1964, when I was posted to the appointment of Schools Liaison Officer for Hampshire, Wiltshire and the Isle of Wight, based on HQ Southern Command, Salisbury. So it was back to school, I thought.

7: Back to School – Face of the Army

The job of Schools Liaison Officer (SLO) for Hampshire, Wiltshire and the Isle of Wight required me to lecture, once a year, about the Army in the 193 schools in my 'parish'. When I took up the appointment in February 1964, I had a small room in the Army recruiting office in Salisbury, in theory clerical support from the recruiting staff, the use of a dedicated army vehicle (a Hillman Husky), a projector and films, and a list of 'my' schools. After about a year in the job, I managed to persuade my boss, a retired Brigadier, to give me a secretary and a separate office elsewhere in Salisbury. I had a three-day handover with my predecessor during which I attended a couple of his lectures and was then on my own. I must admit initially to feeling somewhat daunted by the task, which normally saw me lecturing in two schools every day. I also found it a rather lonely life, having previously been used to a lively and challenging existence in a unit.

By this time Angelika was pregnant and obviously finding life in a strange country, speaking a foreign language, tough. Her English was limited but to her credit she was soon able to make herself understood. To make matters more trying, we were allocated a civilian rented house in Salisbury on the Devizes Road, as opposed to a married quarter, without the benefit of the support of other army families. Apart from next door, which was occupied by an officer learning to fly helicopters, our neighbours were civilians who, knowing we were transitory, were never particularly friendly. I know Angelika was lonely. However, it was only a couple of months before Vivian was born. Angelika's labour started on the Saturday evening so I drove her to hospital. Vivian, a beautiful baby girl, arrived a couple of days later, on Monday 6th April in Tidworth Military Hospital, without complications, but mother and child remained in hospital for about a week. This enabled me to paint the spare room as a nursery for Vivian. Even had I wanted to be 'in' at her birth, I would not have been allowed to by hospital regulations – how times have changed. In case the reader is wondering why we spelt her name the boy's way, I did so as it incorporated my name. In the first few days after coming home,

Vivian would not settle, a matter quickly resolved when an experienced mother explained that a baby needed to be wrapped tightly to feel secure. Soon afterwards we had a visit from Angelika's mother, Hedwig, who stayed for some days helping out. It was to be the last time I saw her as she was to die when we were in Hong Kong.

I had been in the job only a few weeks before I was called to see General Sir Kenneth Darling who was in overall charge of the Army in the south of England. This was the first time I had been seen personally by such a high-ranking officer. To say I was nervous was an understatement. As I was ushered into the large office, the General got up from behind his desk, walked towards me, shook hands and invited me to sit in an armchair opposite him with a coffee table between us. He was small in stature, wore a moustache, had piercing blue eyes and a rather shrill voice. His chest of medal ribbons bore testimony to his wartime service. He had a fearsome reputation. Physically, he reminded me of Field-Marshal Montgomery. After telling him about my background and the job I had taken over, he asked me what I intended to tell my audiences. I started to waffle about terms of service, pay, leave and opportunities, when the General cut in saying, "Nonsense. Tell them where the Army is serving in the world and why we are there. Make it clear we only want tough, independent and properly motivated young men. What we don't want are those who are no good for anything else. I will come and listen to one of your talks sometime in the next three months. You have an important job. Good luck." And with that I was dismissed.

True to his word, the General asked to listen to a talk I had arranged at Portsea Secondary Modern School, located in one of the 'rougher' areas of Portsmouth. The day arrived and I made sure that I had plenty of time to prepare myself for what was going to be an important examination. My audience of senior boys assembled in good time and, unlike many other occasions, were kept under close supervision as we waited for the General to make an appearance. As the clock ticked beyond the scheduled time of start, I decided to get started. As I was metaphorically making my way around the world explaining what the Army was doing, the General, accompanied by the headmaster, came in and sat at the back. By this time, I was well into my stride and not at all fazed by the General's presence. He listened for about twenty minutes and then slipped out without anyone, apart from me, noticing he had gone. The talk had gone well and I left the school feeling positive. It wasn't until the telephone rang about two weeks later, when the caller said he was the General's aide, that I remembered the visit. The Major said the General had enjoyed visiting the school and thought that I had pitched my talk exactly right; well done and I was to keep up the good work! I never saw the General again.

The range of schools in my area was diverse. At one end of the scale I had some top grammar schools, like Portsmouth Grammar School, to good secondary modern schools in socially deprived areas like Swindon, to poorly run schools in prosperous areas. Some schools were good academically; others got good results in technical subjects while others gave their pupils a good all-round education. There were others that did well on the sports field. I particularly remember making a presentation, to mark his outstanding achievements since joining the Army, to the school in Portsmouth where Jim Fox was educated. Fox had become Head Boy of the Army Apprentices College and by that time had made his first appearance in the Olympic Games. He competed in Modern Pentathlon in four Olympics, winning a gold medal with the British modern pentathlon team in the Montreal Games of 1976, a bronze in the world championships in Mexico, and was ten times National Champion. Foxy, as he was affectionately known, once led the charge down sport's super-highway, a swashbuckling, Corinthian hero in an age when sportsmen were men, and women seemed happy to be ladies. After rising through the ranks, Fox became a Captain before retiring from the Army in 1983. Once arguably Britain's outstanding all-round sportsman, tragically 'Foxy' is now a victim of Parkinson's disease.

Many schools in my area had a tradition for sending their pupils into one of the three Services. This was unsurprising given that Aldershot, the home of the British Army, and Portsmouth, a major naval base, were located in my patch. One school, The Priory, in Carisbrooke, IoW, simultaneously had the Head Boy at two of the Army Apprentice Colleges. I arranged for this to be officially acknowledged by a visit and presentation to the school by a senior officer. Sadly, the school ceased to exist in July 1970 when it was amalgamated with two other schools to become Carisbrooke High School. Public relations events, including instructive concerts by military bands, were well received and did a lot to raise the Army's profile within schools. Whereas other SLOs had problems gaining access to schools in their area, I had no such difficulties. Only one of mine, where the headmaster was an unashamed pacifist, did not allow me to lecture to a mass audience but even he allowed to talk to individuals who expressed an interest in an army career.

Winston Churchill died on 24th January 1965 and was buried six days later after a full state funeral, the only commoner to be accorded such an honour. Knowing that the funeral was to be televised, I stayed at home that day and watched the whole thing on our black-and-white

TV. I was transfixed as the wartime hero of our country made his final journey. Such was the impact the funeral had on me, I can still remember vividly the images of the day, in particular the lowering of the cranes as Churchill's coffin passed by on its journey along the Thames. The whole affair was made more poignant as the day was overcast and misty. I remember crying at the solemnity of the procession and the words of the late Richard Dimbleby, the BBC commentator. The whole thing made a deep and lasting impression on me.

The administration of Ian Smith, whose Rhodesian Front party opposed an immediate transfer to black majority rule in the self-governing British colony, declared Unilateral Independence (UDI) of Rhodesia from the United Kingdom on 11th November 1965. Although Rhodesia declared independence from the United Kingdom, the country maintained allegiance to Queen Elizabeth II.

The day after UDI, the United Nations Security Council adopted a resolution condemning it as an illegal declaration of independence 'made by a racist minority'. The UK moved to impose economic and diplomatic sanctions on what they now regarded as a rebel colony. It was at this time that plans were being drawn up for a possible invasion of Rhodesia by military forces from the UK. I draw that conclusion because an order was circulated around Southern Command asking for those who had relatives in Rhodesia to make the fact known. I did and was interviewed by a senior officer who asked me, point blank, whether I would be willing to be part of a force to go to Rhodesia. I said that I would not since Anthony, my first cousin, was a serving in the para-military Rhodesia Police. For that reason, I would not wish to find myself in a position of fighting against him or other expatriates. My name was duly taken off a list of those earmarked to go. Ultimately, no forces were sent to Rhodesia.

Back to the schools. My work was largely routine although, from time to time, it did throw up some surprises. I well remember turning up to a large co-educational school in Basingstoke, prepared to talk to the 4th and 5th year boys. On arrival I was somewhat surprised to be met by a couple of senior girls who, having helped me set up in the hall, took me to the teacher's common room. There I was introduced to a female member of staff responsible, I thought, for career's advice to the boys. Over a cup of tea it came to light that I had been booked in to talk to the 4th and 5th year girls! Explaining that I did not lecture to girls, the teacher said the programme could not now be changed and that the talk would have to go ahead. Entering the hall, I was confronted by well over a hundred chattering girls. What now? I have little recollection of what I actually said but it must have been OK since, at the end, the enthusiastic applause indicated they had enjoyed the talk – or was it the uniform?

Back to School – Face of the Army

I suppose the most rewarding part of the job was when I accompanied headmasters and careers advisers on visits to military units so they could see for themselves the training and care and attention we gave junior soldiers. More often than not, a former pupil of their school would be found for them to talk to, which was always very popular and often served to reassure sceptics that the Army provided good opportunities for the right boy. I also very much enjoyed giving individual advice, particularly those who had ambitions of becoming an officer. I think my own career path of coming through the ranks helped me get a sincere message – that the Army was a meritocracy – across. Another of my duties was to attend career conventions. I remember well going to one on the Isle of Wight with my chum Richard Hutchings, when I was working at the Junior Leaders Regiment. He had arranged for a military boat to take us from Portsmouth to the IoW. There was a large swell running in the Solent in which the boat was pitching and yawing so much so that after some time the display, which we thought had been securely tied securely to the deck, broke loose and went over the side. The sight of us leaning over the side using boat hooks to rescue the display must have been hugely entertaining. But for us it was a very serious matter. Eventually the boards were rescued although not before at least one had been penetrated by a boat hook while the others were soaking wet. Hasty repairs and much use of towels hid the incriminating evidence sufficiently well so our reputations remained intact! Since then, usually over a few pints, this saga has provided much amusement in its retelling!

On 15th July 1965, the Royal Army Service Corps, in which I enlisted in 1954, ceased to exist except in history and the Royal Corps of Transport (RCT) was born. Its role was to provide transport support to the Army in both peace and war. Transport support included road, rail and maritime transport together with port operating and air despatch. As I was not serving in a unit on re-badging day, I attended the parade and festivities at Bulford Camp when new RCT badges were presented. It was a day of mixed feelings as my father had also served in the RASC, a corps which had been responsible for both supplies and transport throughout the Second World War and earlier. In the words of Field-Marshal Montgomery of Alamein delivered in Germany in November 1945:

> *I consider that the work done by the RASC in this war has been quite magnificent. I know well that without your exertions behind, and often in front, we should never have been able to advance as we did. No Corps in the Army has a higher sense of*

> *duty than you have. You have delivered supplies in all weathers and over all roads. You have driven your vehicles in rain, and snow, and ice, and you have never once let us down. Without your supplies our battles could never have been won. It is a fine record.*

As the job was coming to an end, my career manager in the Ministry of Defence telephoned to ask whether I would like to go to Hong Kong. My excitement at the prospect of returning to a place for which I already had a deep-rooted affinity must have been palpable. I was subsequently posted to 56 Squadron RCT, for duties as the Island Detachment Commander.

8: Colony in Conflict – Hong Kong

The 37½ hour flight to Hong Kong in an RAF Bristol Britannia, configured with rear facing seats (for safety), which put down at Akrotiri (Cyprus) and Gan (Indian Ocean), was uneventful until we started our descent into Kai Tak airport, considered at the time to be one of the most dangerous approaches in international air travel. After banking sharply to avoid Tai Mo Shan, Hong Kong's highest mountain, the final approach was over the top of buildings skimming masts so low that you could almost touch them. The plane landed with a bump onto the runway which at its far end led into the waters of Hong Kong harbour. A terrifying experience for the unwary traveller! By the time the three of us landed on 21st March 1966, Angelika was seven months pregnant.

Landing at Kai Tak

We spent the first week or so in a family's hostel north of Kowloon. Rounding the corner, the panorama was breathtaking; we were on the way to the flat we had been allocated on Hong Kong Island. The crescent-shaped bay with turquoise blue water lapping onto the white sand of the beach, with a backdrop of hills covered by green undergrowth, was stunning. On one side of the bay stood an old colonial-style building, which was the world-famous Repulse Bay Hotel, while at the other end was a multi-storey complex, consisting of several spines of ten flats, each having its own balcony looking out to sea. "That's where you're going to live," said the Chinese driver, pointing towards the block of flats. I was 'over the moon'. We settled down quickly to a vibrant new way of life within the military community. We were better off financially although many temptations awaited the impetuous shopper. Juliet was duly born on 27th May 1966 in Mount Kellett Military Hospital, located on The Peak. The hospital was demolished sometime later and has been replaced by flats on some of the most expensive land in Hong Kong.

Hong Kong started out as a fishing village, salt production site and trading post, later evolving into a military port of strategic importance, then – at the time of writing – an international financial centre that has the world's sixth-highest GDP rating. The cession of Hong Kong to Britain, via the enactment of treaties, was completed in 1842 after Britain prevailed over China in the First Opium War. Hong Kong was occupied by Japan for four years during the Second World War. In the post-World War II period, 'Made in Hong Kong' went from a label that marked cheap low-grade products to a label that marked high-quality products. The transfer of sovereignty over Hong Kong from the United Kingdom to the People's Republic of China took place on 1st July 1997, this event marking the end of British rule.

I had not long completed my takeover when, on 6th April, I reported for my first duty officer at Hong Kong and Kowloon Garrison. The 12-hour duty involved sleeping in Osborne Barracks on Nathan Road, the main thoroughfare in Kowloon. On arrival, I was briefed on my duties and advised to read the operation orders during the evening. The responsible officer did say that there had been a demonstration at the Star Ferry complex over a proposed increase in fares, but 'not to worry' as the situation was under control. I decided, nonetheless, that it would be prudent to read, first, the orders pertaining to civil unrest: what a good decision that turned out to be!

At around 8 pm, crowds started gathering in Nathan Road. Demonstrators were chanting and raising their fists in defiance of the odd policemen trying to restore calm: the atmosphere was extremely tense. I was able to watch a lot of what was happening from the window of the duty room and was alarmed by what I was witnessing. Seeing the situation deteriorating before my eyes, I decided to telephone the duty officer at HQ Land Forces, located on Hong Kong

Island, to alert him. His response was, initially, one of indifference until I held the telephone mouthpiece out of the window so he could hear for himself the shouting and chanting. He rang off, saying, "I'll phone you back." He did so about half an hour later. He had spoken to the police who had confirmed that the situation was serious. I was to order the duty unit, in this case a company (60 men) from the Queen's Regiment, to assemble in Kowloon ready for riot control duties.

At around 10 pm, serious violence broke out among the protestors: mobs threw stones at buses and set vehicles on fire. A police station was attacked by a crowd of about 300. By this time riot police had been deployed and fired tear gas but this did not deter the demonstrators. The size of the crowd increased significantly in and around Nathan Road. By midnight the rioters were looting shops and they attacked and set fire to public facilities, including government offices and fire stations. As rioting continued, tear gas was used by the police and in some cases they fired small arms weapons at looters. The Queen's Regiment was deployed with soldiers patrolling the streets with fixed bayonets. Eventually a curfew was successfully imposed at around 2 am. By this time, the senior officer and his staff were in the headquarters and I became a 'bit part' player in the proceedings. That night 772 tear gas canisters, 62 wooden shells and about the same number of carbine rounds had been discharged. The rioting continued for another two days before being brought under control – but not before a unit of Gurkhas had been deployed to assist in keeping order. The Chinese were terrified by the sight of Gurkhas advancing, *kukris* drawn (the traditional Nepalese weapon with an inwardly curved cutting edge) – who wouldn't be! One person died, nearly 2,000 were injured and 260 people received sentences of up to two years' imprisonment for taking part in the riots. Damage to property was estimated to be no less than HK$20 million (£1.6 million). The fare increase was duly implemented. I recall the Brigadier commenting that I had had an 'interesting' first duty!

It was later that month, on Saturday 30th April, when I was again on duty, that I listened on the radio to England beating Germany 4-2 to win the World Cup. Geoff Hurst scoring the winning goal accompanied by Ken Wolstenholme's immortal words '… they think it's all over – it is now' is a moment I have never forgotten.

No sooner had the 'fires' of rioting been extinguished than Hong Kong was engulfed by rarely seen amounts of rainfall and consequential damage. Severe rainstorms occurred during the period 7th to 13th June 1966. The downpour reached its maximum intensity on 12th June when continuous violent thunderstorms and heavy showers resulted in extensive landslides and flooding. In the 24 hours

11th-12th June, rainfall on Hong Kong Island reached a staggering 17.8 inches. Road and drainage systems were blocked or damaged, old buildings collapsed, vehicles were either washed down the hillsides or buried in mud, and stream courses were blocked. Being in charge of the majority of transport on Hong Kong Island, I needed to be located in the operations centre. The problem was living in Repulse Bay some five miles from the headquarters, with the roads impassable: the only way for me to get in was on foot. So I walked in to Victoria Barracks through torrential rain – in places having to crawl on my stomach under torrents of water cascading across the road and, in other places, having to negotiate a way around where the road had been washed away. One of the first jobs awaiting me was to lead a convoy of four Land Rovers, carrying essential supplies to Hong Kong's Peak District, which had been cut off for days. This involved a dangerous journey up nothing more than a narrow track, which had been extensively damaged by the rain. My recollection is that the journey took about two hours to travel no more than two miles. When we reached the top, the crowd which had gathered in anticipation of getting some essential supplies, cheered our arrival. It was a miracle that only 64 people lost their lives in the devastating floods.

Flood damage, HK Island June 1966

On 3rd December 1966, trouble broke out in the Portuguese island colony of Macau when Chinese communist residents were refused permission to open a school. As a result, Chinese 'Red Guards' (supporters of Mao Tse-tung) mobbed the Macau Governor's residence while Portuguese troops tried, unsuccessfully, to suppress them. The Cultural Revolution had started in Hong Kong. Trouble continued to simmer on the island, particularly when the Chinese population adopted what amounted to a disobedience campaign against the government. After some weeks of further trouble, Portugal offered to return Macau to China but – to the astonishment of many – they declined the offer. Consequently, the Portuguese government in Macau became nothing more than a 'puppet' authority under the control of Beijing. Seeing what happened in Macau was a catalyst to further, more serious, unrest in Hong Kong.

Typhoons and tropical storms were (and still are) a regular feature of life in Hong Kong. The main features of a typhoon are surging high winds and heavy rainfall. Typhoons, and to a lesser extent tropical storms, are subject to a system of severity classification, starting from 1 and increasing to 10. During my time in Hong Kong we experienced one with a maximum classification of 10, named Shirley, in August 1968. Wind speeds reached 77 mph and ten inches of rain fell in a 24-hour period. When a storm warning reached Category 6, the military had predetermined tasks to perform. I spent many hours in the operations room dealing with tasks connected to the approach and subsequent impact of many typhoons and tropical storms.

Red Guard Activist, Hong Kong 1966

56 Squadron was the largest sub-unit in the Royal Corps of Transport. The unit included a flotilla of small boats and landing craft, a troop of ambulances and the Island vehicle detachment. The unit had its base at Shamshuipo in Kowloon. As commander of the detachment on Hong Kong Island, I was responsible for a troop of staff cars supporting HQ Land Forces, including the Commander's garage, consisting of a limousine, two staff cars, a Land Rover and two domestic 'runabout' vehicles, a general transport troop based in Lyemun Barracks in the east of HK Island, and a driving school in the same barracks. The Commander's garage was looked after by a senior British NCO; otherwise my NCOs were locally enlisted Chinese soldiers, which overall accounted for about two thirds of the 100 or so men under my command. The history of Chinese soldiers serving in the British Army can be traced back to the 1880s. Many Chinese 'Hongkongers' fought alongside British troops in the defence of Hong Kong against the Japanese. I found Chinese soldiers hard-working, loyal and extremely good drivers but their 'soldierliness' left something to be desired. Language was not a problem although it

could become one at times. I well remember talking to a long-serving soldier who, but for the want of a formal qualification in English would have been promoted, and asking him whether he would agree to taking a two-week English language course. He agreed. My surprise can be imagined when I was telephoned by his instructor, a few days into the course, saying that the soldier was not measuring up and why I had sent him against his wishes. When I interviewed the soldier, he would not concede that he had volunteered to attend the course. In discussion with his immediate Chinese superior, Sergeant Yeung Moon, he explained that it was a matter of loss of 'face'. No Chinese should ever be placed in a position of having to agree openly that something was their fault. I never fell into the same trap again!

I did not find the job of Island Detachment commander particularly stimulating so I was delighted to be offered the job of adjutant to the Lieutenant-Colonel senior RCT officer, when the current incumbent decided to retire from the Army. Essentially, the role of an adjutant is to act as the personal staff officer to a Lieutenant-Colonel commanding a battalion or regiment of around 800 men. The appointment is always in the rank of Captain and usually indicates that the officer is seen as having potential for command himself in the future. It was February 1967. The RCT command in Hong Kong was huge. It consisted of 56 Squadron, which I have already described, a Pack Transport Troop of assorted mules and horses located in the New Territories, a Gurkha transport squadron, and a Movements staff located at Kai Tak international airport. In total, about 800 of all ranks including British, Chinese and Gurkhas. There were also sundry other RCT officers in other posts or learning to speak Chinese at the language school. Amongst these was my old friend Richard Hutchings, who proved to be probably the most elusive of all when it came to requiring him to conform! I did manage to attract his attention one day as he was passing the office after I had noticed the name Miss Slesarenko annotated 'intended wife of Captain Hutchings' on a list of passengers arriving from the UK! That lady, Sigrid, did indeed become his wife but not until there were a few false dawns! Sigrid actually stayed with us in our married quarter for a while until she found accommodation. After they got married, Richard and Sigrid found a nice flat in the New Territories well away from the hustle and bustle of life in Kowloon and from where Richard and I, accompanied by Worthington, Richard's mongrel terrier, occasionally walked. It was on one such walk that I earned the sobriquet 'Boots'. This came about when, after a long walk in the heat of a Hong Kong summer, I became so hot that I dived into a reservoir wearing all my clothes including my green jungle boots! Talking of heat, I well remember another walk through thick, knee-high undergrowth in sweltering hot conditions, climbing uphill, when Worthington refused to go another step. Richard had to carry him some way before he was fit enough to start walking again. For my part, it was the thought of a few bottles of ice-cold San Miguel, followed by a curry cooked by Sigrid, that kept me going when the going got tough as it usually did when Richard was leading a walk! Richard and Sigrid, who retired to their lovely house in Dunkeswell Abbey, in the heart of the Devon Blackdown Hills became very close, lifelong friends after our days in Hong Kong.

'Triad' is a term used to describe a Chinese criminal organisation. Triads engage in a variety of crimes from extortion and money-laundering to trafficking and prostitution, similar to the Italian mafia. As a way of binding the members together, Triad members are usually subjected to an initiation ceremony. A typical ceremony consists of an animal sacrifice, usually a chicken, pig or goat. After drinking a mixture of wine and blood of the slaughtered animal, the recruit will pass beneath an arch of swords while reciting the triad's oaths. Triads infiltrating 'Hongkongers' was always a worry. I was woken one night by the telephone. The voice of the duty officer said I was required in the headquarters as a number of our HK soldiers had been arrested for murder! My mind was racing as I drove into the barracks. It turned out that in a raid on a known criminal premises, eleven of our Chinese had been arrested in connection with a Triad gang murder. I phoned the Colonel who said the matter could wait until the morning when more would be known. I spent the rest of the night in a police station getting the names and as much detail of the circumstances as I could. I was waiting for the Colonel, a large unflappable man who smoked a pipe, anxious to impart what I had found out. "I'll see you after I've had my coffee," was his response, sensing my demeanour! The law took its course and eventually six were charged and convicted of murder. The remaining five were charged and convicted of being members of an illegal organisation and dismissed from the Army.

One of an adjutant's responsibilities is the maintenance of discipline. Over a period of about six weeks, there had been a spate of officers stepping out of line: it was a case of 'too much play and not enough work'! After an initial disagreement with me about the severity of the situation, the colonel agreed to address all RCT officers in Hong Kong. He instructed me to assemble them for a particular date and time, regardless of other commitments, dressed in their best uniform. I was not to tell them the purpose of the meeting. They duly assembled, agog as to what it was all about. The colonel arrived punctual to the second. Without any preamble, he said that he had noted a marked deterioration in the recent behaviour of a significant number of officers. This was unacceptable. He wanted to remind them of what it

| Never a Dull Moment

said on the commissioning 'parchment' signed personally by the Queen, viz: *'We, reposing especial Trust and Confidence in your Loyalty, Courage and good Conduct, do by these Presents, Constitute and Appoint you to be an Officer in our Land Forces ... You are therefore carefully and diligently to discharge your Duty ...'*

And with that, after speaking for no more than a couple of minutes, he walked out. You could have heard a pin drop. It was a master-stroke of getting a message across without labouring the point! There were no further instances of unacceptable conduct!

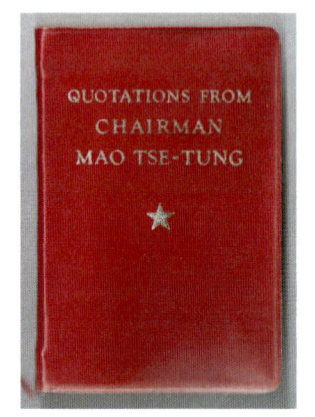

Soon after I became adjutant, increasing signs of tension were evident with demonstrations and labour disputes breaking out in various industries. To the north, the People's Republic of China (PRC) was in turmoil, caused by the ongoing Cultural Revolution, spearheaded by the pro-Mao Tse-tung Red Guards. By May, pro-communists turned labour disputes into large-scale demonstrations, waving Chairman Mao's Little Red Book, against British colonial rule.

Mao's Little Red Book

The Colony was subjected to a wave of terrorism, violence, bombings, murder and intimidation orchestrated by China's Red Guards with the aim of undermining British colonial rule. The most serious of these took place on 6th May 1967 when riot police were deployed. Many were injured and a significant number of rioters were arrested. This type of incident continued for the next four weeks. Another serious incident took place on the Sino-British border when armed militia from the PRC fired at the Hong Kong Police station at

Colony in Conflict – Hong Kong |

Sha Tau Kok. Five policemen were killed. In response, Gurkha infantrymen were deployed and tensions ran high for a number of weeks. Responsibility for patrolling the border, for a six-week period, was rostered amongst the infantry battalions. I remember travelling in a Welsh regiment vehicle, with China on the left-hand side throughout the six or so miles of the border between Hong Kong (Lowu) and China (Sha Tau Kok), in the company of one of their officers. We were on a reconnaissance to examine the condition of the barbed wire border fence. When we got to the crossroads at Sha Tau Kok, with the Chinese Army border post facing us, our driver enquired, "Which way now, sir? Left or right?" The response of his officer is unrepeatable! Whenever leaving barracks, military personnel were armed and I recall carrying a fully-loaded pistol when moving from place to place.

A joint operations centre (POLMIL) was established in the Police Headquarters on Hong Kong Island. Together with other junior army officers I did regular duty stints in POLMIL in the company of an officer from the HK Police. POLMIL was manned on a 24/7 basis for months on end until the internal security situation ceased to exist after 18 months.

Bombings, shootings, demonstrations and riots were commonplace. At the height of the troubles a dawn-to-dusk curfew was imposed. The use of bombs became a favourite weapon of the insurgents. Real bombs, mixed with decoys, were placed to inflict as much chaos and damage as possible throughout the city. A friend of mine, subsequently decorated for his work, and his team of bomb disposal experts were at full stretch. Bombers employed cunning tactics. One was to cut a hole in the floor of a vehicle and then deposit a bomb, real or fake, in the middle of a busy road bringing chaos to the area. Another was to put a live poisonous snake in a box masquerading as a bomb so that when the bomb disposal officer opened the box he would be bitten or suffer severe shock! Bomb disposal officers defused as many as 8,000 home-made bombs, of which only about 1,000 were genuine. The 20-storey Bank of China located in the heart of Hong Kong Island, used by the leftists as a headquarters and hospital, was strengthened with barbed wire defences and festooned by red flags and portraits of Mao Tse-tung. The photograph (see previous page) used on the front of the book *Borrowed Place, Borrowed Time* shows me scratching my ear while playing on the HK Cricket Club ground, with the Bank of China in the background – who said cricket waits for no man!

The troubles were finally brought to an end by an edict from Beijing forbidding the protagonists to cause any further unrest. In total, 51 people were killed including at least one soldier, a firefighter and five police officers. 800 sustained serious injuries while damage to property amounted to millions of pounds. It is a bone of serious contention that the internal security situation was never recognised by the award of a medal by the British Government. The most popular reason was thought to be a fear of upsetting China as negotiations commenced leading to independence from Britain thirty years later in 1997.

Despite periods when life for the family was not without worries, we had a good social life and had made friends within and outside military circles. Our loyal and hard-working Chinese *amah* (a domestic servant whose role combines the functions of maid and nanny), Ah Hing, was a great support for Angelika. Dressed in her white top and black shiny trousers, she was a big favourite with the girls whom she addressed as 'Missy'. Most weekends there was some sort of social function or we met friends in town for a 'beer and a curry'. The girls were happy and thoroughly enjoyed swimming either in the sea or at the Kowloon Cricket Club pool where we were members. Vivian had settled well in school. Life was pretty good and we had enough money for the odd luxury. So it didn't take too much time for me to accept a third job in Hong Kong, this time working as a junior staff officer in 51 Brigade, formed, during the riots, from units of the garrison.

On the down side this meant we would have to move from our lovely flat in Repulse Bay to Kowloon. However, after looking

Angelika, Juliet and Vivian in Perth Street

at the ground-floor flat in Perth Street, with a little garden quite near where I went to school all those years before, we decided to 'go for it'. We did have second thoughts after Angelika saw an arm reach through the bars of the bedroom window one afternoon when she was resting and snatch her bag. Thereafter, windows were never left open.

I was due to take up my post in 51 Brigade in March 1969. Because Angelika was expecting in September and would not be allowed to travel back to the UK so near her confinement, we were able to use the equivalent money to take local leave. I found a two-week round trip to Japan on a P&O liner within the allowance. We had a great trip calling at Kobe, where we sampled one of their famous beef steaks, and Yokohama. On the way out we did sail round the fringes of a tropical storm for a couple of days which was unpleasant. It was during this time that I had to smack Vivian for the first and only time in her life. We were sitting as guests at the Captain's table when Viv decided to be a real pain; nothing was right and, as tension grew, she knocked over a glass of water with the imagined results! I took her to our cabin, gave her a smack and left her there. I suspect it hurt me more to leave her sobbing as I returned to dinner. The incident was never mentioned again until, many years later, Vivian said she had never forgotten the matter! In those days, Angelika still had her German passport so when we got back to Hong Kong she had to pass through the Aliens immigration check whereas I and the girls went through as 'Brits'. Waiting the other side, it was clear that the Hong Kong Chinese immigration official was giving Angelika a hard time. Suddenly, I heard her say in a loud and irritated manner, "Vell, I am telling you zat I'm married to a British object." Of course she meant 'subject'! The Chinese official could not contain himself and without further ado waved her through!

By the time Claire came along on 9th September 1969, we were settled in Kowloon and she was born in the brand-new military hospital at King's Park. There is an apocryphal story that I went to the hospital to see mother and child clutching an evening newspaper rather than a bunch of flowers. That is just not true! I did take the evening paper together with other 'goodies'. Claire was then, and has ever since, been a real joy. The day I was promoted to Major is one I shall never forget. I was picked up at lunchtime and taken to the Gurkha Officers' Mess for a 'beer', I was told. It was New Year's Eve 1970. By the time I was poured out at about 6 pm, I was feeling no pain! When I got home, Angelika reminded me that we were due at the Officer's Club for a dinner dance. When I woke up, she had gone. So I got myself ready and went in a taxi to join the party feeling like death. As I walked in, Angelika and the others fell about laughing.

| Never a Dull Moment

Goodbye Ian goodbye ...

11-3-71

Goodbye Ian goodbye... those were the words sung by Army cricketers last night instead of the original song "Goodbye, Jimmy Goodbye."

The song was for their dependable opening batsman Ian Vaughan-Arbuckle who played his last innings for Army against the Kowloon Cricket Club Saracens last Sunday at Cox's Road.

Vaughan-Arbuckle's superb form helped his side to a 10-wicket win in the Rothmans Knock-out tournament.

He put up an undefeated 51 runs and maintained a 115 runs partnership with West Indian Rockey Daniels who made a 61 not out.

Best

Many cricket followers in the Colony will agree with me when I say that Vaughan-Arbuckle and Daniels are two of the best openers Hongkong has had for the past five years.

Vaughan-Arbuckle will leave Hongkong on Friday with the Cricket Association team for their tour of Ceylon, Singapore and Sabah. But Vaughan-Arbuckle will not return with the team next month.

He will step aboard an Army flight in Singapore and return to the United Kingdom for three months well deserved leave.

He will then attend a 13-month course on Transport before taking up his next assignment.

"May be the Army wants me to remain in the UK for another year, or post me to Germany for the next term," he said.

His absence will be felt by the Army cricketers who have enjoyed his company on and off the field for the past five years.

He skippered the Army side in 1967 and retained the post for the first half of the season that just ended before handing it over to R. Shearburn in January this year.

He also headed the Combined Services XI in 1967.

In 1967 he was selected play for the President's XI and later wore the Colony cap. He has toured with the HKCA side to Singapore and Malaysia, and played against Australian sides on two previous occasions.

Last year, Vaughan-Arbuckle was selected to open the Colony innings against the touring MCC XI, where he made 35 runs.

"I was not good enough to play for the Services five years ago, and I will have prove my capabilities when I return this time during the trial games," he said.

Vaughan-Arbuckle, in fact, first came to Hongkong in 1948 and was educated in a Peak School and later joined KGV.—J. Pulle

Apparently I looked so pale and ill nobody found it in their heart to be angry with me!

It was about this time that I had another of those troublesome duty officer stints. The telephone rang in the duty officer's room. It was around 10 pm. "Hello, sahib. Sergeant Bahadur Gurung, duty NCO 28 Squadron Gurkha Transport Regiment speaking. Guardroom being attacked, permission to open fire?" In shock, my immediate response was 'No' before asking him for more information. He explained that some men were attacking the guardroom with knives and that, in his orders, it said that in the event of the guardroom coming under attack he was to seek permission from Brigade HQ, if necessary, to open fire. The guardroom opened onto a main road protected only by a chain-link fence. There were a couple of drunken men stabbing the guardroom main door with knives. I telephoned the civil police seeking assistance. They were soon on the scene and arrested the 'attackers' who turned out to be drunk. Good soldiers as they undoubtedly are, I quickly learnt Gurkhas are likely to interpret instructions literally and do relish a 'punch-up'!

My five-year tour in Honk Kong finished on a 'high' when I was selected for the Hong Kong cricket team to tour Ceylon (now Sri Lanka), Malaysia, Singapore and Thailand. This article in a newspaper (opposite) featured my departure.

So, the three girls, aged 7, 5 and 2, and Angelika travelled home on their own and I followed once the cricket tour had ended. We had arrived in Hong Kong in 1966, with one daughter and left with three at the end of my five-year tour of duty. Life in Hong Kong, which I have described in detail elsewhere in the book, was a wonderful experience in military, sporting and family life terms. Actually, I was so fond of the way of life, I did try unsuccessfully to obtain a job in Hong Kong with British American Tobacco. As things turned out, it would have been a grave mistake on my part to have left the Army.

After leave, I was to attend a year-long professional transport course studying transport methods under the auspices of Southampton University.

9: Mid-Career Postings

Sixteen rather anxious officers assembled in April 1971 at the Army School of Transportation, Bordon, Hampshire, from all over the world, to attend the year-long Advanced Transport Course. The aim of the course was to prepare students to occupy command positions in the Royal Corps of Transport. I had no wish to attend this course but, having taken advice, felt it was in my career interests to do so. I knew a few of my fellow students and by and large got on well with them. There was only one exception, an Australian who spent the whole time telling us how much better paid he was than us!

Because we were going to be in the area for less than a year, we did not qualify for a married quarter. Instead we found rented accommodation in Farnham which belonged to a fellow RCT officer who was on secondment in the USA. It was a comfortable house in Brambleton Avenue within walking distance of a primary school for Vivian and Juliet, a kindergarten for Claire, the town and an easy drive to work for me. I was away a lot visiting units, completing modules of the course and planning fictitious operations. The course was militarily interesting and worthwhile but I did not feel the same about the month we spent at Southampton University preparing to take the qualifying examination for the Chartered Institute of Transport. Among subjects studied was Quantitative Method which involved higher mathematics. Given my numerical dyslexia, I struggled to grasp even the fundamentals of the subject, a fact that I brought to the attention of the Commandant who was entirely uninterested in my problems! He merely advised me to enrol for extra maths at the local polytechnic, as though I had spare time on my hands! Needless to say I failed the exam and did not qualify for the CIT. This did not, however, affect my overall result in which I placed third on the course.

As part of the course, in syndicates of four, we were attached to a large and small seaport to study their differences in operating and management systems. Our syndicate was attached to the Mersey Docks and Harbour Board in Liverpool, and to Felixstowe Port as the small operator, although they are now one of the largest ports in the

UK, if not the largest. The difference was marked. In Liverpool top managers were distant and removed from the reality of what was happening dockside, whereas in Felixstowe each man knew the 'gaffer' and had ample opportunity of talking directly to him. We spent two weeks in Liverpool and one week in Felixstowe. Quickly identified as army officers in Liverpool, a senior docker, who was also a Territorial soldier, took us under his wing. In his care, we really did get an insight into a docker's tough life. I remember him telling us that trouble was brewing over a new dock, the Seaforth Grain Terminal, which was to open shortly using unregistered dockers. Management had not spoken to the workforce and serious trouble was ahead unless they made their plans clear. During our final meeting with the Chairman of Mersey Docks & Harbour Board, I mentioned this to him. His reply was that he had heard nothing and in any case the new terminal was a long way off. In fact, the terminal was ready for use by late 1972 but due to prolonged industrial relations problems it was not fully operational until 1974! The opposite was the case in Felixstowe where the managing director got out of his Rolls Royce each morning at the gate and walked around the entire harbour before going to his office; he did the same each evening, regardless of the prevailing weather. He knew most of his workforce by name. He told us that the two hours he spent 'walking and talking' were by far the most valuable in his day. A salutary lesson for all those in positions of authority: 'Time spent making oneself available is essential to good relations.'

The final exercise, which lasted two weeks, involved planning the logistics for an imaginary invasion over the Scottish coastline between Ullapool and Kyle of Lochalsh. I remember little of what plan we evolved but I do remember clearly the outstanding beauty of this coastline and the generous hospitality of the Scottish people, even though I do not like whisky! What a shame it is that the UK does not have reliable weather since there can't be many areas more attractive and hospitable anywhere in the world.

I received a call during the course saying that my mother was very seriously ill in Tunbridge Wells. I travelled back immediately but she died before I got there. As mentioned earlier, her funeral was held in the chapel of the Blessed Sacrament Convent attended by an aged nun who had taught her and her one surviving sister Ayelish (Fane-Saunders) and her husband Bernard. Personally, I think her death was a blessed relief from the misery and poor health she had suffered for some years through smoking and over-drinking. My mother's death left my father living in a flat which was too large for him and he quickly took the decision to move to Brighton. Before doing so, he asked me what of my mother's possessions I would like. I chose the heart-shaped mirror she was given on her marriage and a nice Delft cake dish, for which my father charged me £8!

I finished the course in May 1972 and, after leave, took up my new position as officer commanding C Squadron of the Depot Regiment RCT in Buller Barracks, Aldershot, where I had been stationed on three previous occasions. In the meantime we had bought our first house, in King's Road, Haslemere, a semi-detached property within walking distance of the town centre and railway station with its fast link to London.

The job was to train recruits. Having done this as a junior officer, I suppose it was reasonable that I was now to put that experience to good use. To carry out the role, I had a number of NCO instructors and a small administrative staff. At any one time there would be around 90 recruits undergoing their eight-week basic training. Although the job was repetitive it was never dull. When I took over the unit, the wastage rate – those who left the Army

123 King's Road, Haslemere

for whatever reason before completing their training – stood at around 30%. This was far too high and suggested that there was something wrong. After a few months, I worked out that a large number of the junior instructors (Corporals), who had most contact with the recruits, were altogether unsuitable for the work. Some were bullies who made life a misery for any recruit who showed weakness while others did not have what it took to be good instructors and mentors. I recommended the removal of about 40% of my junior staff. This did not meet with any great support from my commanding officer but eventually he reluctantly agreed, setting me a target of reducing wastage to less than 10% within six months of the changeover, with the threat that if it did not work it would be me who got the sack! The target was achieved and my judgement vindicated!

In January 1971 Idi Amin, who had been a Sergeant in the British Army, seized power in Uganda after a military coup and gave himself the rank of Field-Marshal. In August 1972, Amin declared what he called an 'economic war', a set of policies that included the expropriation of properties owned by Asians and Europeans. Uganda's 80,000 Asians were mostly born in the country, their ancestors having come to Uganda from the Indian subcontinent when the country was still a British colony. Many owned businesses, including large-scale enterprises which formed the backbone of the Ugandan economy. On 4th August 1972, Amin issued a decree ordering the expulsion of the 60,000 Asians who were not Ugandan citizens (most of them held British passports). This was later amended to include all 80,000 Asians, except for professionals, such as doctors, lawyers, and teachers. A plurality of the Asians with British passports, around 30,000, emigrated to Britain. A small percentage of those who fled to Britain joined the Army. One of the first to enlist was Suryakant Patel who came to my unit for training. He proved an excellent young man who was chosen as Best Recruit of his intake – a fact that was seized upon by the press who turned up in their hordes for his Passing Out Parade.

I was happy and highly motivated by the important job of training recruits and until then had never experienced a problem with any of my superiors. It was therefore a great shock when my first report contained serious criticisms of my performance. In particular, it said that my judgment was suspect, that I was more interested in sport than the job and, most damning, that I allowed the unit to exist without proper direction. I knew my superior did not like me but I was genuinely hurt by the remarks. After discussing the report with various people whose advice I trusted, I decided to appeal the report, not something which was a routine matter. After being interviewed by two senior officers, the report was forwarded with their recommendation to the Ministry of Defence Appeals Board. In due course I was informed that my appeal had been upheld. The overall grading would be upgraded and the non-recommendation for

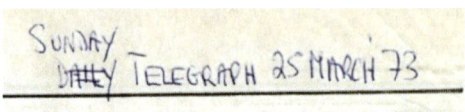

Sunday Telegraph 25 March 73

Ugandan is top recruit

MAJOR I. M. Vaughan Arbuckle congratulating Driver Suryakant Patel, 20, a Uganda Asian expelled by President Amin last October, when he passed out as Champion Recruit at the Aldershot training depot of the Royal Corps of Transport. He is the first Uganda refugee to complete training as a British soldier.

After seven weeks' basic training in drill, rifle-shooting and other military subjects, Driver Patel was adjudged the best of the 21 recruits in his intake. "He is smart, enthusiastic and an extremely hard worker," said Lt. Robbie Campbell, his squad commander. "We can do with more soldiers like him."

Driver Patel's parents have returned to India, but he came to Britain with his elder brother and cousin. After two months at the resettlement camp at R.A.F. Greenham, Berks, they moved to Cardiff, where Driver Suryakant enlisted on Jan. 23.

Mid-Career Postings |

promotion overturned. Part of the problem was that I was Captain of Army Cricket at the time and my superior assumed that I had let my military duties slip. Nothing could have been further from the truth for I always made a point of leaving clear instructions and catching up every time I was away. Fortunately, that particular commanding officer was replaced shortly afterwards and my career was back on track.

It was during this period that Vivian and Juliet started at St Margaret's School, Midhurst. St Margaret's was an independent school for girls run by the Sisters of Mercy. It catered for both day pupils and boarders.

St Margaret's Badge

We decided to send the girls there as boarders, knowing that, sooner or later, I would have to go overseas and wanted to give the girls continuity of education, something that I had never had. The decision was alien to Angelika as very few children in Germany board. We went to have a look at the school with my Aunt Ayelish and decided that, although it was not particularly academic or sporting, it was a happy place where the girls' interests and welfare would be uppermost. In the absence of their grandmother, Ayelish got involved as she no doubt felt we needed guidance over which school would be suitable. There was a good feel

Vivian, Juliet & Claire circa 1977

about the school which provided an excellent, well-balanced, quality education within a happy secure atmosphere based on sound Christian values. Although run by Roman Catholic nuns, the school did not require their pupils to be of the RC faith.

Later, Claire would also attend St Margaret's. Another important factor in our decision was that the basic fees were covered by the allowance I received. On my salary, there was no way that I could have afforded to fund their private education. It was strain enough covering the extras of them attending a private school. There is little doubt that all three girls would probably have achieved better academic results had they gone elsewhere. Against that, all three were happy at the school where they made lifelong friends and passed their O Levels. The school closed in 2009 after 121 years because the ageing Sisters of Mercy nuns wanted to step down from their trustee responsibilities.

My next job, which I started in August 1974, was in the Equipment Management Directorate of the Ministry of Defence, Whitehall. My office was on the ground floor of the Old War Office building, in Whitehall Place, opposite the modern MOD building. The room, which I shared with two others, was large with a high ceiling, an oak door and original brass fittings and two huge windows protected by blast curtains in case of a bomb attack by the IRA, which was lethally active during this period. I was responsible for briefing a General, lecturing various courses on equipment husbandry and acting as secretary to two policy-making committees. Not a particularly dynamic post but an important one which, if completed satisfactorily, would earn me a qualification to enhance my chances of rising to the rank of Lieutenant-Colonel. I therefore took the job seriously but, with the blessing of my boss, continued to play cricket for the Army. We remained in our house at Haslemere from where I commuted daily the 55 minutes by train to London. My two successful years in this post ended in August 1976.

In an earlier chapter I have covered my father's marriage to Trudie (Lynch). As a holder of Top Secret security clearance, I was required to inform the authorities of any change in my personal circumstances. As this included immediate family, I submitted the relevant paperwork about Trudie, my father's new wife. Good job I did, for in August 1975 it came to light that her brother Mel Lynch (37), a New York fireman and his accomplice, Dominic Byrne, were involved in the kidnapping of Seagram Whisky heir, Samuel Bronfman II. The kidnappers initially demanded a ransom of $4.6 million but, ultimately, settled for $2.3 million which was handed over. The 21-year-old Bronfman was kept in an apartment in downtown Brooklyn for nine days. It was thought that there was a possibility of an IRA connection

Mel Lynch arrested by the FBI

stemming from several findings: both Lynch and Byrne were born in Ireland; Lynch had made several trips to England and Ireland in the past year; Byrne spoke to friends about making a 'big score' to help 'the cause'; the odd ransom sums, first $4.6 million, then $2.3 million, convert approximately into two million and one million pounds Sterling. Lying in wait when the ransom was handed over, FBI agents recorded the vehicle's licence number, tracing the car to its owner Mel Lynch. Two days later, on 17th August, a team of FBI agents and New York police raided the apartment where Lynch resided. There they found Bronfman tired and hungry but unharmed. The ransom money was recovered at another apartment. Lynch and Byrne were arrested and charged with kidnapping and extortion.

They were tried in December 1975. At the trial, Lynch's defence attorney alleged that Bronfman was himself in with the plot having previously entered into a homosexual relationship with Lynch. Jurors partially believed the submission and acquitted Lynch of kidnapping but found him guilty of extortion and sentenced him six years in prison. In the end he served four years before being released in 1980. Fortunately, as I had never met the man, this matter had no bearing on my security clearance. But that was not the end of the story!

In August 1976, I was posted to Sennelager, a large British Army garrison on the edge of the Lüneburg Heath in northern Germany, as second-in-command of 7 Tank Transporter Regiment. Vivian and Juliet continued to board at St Margaret's while Claire, who was now seven, came with us to Germany where she attended the William Wordsworth School, run by the British Forces Educational Services. My arrival at 7 Tank Transporter Regiment was a massive embarrassment as I had lost my suitcase, containing my uniform and other personal possessions, on the way to Germany. Travelling by car to the Dover cross-channel ferry from the West Country, where I had been playing cricket, a suitcase had worked loose and was blown off the roof rack. This did not become apparent until I had boarded the ferry by which time it was too late to do anything. I was therefore forced to arrive without any uniform to wear. My new commanding officer, Peter Mears (and his wife Ann) who has since become a lifelong friend, was less than impressed! Fortunately, a member of the public had retrieved the suitcase from the road and handed it in to a police station who contacted Angelika; she was also less than impressed! I got the suitcase back when she joined me from the UK a couple of weeks later. In the meantime I managed to cobble together enough uniform to tide me over.

As second-in-command of the regiment, I was responsible for all matters connected with the operational readiness of the unit: I wrote

| Never a Dull Moment

the operational plans, I allocated places on all external courses, I ran the regimental training wing, and I was responsible for briefing visitors to the regiment. My workload was heavy. I well remember the commanding officer, Peter Mears, leaving the office one evening as I was struggling to deal with piles of files stacked up on the floor of my office. As he passed my door, he cheerily enquired, "Everything OK?" To my surprise, I answered, "Frankly, no!" prompting the Colonel to come in and sit down. I explained that my workload had been very heavy for a long time and I was fed up working late every night. "What you need is a holiday," he suggested. I explained that we had arranged one when the girls came back for the holidays and that was all we could afford. He then suggested that I nominated myself to go on a cross-country skiing course in the Harz Mountains. I agreed and spent a day short of two weeks at the Army's Winter Warfare Training Centre, Silberhutte. This was a relaxing and thoroughly enjoyable time thinking of no-one but myself. As a major, I was by far the highest-ranking person on the course – a fact that the German instructor was quick to seize upon. Whenever he chose a student to try a technique first, it was usually me. On the penultimate day of the course, after successfully passing the final test, I was chosen to demonstrate a technique known as 'organ peddling' where, at the end of a slope, a series of bumps had to be negotiated. The experience was a disaster!

7 Tank Transporter Regiment RCT on parade to say 'Farewell' to Colonel Peter Mears

Mid-Career Postings

My legs shot upwards towards the sky and I came down with a real bump, both winded and with a severe pain in my shoulder. A trip to hospital confirmed that I had broken the right-sided collar bone. Arm in a sling and on painkillers, the 'boss' was not impressed when I reported back for duty unable to write for a time! No computers in those days!

The wartime role of the regiment, which had sub-units in Fallingbostel and Hamm, was to move the forward tank regiments from their peacetime barracks to their wartime locations in northern Germany.

Each tank transporter was able to carry one main battle tank, in those days the 55-ton Chieftain. The idea of having vehicles capable of carrying a tank was to save valuable time and money by lessening the wear and tear on the tank and their crews.

Antar Tank Transporter with a badly loaded Chieftain main battle tank

The procedures were practised regularly, and tested by the NATO Operational Readiness Team (ORT) who descended, unannounced, to initiate a test exercise. These ORT tests were hugely important. If deficiencies were identified in plans, they had to be corrected without delay and were then re-tested. Within the regiment, it was my responsibility to prepare plans to respond to operations, which could be called at any time of day or night. The first 'trigger' was to get key personnel to barracks from wherever they lived. This meant using all available means of communication. The code word used at the time, requiring all to report into barracks without delay, was 'Razor Blade'. On one such test exercise, not realising I was already in barracks, the messenger knocked on the door of my married quarter in the early hours of the morning. Angelika answered, in her dressing gown, to be confronted by a soldier quoting 'Razor Blade'. She told the soldier to wait and reappeared with a bag which she asked him to deliver to me. I was in the middle of some crisis in the operations centre when the soldier said, "Your wife asked me to give you this." It was my spongebag containing my razor!!

I well remember a patrolling exercise in southern Germany, of which I was in charge, designed to test the map-reading skills of junior non-commissioned officers aspiring to promotion. One of the patrols was many hours overdue at a checkpoint so I decided to send out search parties to find them. I went with my driver to search a densely wooded area which stretched for many miles. After some hours, late that afternoon, I found the patrol tired, hungry, disorientated and dispirited so decided I would lead them out of the forest. After walking for about an hour and a half, I realised that I too was lost! Thinking I knew the way, I had made the mistake of not checking the direction on my compass. After another hour or so, as the light was fading, it was clear that I had been going round in a circle. By this time the patrol was grumbling and I was at my wits' end. Panic was setting in. It was time to swallow my pride and admit I was lost. I was near to tears. At that moment, I saw the lights of a car and knew that was the only road in the area and was where we needed to be. About an hour later, the patrol stumbled out onto the road only a few hundred yards from where I had left my vehicle. Never again would I take anything for granted when leading others using a map and compass!

At the end of the Second World War, there were over two million Poles stranded in Europe. After the war, without an independent homeland, many Poles faced a future in exile. Some emigrated but some remained in Germany, and were absorbed into military employment.

In 1947 the first two British units employing Poles (henceforth known as Military Service Organisation (MSO)) were formally established. These two units were based in Fallingbostel and Hamm: from these the proud Polish tank transporter tradition within 7 Regiment was developed. Unit titles changed over the years, but the personnel were the same: loyal and hard-working with an outstanding reputation amongst the customer units. It has to be said, however, that their military skills sometimes left a lot to be desired.

During another ORT, the MSO squadron was chosen for particular examination. The unit had to deploy to their war location where they

Mid-Career Postings |

were to be subjected to a simulated air attack by the RAF. Peter Mears and I decided to pay the unit a visit to see how their preparations were going. On arrival, the first thing we saw was a sentry wearing his respirator (gas mask) in response to a simulated gas attack. Fine, except that he was using a finger to hold the rubber seal away from his face rendering the mask quite useless. When the RSM told the soldier in no uncertain terms to remove his finger he did so but it was immediately obvious that he could now no longer breathe! Seeing this, he removed the respirator. Further examination of the mask, revealed that it had clearly never been worn, since the cardboard packing was still in place. No wonder the man could not breathe!

That small crisis overcome, we moved through the location to the unit headquarters where, to our amazement, tents had been erected with comfortable chairs inside and a white tablecloth adorning the table. This was supposed to be war! To make matters worse, white marker tape, which could be seen for miles, was attached around most of the trees. When asked by the commanding officer why this was so, the senior MSO officer replied, "Simulated dannert vire, sir" – and he was deadly serious! (Dannert Wire is a type of barbed wire or razor wire that is formed in large coils which can be expanded like a concertina. In conjunction with plain barbed wire and steel pickets, it is used to form military wire obstacles). We could not contain ourselves and a tricky situation was defused. Although the MSO connection ended in 1985, the links with this special group of men remain. They made a deep impression on everyone who ever had the privilege of serving with them. Their ethos and traditions will not be forgotten.

We were allocated a nice married quarter within walking distance of the barracks and Claire's school and, from where, I could run without having to get in a car. Sport played an important part of regimental life. I captained the unit cricket team while spending a lot of time on the British Army golf course. The unit had a talented group of golfers who did well in the Army Cup competition. As we were relatively close to Bielefeld where Angelika's family lived, we saw a certain amount of them without it being close enough for them to pop in unannounced! It was always nice to have the girl's home during the school holidays.

On 7th June 1976, the British Army of the Rhine (BAOR) celebrated the Queen's Silver Jubilee with a review by The Queen of the mechanised 4th Armoured Division on the Sennelager Training Area. Two thousand seven hundred men and some 600 guns, tanks, vehicles and helicopters 'marched' past Her Majesty in a never-to-be-forgotten show of power, precision and pageantry. It was quite simply a parade without equal. Our regiment was involved in getting the tanks and armoured vehicles to their harbour areas at the right time, a complex plan requiring attention to detail and minutely perfect execution. The plan worked. Along with all other units involved, we had a regimental tent to which we adjourned for a well-deserved celebration after the parade. The only sour note was that the commanding officer was allocated a mere five Silver Jubilee Medals to award in a regiment of over a thousand men: what other nation would be so penny-pinching in rewarding its army?

Queen's Silver Jubilee First Day Cover

When Germany was divided into three zones in 1945 at the end of the Second World War, the agreement made provision for each of the occupying powers of Britain, U.S. and Russia to have a military mission in the two other zones. The aim of each mission was to maintain liaison between the military commanders; they were known as BRIXMIS and SOXMIS (acronyms for British Military Mission and Soviet Military Mission respectively). What actually happened was that both became intelligence-gathering outfits. Instructions throughout the British zone were that any SOXMIS car had to be reported without delay. Each soldier was issued with a card explaining what to do in the event of sighting a SOXMIS vehicle. Given the importance of our unit's war role, it was hardly surprising that we often had sightings of SOXMIS vehicles which had to be reported. I well remember one incident when a chasing unit vehicle was involved in a minor collision with the SOXMIS car.

As my two-year tour was coming to an end, I was delighted to be told that my next appointment was to be one of three British army officers at the NATO Headquarters in Izmir, Turkey.

But what to do for Claire's schooling was the question since there were no English-speaking schools in Izmir? The choice was clear: either I turn down the posting or Claire went to St Margaret's with Vivian and Juliet. The problem was we thought Claire might not be robust enough to cope with being a boarder. To us she seemed fragile and lacking in confidence. After speaking to her headmaster, he seemed confident that she would do well, particularly as she would have her two sisters to support her. "If you don't believe me, come along and see what she's like," he said. We did and, watching her in the playground, were astonished to see that Claire was clearly a leader among her peers. So a place was booked for her to start at St Margaret's at the start of the Christmas term 1976, when she was seven.

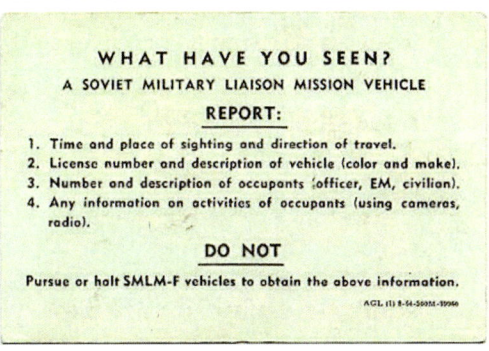

Soviet Military Mission report aide-mémoire

10: Sporting Memories

> *I tend to believe that cricket is the greatest thing that God ever created on Earth ... certainly greater than sex although sex isn't too bad either. But everyone knows which comes first when it's a question of cricket or sex – Harold Pinter*

Sport has always been a passion and a very important part of my life: with justification, some might say far *too* important. I remember one heart-wrenching occasion when, yet again, I was off to play cricket one Sunday and called goodbye to the girls, who were still in bed. Claire, who must have been about four years old at the time, stood at the top of the stairs and, waving, called out, "Bye bye, skipper." I was captain of the Army cricket team at the time and obviously spending too long away from home!

From my very earliest days, I can remember my father encouraging me to play all games, particularly emphasising the need for fair play. One of his favourite mantras was 'Cheats never prosper'. It is therefore much to my shame that I once failed to 'walk' in a cricket match, knowing that I had hit the ball, even though I was given 'not out' by the umpire. It was when, as captain of the Army, we were playing against former cricketing friends who were touring the UK with Hong Kong. Such was my guilty conscience, that I have never forgotten this incident.

As an only child it was never easy for me to practise my skills, although any flat surface on which to hit or kick a tennis ball was where my parents knew they would invariably find me. I was always in trouble with my mother for ruining sundry pairs of shoes. As I only ever had one pair at a time, I can remember doing my paper round with the sole of a shoe being held on with a piece of string. It was as a result of my obsession with playing games that I developed a chronic cartilage condition in both my knees. Very often at the end of a day, the pain was so intense that I would cry myself to sleep. Eventually my mother took me to see a specialist who decided that my legs would have to be immobilised to allow the knees to recover. This resulted in my legs being put in Plaster of Paris, from the hip to the ankle, for six months. Even this did not prevent me from playing cricket for the school. The look of amazement on the face of the opposition when I came out to bat wearing no pads was a source of great amusement to my team mates! Although the treatment worked, the muscle definition in my legs never really recovered so that my legs have always looked rather 'weedy'.

As recorded in chapter 4, my father was an accomplished sportsman, having represented Bedford Modern School, the Royal Military Academy and a variety of clubs at cricket, rugby, boxing and athletics. Watching me open the innings for the Army at Lords against the Royal Navy in 1972, I know was a very proud day for him, although he never said as much. But then he seldom revealed his emotions; something about the Victorian attitude of 'stiff upper lip' and all that. What is clear to me is that any sporting talent I have had came from the same gene pool as that of my father.

Having had a level of success at most sports, none has matched that which I have enjoyed at cricket. For that reason alone, cricket is and always has been my first love. Playing cricket has not only given me some of the happiest moments of my life – it has also been responsible in forging some lifelong friendships as well as enabling me to meet and play against some of the most famous in the game. I am particularly proud of having played against Imran Khan when he and I were opposing captains of Oxford University and the Army. Unlike the modern era, over half of the players that made up university teams in the 1970s had county experience while some, like Imran, had played international cricket. Imran opened the bowling while I opened the batting so our opposition was up close and personal! Our first encounter was at Aldershot in 1974. The Army batted first and were doing quite well. I was 40-odd not out when Imran came back for his second spell. A fast, in-swinging bouncer reared up and hit me in the mouth. With blood everywhere, I was taken to the medical centre where a couple of stitches were administered to the wound. I took no further part in the match. I next faced Imran at The Parks, Oxford, a handsome tree-lined ground, this time playing for the Combined Services. On arrival at the ground, Imran could be seen working up a real sweat in the nets as he went through a thirty-minute practice session bowling at one stump. On this occasion, I batted in the middle order and did not face Imran. Imran was a fine specimen of a man, with a gym-honed body, a mane of shaggy dark hair and a deep voice. One or two of us were invited to a party in Keble College after the first day's play. Imran was there, wearing hip-hugging flairs, a garish flower-patterned shirt splayed open to reveal his chest, and a chunky gold necklace with a dangling medallion. No other man in the room stood a chance with the female undergraduates who had eyes only for one man! He was physically terrifying and it was as though he had something to prove. Perhaps his competitive instinct contained an element of revenge, the Pathan principle of *badal*. After leaving Oxford, Imran went on to play for Sussex and led Pakistan to many famous victories, including the World Cup in 1992, and in doing so established himself as one of the greatest all-round cricketers of all time. After marrying and later divorcing Jemima (née Goldsmith) and raising money to build a cancer hospital in memory of his mother, who had died of the disease, Imran went into politics. Who knows? – his obvious leadership and popularity in Pakistan, particularly amongst the underprivileged, might one day lead to high office.

But Imran was by no means the fastest bowler I faced. Two others come to mind. The first was Harold Rhodes of Derbyshire who, had it not been for a suspect action, might well have played in many more test matches than he did. Rhodes came to Hong Kong with Joe Lister's XI in 1968 along with such cricketing luminaries as Geoff Arnold, Derek Underwood, Dennis Amiss and former England captain Mike Denness. Opening the batting for Hong Kong, I managed to survive a couple of the fastest overs I had ever faced from Rhodes before eventually falling victim to the left-arm spinners of the 'great' Derek Underwood. The fastest of them all was, without doubt, Andy Roberts. In the words of the great West Indian Sir Vivian Richards: "There are few bowlers better or quicker than my own Antiguan colleague, Andy Roberts. He was lethal in every way. Andy had the knack of really hurting batsmen." Small wonder, therefore, when opening the batting for the Army against Hampshire, for whom Andy Roberts was in the process of qualifying in the second team, my fellow opener Len Sanderson unusually offered me first strike. As I watched Roberts pace out his considerable run, I should have known he was going to be fast, but I didn't know just how fast! The first ball crashed into my pads and really hurt; the second fizzed past my head at an alarming speed (no helmets in those days) – and only once during that over did I make contact with the ball which flew off the edge to third man for four runs. At the end of the over, all was revealed when Len told me the bowler was Andy Roberts, reckoned to be the fastest on the county circuit at that time. I should have known there was something afoot when Len offered me first strike!

Although I used to have a 'knock around' with my tutor in India, it was not until much later that my interest in cricket blossomed. After returning to England, I remember well listening to the 1948 FA Cup Final between Manchester United and Blackpool, which United won by 4 goals to 2. After that match I became a lifelong United fan. Being able to reel off that United team has stood me in good stead in convincing people of my United pedigree. For example, there was the time, when I took the RCT band to Old Trafford in October 1982 for a cup game against Spurs. As a guest of the club, I found myself sitting next to the great Sir Matt Busby, by then retired, who quickly engaged me in conversation. In reply to his question, I reeled off the cup-winning team of 1948, after which he agreed that I was a true United supporter. At half-time, he asked me into the Director's lounge where I met the current manager Ron Atkinson. I remember Sir Matt forecasting, early in the game, that United were playing poorly and would lose – they did: 1-0. After arranging to leave my copy of his book, *There's Only One United*, at the ground, Sir Matt, true to his word, signed it – along with the Manchester United Secretary, Les Olive.

My close association with The Reds has continued over the years, principally through Harold Riley whom I first met when he was doing his two-year National Service at Buller Barracks, Aldershot, in the early 1960s. A talented footballer, Harold played for the Army but chose (wisely) to pursue his career in art rather than with Manchester United for whom he was registered as a junior professional. Aged 17, Harold won a scholarship to the Slade and went on to study in Florence and Spain before returning to Salford, his home town, where he has lived and worked ever since. It was his deep affection for his home town that cemented his close friendship with LS Lowry. Together they worked on a project to record the area and its people. Harold has painted Popes, American presidents and royalty, but it is probably his paintings of footballers and golfers which have made him famous. Harold used to turn out in the evening inter-unit cricket league. Harold's dog, a Boxer – Bonzo by name – was well-known around the barracks. One evening, during a cricket match, Bonzo spied a lump of willow to which he took a fancy. How was he to know that the bat belonged to the Brigadier, a cricketing fanatic, as he cocked his leg for a pee! When I was posted to Liverpool, many years after we had lost contact, I saw Harold being interviewed on local TV. This led to us re-establishing contact and Harold accepting a commission to paint Princess Alice, Duchess of Gloucester, who was to make a visit to the regiment I was commanding at the time: more of that later.

Through my friendship with him, Harold's close links with the club have enabled me to meet some of the 'great and good' at Old Trafford, including Sir Alex Ferguson and Sir Bobby Charlton, who was my host for a European night at Old Trafford. What a marvellous man – who has done such great work for the English game of football. With Lynn, my partner, I attended, in November 2009, the unveiling of Harold's collection of ten portraits of Manchester United 'greats' at a special evening at Old Trafford. The chosen ten were: Duncan Edwards, Sir Bobby Charlton, George Best, Denis Law, Bryan Robson, Eric Cantona, Ryan Giggs, Paul Scholes, Wayne Rooney and Christiano Ronaldo.

With Sir Alex Ferguson at Harold's Exhibition November 2009

A visit to The Archive, where Harold works, is like entering an Aladdin's Cave of art. Books adorn one side of his studio, from floor to ceiling, while on other walls hang some of his paintings. During one of my visits he was working on a life-size painting of Dennis Law, of legendary fame at Old Trafford. In another room, there are glass cabinets housing every camera he has ever owned, together with many gifts he has been given over the years and sample artefacts incorporating his designs. The Archive, which was provided for him by Salford City Council, will surely one day become a 'museum' to Harold's work. Ashraf, Harold's lovely wife, a practitioner of Rakki, is a real gem who does her best to protect him from a constant stream of demands on his time.

Although I attended a rugby-playing school, I was a far better at football, so it was natural that I played football for a team outside school. This was the Peterborough Sea Cadet team in the local youth league. At that time I was a useful goalkeeper and had a trial for Peterborough to play in the national youth championships. However, I was considered too short to be a goalkeeper so I converted to a right-footed winger, a position where I was able to use my speed. Later on,

Harold and Ashraf

I played regularly for The Army Crusaders. During my time at school, I used to watch The Posh (Peterborough United) every weekend when they played at home. A formidable force in non-league football, winning the Midland league on no less than five consecutive seasons, they became well-known for their FA Cup giant-killing acts in the 1950-60s. Their scalps included Portsmouth, Newcastle United, Notts County, Swansea Town and, most famously, The Arsenal. Those few occasions when a cup run included a weekday replay were too big a temptation for me not to play truant to see the game. If I had been caught doing so, the punishment would almost certainly have resulted in me being expelled – not that that put me off!

During the four years that I represented the Army at cricket, I worked in Aldershot, which as well as being 'Home to the British Army' in those days, was also home to Army cricket. I suppose it was therefore natural for the BBC to approach the Army to find someone who might be suitable to play a cricketing part in a TV screen adaption of the classic story of a village cricket match, *England, Their England* by AG MacDonnell. I jumped at the chance to audition for the character Robert Southcott. The Green at Tilford, Surrey, where cricket has been played since 1886, was an ideal location for the film. One of the most picturesque in England, the cricket ground is surrounded on two sides by houses and on the third by a stream.

The famous Barley Mow pub provides a focal point and 'watering hole' for the ground. Robert Southgate is described in the book as 'a singular young man, small and quiet who wore perfectly creased flannels, white silk socks, a pale-pink shirt, and a white cap. He looked as if a fast ball would knock the bat out of his hands. The producer obviously thought I had the necessary attributes to play Southgate and

The Green at Tilford with The Barley Mow in the background

I was offered the role! The main opposition bowler in the story was the local blacksmith, a huge man with arms like tree trunks, who wore a snake-buckled belt and who is first 'seen' loosening his braces to enable his formidable bowling arm to swing freely in its socket. To my considerable dismay, it was a Surrey policeman, six feet five inches tall, who was to play the part of the blacksmith! The blacksmith bowling is one of the classic cricketing pieces of all time. Suffice it to say, the policeman, entering wholeheartedly into his role, did his best to knock my block off, much to the amusement of the director. After many failed attempts, I did manage to smash him for six, which the role required, and I was duly paid fifteen shillings for my trouble! The resulting film, shown on BBC one Sunday evening later that year, was great, although friends I had prompted to watch, including my father, were disappointed that the shots of me were too far away for me to be positively identified by anyone other than my colleagues in the Army team, who were duly disparaging about my performance!

Returning to the UK in 1971, after a very successful five-year period of playing cricket in Hong Kong, where I had captained the Army and Combined Services, and played for the Colony side, I had high hopes of a place in the Army side, but the two-day trials went badly and I did not even get short-listed. This was a massive disappointment and I resolved to work hard and have a good season playing for my Corps and in club cricket. It went well and I qualified by playing ten matches to become a playing member of the MCC.

The 1972 season started well and I was immediately 'in the runs'. One of my early-season matches was for the Aldershot Services against the MCC, in which I enjoyed a substantial partnership with the current Army captain, Chris Russell, who had played county cricket with Kent before joining up in the Royal Army Educational Corps. In this match

I scored a hundred, but it was still a complete surprise when I was selected to play for the Army against the Territorial Army. I had a reasonable debut and went on to play in the most of the remaining Army games. Being selected for the Inter-Services tournament, the last to be played at Lords (until 2008), still came as wonderful surprise. Being presented with my Army cap before the first match against the RAF was a huge moment in my life. Walking out through the Long Room at Lords was surreal. Not in my wildest dreams could I have imagined such a moment. I remember being nervous, elated and terrified as we took the field on the first morning of the Inter-Services Tournament. We outplayed the RAF and won with something to spare.

The second match against the Royal Navy was completely different. A keen rivalry has always existed on the sports field between the Army and the Navy, with matches being fiercely contested in an atmosphere of mutual respect. Batting first, the Navy scored about 180 in their allotted fifty overs. All was well until we lost a couple of quick wickets. This brought me to the crease with us needing about 60 to win in ten overs. When we lost two more wickets cheaply, pressure started to mount. In came Roland Fahey, a vastly experienced player and a great wicketkeeper, but not the fastest between the wickets! I called him for an easy run but he was slow setting off and was run out. The next man in was Richard Shore, a fast bowler, but not the most agile of batsmen. Anxious to shield him from the strike, I called him for a run and he too was run out! It was the end of the over. At this point we needed two runs to win with the last man, Paul Presland, at the non-striker's end. My father was watching all this from the Mound Stand. After the second run out, the man sitting next to him turned and asked 'Who's the madman trying to commit suicide?' The Navy's fast bowler, Gavin Lane, started his run-up from the pavilion end. The ball was short and fast and headed my way. Instinctively, I leant back and hooked the ball, which flew first bounce over the boundary: a great moment and one of immense relief to me for, if we had not won, my coolness under fire might well have been brought into sharp focus! We had won the game and the 1972 Inter-Services championship and I had finished 30-odd not out. It was a fantastic moment and I was on 'cloud nine'. The celebrations started in our dressing room, continued over the beating of retreat on the ground by the Parachute Regiment and long into the night at one of the best night clubs in London.

My introduction to cricket in Hong Kong could not have gone better. In a traditional pre-season game, the Army, who had been league champions in 1965, played The Rest at the Army ground, Sookunpoo. Opening the batting with the legendary West Indian Rocky Daniels, I scored a 100 against the top bowlers in colony cricket and went on to have an excellent season. The Army won the First Division that season under the capable leadership of Tony Vivian. I was awarded my first Colony cap in 1968, during Hong Kong's tour to Malaysia and Singapore, when we played Malaysia on the Padang, Kuala Lumpur. On a turning wicket, Hong Kong were outplayed but, batting with Ian Lacy-Smith, a policeman, we hung on for a draw in fading light, facing the last 58 balls without scoring a run. The tour manager, Ted Wilson, remarked in his speech, at the post-match dinner, that Hong Kong's 'two night-fighter pilots' had done well to force a draw!

Hong Kong, always a popular place for touring sides, hosted a number of teams during the five years I was there. In 1967, I played against the Cricket Club of India, which included in their ranks the great Indian batsman-cum-wicket-keeper, Polly Umrigar and, in 1968, Joe Lister's International Team. It was against that team that I described, in an earlier chapter, my experience of facing some world-class bowling. The Melbourne 29-ers visited in 1970. In their party was the future captain of Australia, Kim Hughes, and other budding State players. The wicket at Chater Road, reckoned to be the most expensive cricket ground in the world, presented real problems that day. The post-race report in the South China Post the following day described my 'knock' of 62 as 'An innings of courage and technique on a fiery wicket.' Later that season (March 1970) the MCC came to town under the leadership of Tony Lewis. In the game against Hong Kong, played in Kowloon, the MCC batted first and scored 199 without loss, with Alan Jones 104 not out and Geoffrey Boycott 74 not out, in their fifty overs. The overcast conditions made batting difficult on the matting wicket. Peter Mitchell, who had played for the Army in the UK, bowled seventeen overs for a mere 40 runs against two world-class players. At one point, Mitchell challenged Geoff Boycott 'to hit the bloody ball', to which 'Boycs' replied, in his own inimitable way, "When thou bowls ball at wicket, I'll play, lad!"

I got to know Geoff Boycott from hosting him during the days he spent in Hong Kong and have kept in touch with him intermittently ever since. After a top-scoring 35 in Hong Kong's innings, in the match against the MCC, Geoff was most encouraging about my batting and became a source of inspiration and example to me.

In dedicating his autobiography, Geoff was kind enough to say, *'For Ian with fondest memories of Hong Kong 1970 and with warmest regards for his friendship.'* I also got to know John Hampshire during the same tour and enjoyed a round of golf at Fanling with him and Geoff Arnold, both England cricketers. Geoff B passed through Hong Kong on his premature return to the UK from the Ashes tour in August 1971, with

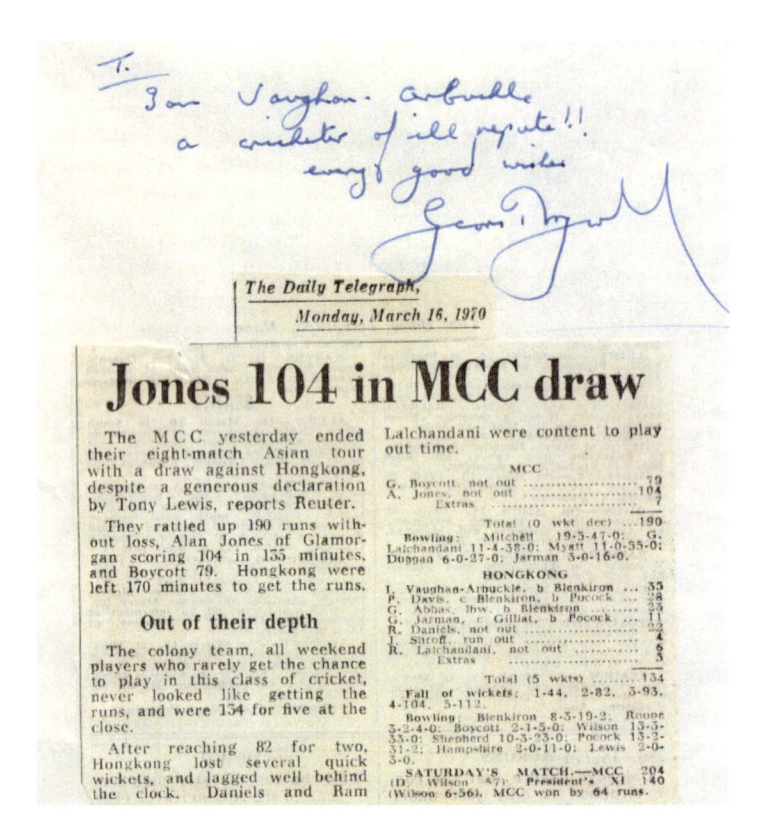

> T.
>
> Ian Vaughan-Arbuckle
> a cricketer of ill repute!!
> every good wishes
> Geoff Boycott

The Daily Telegraph,
Monday, March 16, 1970

Jones 104 in MCC draw

The MCC yesterday ended their eight-match Asian tour with a draw against Hongkong, despite a generous declaration by Tony Lewis, reports Reuter.

They rattled up 190 runs without loss, Alan Jones of Glamorgan scoring 104 in 135 minutes, and Boycott 79. Hongkong were left 170 minutes to get the runs.

Out of their depth

The colony team, all weekend players who rarely get the chance to play in this class of cricket, never looked like getting the runs, and were 154 for five at the close.

After reaching 82 for two, Hongkong lost several quick wickets, and lagged well behind the clock. Daniels and Ram Lalchandani were content to play out time.

```
                MCC
G. Boycott, not out .......... 79
A. Jones, not out ............104
Extras ........................7
        Total (0 wkt dec) ...190
Bowling: Mitchell 19-5-47-0; G.
Lalchandani 11-4-38-0; Myatt 11-0-55-0;
Duggan 6-0-27-0; Jarman 5-0-16-0.
            HONGKONG
I. Vaughan-Arbuckle, b Blenkiron ... 33
P. Davis, c Blenkiron, b Pocock .... 28
G. Abbas, lbw, b Blenkiron .......... 25
G. Jarman, c Gilliat, b Pocock ..... 11
R. Daniels, not out ................ 22
R. Sircoff, run out ................. 4
R. Lalchandani, not out ............. 5
Extras .............................. 3
        Total (5 wkts) .........134
Fall of wickets: 1-44, 2-82, 3-93,
4-104, 5-112.
Bowling: Blenkiron 8-3-19-2; Roope
3-2-4-0; Boycott 2-1-5-0; Wilson 13-3-
35-0; Shepherd 10-3-23-0; Pocock 13-7-
31-2; Hampshire 2-0-11-0; Lewis 2-0-
3-0.
  SATURDAY'S MATCH.—MCC 204
(D. Wilson 87); President's XI 140
(Wilson 6-56). MCC won by 64 runs.
```

a broken forearm after being hit by Graham McKenzie in the tour match against Western Australia. This was cruel luck considering he was only 18 runs short of Wally Hammond's record of 1571 runs, set forty years before, on a tour of Australia.

Taking up his invitation, I went to see Geoff playing for Yorkshire against Sussex at Hove. Arriving at the ground a few minutes after the start, I was disappointed to see that Geoff had been dismissed without adding to his overnight score of 90. Waiting for the inevitable dust to settle, I called at the Yorkshire dressing room about an hour later to be told that he was in the nets practising, where he remained for about an hour! Another example of Geoff's single-mindedness occurred in the dressing room before the game against Hong Kong. MCC had won the toss and Geoff was putting on his pads to open the batting. Rocky Daniels, who knew Geoff from a previous encounter, attempted to engage him in conversation: "Do you mind, lad (everyone was 'lad')? I'm trying to concentrate," was his reply. Geoff has been criticised throughout his career as a selfish cricketer, not a team player. To my mind, he was misunderstood and certainly not liked by the 'blazerati' at Lords. He was the consummate professional for whom nothing but the best would do; what's wrong with that? He has a wonderful cricket brain and is now in the top flight of cricket commentators. A controversial figure perhaps but, without doubt, one of the most accomplished opening bats England has ever had. I liked and respected him, although I never thought he would make a good captain. He was far too selfish. Imagine my surprise when in Berlin working in the mid-1980s, before the Berlin Wall was dismantled, I came across a piece of graffiti on the wall which read: 'Geoff Boycott, we love you.' Germany is not a country one would link with cricket, which made the discovery all the more interesting. I sent the photograph to Ann, Geoff's partner at the time, and was pleased to see the picture reproduced in his 1986 autobiography, albeit without a credit!

Geoff Boycott (centre) with Daily Mail cricket correspondent Alex Bannister (left) and Hongkong Interpreter Ian Vaughan-Arbuckle at the HKCC bar yesterday.

The Berlin Wall with East Germany on the other side

I continued to enjoy modest success playing for the Army and Combined Services. The Army won the championship in 1969-70 and the Rothmans limited overs competition in my last season. The definitive history of cricket in Hong Kong, which includes some references to me and a photograph of the 1969-70 title, winning Army team, is included in Peter Hall's excellent book *150 years of Cricket in Hong Kong*.

I bade farewell to Hong Kong cricket while touring with the colony team through Singapore, Sri Lanka and Sabah. During that tour I shared a room with Charles Rowe, who had already represented England Schools and was later to play for Kent. The tour was a great experience although for me not altogether successful for I failed to make any 'big' impression with the scorers. Sri Lanka was a real eye-opener. The potential they showed suggested they would surely be a force in world cricket in the future, and what a force they have since become, having won the World Cup and taken the scalps of most of the cricketing nations. I well remember attending the final of the Schools Cup played in front of a crowd of 30,000 screaming schoolchildren in the Colombo stadium.

Throughout the Indian subcontinent cricket is a religion. On any spare, reasonably flat, piece of ground, little boys can be seen trying to emulate their national cricketing heroes – more often than not using a plank of roughly hewn wood as a bat.

Elsewhere I have described watching knock-up games in India played as though their very lives depended on the outcome. But nowhere is the enthusiasm for the game greater than in Pakistan. It was therefore a shock when, in the summer of 2010, Pakistan were involved in the spot-fixing scandal, an indefensible and terrible thing for the great game. Political strife, warfare and trouble have been part of that region for centuries. Corruption is the problem of every cricketing nation, England included. That doesn't exonerate or excuse those involved but the smugness and self-righteousness along national boundaries help no-one. Pakistan has constantly brought fine things and great players to cricket. Contradictions abound in Pakistan cricket. The captaincy has always

I will play for Pakistan!

operated on an unfathomable basis. Yet Pakistan, under Imran's outstanding leadership, brought us one of the great displays when they won the World Cup in 1992 against all the odds. Few know that cricket is an Indian game accidentally discovered by the British. We English are just learning to be less proprietorial about cricket, to understand that its racial and cultural mixture is its strength. It is in our nature to mistrust other cultures and their motives. That cricket continues to teach us lessons of understanding while competing against nations like Pakistan can only do us good. Long may the great game be played throughout the world, particularly in troubled lands like Afghanistan.

I was fortunate enough to play Army cricket for five seasons, 1972-76, the last three as captain. In my first couple of seasons, the Army fixture list consisted of matches against a few minor counties, one or two premier clubs, representative teams and Oxford University. This all changed when General Sir James Wilson became President. Being from Lancashire, an Oxford 'Blue' at cricket and a football sports writer for the Sunday Times, he had definite ideas on how sports teams should be run. He was not merely a figurehead but someone who took a close personal interest in the team. We were very soon playing against county Second XIs, including Lancashire, Kent, Sussex, Hampshire and Surrey. Whereas, in the past, ranks were used both on and off the field, Jim Wilson decreed that, when representing the Army, rank was no longer to be used. In other words, there was to be equality within the team regardless of rank. This made for a very happy dressing room, in which everyone's view was taken account of and contributed greatly to the success of the team.

During my time as skipper of the side, I valued greatly the General's wise counsel and encouragement. It was clear to everyone that he thoroughly enjoyed being part of what was a very successful and happy period in Army cricket. We only lost the Inter-Services championship once during the time I played. That was in 1974, my first season as captain, when we were bowled out for less than 100 at Portsmouth by the RAF and comprehensively beaten by the RN. During the next two seasons we won the championship, with a side of many gifted players. I remember particularly Len Sanderson, a fine left-handed opening bat and change bowler; Richard Davies, a wonderfully gifted batsman and outstanding fielder, who played for Warwickshire and England Schools; Paul Presland, our opening bowler who played for Bedfordshire, and would have undoubtedly played county cricket had he not been in the Army. And probably the finest all-rounder ever to play for the Army up to that era Bill Dover, a right-arm off-spinner and left-handed bat. To these I would add

Richard Peck, opening batsman; Rocky Daniels, an all-rounder whom I have mentioned earlier; Roland Fahey, a fiercely competitive wicketkeeper and senior professional; and Vic Nurse, an all-rounder who hailed from the West Indies. It was a privilege to play with and captain such a fine side. As for myself, I think my modest contribution was as captain. Like Michael Brearley, who captained England but was never thought to be a good enough player to get into the team as a batsman, I probably fell into the same bracket. In dedicating his autobiography, Jim Wilson wrote of me: 'A fine captain and leader of a very good Army team, whose performances gave me much pleasure.'

During my time involved with Army cricket, I attended and passed – the first serviceman to do so – the 1976 MCC Advanced Coaching Certificate at the National Sporting Centre in Shropshire. The two-week course, of continual assessment, was under the tutelage of eminent players like AC (Alan) Smith, Warwickshire and England, Ken Suttle, Sussex and England, and Les Lenham, Sussex. As the 1976 MCC Cricket Coaching Book was being compiled at the time, use was made of the course to demonstrate certain aspects of the game. To my embarrassment, I duly appeared on pages 134a and 134b, demonstrating coaching techniques. The coaching course encouraged

The Army 1976 – Inter-Service Champions
Back: Paul Presland, Richard Davies, Vic Nurse, Tony Snook, Nigel Scott, Len Sanderson & Steve Dove-Dixon
Front: Richard Brooks, Richard Peck, me, Bill Withall, Bill Dover & Rocky Daniels

Sporting Memories

me to arrange a successful coaching course for players of army standard at Sandhurst. During my tenure as 'skipper', I relied heavily on the wise counsel of Ron Bell, the professional at Sandhurst who had played for Sussex in the 1960s. Tragically, Ron's life was cut short when he died of cancer in 1989, aged 58.

At the end of the 1975 season, after we had beaten the RN by seven wickets to win the championship, Jim Wilson came into the dressing room to say goodbye, as he was shortly leaving the Army, and to congratulate us on our performance. Saying how much he had enjoyed being involved with us as a group, he offered to help anyone in the future: "Just get in touch and I will see what I can do." Len Sanderson, who was a Lance-Corporal at the time, took the General at his word. At his invitation, they met in London. Jim Wilson, who was on the board of Gallagher's (cigarettes), got Len a job in their advertising department. To cut the story short, within five years of leaving the Army, Len was working for the Daily Telegraph, selling advertising and within a few years became their Advertising Director with a seat on the Board. Who said that Britain is a society without opportunity? Jim Wilson was replaced by Major-General Bill Withall, who himself had played for the Army, as Chairman of Army Cricket. He was another tremendous supporter and encourager of the team and someone whose wise counsel I valued and appreciated. He was Chairman in 1976, my last year, when we won the Inter-Services title, played at the RAF Ground at Vine Lane, Uxbridge, in fine style.

I remember being somewhat surprised to find myself selected for the Combined Services to play Pakistan on 11th and 12th July 1974 as there were others who, in my opinion, deserved to be selected before me. Opening the batting, I scored a meagre 2 runs in both innings, being despatched both times by Naseer Malik. Pakistan, who played and drew three games against England on that tour, put out a team against the Combined Services which included Wasim Raja, Majid Khan (Imran's cousin) and Asif Masood, all international players of particular note; but it was the great Safraz Nawaz, the first exponent of reverse swing, who destroyed the Combined

After the toss with Robbie Robinson, Navy skipper

Services second innings by taking a hat trick and four wickets in four balls! Pakistan duly won the game by seven wickets.

Despite my poor performance in that game, I was selected to be Twelfth Man for the Combined Services against England Young Cricketers at Lords later that season. I don't remember who exactly was in the EYC team but it certainly included Graham Gooch, Ian Botham and David Gower, all of whom were subsequently to captain England at various times. The Twelfth Man duties included taking drinks onto the field, substituting any player who got injured, and ensuring that players' every need was catered for! Imagine my surprise when, during a visit to the toilets, I found myself standing next to Jack (JT) Ikin, the England manager. In the knowledge that Jack Ikin had been my father's driver throughout the 8th Army campaign in North Africa, I introduced myself to him. His surprise was tangible when he said, "My God, I never thought I would meet Hector's son in the bogs at Lords." I spent an interesting couple of hours in conversation with Jack that ranged over his time with my father and his own illustrious playing career with Lancashire and England. He was absolutely charming and spoke warmly of his time with my father.

In 1975, we played Kent 2nd XI at the county ground at Canterbury. After winning the toss, I opened the batting, as usual, with Len Sanderson. One of the Kent opening bowlers was a tall, well-built West Indian who, being on a month's trial, was out to make a name for himself. He was fast without being worryingly so. The main problem in facing him was his ability to make the ball rear up from a good length, due to his considerable height. I hadn't been in long when I was hit on the wrist by such a ball. The resulting pain was intense so I knew, instinctively, that something was broken, correctly confirmed by a visit to hospital. Returning to the ground with my lower arm and wrist in plaster, Les Ames, the Kent coach and former England wicket-keeper, in commiserating with my circumstances, gave me a ticket to the main pavilion at the first World Cup Final between Australia and the West Indies to be played at Lords on 21st June 1975.

Arriving at the ground, I made my way to the balcony of the main pavilion and looked for my seat. The pavilion was full, in the main with members wearing the distinctive yellow-and-red colours of the MCC. To my consternation, a large man wearing a straw boater and MCC tie was sitting in 'my' seat. Plucking up courage and clearing my throat, I challenged him, "Excuse me." All heads turned in my direction while my man continued to munch on his sandwich. "Excuse me," I repeated. This did the trick and he looked in my direction. "I think you are sitting in my seat." "What makes you think that?" he replied in a rather sarcastic tone. By this time all those around were taking a keen interest in the proceedings. I passed my ticket to him. After examining it and with a smirk of triumph on his face, he said, "Well, young man, you clearly have never been to Lords before; otherwise you would know that this is the Members' Pavilion where seats cannot be reserved. You want the stand over there," he said, pointing in the direction of what I now know to be the Main Stand. Laughter broke out among those who had overheard our exchange. My acute embarrassment can be imagined and, at that moment, I wanted the ground to swallow me up. Anxious to remove myself from the situation without delay, I headed for the exit, only to be stopped by another member saying, "If you have managed to get into the Members' Pavilion on such an important occasion without being a member, you deserve to be here. Come and sit next to me." So I spent a pleasant day, with the best view in the ground, watching what turned out to be a truly memorable high-scoring match won by the West Indies by 17 runs.

After a season captaining the Army in Germany, I retired from playing serious cricket in 1978. My complete retirement was hastened when, playing in a casual game, I saw two balls coming towards me. Picking the wrong one to catch, the ball hit me in the chest and I fell over. 'Enough is enough,' I thought and have seldom played again. After moving to Wantage in 2007, I became a qualified umpire and thoroughly enjoyed officiating in the Oxfordshire League. Since moving to Dorset, I have been appointed to umpire in County representative matches at youth level and in the Premier league. Looking back, I wish that I had taken up umpiring earlier in the belief that, with my strong playing experience and innate officiating ability, I could have progressed up the umpiring 'ladder'. Alas! age is now against me although I hope to remain an effective umpire for a few more years.

I have had some wonderful times playing cricket, have made some lifelong friends, and been to many places and grounds and, most importantly, the game has given me some great times. Cricket is unique. It has grace, charm and athleticism, and builds character. The game is played with a generosity of spirit that is as refreshing as it is, currently, unfashionable. It remains essentially a very English game. Long may it prosper.

Soon after returning to the UK in 1948, my father took me to Highbury Stadium, Arsenal's ground in north London (sadly since replaced by the Emirates Stadium), to see England play Switzerland. As a ten-year-old, I remember feeling overwhelmed by the sense of occasion created by a crowd of 48,000 England supporters, fanatically patriotic after the war. England won easily 6-0 with a very strong team including such footballing idols as Alf Ramsey – who subsequently managed England to a World Cup triumph in 1966, Billy Wright – who won over 100 international caps, and Jackie Milburn – still hailed as the greatest centre-forward to emerge from Newcastle; but my abiding memory is of the one-and-only Stanley Matthews, who gave the Swiss left back a torrid time. As Stan Mathews yet again dribbled his way past, the Swiss player, by this time utterly demoralised, executed a perfect rugby tackle on his tormentor. Getting to his feet first, the Swiss player shrugged in a gesture of resignation. Matthews responded by patting his opponent on his back before placing the ball for the free kick. Surely this was a lesson in sportsmanship from which modern players could learn a great deal?

Athletics, particularly running, seems to have been part of my life for as long as I can remember. At school, it was cross-country in the winter, and track races and long jump in the summer. Although I did not particularly enjoy running across heavy ploughed fields, ankle-deep in mud and often through small streams wearing flimsy plimsolls, there is no doubt that I gained a lot of strength from cross-country. But it was the mandatory, often cold, shower afterwards which was the 'killer'. Never in the prizes, I was nevertheless a useful runner and always picked to represent my House. After joining the Army, running became an important part of everyday life, and I continued to enjoy other aspects of track and field, particularly long jump.

Weekly runs in boots were a regular feature throughout my career, and then there was the Battle Fitness Test (BFT), which included a timed run over three miles, adjusted for age, which had to be passed. Unlike many for whom running did not come easy, I never had a problem passing the BFT. I suppose I really began to get seriously into running when I became too old to play other games. When working in Liverpool, I joined Sefton Harriers, a very old and famous club that met on a Saturday afternoon in Sefton Park. It was with Sefton that I first learnt about serious training. I particularly enjoyed my training runs along the sands at Formby. On moving to Norfolk, I joined West Norfolk AC before forming in 1987, with Bob

Track and field championships in Hong Kong circa 1967

Hancock and Peter Duhig, Ryston Runners. With a view to creating a team spirit within the club, the idea of running 195 miles around the Norfolk County boundary in a relay took shape. After a great deal of sometimes heated discussion over a 'few' beers at Rose Cottage, the outline principles of the run were agreed. This spawned an event known as the Round Norfolk Relay, first run in August 1987. So successful was the inaugural run that two other teams were invited to run the following year. Since then the event has gone from strength to strength. On the tenth anniversary of the RNR in 1996, we were privileged to have Kelly Holmes as our guest of honour

The 'Great' Kelly Holmes and the Race Director

I am proud of having directed all but one of the races which, in 2011, celebrated its 25th anniversary. Over the years, many people supported me in staging the RNR. Of those, I have particularly valued the immense contributions of Rod Baron – who, among other things, designed and maintained the website (*www.roundnorfolkrelay.com*) and automated results package – Tony Hunt and Rob Saines. I retired from organising the event after the 2011 race.

In 2005 I was approached by the Borough Council of King's Lynn & West Norfolk to organise a half-marathon which would help raise the profile of the town. I agreed but soon decided that it would not be possible to fashion a 13.2-mile course around the town. After further discussion, it was agreed that the event would be run over ten kilometres (6.2 miles) through the town centre. A sponsor was found, and after a great deal of work and help from friends, including Tony Hunt, Rod Baron and others, the inaugural event took place in May 2006 attracting 1,577 runners. The race was won by a Kenyan runner, Patrick Macau, who has since become a leading performer on the world stage. Unfortunately, a fit and healthy 25-year-old local man who played competitive football, Duncan Gooderson, collapsed after finishing. Despite getting immediate attention from Dr Paul Garner – a personal friend who had agreed to be the race doctor – and paramedics, he was pronounced dead at Lynn's Queen Elizabeth

| Never a Dull Moment

Ever-decreasing CIRCLES

MARTIN DUFF PROFILES THE ROUND NORFOLK RELAY, A QUARTER OF A CENTURY OLD AND STILL GROWING

ORIGINALLY conceived as a small event for local clubs, the Round Norfolk Relay celebrates its 25th running this weekend with an expansion to 58 teams this year.

Held over 17 stages and over a total distance of 195 miles, the event starts at Lynnsport, Kings Lynn, very early on Saturday September 17 and runs continuously through the night, before finishing back there the next day. There is a staggered start for squads of differing abilities that is designed so that all 60 teams finish at roughly the same time on Sunday morning as the King's Lynn Town Band plays them in.

While other races such as the Green Belt and Welsh Castles relays are also spread over two days, the Round Norfolk event is the last of what was once a whole string of continuous relays up and down the country. There was the legendary London to Brighton relay, Bristol to Weston, Manchester to Blackpool and many others.

Long-serving race director Ian Vaughan-Arbuckle, who is stepping down after this year's event, said: "The Birketts Round Norfolk Relay is the only long-distance race that requires each team to carry a standard baton which is passed between runners at changeovers."

Vaughan-Arbuckle says the issue of whether to carry a baton was brought up at an early meeting. "After some time, a person interjected that, in his experience, a baton was carried in all true relays whether on the track or elsewhere," he remembers. "That person was Olympic Games 10,000m fourth placer Tony Simmons, who ran stage three in 1993. No further discussion ensued and the matter has never been raised since."

Originally starting in Downham Market, the race has outgrown its original surroundings and, with increasing traffic congestion, has moved largely off-road, even venturing on to Norfolk's sandy beaches.

Athletes race through the night in the Round Norfolk Relay

There are four team classes, led by the premier "club class" competition, where teams must include five women and six masters. There are also open, veteran and women-only team awards to be won. Junior athletes' participation is limited to shorter stages.

》 SEE roundnorfolkrelay.com

Ron Hill to start 2011 race

RON HILL, the former European, Commonwealth and Boston Marathon champion, is guest of honour this weekend and he has agreed that the family trophy can in future carry his name. Dame Kelly Holmes has been a previous guest of honour and the award for the best performance irrespective of age bears her name.

Vaughan-Arbuckle said: "The race is a test of the organisational prowess of a club and is much more than just a normal relay, for it requires special preparation, planning and support. It is not an event for a club without a spirit of adventure, but the sense of satisfaction and achievement after completing the race is second to none."

Silver anniversary: 58 teams will take part this weekend

Facts and Figures

- The past 25 years will have seen 611 teams and 11,152 runners contesting the race, running a total of 126,906 miles.
- Norwich Road Runners' Richard Sales has achieved the most stage wins (17) since his first in 1988.
- Iva Barr, 82, of Bedford Harriers, is the oldest to have taken part when she ran last year.
- Tony Simmons' Vauxhall Motors team from 1993 hold the record for the fastest average pace at 5:58.4 per mile over the course.
- Ryston Runners AC is set become the only club to have competed in all 25 races, while Norwich Road Runners will have raced 23 times and the Stragglers 21.
- Paul Firmage of Ryston has competed in 22 of the 24 races, followed by his club colleague Andy Smith and Sales with 20 appearances. A further 90 runners have made 10 or more appearances in the race.

Hospital. As race director, I was chased and hassled by the press and media until I gave them an interview to explain what had happened. To my disappointment and anger, the local newspaper slanted their report to suggest that the race organisation must have been at least partly to blame, whereas nothing could have been further from the truth. Duncan received immediate and sustained attention, a fact subsequently acknowledged by his family and at the coroner's enquiry, which ruled that Duncan had died of Adult Sudden Death Syndrome. I attended his funeral and spoke with his parents who thanked me for all that had been done to try to save their son. With their agreement, I arranged for a memorial trophy to be awarded for the first local runner in the race. The following year the trophy was presented by his parents. Known as the Great East Anglia Run (GEAR), the race has gone from strength to strength over subsequent years, attracting such athletic luminaries as Dame Tanni Grey-Thompson.

From 1987, the next few years resulted in me running in eight marathons: London, New York, Berlin, Paris, Mallorca, Rome, Rotterdam and Macau. London on 17th April 1987 was the first I ran. Being the first, I was mindful of the stories of people 'hitting the wall' which is where the body literally runs out of 'fuel' and can no longer function. Examples of this can be seen in any marathon, but I suppose the most famous is that of Dorando Pietri in the 1908 London Olympics Marathon when he staggered across the line after being helped by an official, only to be disqualified. Terrified of running out of 'steam' myself, I decided to take things easy until I reached the last couple of miles. As I passed through Docklands, about two thirds into the race, I must have looked in trouble since a buxom woman suddenly stepped into the road holding up a placard which read: 'Stop here for your kiss of life'. I did not need the kiss and finished in a respectable 3 hours, 24 minutes and 30 seconds.

Our club coach had set a standard for the marathon, which he considered was 'decent', of under three hours. Although I never did achieve this, the following article of my run in Rome in 1987 will attest to the fact that I did get close to the three-hour mark.

'A right load of old cobbles'
Road Runners Club Newsletter No 124

"MILES and miles and miles of cobbles" so said David Coleman when describing the marathon course in the 1987 World Championship held in Rome. Having myself participated in the 6th Romaratona Elite on 1st May, 1987, which was used by the Italian Athletic Board as a dress rehearsal for the 1987 World Championship Marathons, I can vouch for the fact that about 1/3 of the course was run over cobbled streets.

The Rome Marathon, first held in 1982, was the brainchild of Franco Fava a member of the Italian Athletic Board and a marathon runner himself. Although the course has altered to some degree, it remains essentially the same today as it was in 1982.

My trip to Rome, some 36 hours before race day, was uneventful, apart from the usual problems caused by my surname! This time the Alitalia staff at Heathrow could not identify me on the passenger list when I reported for the flight. In desperation I asked to examine the VDU myself. and, having located a Mr. Carculckle, was able to convince them that he and I were almost 'certainly the same person! So far so good, but race registration in Rome that evening proved to be more of a problem. The Olympic Stadium is an enormous place and particularly lonely when empty, as was the case when I arrived to register. "If only I could find someone to ask" I thought, as I walked around the deserted perimeter trying to locate race registration. "Funny, even though it's nearly 8 p.m., surely others arriving for the event would also want to register?" but nobody! Just as seeds of doubt were forming in my mind, I saw an official in uniform. "Marathons registration?" No reaction. "Romaratona" I said running on the spot like an idiot. "Ah Si Si senor" said my savior beckoning me to follow him. After walking to the other end of the stadium we approached a mobile caravan where, to my delight and the obvious relief of my guide, I made contact with a pretty young woman who confirmed that she was indeed responsible for race registration: TG for that. :Where is everybody?" I enquired. "Most of runners already been – what size T-shirt?" She was anxious to close for the night.

Next afternoon, after a good night's rest, some pasta and a gentle day of sightseeing, I made my way back to the Olympic Stadium for a final loosener. Seeing other kindred spirits with the same idea, I decided to join them for a run around the Marmi Stadium. This gladiatorial type amphitheatre, built by Mussolini for the 1940 Olympic Games and surrounded by 60 twelve foot high marble figures, one for each province of Italy, has a very special aura about it. After a couple of laps, I found myself running alongside the great Grete Waitz. A few words pass between us before she excuses herself and moves ahead – oh well! After only 3 miles or so I am dripping wet, a far cry from training runs with my club mates from Ryston Runners around Downham Market, but at least there is no adverse reaction from my troublesome ham-string. That evening, alone in my hotel room, I think of Dorando Pietri, the Italian, and Jim Peters both of whom had collapsed from exhaustion close to the finish of the 1908 Olympic

Sporting Memories |

event and the 1954 Empire Games marathon respectively.

"A combination of heat and too fast a pace will almost certainly mean failure, so keep to your race plan." Good basic advice from our club coach Bob Hancock, but so often forgotten by inexperienced marathon runners in the "heat" of a race. "Remember 6.50 minutes per mile is all you need to duck under 3 hours but what's that in kilometres?" I think to myself before going off to sleep.

The race was scheduled for a 5 p.m. start, so I decided to remain in the hotel all day leaving just enough time to travel in comfort to the stadium. "Sorry senor no public transport, today holiday" says the receptionist in reply to my request for an underground ticket.

So, after an extortionate and nerve racking journey across Rome in a taxi, I arrived at the Marmi Stadium in a real sweat. Just time to produce the mandatory blood sample, carry out the normal pre-race ritual, plus one for luck, and then await call forward into the Olympic Stadium. I judge there to be about 100 runners, and identify a number of Frenchmen and Germans, but no other Brits so far as I could tell.

As we enter the magnificent but empty Olympic arena, via the inter connecting tunnel from the Marmi Stadium, I follow others towards a table lined with bottles of water, have a swig and continue jogging around the track. Suddenly and unexpectedly a gun fires and, to my horror, I realise that the race has started about 200 metres away. Out of breath and almost lapped, I leave the stadium and head off towards the centre of Rome in the shade of trees via the Olympic Way and Angelico Viale. I catch a glimpse of Grete Waitz some way ahead, but dismiss unwise thoughts of trying to catch her. A wise move since I hear afterwards that she had to retire after about 20 kms due to the heat. Check my watch after about 7 kms and judge my pace to be about 3.45 per km, 15 secs faster than I need to beat 3 hours – be careful! As we enter St. Peter's Square there is plenty of support but no sign of his Holiness. Not so much shade now and the sun is pretty strong as we cross the Tevere. Through 15 kms in 61 mins – too fast? Perhaps not, but be careful. Vast and enthusiastic crowds at the Colosseum and past the imposing monument to Victor Emmanuel II where I catch sight of the leaders, Bordin and Diamantino going at a terrific pace. "Damn these cobblestones" which are really taking a toll of my legs now. My thoughts turn to the fuss made over the few hundred yards of cobblestones on the embankment in London. Should they really be allowed to tamper with the natural course by laying carpet over the cobbles – I think not.

At 30 kms my legs are really tired and sore, and the cumulative effect of negotiating 4 of the 7 hills of Rome is beginning to take its toll – I did not feel good at all and there were still 12 kms to go. My pace had now slowed to 4.20 per km but I was still on to break three hours. I tried to recall the advice I had been given by my club mates, but the feeling of tiredness seemed to dominate any other sensation. By the time we reached the Vatican, on the way home, with about 9 kms left, morale was very low indeed. Suddenly the public address announced "Arbuckley Gran Britagna..." plus an Italian name which draws great applause. I soon realised why this was when the diminutive figure of an Italian woman passed me escorted by a police motor cycle. "Must be the leading woman" I thought as I picked up my pace to stay with her. In fact she turned .out to be 19 year old Maria Febbrari, the second woman home. I passed Febbrari with about 7 kms left, but J am passed myself by Deiter Kleinmann, a well known German author on running. I tucked in behind him with fantasy thoughts of racing him for the Veterans' Gold – anything to keep my mind off the pain and fatigue. 4 kms to go and 20 minutes left to beat three hours – should be easy but… I dig deep but there's not much there. We have now closed on a Frenchman. "England versus France and Germany!" We turn left into the Viale dei Gladiatori and l could see the Olympic Stadium – 2 kms remain and the crowd were doing their best to lift us. Still 8.30 seconds left. I entered the stadium and the marshal indicated two laps. On no! Those two laps seemed to take an eternity. As I crossed the line the clock showed 3.00.54 seconds. So near and yet so far. Failure yes, but a real sense of pride in having improved on my personal best by over 3 minutes and, as the only Brit there, I had finished 36th in my first 'Elite' marathon.

The Rome Marathon is run over a course which passes through 2,000 years of civilisation and has the thrill of negotiating some of the great masterpieces of architecture in the world. It is certainly a demanding course with its cobbles, uneven surface and many twists and turns. It is also hot and very humid. A tough and demanding course by any standards, but not, in my view, one which deserved the plethora of adverse comment it got from some of our own athletes and officials who decided in advance of the World Championships that it was not for them.

RESULTS
Men   h. m. s.
1.   Gelindo Bordin, Italy   2 16 03
2.   Silveira Diamantino, Brazil   2 16 35
3.   Michalangela Arena, Italy 2 18 55
Women
1.   Maria Araneo, Italy   2 56 00
2.   Maria Febbrari, Italy   3 02 00

Running marathons was a great way of seeing a few of the big cities of the world. I shall never forget, particularly, starting over the Verrazano Bridge, running through the eight districts of New York to finish in Central Park. In a state of collapse at the finish, I was taken to a recovery tent. As I was woken by a stethoscope on my chest, there looking down on me was the spitting image of 'Hot lips', the well-endowed, female military doctor in the TV series *Mash*. When I blurted out, "Hi hot lips," she replied, "Not much wrong with this guy," and moved on! Berlin was great. The race was started by Emil Zatopek, the legendary Czechoslovakian runner, in front of the Reichstag (government building), and wound its way through the city a few years before the Wall, separating East and West Berlin, was demolished in 1989. Finishing in the stadium used for the 1936 (Nazi) Olympic Games was one of those moments which turned my thoughts to Swastika-waving Germans and Hitler's snub of the great Jesse Owen.

Rome – Olympic Stadium

Berlin Olympic Stadium

My main memory of Paris, apart from 'hitting the wall' and finishing in a state of collapse, was being passed by a number of Parisians who joined the race at various points well after the start! I particularly remember noticing one man stripping off in the crowd at about twenty miles and sprinting past me; I saw him at the finish, jabbering away, with the medal around his neck – "C'est la vie!" London, the first marathon I ran, has – as everyone knows – a special atmosphere. Macau, the former Portuguese colony, south of Hong Kong, was an 'opportunity' run as I was working temporarily in Hong Kong. I ran a personal best at the time of just over three hours.

| Never a Dull Moment

Anyone who has been a runner knows that being injured is part of the sport; I was no different. Injuries came and went, usually as a result of over-training, but there was one which caused me more distress than any other. This is described in the following article I wrote for the Road Runners Club Newsletter in January 1986.

'It's only sport'
Road Runners Club Newsletter, Number 127

WATCHING the thrilling and highly motivating scenes from the London Marathon on TV, at my temporary home in Northern Germany, my thoughts turned, somewhat selfishly, to the misfortune which had recently befallen me.

My training had been proceeding well and, within excess of 600 miles in the 'bank' since 1st January including some modest success in the local cross country scene, I was looking forward to breaking 3 hours for the marathon. My problems started when, after a race in quagmire conditions, I put my shoes in the washing machine with disastrous results! Worse still, replacements were not readily available in Germany. In desperation, I bought a shoe off the shelf which had rave reviews and which subsequently proved to be very comfortable on short runs. Yes, I know, every runner should have more than one pair of shoes!

After a good 25 km run in my new shoes, spirits were high and I looked forward with eager anticipation to the Rotterdam Marathon the following weekend. Next morning, as I staggered down the stairs half asleep to make the morning tea, there was a sharp pain in the area of the Achilles tendon of my right leg. The pain persisted through that day and was particularly bad when going up or down stairs. For 24 hours I managed not to panic, rationalising that it was nothing more than a minor strain which would disappear. By Wednesday, when the pain was no better, morale worsened as I realised my chances of running were diminishing as time passed. Ice treatment, expensive cream, anti-inflammatory pills and complete rest had ensured that, by Friday, I was pain-free when walking. That evening I had a successful jog of about 3 miles, although some slight discomfort persisted in the troubled area.

Next morning my world all but collapsed when, taking the dog for his constitutional, I tried running a few steps only to experience the same stabbing pain in my leg. I knew immediately that the marathon was out. The doctor's parting words to me earlier in the week "Remember you are not as young as you were", were of little comfort as I unpacked my bag. Irrational thoughts, including retirement, twinged with more than a touch of self pity, pervaded my mind for the rest of that day.

Sporting Memories

My motivation returned, 24 hours after watching London, with a most exhilarating bicycle ride in the local military training area, which stretches for hundreds of miles through forest and gently undulating heathland. It was a superb evening with the departing sun streaming through the trees. In the space of about an hour, I saw an abundance of wild life, including deer, wild boar and red squirrel. Positive thinking returned to me as I thought how lucky I was to experience such pleasant surroundings with my health in tact – but the injury was not healing.

For the next few weeks, a round trip of over 100 miles, three times a week, for physiotherapy seemed to help, but a few short strides always reminded me that my leg had not healed. Meanwhile, I had purchased a copy of Joan Benoit's road running coaching video in which she extols the virtues of a floatation vest to enable injured runners to run suspended in the water. Just what I wanted but where could I get one?

Shopping trips to local sports shops confirmed that the German retail sports trade had not heard of the item. As luck would have it, the May edition of Runners World magazine carried an advert for the "Wet Vest". A call to their office in the U.S.A. revealed that the item was on trial in Germany, and I might be able to get a vest through a contact they gave me. I eventually made contact with the right man, and the item duly arrived about 10 days later. By this time, I had been "off the road" for 5 weeks.

Armed with my Wet Vest, I made my way to the local indoor swimming pool at 7 a.m. on the Sunday, so as to avoid the crowds, and enable me to get used to running suspended in water with a minimum of fuss... some hope! As I emerged from the changing room into the pool area, feeling somewhat self conscious, I was acutely aware of an unfriendly looking official observing the considerable number of intently serious Germans breast stroking their way, in metronome fashion, up and down the excellent pool. I was also aware that the official was watching my every movement with more than a passing interest. Undaunted, I started to get into my Wet Vest, but noticed that he majority of Germans in the pool were by now extremely interested in what I was doing, so much so that one or two were zig-zagging across each other's paths! The sound of heavy steps alerted me to the fast approaching pop-bellied official, with a ruddy complexion, dressed in his all-white uniform. His disapproving finger wagging was warning enough. "Das ist nicht in ordnung..." My plea, in broken German, that I was an injured runner who wished to "run" in his pool did nothing to ease the tense atmosphere. Indeed, one or two of the swimmers had now stopped swimming, and seemed to be enjoying the situation. I felt helpless and furious, but there seemed no alternative but to leave, clutching my virgin Wet Vest.

My long suffering wife, by now used to my eccentric activities, seemed not in the least surprised that I had met with a rebuff, but agreed to accompany me back to the pool after breakfast to see whether she could help explain my predicament in her mother tongue. To begin with, Herr Dollar listened to what my wife had to say, but obviously with little interest or sympathy until, quite suddenly, he broke into a broad smile at something my wife said. The conversation then flowed for a few minutes, my only contribution being an occasional nod, before we left after the mandatory hand shake.

On the way home, Angelika, my wife, explained that it was her comment "I don't suppose you have ever lived with a runner who can't run" which seemed to have made the difference! She was to take the jacket back to Herr Dollar later in the morning to substantiate that the Vest was indeed an aid to running and not another floating device which would cause further complaints from his regulars. However the box, in which the West Vest arrived, covered in sticky tape indicating that it had come from FC Borussia Munchengladbach, the late European football champions, and the discreetly concealed bottle of Schnapps seemed to do the trick! It must have, because the next day I was given permission to use the pool.

The Wet Vest is simple in design and very effective. It is made of a light-weight material, padded for buoyancy and fastened by Velcro tabs across the front and at the beaver tail. Specifically designed for deep water running, the vest allows cardiovascular exercise, improved muscular strength and endurance without any risk of injury. Running in water with the whole body, apart from the head, submerged is somewhat strange at first, but there is no doubting the value to be derived from this excellent concept. It is not a substitute for running, but could and does successfully augment daily training schedules. Meanwhile, my personal experience has indicated that the Wet Vest is of inestimable value to the injured runner. I have been using it 3 times a week with each session being conducted at 3/4 effort for between 30 and 40 minutes.

But it wasn't until I visited an osteopath in U.K. that my "Achilles tendon" was eventually sorted out, 9 weeks after the problem developed. He diagnosed that a badly misplaced ligament in my lower back was the real cause of the injury. To my enormous relief, 3 days after his manipulative treatment, the discomfort disappeared and I returned to running on the road. Ten days later I ran at the VI European Veterans Championships in Brugge and, although I had a very poor run, it was extremely good to be back.

As all the text books indicate, much can be learnt from an injury, and I have been no exception. Most importantly, I am now able to place my sport in context to the rest of my life. In the past I was probably too obsessive over my running but I now feel more able to keep it in perspective with the bigger picture of life as a whole. My round trip to Brugge, of 755 miles in a day, to run a mere 10 kms, so soon after a major injury did seem somewhat excessive. To my family and friends, it has merely served to reinforce their already held conviction that I continue to suffer from a large overdose of veteran's inveterate madness.

Those who have run marathons will attest to the fact that it is well-nigh impossible to run more than one decent marathon in a year. Quite apart from the hours of commitment to training, it is the wear and tear on the body which eventually takes its toll. My body was no exception! I therefore decided to concentrate on shorter distances up to the half-marathon. This brought me some modest success. I found that I also enjoyed the cut-and-thrust of track running and started competing in 5,000 and 10,000-metre races. After competing in area and national championships, I decided to join club mates Peter Duhig and Cath Turner (now Mrs Duhig) who were going to the World Veteran Championships in Turku, Finland, in July 1991. I ran in three events: 5,000m, 10,000m, and the cross-country for 50-year-old men. After successfully negotiating the 5,000m heats, I finished a modest 14th (out of 18) in the final which was won by a Mexican, former Olympic competitor, Antonio Villanueva. It was a sobering experience. In the 10,000m there were no heats so it was with no less than 63 other athletes that I lined up for the 25-lap final. Running a reasonable race, I finished 25th in 35½ minutes. The race was won by the great New Zealander, Ron Robertson, who also won the 3,000m steeplechase and the cross-country. In the same cross-country race, in which there were 77 runners, I finished 18th – and 4th British finisher – narrowly missing out on the team Gold Medal, made up of the first three British finishers!

It wasn't until I attended a training weekend at Annan in Dumfriesshire with Steve Ovett, Olympic gold medal winner and world record-breaker, and his coach, the great Harry Wilson, that I came to the realisation that the longer distances were not really best for me. During a series of tests on the track and afterwards during a face-to-face discussion, Harry suggested that I would do far better running 800/1,500-metre races. But wasn't I too old to convert to those distances, I asked? Harry persuaded me, based on the trials he had put me through, at least to give it a try. I was not to be disappointed.

Listening to Steve and Harry during that weekend was a real privilege and taught me a great deal. Harry had been Steve's coach from 1973 until he retired in 1986, after winning the Commonwealth Games 5,000 metres. Describing Harry in his autobiography, Steve says he was 'dogmatic, a brash extrovert, with peak cap and whistle shouting at you ... he was a little over the top, but then that was Harry'. Their relationship was obviously very special and not a stereotype 'coach runner relationship': it was more a friendship born out of mutual respect. This came out during the weekend. I kept in touch with Harry over the years and it was a mark of the person that he was always willing to give of his time to an ordinary club runner. Sadly, he died in May 1999, aged 77.

I also attended a training weekend with Bruce Tulloh, who won the European 5,000-metre title in 1962, during a particularly strong period in the sport. He was also runner-up in the National Cross-Country Championships when all leading stars saw the event as one not to be missed. Bruce ran without shoes on the track and was the first barefoot runner and the seventh Englishman to break the under-four-minute mile. He also ran across America from East to West. After retiring from competition in 1965, Bruce turned to coaching, in which his greatest success came with Richard Nerurkar, whose most notable success was a 3rd in the World Cup Marathon. It was with Richard's help that Bruce organised the weekend I attended at Braunton in Devon, where there were plenty of sand-hills for him to put us through our paces.

In a letter to me sometime later, Bruce noted that 'by moving down from the marathon to 5k and 10k, and then to 800m, you have gone in the opposite direction to most of us!' As a result of an exchange of letters, Bruce included, on page 62 of his book *Running over 40*, a quotation of mine on training, and on page 115 a photograph of me racing in Battersea Park. Success at the shorter track distances came regularly in both local and regional competitions. Through running I have formed many lasting friendships. Of those, my relationship with Tony and Eileen Hunt, Peter and Cath Duhig, and Rod Baron have been important to me, and I want to thank them for their help and friendship over many years.

Knowing that I was going to the World Championships in 1993, I had trained very hard in the preceding twelve months – and my results bore this out. I had a fine year on the track, winning local, regional and national races at 800m and 1500m. The Veterans' 1,500m championship best of 4 minutes, 50.5 seconds I set in the Civil Service Championships 1993 still stands as I write. So it was with confidence high that I arrived in Japan for the 10th World Veterans' Championships in October 1993, along with 12,178 other athletes from 78 countries, including fellow

Ryston Runner and coach, Bob Hancock,. Watching the competition from the stands one day, I found myself sitting near the great Kenyan, Kip Keino. Knowing that Bob had previously coached the Kenyan team, including Keino, I mentioned he was at the games. As a result, they met later to chat about old times over a few beers.

Although I had pre-entered three events, the final programme realistically allowed me to run in only one, so I decided on the 800m. I was drawn in the first of three heats, from which the first two in each heat plus the two fastest losers would progress to the final; this made the task of qualifying for the final all the more difficult. There were fifteen in my heat which resulted in plenty of barging and pushing as we jockeyed for position. Entering the final straight of the second and final lap, I was lying fifth. Knowing that I must be at least third to stand any chance of making the final, I pushed hard and managed to squeeze past a Japanese runner into third place. I now had to wait to see what happened in the other two heats. The second of these was very fast, and produced three runners inside my time. The third heat was less competitive, although the first three runners were well ahead of the others. It was therefore a very nervous forty minutes as I waited for the list of those who had made the final to be posted. To my relief, I had made it by the skin of my teeth as one of the fastest losers with a time of 2 minutes, 15.16 seconds. I was now able to tell Vivian, who was teaching in Japan at the time, that I would, after all, be running in the final if she wanted to come.

The day of the final was fine and sunny. I was very nervous as I went through my warm-up drills on the practice track. Bob was there to help and encourage me. Sitting in the forming-up area, with runners from the USA, Canada, Denmark, Japan, Russia and a second 'Brit', was as tense a situation as I had ever experienced. Eventually we were led into a packed stadium. It was just as I had imagined it would be to take part in a major athletics championship. Vivian had said she would be there but I could not see her. We were individually announced. I was in Lane Six. The gun went and there was the usual sprint for the 200m mark, at which point lanes could be broken. At the end of the first lap I was in fourth place, but I knew the pace was too fast for me. Down the back straight, my mouth felt dry and my legs were beginning to feel heavy. Coming into the home straight, I was still fourth but was fading. Finishing was a blur, although I knew that I was out of the medal positions. The race was won by John Ross, my fellow Brit, from one of the Americans, with a Dane in third place. I finished seventh in a time just a few tenths outside my personal best set in the heats.

Tenth World Veteran's Track & Field Championships October 1993 – M55 800m Final – I'm fifth from the right

It was great meeting up with Vivian and her boyfriend after the race and having a meal with them that evening. The experience of Miyasaki has remained with me all these years. I remember the friendliness, the dedication, the efficiency and the generosity of the Japanese people who came out in their thousands to support the Games, including the Crown Prince and his bride.

Those of my friends and family who do not run have often asked me why I do it and what I get out of it. I think these questions are interlinked. Apart from the obvious benefit of increasing cardio-vascular fitness, running creates a sense of well-being and a feeling of heightened mental acuity. A run makes you feel good and even superior. A run will often reduce tension and it often produces clear thought to enable a problem to be solved. I don't remember where this quotation came from but it encapsulates for me what running is all about: *'It is the lone runner who is most likely to experience the satisfaction of athletic achievement.'* Running requires nothing more than a pair of shoes, it can be done at any time during the day or night and, importantly, it can be done alone. In a nutshell, to run is to live. It was when browsing around Waterloo Station, on the way home after a hectic week in the MOD, I came across Percy Cerutty's book *Be Fit or Be Damned* which became my 'bible' and has inspired me to maintain a level of fitness wherever and whatever circumstances I have found myself in.

Sporting Memories |

One of the greatest athletic feats of all time was the breaking of the four-minute mile barrier by Roger Bannister, then a student at Oxford University, at the Iffley Road track on 6th May 1954. Fifty years later, on 6th May 2004, I attended a meeting, with friend Rod Baron, at Iffley Road to commemorate the original feat. In front of some of the 'greats' of middle-distance running, including John Landy, Sir Roger Bannister, Doug Ibbotson, Chris Chataway and Seb Coe, the mile was 'replayed' with Roger Bannister ringing a bell to signal one lap to go, but this time it was an Australian, Craig Mottram, who won the day and in doing so broke the four-minute barrier. It was an afternoon I shall never forget as I made my way around getting the signatures of many great runners.

Running, particularly as a way of people keeping fit, is an important part of life in Germany. I regularly used to run in these excellently organised meetings. Most villages organised at least one *Volkslauf* (People's Run) a year. Apart from providing good training, it enabled me to meet Germans and to get to know the local area. Whenever possible, I tried to get Angelika and the girls to come with me. Eventually, I did get the girls to run once or twice although I was never successful in getting Angelika to don a pair of running shoes! Even at that early stage, Claire showed some ability, so it was no surprise that later in life she became a talented runner. Imagine how proud I was when I watched her qualify for the Army team after placing fourth in the Army Cross-Country Championship over a demanding course in Bordon. Knowing how important this race would

Women's Inter Service X Country Championship, Aldershot 1994
Claire on extreme left number 44, Kelly Holmes number 45

| Never a Dull Moment

ATHLETICS / Success for Ryston Runner
Claire crowns excellent season

RYSTON RUNNER Claire Vaughan-Arbuckle, an army lieutenant, has crowned an excellent winter season with her selection for the Combined Services cross country squad shortly to face the British Athletic Federation and Combined Universities teams.

Claire finished 12th overall, and 6th in the victorious army team which included Kelly Holmes the British 800m record holder, in the Inter Services match last week.

COMPETITIVE

She demonstrated with a determined and gutsy run how much she has matured and improved in her first year of competitive athletics.

Earlier in the season she had indicated good form with a series of impressive runs to win the Southern Area Seniors' League, fifth place in the Norfolk County Championships to win her first county vest, and 17th at Colchester in the Eastern Counties' Championships.

Shortly to take up a two year appointment in Northern Ireland, Claire has received recognition of her athletics potential with an invitation to join a squad of elite athletes to undergo special training.

KES students selected for Norfolk team

THREE pupils from King Edward VII High School, Lynn, Helen Atthowe, Gemma Bonnett and Donna Scott, have been selected to represent Norfolk schools in the English Schools Cross Country Championship at Liverpool on Saturday, March 5. This is a great achievement and reward for their dedication and effort.

Claire Vaughan-Arbuckle – great season

be, I took a day off from work and travelled down so that I could support her. As she had no idea I was there, it was clearly a shock – and I hope a spur – when I popped out from behind a bush to shout some words of encouragement. At that time I think she was in sixth place and needed to finish in the first four to be selected for the Army. To my delight, she did make up the two places. I then watched her run for the Army, in the same team as Sergeant Kelly Holmes, who was, of course, later to become Dame Kelly, double Olympic Champion at 800 and 1,500 metres.

I have 'flirted' with a few other sports including golf, boxing, modern pentathlon, *langlauf*, hockey and squash. My introduction to golf was via a friend of my father who took me to a course in Bedford. I 'graduated' from there to playing in Aldershot on a casual basis, but it wasn't until I got to Germany that I played regularly. My 'boss' at the time, Peter Mears, had a number of low-handicapped players in his unit whom he encouraged with a view to winning the Army team championship. As I played more golf and gave up cricket, my game improved to the point where I was playing off a decent handicap of 15. My 'home' club was Sennelager Golf Club, where the course was fairly easy until it went through the pine woods. My golf style was very much that of an ex-cricketer, a matter commented on by a friend who, having watched me drive off, remarked to a packed first tee, "Crude but effective!"

There was not much golf in Turkey, where I worked after Germany, principally because the Turks had ploughed up the golf course to spite the Americans who generally sided with the Greeks over the struggle for Cyprus. But I did return to the game when I was posted to Liverpool. Living in Formby, with a neighbour and a General who played, I got back into the game. With the likes of Birkdale, Formby, Lytham St Annes and Royal Liverpool all within easy reach, it was a wonderful opportunity to play some of the great English golf courses.

I was invited to play in a Pro Am tournament at the Royal Liverpool Golf Club where I partnered a professional named Guy Hunt. On introducing myself to him in the locker room, he seemed somewhat 'distant' and said he would see me on the first tee. I duly met him there and it was soon our turn to tee off. He went first and promptly hit his ball 'Out of Bounds' on the right-hand side. My remark of "Hard luck!" was ignored. I was then announced over the tannoy, "On the tee, Lieutenant Colonel Ian Vaughan-Arbuckle"; there was an audible 'titter'. I was terrified with spectators all around the tee and the clubhouse glass windows within easy reach of a hooked drive, a shot I was prone to produce. Not able to look up after hitting the ball, I was relieved to hear applause punctuated by the odd 'Good shot', and to see my ball sailing straight down the fairway. I can't remember how many points we scored but it was good enough to secure second place and a new golf bag, presented at the evening dinner, which I attended alone, by Fred Truman, the iconic fast bowler.

My father introduced me to boxing on the pretence that I needed to know how to defend myself in everyday life. My first fight in the ring was as part of a cub-scout match in Hong Kong. I remember little of the fight except that I left the ring crying with a bleeding nose, which turned out to be broken. I can't remember climbing into a ring again until I was at King's School where boxing was mandatory. Boxing for my house team, I was again on the receiving end, so when it came to boxing at officer cadet school I was very nervous. Paired with someone of roughly the same size, we were expected to knock 'six bells' out of each other, in a fight of three rounds each of two minutes' duration, to demonstrate courage, resilience and aggression. Seeking out my opponent before the fight, we came to a pact to 'take it easy' on each other. Soon after the bell to start the first round, he hit me on the nose which immediately started to pour with blood. At this, I lost my temper and waded into my opponent with arms flailing, some of which must have landed since the fight was stopped in my favour. So ended my career in boxing!

From my early days I have followed boxing. I well remember, when I was a boarder at King's School, my housemaster, Mr 'Nosey' Parker, knowing that I was interested, invited me and another boy to listen in his room to the World Middleweight title fight between Randolph (Randy) Turpin and the American Sugar Ray Robinson, who had lost only one bout in his 132-fight career. He even gave us a cup of chocolate during the fight! It was 10th July 1951 and I was 13. The first few rounds were even, but in the sixth, Turpin took the fight to his opponent. Robinson was cut above his eye and the excitement grew as a British win became a reality. Turpin, who was in the lead, managed to stay out of trouble until the last couple of rounds. Realising that he needed a knockout to win the fight, Robinson threw everything at Turpin, who was forced to hang on until the bell. We waited anxiously for the verdict: a win on points for Turpin to become Middleweight Champion of the World. It was a great moment in British sport.

My experience of Modern Pentathlon was brief. I was spotted as someone who could run 3 km cross-country, shoot pistol and stay on a horse to cover twelve jumps in 400 metres, leaving me to learn to swim 200 metres freestyle and fence *épee*. After six months' intensive training, I took part in my first, and only, championship, the Army team competition. So nervous and overwrought was I that, apart from the run in which I scored over 1,000 points, the two-day competition was an unmitigated disaster. So ended my brief foray into the world of modern pentathlon! Hockey was different as I had played this briefly at school. Having good hand-eye co-ordination and a reasonable turn of speed, I took to the game well and in time became a decent forward. I eventually captained my Corps team and played for Guilford Hockey Club in their third team at weekends.

It will be obvious from the foregoing that physical training has invariably been a part of my life. In fact, I have always enjoyed training and the resultant feeling of well-being. 'Fit in body, fit in mind' is a mantra in which I have always believed. Fun and fitness go hand-in-hand. If you enjoy your training, benefits will follow. Sometimes it will be necessary to work hard to achieve your goals, but the pleasure to be derived from achieving them will more than adequately make up for the pain. Running should add enjoyment to your life, not restrict it. Enjoy the freedom of being a runner, of being in control, of being strong and fit. I well remember the sheer joy and exhilaration of running through virgin snow over miles of countryside in Germany with only wild animals for company. Enjoy the changing seasons, the freshness of a morning run and the wind in your face. Remember, whatever speed you run, there will be others who would love to be running but are unable to do so. There are no short cuts to sporting success. What effort you put into practising or training will determine how successful you are. In running, regardless of age, hard intensive work, with suitable recovery periods, is the only sure way of improving. General all-round fitness greatly enhances one's life. Injuries form part of a sportsman's life and I have had my fair share of them, including one or two very serious ones. In fact, it was the constant wear and tear on my left knee, brought about by running 'left about' on the track, which gave rise to the arthroscopy I had on my knee in 1994 and precipitated my early retirement from competitive athletics. And only recently have I had to undergo a further operation to my left knee, which revealed such a serious deterioration to the meniscus cartilage that my running days are over. So, I shall now turn to cycling and walking for my exercise.

I was ten when the 1948 Olympic Games were held in the UK. Coming just after the Second World War, they were known as the Austerity Games. The Games were nonetheless well attended, popular and successful, and a credit to the country. I remember little detail of the stars as there was no TV in those days but I did listen to the commentary on the wireless. My heroes from 1948 were Emile Zatopek (Czechoslovakia) who won the 10,000 metres and Tom Richards (GB) who was second in the marathon.

Olympic stadium, London

| Never a Dull Moment

Imagine my delight when I got a ticket to attend the morning track and field session of the London Olympics on Saturday 4th August 2012. Getting to the Olympic Park early, I had plenty of time to walk around to see the magnificent facilities and soak up the atmosphere before taking my seat in the main stadium. Hundreds of volunteers were on hand to guide and offer spectators advice, while members of the armed forces took care of security matters in their normal professional and unobtrusive manner. The Olympic Park was quite superb and testimony to British planning, design and construction, while the organisation was faultless. The stadium must rank alongside the greatest athletic arenas in the world and the performance of our athletes scaled heights that we could only have dreamt of, particularly that of Mohamed (Mo) Farah who took Gold in the 10,000 and 5,000 metres, a feat replicated by only seven other athletes in the history of the Olympics, including Lasse Viren, Emile Zatopek, Miruts Yifter and Abebe Bikila. I shall never forget my experience and I feel privileged to have been there. On the way home, I reflected on how Britain could still stage a major event which those lucky enough to be present would never forget.

It is to be hoped that the country's success at these games will be seized upon to improve sport in schools and communities if the legacy of the Games is not to be lost. An important aspect will be to bring back competition in every school so that our younger generation learn how to be magnanimous in victory and gracious in defeat.

Usain Bolt at 100 meters start

11. NATO's Fragile Flank – Turkey

Told that my next job was to be in Headquarters Land South East, my immediate reaction was, 'Where on earth is that?' Not even Peter Mears, my boss, knew the answer – it was before the Internet became the font of all knowledge. Eventually, I found out that it was located in Izmir (Smyrna in ancient times) on the western shores of Turkey off the Aegean Sea. I was to be one of four British Army officers in the headquarters staffed predominately by Turkish and American personnel. My job entailed planning for the logistical support of NATO operations on its southern flank, particularly the Allied Command Europe Mobile Force which was earmarked to reinforce Turkish Army units at the first sign of trouble in the region. Trouble, in those days, was expected to come from the Soviet Union. I would be taking over from John MacDonald, an officer with a formidable reputation who had played rugby for Scotland and was justifiably tipped for high rank: he eventually reached the rank of Major-General.

We decided to travel by car and ferry from Germany to Turkey. After a trouble-free journey, we arrived in Izmir on a Friday in June 1978 in a state of heightened anticipation of our new life in a foreign country about which we knew little: we not to be disappointed. Soon after leaving the docks, driving along the seafront main road, following the directions I had been given for the American forces' hostel where we were to stay, the traffic slowed to walking pace. As we neared the obstruction, I could see there was a temporary, unmanned barrier across the road. As each car reached the obstruction, the driver was getting out, lifting the barrier, driving through, replacing the barrier and driving on. When my turn came, I just did what others had done and went through the barrier. Just as I was getting back into the car, there was a shrill blast of a whistle as a policeman made his way towards me. He spoke no English but his anger was palpable. With a wave of his arms and much shouting, he obviously wanted to see my papers. I first produced my driving licence, followed quickly by my passport, when it was clear that the driving licence was not what he wanted. By this time another policeman was on the scene and a sizeable crowd had gathered to enjoy the spectacle of someone with foreign number plates in trouble with the police. The 'lead' policeman was becoming even more animated as he jabbered away in Turkish without being able to make himself understood. Clearly, I had breached the law by ignoring the barrier. In mitigation, I wanted him to understand that I had only just arrived in Turkey and was merely following everyone else who had lifted the barrier. That my efforts had failed was obvious when he drew his pistol, spreadeagled me over the car and frisked me. Angelika was still in the car.

At this point, a man emerged from the crowd and asked in good English whether he could help. He was a student at the local university. After I had explained what had happened, he relayed the story to the policeman who then seemed to calm down somewhat. I produced my NATO travel order, my military identity card and apologised profusely, through the student, for what I had done. This seemed to 'do the trick' and we were allowed to go on our way, still on the wrong side of the barrier! I had had a lucky escape for the Turkish police have a fearsome reputation. If one needed evidence of this, one need look no further than the true story portrayed in the film *Midnight Express* of an American convicted of drug smuggling. There was also the true story of two American sailors arrested and convicted of urinating on a statue of Kemal Ataturk, the founding father of modern Turkey, who were sentenced to ten years in jail for the offence! As duty officer at the NATO headquarters, I once had to visit the unfortunate sailors who, although well looked after, were obviously very unhappy.

Until my handover was completed and my predecessor had vacated the flat, we lived in the Kordon Hotel, a family hostel run by the Americans mainly for their personnel. It was soon to become obvious that the Americans kept themselves to themselves and did little to foster good relations with the Turks. They had their own school, their own shops, a large recreational facility, including a swimming pool – and, until just before we arrived, their own golf course. To demonstrate their anger with American foreign policy prevailing at the time, which favoured the Greeks in their spat with Turkey over Cyprus, the locals ploughed up the golf course one night! Very cunning, for nothing else would have had such a morale-sapping impact on the Americans. Americans were hardly ever to be seen using the local economy. In my experience, this is fairly typical of the average American serviceman abroad who seldom strays outside his own environment, and knows or cares little about the people and country in which he is serving. Small wonder therefore that Americans seldom win the hearts and minds of those in whose country they are serving.

We eventually moved into a first-floor flat on the main waterfront road with a magnificent view over the Bay of Izmir with its lively traffic of small and medium vessels.

Izmir waterfront

Coming from a busy and demanding job in Germany, I very soon realised that the pace of life on NATO's southern flank was significantly slower. I shared an office with three Americans and one Italian officer. Initially, our 'boss' was an American but he was replaced by a Turkish colonel named Arafat Beyaz, who had commanded a parachute battalion during the Turkish invasion of Cyprus in 1974. A squat, well-built man with strong facial features, he initially struggled with life behind a NATO desk principally because he neither spoke nor read much English. His copy of the *Concise Oxford Dictionary* was a constant and much-used companion. Once I got his trust, he began to use me as his personal staff officer to help him understand papers and to draft replies. I know he found the Americans difficult and not particularly helpful so I was quite happy to do this. One of the Americans, a Lieutenant-Colonel, made it clear that he disliked the Turks and, when asked by Beyaz, would often reply under his breath, "My nerves!" Despite their impressive paper qualifications (most had degrees of one sort or another), I found them, with notable exceptions, a pretty unimpressive bunch and took great pleasure in pointing out that it was the *Concise Oxford,* and not *Fowler's English,* that was the official dictionary in NATO!

My three fellow British officers all worked in the Planning Directorate: the senior British officer was Brigadier Dennis Fuller; he was replaced towards the end of my tour by Terrence Holloway, while the two Lieutenant-Colonels were Nigel Roberts and John Leonard; John's wife taught their children at home. Most visitors to the headquarters were American or Turkish so it was a pleasant surprise when the visit of British General Sir David Frazer, Deputy Supreme Commander Allied Forces Europe, was announced. Well over six feet tall, and in dress uniform wearing an impressive array of medals, the General made an immediate impact by answering the guard commander in Turkish and speaking to every man. So often on such occasions others would just walk along the guard without talking to any of the soldiers. That is not the way of the British Army. We were required to wear our best uniform with medals for David Fraser. At that time, I had no medals – a fact that was seized upon by my American female clerk, with less than five years' service, who already had four medals. She found it difficult to accept that a Major with over 25 years' service had a bare chest. With perhaps less tact than I ought to have had, I explained that, in the British Army, medals were awarded only for campaigns and not for routine service and qualifications. Every American who served in Turkey received a medal.

One evening as he was relaxing, the telephone rang in Dennis Fuller's flat. The caller announced himself as General Hackett. At first Dennis Fuller was wary thinking the call was a hoax but he soon realised it was General Sir John 'Shan' Hackett talking. The General had just published a book, *The Third World War, August 1985,* which ultimately sold three million copies in ten languages. Subsequent events showed that General Hackett had been prescient, for the novel predicted the disintegration of the Soviet Union (which eventually happened in 1991) and paid special attention to the strategic importance of oil in the Middle East. Hounded by the world's press, Shan Hackett decided to accept an offer by his dentist to spend a week or so in his holiday flat in Turkey. The General had arrived in a hurry and turned to the British Army to help organise his stay. I was deputed to pick up the General and Mrs Hackett at the house by the sea near Bodrum where they had been staying. On arrival, they were nowhere to be found. Eventually, I found them sitting in a shack beside the sea, drinking *chai* and chatting to the locals. The General invited me to join the group and I soon realised he spoke some Turkish, whereas I spoke none. Travelling back to Izmir, the General explained that, knowing he was coming to Turkey, he had picked up a book and learnt a few phrases. He was clearly annoyed that I had not attended a language course before taking up my post, and resolved to do something about it when he got back to London. When my successor was chosen, his posting order noted that he would be required to attend a short course to learn Turkish!

As I have already indicated, my official post was hardly justified, as there was not enough work to require a full-time officer. Had it not been NATO-funded, I doubt that it would have existed in the British Army. This was worrying from a career standpoint as I was entering the zone for promotion to Lieutenant-Colonel and keen to enhance my chances with a good report: difficult without a challenging job. When I raised this matter with my superior, he told me that I would not have been selected for the post unless my promotion was pretty well assured. I should therefore relax and play a full part in life around the garrison to help ensure that the British element was seen to be making a significant contribution to life in the garrison. Shortly afterwards, I was summoned to see the American General who wanted me to create a soccer programme as a replacement for American football for which the essential kit had not arrived. This I did with the help of the Italian officer who worked alongside me, and a couple of Turkish soldiers who spoke English. Before too long we had matches arranged between the Americans and the game was proving very popular, so much so that I arranged for a representative team to play the local Turkish school. We got thumped but the venture was a great success for public relations. Overleaf is an article which appeared in a local newspaper:

An amusing aside to this whole matter occurred when I was standing in the queue at the Base Exchange (shop) one morning when I overheard two American women discussing the soccer program *(sic)*. It went something like this: First woman, "Yeha, my son is playing; he is coached by some Italian and seems to like it." Second woman,

Izmir AYA select soccer team

The Izmir, Turkey, AYA select soccer team is comprised of the best players from the 11 competing youth teams. Members pictured are (kneeling from left) Earl Cheney, Sam Jordan, Mike Johnson, Tony Bruno, Anthony Gaviola, John Stringle and Dan Nagley. Standing (from left) are coach Ian Vaughan-Arbuckle, Gerry Thomason, Earl Williams, Derek Washington, Mark Catan, Neil Clark, Mark Rankin, and Tim Blaymeir. Not pictured is Mark Queen.

No-show grid gear raised problem
Soccer proved popular substitute

IZMIR, Turkey — "When in Turkey, do as the Turks do."

That could well be the motto of the American Youth Activities (AYA) program here which found a unique way to put the old cliché into practice.

When new football equipment, ordered earlier in the year, failed to arrive this fall, the AYA was faced with the possibility of no competitive sports for children ages 6-14 this season. But this American community of 3,000 decided that the children needed something, and so the idea of fielding a soccer team was born.

Response was to the idea was immediate. Some 150 boys and girls were enrolled and assigned to 11 teams in three divisions.

Equipment, in the form of uniforms, balls and nets were purchased locally. Turkey, a country where soccer is a household name, provided easy access to the gear.

The American community soon found an important local asset in developing the program, the people. As a part of NATO Headquarters, the Azir community was blessed with numerous English, Italian and Turkish residents who were both familiar with the game and willing to help. Within a short time, many volunteered to coach the teams and provide officiating for American youth teams.

As the season progressed, so did the ability of the American players. The Turkish communty watched the development of the team and asked if the Americans would form a team to play Necatibey, a Turkish team from a nearby school. The Americans agreed and the game was scheduled.

Before an enthusiastic crowd of Americans and Turks, with the Turkish press in attendance, the Americans battled the Turks to 0-0 tie. As a result of their performance, the Azir American soccer team, born just a few months ago, now was recieving more offers from Turkish children's teams, requesting competition.

The Azir team is taking a holiday break but hopes to resume play next spring when more than 200 American youngsters will do as their Turkey counterparts have been doing a long time — playing soccer.

"M'boy likes it also. His coach has a funny name with two parts. We reckon he's Turkish but don't rightly know." I took a certain pleasure in being able to put them right – that I was, in fact, British! Through Facebook, I have since been contacted by a couple of the former Izmir All Stars who, encouragingly, continued playing soccer as they grew up and are now dedicated supporters of the game. It was while coaching the American children that I realised the difference in our two ways of speaking English. In an attempt to gain control of the children, I blew my whistle and told them to 'pick up your boots and form a queue in front of me'. To my astonishment no-one moved. My assistant, a American sergeant shouted, "Pick up your cleats and get into line." The reaction was instant!

The Turkish Army is generally credited with playing a major role in the founding of the Turkish Republic. Kemal Ataturk himself rose to prominence through the military establishment and, as Inspector-General of the Army in Anatolia, rallied troops and patriotic groups to the independence movement. The fighting qualities of the Turkish soldier *(asker)* are legendary as Gallipoli, the War of Independence and Korea have testified. Strong, tough and fatalistic, the *asker* has proved himself a significant adversary by accepting courage as the norm and despising weakness. Discipline in the Army is harsh and uncompromising. I witnessed summary punishment in the corridor of the headquarters when an officer repeatedly slapped an *asker* across his face while the soldier stood to attention and took it. When I enquired what had prompted this treatment, I was matter-of-factly told that the soldier had answered the officer back, something that was totally unacceptable in the Turkish Army. Another incident, I know to be fact, involved a Turkish unit opposing the Greeks in Cyprus. A friend of mine, who was serving as a UN observer, witnessed a Turkish soldier being executed by firing squad. During a subsequent liaison visit to the unit concerned, he enquired about the circumstances leading to the execution, and was told that the *asker* had been found asleep at his post, on active service – a crime punishable by death!

With history everywhere, it is tempting to portray Turkey as a somewhat quaint, backward country that adheres to tradition, but this is far from the truth. What we saw was a healthy combination of ancient tradition and contemporary outlook. Modern Turkish ways are tempered by Islam and time-honoured traditions of hospitality. Turks are fiercely patriotic. I shall never forget the visit of West Bromwich Albion to play a Turkish team in the European football competition. The local stadium held 60,000 fanatical Turks who screamed threateningly at the British team whenever they got the ball. There was a brigade of Turkish troops (3,000 men) on duty to enforce the law that evening.

Turkey, particularly the west coast along the Aegean Sea south of Izmir, is remarkably rich in the remains of antiquity. Many sights we visited come to mind such as Pergamum, Miletus (where we bought a *kilim*), Didyma and Troy – but it was Ephesus which has left the most vivid

Ephesus amphitheatre

The Library of Celsus, Ephesus

lasting memory for me. The history of Ephesus can be traced to the Bronze Age, but it is the Roman period which really demands attention. I particularly remember standing at the very top of the amphitheatre listening, with great clarity, to Angelika speaking in a normal voice from the stage.

A part of Ephesus I remember well is The Library of Celsus built c AD 125. Celsus paid for the construction of the library with his own personal wealth and is buried in a sarcophagus beneath it. Designed with an exaggerated entrance, the building faces east so that the reading rooms could make best use of the morning light. We were there in the morning and I remember vividly the large bird of prey swooping down to pick up a sizeable snake with its talons from the front of the building and flying off as the snake wriggled furiously in trying to free itself.

We also visited Mary's House, purported to have been the last home of Mary, mother of Jesus, a few kilometres from Ephesus where we had a meal sitting under an olive tree, perhaps the one illustrated in the picture below. It is a popular place of Catholic pilgrimage which has been visited by recent Popes. On the way, an amusing sign outside a shack on the side of a dusty road caught our attention: it read: *Hier kocht Mutter* – or, for those who don't speak German: 'Mother cooks here' – testimony to the influence of former Turkish *Gastarbeiter* (guest workers) in Germany.

Mary's House

When the girls joined us for their holidays we had some great times. They loved the warm weather, the swimming, shopping with Angelika in the American facilities and generally experiencing a completely different way of life. It was always very sad seeing them off from Izmir for a flight to Istanbul, where they would be met and chaperoned by British Airways staff to catch the flight to London. At London, they would be met by a car and driven back to school at Midhurst. I know they enjoyed the notoriety, among their peers, of spending their holidays in a country like Turkey. I remember well my emotions welling-up inside me as I said goodbye to a tearful and seemingly vulnerable Claire. I should not have worried as I now know just what a tough 'cookie' she was. We all thoroughly enjoyed going out in the evening for a meal together on the Izmir waterfront. Lamb kebab, yogurt and green salad, for me washed down with a pint (or two) of cold Effes beer, was our favourite. During a camping holiday together with the other 'Brits' a tragedy was narrowly avoided. The girls, who were all competent swimmers, were playing in the water in no harm whatever. Next thing I saw was Vivian waving from a Lillo. At first I thought she was just waving 'hello' but as her waving continued and after shouting for her to come in, I realised she was being swept out to sea by a gusty wind. Not a strong enough swimmer to rescue her myself, I sought help from a friend. He brought her back safely none the worse for wear although a little shocked. It was during our time in Turkey that Vivian, who was (and still is) a classical beauty, had her first boyfriend, the son of pleasant American colleague of mine. I remember the surprise of seeing Viv holding hands with this boy at an American football game. On seeing me, Vivian blushed bright pink but, to her credit, she held on to his hand! Claire too developed an interest in boys, not Americans but local shoe-shine boys. She seemed to be fascinated by them and their way of life. Coming from the poorer districts of Izmir, where often there was no electricity or running water, these boys worked 7 days a week earning a paltry £1.50 – £2.50 for a day's hard graft. Claire pestered us to allow her to bring a shoe-shine box back to the UK. Fortunately we could find no room in our baggage allowance to accommodate such a large item.

Shoe-shine boys

Running to keep fit was a part of my life in Turkey, although the danger from wild dogs which might have been carriers of Rabies was always present. My regular running partner in those days was a Lieutenant Colonel Giovanni Peppini a member of the elite Italian Alpini Regiment, the equivalent to our SAS. I wrote this article (overleaf) for *Reader's Digest* magazine without knowing whether it was ever published in the US.

It was with some surprise when an order was issued by the American General that no running was allowed in the town. This

"The early bird catches the worm".

For the past year or so, I have been running every morning with an Italian friend of mine, Giovanni Papini, along the waterfront in down town Izmir, Turkey.

During this time, we have had to contend with a variety of hazards including attacks by stray dogs, abuse from the locals, the dangers of unmarked potholes and over zealous pigeons to say nothing of the discomfort of the extremely high humidity experienced in this part of the world. However, most of these would be classified as 'ordinary' by runners and pale into insignificance when compared with our most recent encounter.

It was 5.50 am. We were on our third mile of the normal four when a taxi drew up alongside us and a moderately pretty girl leaned out of the window to comment "You crazy people" to which we responded with our normal friendly wave and smile.

The taxi then moved off but stopped again about 200 yards further on. As we drew level the same girl enquired "You crazy men where are you going?" but before we had time to answer she said "I like to look you-you like nice time with me-we go now?"

All things considered we had to reject the girls offer but agreed that there must, after all, be some thing in the adage "It is the early bird that catches the worm!"

Ian M Vaughan-Arbuckle.

followed the assassination of an American soldier who was shot in the back while out walking in uniform in the town. Giovanni and I decided to ignore the order on the basis that it applied only to Americans. A few days later, I was summoned, along with Giovanni, to see the General, having been spotted by him out running that morning. Explaining that I thought the order applied only to Americans, the General asked to see the order and had to agree that the wording was loose enough to create doubt as to whether we had deliberately disobeyed an order. In truth, I had taken a calculated risk because I thought (as, incidentally, did the senior British officer) that the order was daft.

Militarily, life was pretty dull, although I did take part in a couple of NATO test exercises, one in Naples and another in Erzurum, bordering the USSR, both very different in content and approach. In Naples, it was civilised and well organised by the Italians, whereas the same could not be said for Erzurum, which was staged by the Turkish General Staff. After a welcoming reception and dinner, the vast majority of delegates, including the American general and his senior staff, were struck down overnight with food poisoning. This left the field open to the Turks, and those who remained free of infection by not eating the meat, to run proceedings. I was not alone in wondering whether it had been a dastardly plot to undermine American morale. The net result was that the exercise was run by a Belgium officer for three of the five days. That apart, I remember two other aspects of the exercise. The first was confirmation of the toughness of the Turkish soldier who was operating in below-freezing conditions wearing uniforms which would not have looked out of place during the Second World War, and using weapons which were equally antiquated. The second was the flight back to Izmir using Turkish Airlines (TA). As usual with TA, the flight did not take off until the aircraft was full. One of the last seats to be filled was the one next to me. To my utter amazement, the seat was eventually occupied by an unshaven Turk wearing traditional dress, with a mouthful of gold and carrying a bird of prey on his arm! The body odour and associated smells from him and the bird were revolting, not improved by the fact that his bird kept blinking at me! About halfway into the flight, we passed through a seriously frightening electric storm with the aircraft lurching, shaking and dropping like a stone as it ploughed its way onward. After about fifteen minutes of sheer terror, the aircraft settled down. As the wheels touched down on tarmac at Izmir, the passengers broke out in simultaneous applause, more in a gesture of relief than any compliment to the captain who should have surely avoided the storm. But then avoidance of trouble is not part of the Turkish psyche!

About a month or so before we were due to leave Turkey, Arafat Beyaz called me into his office and said, "You come dinner with wife at my house tonight?" This was totally unexpected as I had rather given up hope of him reciprocating our hospitality. I replied that I was otherwise engaged that night, to which he said quizzically, "Tomorrow?" "That would be fine," I said, adding, "What time would you like to see us?" "I send car 6 pm for you so you can drink with me." Rather unconventional, I thought, but a great compliment since, as far as I knew, no other foreign officer had ever been to his house. I had no idea what to expect and told Angelika so when she asked me what to wear.

The car arrived and fifteen minutes later we were at his flat on the other side of town. His wife, a rather dumpy woman with a warm smile who spoke no English, welcomed us into their sparsely furnished sitting room. As an aperitif, we were given a 'shot' of *raki*, a Turkish unsweetened, anise-flavoured, hard alcoholic drink. This was followed almost immediately by a buffet consisting of numerous dishes of delicious food including a variety of cheeses, hummus, yogurt, green salad, kebabs, *yufka* bread, and a number of sweet dishes to finish. This was washed down with beer with a strong black coffee to finish. After eating, Arafat produced photographs taken at various stages of his career with him carefully explaining the circumstances of each. It was a fascinating insight into his career, his personal view on many topics, including the position of the Army in Turkey and what he thought about Americans – which was not what they would have wanted to hear. His wife played little part in the conversation. The drink kept flowing throughout the evening so that by the time we left, well after midnight, I was feeling no pain! After that evening, my relationship with Arafat became far closer; it was as though a barrier had been broken down so that we were now able to enjoy a laugh together, and I felt much more relaxed with him.

About a week before we were due to leave, Arafat called me into his office and asked, "What you take out of Turkey?" He meant antiquities, rugs and anything else which could have caused problems since there existed very strict rules about taking anything of historical value from the country. I told him that I had been collecting swords and daggers, and that I had about twenty which I intended taking with me. "OK, I come with you to boat and you have no trouble." True to his word, he was at the dock, in full uniform, to ensure that we had a hassle-free departure. As I reflected on our relationship, I have regretted that it was only in the latter stages of my time working for him that we established mutual respect and understanding. My time in Turkey would have been so much more rewarding in many ways, had I felt able to seek his views and advice earlier on.

No visit to Turkey would be complete without visiting Istanbul. We went there for a few days and marvelled at the wealth of treasures and diversity in this great city, for so long the gateway to Europe. We visited the Sultan Ahmed Mosque, colloquially known as the Blue Mosque for the blue tiles that adorn its inner walls, Topkapi Palace, Hagia Sophia Museum and the Grand Bazaar, one of the largest and oldest in the world.

As a military man, I had to visit the Ataturk Museum dedicated to the life of Mustafa Kemal Ataturk, founder of the Republic of Turkey. It is located in the house Ataturk rented and where he lived with his mother and sister until May 1919. The museum houses personal belongings of Ataturk, clothes, historical documents, personal collections, photographs and paintings.

The only British naval officer in Turkey, who was an expert on the Gallipoli Campaign, April 1915-January 1916, organised a tour of the battlefields which we went on.

Grand Bazaar, Istanbul

It was a simply riveting experience to see, at first hand, some of the key places fought over at the time. After the failure of the naval offensive, ground forces were sent to secure the Gallipoli Peninsular without really appreciating what they were in for.

The British forces (not including Australian and New Zealand) tried to land at five points around Cape Helles but met fierce opposition and established successful footholds on only three of them before asking for reinforcements. Meanwhile the Turks took advantage of the British halt to bring as many troops as possible onto the peninsula. Amid sweltering heat and disease-ridden conditions, the deadlock dragged on into the summer of 1915. I well remember standing at the point known as W Beach and being able to visualise the terrible carnage that took place there.

Early one day, the Lancashire Fusiliers started to disembark from a converted merchant ship down a gangplank into small boats

W Beach, Gallipoli

before heading toward the beach. The Turks, who had two machine guns in enfilade, one on either side of the beach, held their fire until they were able to target the maximum number of British soldiers, as they embarked and disembarked. When they did open fire, they cut down huge numbers of British soldiers.

At one point, the pilot of a spotter plane reported back that the sea was bright red from the blood of British soldiers. The Lancashire Fusiliers lost 600 men that day. Showing great courage, the Fusiliers eventually silenced the Turkish guns, and in doing so, were awarded six Victoria Crosses, all before breakfast! W Beach was only one of many such actions that took place that terrible summer. Turkish soldiers under the command of Lieutenant-Colonel Mustafa Kemal (who was later to lead his country) fought like tigers. Faced with only bayonets with which to repel their enemies, Mustafa Kemal issued the following order: *"I do not order you to fight. I order you to die. Until the time passes until we die, other troops and commanders can come forward and take our places."* After visiting various places where action took place, we visited the British Cemetery at Cape Helles where hundreds of British soldiers are buried. The place is immaculately maintained by the War Graves Commission, and provides a fitting and poignant memorial to those who fell. There are many such places on the Cape Helles Peninsular.

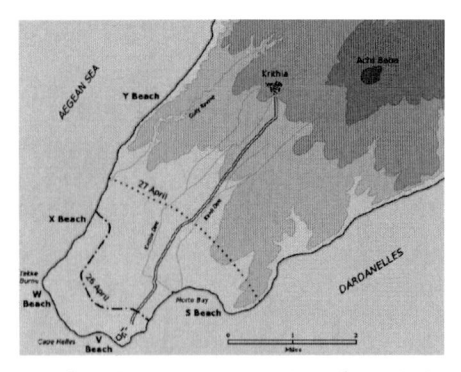

At the end of my tour of eighteen months, I left Turkey with mixed feelings. My job was not particularly challenging but my tour ended on a happy note when I was selected for promotion to Lieutenant-Colonel. We made some good friends, we had lived in a country full of ancient history, and I had had the privilege and pleasure of serving alongside military men from different countries. Towards the end of my tour, I wrote an article for the *British Army Review* (Number 63, December 1979) entitled *Landsoutheast – The Fragile Flank,* which considered Turkey's strategic importance and her ability to meet the threat to NATO's south-eastern flank. The piece drew to the attention of people who've never had to suffer for an idea or fight for a patch of land, to the passion of ordinary Turks for their country. Things have now moved on. Headquarters Land South East no longer exists – and today Turks find their outlet, not in martial ardour but in simple pleasures: family, food, music, football and friendship.

12: COMMAND WITHIN THE TERRITORIAL ARMY

I was appointed to command a Territorial Army (TA) Regiment, known as 156 Transport Regiment, Royal Corps of Transport. Split between Liverpool and Manchester, with a theoretical strength of around 1,100 personnel, the regiment was one of the largest TA units in the Army. I say 'theoretical' because, due to poor recruiting, it was well below that figure when I took command. As anyone who has lived in that part of Britain will know, the basic character of the Scouse (Liverpudlian) and Mancunian is very different: that is in addition to the fierce rivalry which exists between the football teams of these two great cities! Being a lifelong supporter of Manchester United was, I thought, going to prove a tricky path to tread, with the majority of my soldiers coming from Liverpool, but I need not have worried. I must admit to being somewhat disappointed when I first heard about my new job as, being a former pupil at the junior leaders' unit and, essentially, a practical soldier, I would have been ideal to command the Junior Leaders' Regiment which was 'up for grabs' at the time. As it transpired, however, I need have no anxieties, for the challenges which faced me during my 2½ years in the North West were almost certainly more interesting than had I been made responsible for the training of junior leaders. As commanding officer, I would be responsible for training the regiment to meet its war role, to lead them in war should that happen and, in a unique and very personal way, be totally responsible for their success or failure. A humbling task but one to which I was enthusiastically looking forward.

The TA is the spare time volunteer force of the British Army, sometimes known as 'Terriers' or 'Part Timers'. With around 35,500 members, the TA forms about a quarter of the overall manpower strength of the British Army. TA soldiers regularly volunteer to serve overseas on operations, either with TA units, or as individuals attached to regular units. Over one thousand TA soldiers are deployed overseas on operations each year. TA members have a minimum commitment to serve 27 training days per annum. This period normally includes a two-week period of continuous training either as a (TA) unit, on

| Never a Dull Moment

courses, or attached to a regular unit. While engaged on military activities, territorial soldiers are paid at a similar rate as their regular equivalents.

I arrived in Liverpool on a Sunday in September 1979. During the fourteen-day handover of the regiment from Cecil Tanner, with whom I had previously served in Germany, I lived in the Liverpool garrison Officers' Mess. Angelika joined me after I took over the 'tied' married quarter we were allocated in Larkhill Lane, Formby, close to the red squirrel reserve and on the edge of Formby Sands, a beautiful spot on the Lancashire coastline, much sought after by the elite of Liverpool. At this time the girls were still happily settled at St Margaret's. We soon had an addition to the family in the form of 'Whisky', a West Highland Terrier. A grand little dog, plucky, headstrong and highly intelligent, he was to be part of us for fourteen happy years. Having been spoilt for walks in Formby, Whisky loved nothing more than walking. I well remember taking him up Scafell Pike on a cold winter's day, so cold in fact that he started to shiver uncontrollably so I had to put him in my rucksack for the downward journey.

'Whisky' on Scafell Pike, painted by Jennifer Bell

One of the visits we made during the handover was to Lord Derby (Edward John Stanley, 18th Earl of Derby MC) at Knowsley Hall in Liverpool. At that time, Lord Derby was Chairman of the Territorial

| 236 |

Army Association and made a point of meeting all new commanding officers to Liverpool. With a strong military background, Lord Derby had been awarded the Military Cross for actions while serving in Italy with the Grenadier Guards. He knew a great deal about the Army and had served in the TA.

Knowsley Hall, Liverpool

We arrived on time and were shown into the drawing room by the butler who said, "His Lordship apologises for being delayed but will be with you shortly, gentlemen. In the meantime, please do make yourselves comfortable." We sat down feeling somewhat awkward in the enormous room dominated by portraits of Lord Derby's ancestors – who seemed to be viewing us with a certain disdain – surrounded by priceless pieces of furniture and antiques. I could not help noticing a trolley of drinks was in evidence. Lord Derby arrived about five minutes later, apologising profusely for keeping us waiting. After the introductions, he invited us to help ourselves to a drink from the drinks trolley. I did not normally drink spirits but noticed that it was basically a choice between whisky and gin or a soft drink. I went for the gin and picked up a small bottle of tonic water as a mixer. Lord Derby was clearly observing me as I searched for a bottle opener and asked, "Can I help?" When I replied that I was looking for an opener, he said, "It's clearly a long time since you had a gin as all bottles of tonic now have screw tops." My embarrassment must have been palpable but after a good chuckle we spent about half an hour discussing the TA before the butler came in and discreetly reminded Lord Derby that he had another appointment. We left.

During the handover, I came to the conclusion that the regiment was efficient and effective but it seemed to lack *esprit de corps* or, put another way, morale – defined by Alexander Leighton as 'the capacity of a group of people to pull together persistently and consistently in pursuit of a common purpose'. Morale is a fundamental responsibility of any CO, since from that everything else will flow. My view on the state of the regiment was shared by Donald Gibbs who had been the Honorary Colonel (the ceremonial head of the regiment) for many years. He had served with the King's Regiment during the war and held a number of civic positions in Manchester. He was the Chief Executive of Broughton House, a residential home for ex-servicemen in Manchester. During our initial discussions, I told him that my priority was to get the regiment up to its full strength by making soldiering challenging and fun – in other words something people wanted to be a part of. He agreed and told me that, in his view, the four squadrons (three in Liverpool and one in Manchester), which made up the regiment, to a large degree did their own thing. They largely acted independently without direction. I was determined to change this. If we were a regiment in name, we should be seen and act as such, not a group of squadrons thrown together for operational reasons only.

Soon after taking over as Commanding Officer (CO), I spent a whole weekend visiting the units and meeting as many people as possible. By the time I had reached my final destination, the headquarters, I was tired from meeting vast numbers of people and talking incessantly. In the car park there was a soldier underneath his vehicle carrying out some maintenance. I bent down to speak to him and, after asking him a couple of things about himself, I said, "Do you enjoy the TA?" This brought an immediate response. He came out from under the truck, sat upright, looked me in the eye and replied, "Do I enjoy the TA? Corse I f…ing do – I wouldn't be here if I didn't enjoy it!" Hearing this, the Regimental Sergeant-Major who had been with me throughout the weekend, started to lambast the soldier for addressing me in that manner. I interrupted and thanked the soldier for being frank. This soldier's answer to a rather stupid question taught me an immediate and very valuable principle of volunteer soldiering: that is, if the soldiers did not enjoy what they were doing, they would quickly resign from the TA. I never forgot that principle during my time with the TA.

As I settled into the job, it became more and more apparent to me that the squadron in Manchester wanted to retain their self-styled independence rather than adopt my ethos of being part of the regiment. I spoke to the squadron commander, who was an executive in the insurance world, about this and asked him to embrace my directive. He agreed. Soon afterwards, however, I attended a regimental dinner in Manchester where I was formally welcomed by the squadron commander in his speech, as a guest along with the other guests of the evening. Being treated as a guest in my own regiment was the last straw! After discussing the matter with the Honorary Colonel, I sacked the squadron commander. Not a pleasant thing to have to do but essential if I was to achieve my plans for the regiment. I appointed a new squadron commander who was fully behind my plans and very soon the Manchester squadron became a leading 'player' in the regiment.

The regiment's war role was to fly into Germany, draw up reserve vehicles held in depots, and distribute ammunition to British units. The task was complex and required detailed plans for the many phases involved. I decided to put the plans to the test and, accordingly, the regiment went to Germany in the summer of 1981 to practise its war role. Flights were arranged from Speke Airport to move 600 men to Germany. From there, some were transported to various depots to draw the vehicles while others moved directly to a field base we established in southern Germany. From there we spent the next ten days or so delivering live loads of ammunition, as though in war, all over the British Zone. There were small packets of our vehicles on the move all over West Germany. The exercise was a great success. The soldiers performed brilliantly and were a great credit to themselves and the regiment. I was delighted and proud to be leading them. I had told everyone that there was to be no drinking of alcohol until after the task had been completed. Also, at their peril would they try to smuggle duty-free booze or cigarettes back into the UK on the return journey as Customs had warned me they would be hard on anyone caught trying to do so.

One day, while out and about, checking on the progress of various tasks, I came across a small 'packet' of my vehicles parked outside a *Gaststätte* (German pub) in a small village. The sentry told me that the rest of the 'lads' were inside having a 'pee'. The look on their faces when the soldiers, who were drinking beer, saw me spoke volumes! The Corporal in charge was the regiment's goalkeeper so I knew him quite well. I told him a leave and said that I would be reporting the incident to his squadron commander. Later that night he was 'up in front of me' on a disciplinary charge of disobeying an order. When I asked him whether he had anything to say, he replied, "It was a fair cop. I just thought one beer would be OK." In sentencing him to be demoted to private soldier, I wondered whether he would continue to remain in the TA. Typical of the Scouse, he took his punishment and was in goal when the regiment won the TA Football Challenge Cup the following year! As for smuggling, all was well until the last flight into Speke when a soldier was found to have 1,000 duty-free cigarettes in his rucksack. Needles to say, he received a hefty fine and left the TA; there's always one! Actually, considering the numbers involved, the discipline was excellent.

Our social life was pretty hectic. Seldom did a week go by when Angelika and I were not attending some function or hosting our own parties. Much emphasis is placed on the social and sporting side of life in the TA. Civic dinners, cocktail parties, charity 'do's, regimental dinners and private parties were a constant feature in the life of regulars serving with the TA. I particularly remember one such function. We were invited to dinner, soon after I took over the regiment, with the General who lived just outside Preston. I told my driver where we were going and to be at the house in good time. He turned up late and in the wrong dress! By the time he returned, having changed into the correct uniform, we were going to be pressed for time. We arrived about ten minutes late at the General's house to find the car park full. There was a buzz of conversation as the front door was opened by the house sergeant. Mrs Hicks, the general's wife, greeted us with the words, "Oh dear, I must have forgotten to write Black Tie on your invitation." I was dressed in a suit while Angelika was in a cocktail dress! You can imagine my embarrassment as we entered the packed room with everyone else in dinner jackets and long dresses. To her credit, Mrs Hicks admitted that the error was hers and my blushes were partly spared, even though a couple of my fellow commanding officers thought the whole thing hilarious!

Whenever we could, Angelika and I would visit an antique fair, of which there were many in the Liverpool area. It was during this time that I started collecting Sweetheart Brooches, the first being my mother's. Sweetheart brooches are basically small brooches depicting the regimental or other service crest of a soldier, sailor or airman, and were worn by military wives or girlfriends. Particularly popular around the era of the Great War (1914-18), they were often given to wives or girlfriends (hence 'sweetheart') by servicemen as mementos and reminders of their absent loves. They would be worn by the lady as a token of fealty and regard, and also to show their pride in having a husband or sweetheart who was serving his country. Whilst regimental or other service insignia are generally self-coloured base metals, it is not unusual for sweetheart brooches to be made in precious metals (silver or gold) and colourful enamels. After amassing a collection of about 150 brooches of the RASC, its predecessors and successors, when I left the Army, the collection was purchased by the RCT Museum and remains there today.

Being a transport regiment, we were tailor-made to step in whenever there was a civil crisis. The winter of 1981-82 was particularly severe. In early December and again in mid-January, heavy snow arrived and roads became impassable with local authorities unable to keep up with the demand for their services. Supplies of rock salt, at that time used to melt snow and ice from roads, ran out. The regiment, with its fleet of 16-tonne vehicles, was tasked with the job of transporting the road salt from Wales to various depots in the South West. The job took about a week to complete but left the vehicles, which were new, in a terrible state. The job of removing the salt from the vehicles took ages, with many of them having to be repainted. During the 1979-80 threatened Firemen's Strike on

Command within the Territorial Army

The Vaughan-Arbuckle collection of Military Sweetheart Brooches:

•
- These brooches were collected by Lieutenant Colonel Ian Vaughan-Arbuckle, during his service years of 1954–1987. His father also served with the Corps.

- The collection of 244 sweetheart brooches span manufacture dates of:
  - Queen Victoria
  - King George V, prolific manufacture during WWI
  - King George VI, prolific manufacture during WWII
  - and Queen Elizabeth II

and covers the history of the:
  - Army Service Corps;
  - Royal Army Service Corps; and
  - Royal Corps of Transport

| Never a Dull Moment

Merseyside, the regiment were put on stand-by to man a fleet of ancient 'Green Goddess' fire engines previously used after the war by the Auxiliary Fire Service. I was to be the Chief Fire Officer for Merseyside (perish the thought!) and spent many days with the incumbent in his office, talking through possible tasks and procedures while some of my officers and NCOs did the same at their level. I was given fire-protection clothing and a radio so I could communicate direct with the control centre. To my relief, the strike was called off and our involvement proved to be minimal.

A Green Goddess

Knowing how keen the cities of Manchester and Liverpool were on sport, and talking to the soldiers, I could not understand why the regiment had not had more sporting success. I therefore set about increasing participation in sport. In conversation with one of the senior NCOs, I discovered that there were a number of soldiers who belonged to amateur boxing clubs and that three of them had boxed at international level. Why therefore did we not have a boxing team? It seemed that no-one had ever tried, so I set about arranging a boxing evening in the presence of the Chief Constable of Merseyside, Ken Oxford, who was himself a successful boxer. The evening was a resounding success which led to the formation of a regimental team. The next year, the team went on to beat the all conquering Parachute Regiment by six bouts to five in the final of the TA competition, a very proud moment which led to a number of other boxers joining the regiment. Applying the same principle, I set about forming a cross-country team which competed locally and also had success in TA competitions. Football is a religion in both Liverpool and Manchester, so it was a surprise to me that the regiment had never won the TA Challenge Cup. With suitable encouragement and support during my first season, I let it be known that it was a priority of mine to win the cup. The next season we got to the final, only to be narrowly beaten. The following season, 1981-82, we made amends by beating the Parachute Regiment 3-1 at the Aldershot Military Stadium to win the cup: another very proud moment. The mix of interesting military training and sporting success lifted the profile of the regiment which, in turn, had a positive effect on recruiting. I recall that at one point we could boast of being well over 80% of our target strength. The wastage of soldiers leaving was also reduced, proving the adage that recruiting and retention will take care of themselves if the soldiers like the regimental 'diet'.

But it was most certainly not a question of 'all sport and no work' – far from it. Training at squadron level took place on drill nights (once a week) and at weekends. A varied and interesting training programme ensured a good turnout most weekends. Driving, our bread and butter, was a priority and hugely popular because it gave the soldiers a chance to obtain a valuable HGV 1 licence to drive heavy vehicles. I also ensured that the soldiers were properly trained in military skills like shooting, first aid and map reading, and that they were all physically fit.

Just under a year after I arrived, the regiment was given the honour of a visit by HRH Princess Alice, Duchess of Gloucester, Colonel-in-Chief of the RCT, the first TA regiment to be so honoured. On Saturday 7th June 1980, an idyllic summer's morning, Princess Alice arrived to review the regiment at Grantham. As I stood nervously at the head of the regiment drawn up on parade, I began to worry that something had gone badly wrong when her ETA had been exceeded by around ten minutes. Just as I was weighing up what to do, a small black car drove onto the parade ground. This cannot possibly be HRH, I thought, since she was to travel in a royal limousine flying the appropriate standard. To my surprise and astonishment, Princess Alice got out of the car and, after being greeted by the Lord Lieutenant of Lincolnshire, mounted the dais. After a Royal Salute, I marched

I salute HRH Princess Alice, Duchess of Gloucester, at the start of her visit

forward to invite Princess Alice to review the parade. As we got into the open-topped Land Rover, Princess Alice said, "I'm so sorry for being late but my car broke down. I do hope the driver will not get into trouble as it was not his fault. Thankfully, my police escort car was able to bring us here." Despite this slight hiccup, the parade, culminating in a march-past of 250 men and a drive-past selection of the regiment's vehicles, went off well.

Before lunch I presented Princess Alice with a Caithness Crystal Glass rose bowl inscribed with the regimental crest which she seemed to like. We then sat down to lunch in the Officers' Mess, during which I was able to reassure Princess Alice that her car had been recovered, that the driver was OK, and that it would be repaired and ready for her to travel home in. She seemed pleased. Despite all the fussy instructions, I had received before her visit, Princess Alice was totally relaxed throughout her four hours with us. She showed a genuine interest in everything we did and the people she met. One of these was my old friend from National Service days, Dr Harold Riley, the world-

From
The Lady-in-Waiting to
HRH Princess Alice,
Duchess of Gloucester

KENSINGTON PALACE, LONDON W8
Telephone 01 937 6374

9th June 1980

Dear Colonel Vaughan-Arbuckle,

Princess Alice, Duchess of Gloucester has asked me to thank you and All Ranks 156 Transport Regiment very much indeed for the beautiful Caithness glass goblet you so kindly gave her after the Parade on Saturday.

Her Royal Highness was very touched by your generosity and kindness in giving her such a lovely present and one that she will always treasure.

Her Royal Highness was very impressed by the smartness of the Parade and she was delighted to be able to meet so many of the Regiment afterwards.

Princess Alice has also asked me to thank you very much for the lovely flowers you gave her.

Yours sincerely,

Jean Maxwell-Scott

Miss Jean Maxwell-Scott CVO

Lieutenant-Colonel I.M. Vaughan-Arbuckle RCT

renowned artist who had agreed to paint an activity of the day. There was a lovely moment during the pre-lunch drinks when the Lady-in-Waiting, latterly Dame Jean Maxwell-Scott, said she had something for me. Passing me a small package, which I promptly put in my pocket, I spent the next hour wondering what it was. I should have known because there was a tradition in the regiment to give the Commanding Officer a joke present at camp. During my next visit to the loo, I found out. It was a carrot, something the lads had tried to pass me a few times without success, so they had cunningly enlisted the help of royalty to win the day and I fell for it! This prank had all the good-humoured hallmarks of a Scouse send-up which caused a good deal of fun throughout the regiment! That day, which will live on in the folklore of the Regiment, ended with a dinner-dance in Grantham. The letter I received after the visit is shown opposite.

Some months later, Harold invited Angelika and I to dinner, where we met for the first time, Ashraf, Harold's lovely wife.

Over a glass of champagne, Harold unveiled the picture he had painted of Princess Alice at Grantham which he had called 'Waiting for the Parade'. The picture, illustrated below, was of Princess Alice with her head inclined to the left watching as the parade approached.

Waiting for the Parade *by Harold Riley*

| Never a Dull Moment

The picture was a masterpiece and captured the essential moment of the day with Princess Alice radiant in her lovely dress. Such was the quality of the picture, we decided it should be presented to the Royal Corps of Transport, rather than staying in the regiment. I heard later that the Director-General thought that, because it was a view of the back of Princess Alice, it was not acceptable. To my mind this was ridiculous, proved by the fact that Princess Alice liked the painting so much that she used it for her personalised Christmas cards that year! The last time I heard, the picture was hanging in the Officers' Mess at Grantham for everyone to admire.

The Liverpool riots of July 1981 were a civil disturbance in Toxteth, an inner-city district, which arose in part from long-standing tensions between the local police and the black community. One main cause of poverty in the area was containerisation at the nearby Liverpool Docks, ending thousands of waterfront-type jobs which had been associated with the city of Liverpool for generations. With the economy in recession, unemployment in Britain was at a fifty-year high in 1981. Toxteth had one of the highest unemployment rates in the country. Over the following weekend, small disturbances erupted into full-scale rioting, with pitched battles between the police and youths in which petrol bombs and paving stones were thrown, and the police used CS gas for the first time in the UK outside Northern Ireland. In all, the rioting lasted nine days, during which one person died after being struck by a police vehicle trying to clear crowds, 468 police officers were injured, 500 people were arrested, and at least seventy buildings

Riots in Toxteth, Liverpool

were damaged so severely by fire that they had to be demolished. About 100 cars were destroyed, and there was extensive looting of shops. Such was the scale of the rioting in Toxteth that police reinforcements were drafted in from Cumbria, Birmingham and Devon to try to control the unrest. The subsequent Scarman Report recognised that the riots did represent the result of social problems, such as poverty and deprivation. The Government responded by sending Michael Heseltine, as 'Minister for Merseyside' to set up the Merseyside Task Force and launch a series of initiatives, including Kevin Keegan setting up a programme of activities for the youth. This included football for the underprivileged. I attended a meeting and offered help which Keegan refused on the grounds that he did not want the Army involved!

Serving with the TA meant that the regular staff worked most weekends and had Monday off. I spent the occasional Monday morning playing golf at Formby Golf Club with Gavin Mackay who commanded the Signals Regiment. Very few played golf on a Monday so we usually had the course to ourselves. We were therefore surprised to see a group of four lads ahead of us but soon realised they were just fooling around on the links. We warned them that it was dangerous to play on the course and that, anyway, they were trespassing. All was well until the 15th hole, which is a 'blind' drive. In other words, it is not possible to see much of the fairway from the tee. I drove off and the ball disappeared over the hillock which straddled the fairway. There was a shout from the direction in which I had hit the ball. Almost immediately, one of the boys, whom we had seen earlier, appeared waving his arms, shouting that another boy had been hit. Both Gavin and I ran to the scene where we saw a boy lying on the ground. His face was ashen grey with my golf ball lying close by. The boys pulse was very shallow. I could not see any mark on him until, in the process of turning him over, I noticed blood oozing from behind his ear. I now know that where the ball had hit him is one of the most dangerous places on the body. The boy's heart stopped. I started administering CPR while Gavin ran back to the club house to call an ambulance. A trickle of blood appeared from the corner of the boy's mouth. I continued CPR but to no avail. Sometime later the ambulance arrived and the boy was taken away. I heard later that he was declared dead at Southport Hospital. Months later, Gavin and I appeared at the Southport Coroner's Court where the incident was examined. In his summing up, the Coroner said the affair had been a terrible tragedy and totally exonerated me from any blame while acknowledging that we had done our best to save the boy's life. I remember the Coroner saying, "Golf courses are very dangerous places and not somewhere to

| Never a Dull Moment

Service of Remembrance 1981 at the graveside of R.G. Masters VC, St Cuthbert's Church, Southport

Lord Leverhulme and Lt. Col. Arbuckle arrive at the George Masters centre for the official opening.

Freedom day for volunteers

VOLUNTEER soldiers were given the Freedom of the Borough of Sefton at the weekend.

The Mayor, Councillor Bill Bullen, handed over to the Commander of 156 Transport Regiment, Lieutenant-Colonel I. V. Arbuckle, a casket containing the freedom scroll.

It is the 238 (Sefton) Squadron of the Royal Corps of Transport Volunteer Regiment which has been given the Freedom.

The award entitles the Squadron to march through the streets on all ceremonial occasions with colours flying, bands playing and bayonets fixed.

Bootle Council granted the Freedom of the Borough in 1948 to the Old 40 Royal Tank Regiment and Southport did the same in 1953 to the 22 Column RASC.

After the Freedom ceremony and accompanied by the staff band of the Royal Corps of Transport, the Squadron marched to Strand Road for the formal opening of a brand new TA Centre.

There, Colonel The Viscount Leverhulme, President of the TA Association (North West) and IoM, unveiled a commemorative plaque.

The new centre which will house the 300-strong squadron and its equipment, is to be known as The George Masters Centre.

It honours the memory of the late George Masters, who while serving with the Army Service Corps, was awarded the Victoria Cross at Bethune in 1918.

One of the most interesting spectators of Saturday's ceremony was George's youngest brother, John, now approaching 90, of Forest Road, Southport.

"It brought back many memories," said John. "One of my brothers served in the Dardanelles during the First World War. The other three of us went to France. But it was all a long time ago and George would have been 104 had he lived till now."

| 248 |

be fooling around." The story got into the national press. Over a year later, I answered the door to a lady I did not recognise. She introduced herself as the mother of the boy who had been killed. She wanted to thank me for trying to save her only son, and to tell me that she had recently given birth to a healthy boy; she thought I would like to know. This news enabled me to bring closure to the matter.

Shortly after taking over the regiment, I discovered that a holder of the Victoria Cross and Croix de Guerre, Private Richard George Masters, of the Royal Army Service Corps – a predecessor of the RCT – and a native of Southport, was buried somewhere on Merseyside. When his grave was found, it was in a terrible state and clearly never visited. I had the grave refurbished and set about finding surviving members of his family. A simple ceremony of remembrance at his graveside, at St Cuthbert's Church, Southport, is held annually on the anniversary of his death every 4th April.

The Sefton squadron occupied a TA Centre which was built around the time of the First World War when horses were used for moving materials. I managed to persuade the powers that these old, dilapidated premises needed replacing, and within eighteen months a brand-new, state-of-the-art TA Centre in Bootle was ready for occupation. It was decided to name the centre after George Masters VC, a fitting tribute to a fine local soldier. It was around the same time that the squadron was awarded the Freedom of Sefton, an honour they accepted with a formal ceremony and march through the town.

As the time drew near for me to move on, I realised that we needed to buy another house, having sold the one we owned in Haslemere at the time I was posted to Turkey. East Anglia, which was not yet popular and where prices were reasonable, seemed to be the place of the future. I started looking around guessing that my next job might well be at Grantham. Talking houses at some party or other, someone asked me whether I had ever looked in the *Exchange and Mart*. This had never crossed my mind, as I thought the magazine was for everything bar houses. To my surprise, in the very first copy I bought, a house was advertised in Hilgay, a Norfolk village. The advert read something like this:

> Norfolk Village. Two semi-detached workers' cottages converted into one house by private builder. 4 beds, kitchen/breakfast room, dining room, large sitting room, cellar room, 2 baths, double garage and parking, ¼ acre garden. Original features retained. £34,000.

| Never a Dull Moment

I called the number immediately. Yes, the advert was authentic and, no, there had been no other enquiries. Could you please send me a plan? "Sorry, I don't have a plan but I can send you a sketch," replied the man in a broad Norfolk accent. The plan duly arrived and we decided to go and see the place for ourselves. It rained incessantly all the way down through the Derbyshire hills and into Lincolnshire. As we drove over the Fens, Angelika announced, "I'm not living here; this is a most depressing place." I had to agree that it was flat, without trees, and the villages looked forlorn.

All that changed as we drove through Downham Market, only three miles from Hilgay, a nice, rather quaint, small market town having its own railway station on the main line to London, a golf course and other essential amenities. We drove into Hilgay and stopped at the garage where we were served by a most pleasant man who, within a conversation of no more than ten minutes, had given us a complete rundown on the village. As we were about to leave he said, "Nice talking with you. I do hope you finish up buying the house." What a change from the sort of abrupt manner usually prevalent in Liverpool! It did not take me long to realise that this house was a real bargain, particularly after the builder had dropped his price to £31,500 after only a hint from me that we could be interested. He also offered to incorporate any modifications we wanted, like a firebox grate and the original door and window furniture. We shook hands there and then and drove back to Merseyside feeling very pleased with our days' work.

My hunch that my next posting would be to Grantham was correct. The social lead-up to my departure was frantically busy. I visited all four squadrons where I was royally entertained, including a regimental dinner, during which I was presented with a silver salver by the officers – a prized personal possession. When a

Commanding Officer

| 250 |

CO takes over, it is normal to display a photograph of the new man so that soldiers get used to recognising him. Under one such photo of me, a 'wag' had written 'Wacha wak', meaning 'Hello, mate' in Scouse. It took me over a year of nagging to have all but one of these photos removed as, by then, I thought everyone should know me. If not, I was not doing my job. The one that remained was in the Bootle TA Centre, which stayed there throughout my time. As we arrived at the farewell dinner dance thrown by the Sergeants, there at the top of the stairs was this wretched photograph with the caption 'Tera La' which, in Scouse, means 'Goodbye, lad' – to which the Regimental Sergeant-Major referred, with much amusement, in his speech.

All officers aspire to commanding their regiment and I was no different. There were plenty of challenges and I worked hard to ensure that the regiment was successful, respected and that the soldiers enjoyed what they were doing. It is a privilege to be given command and one which I thoroughly enjoyed.

My tour in command came to an end in April 1982 and, as I had predicted, I was posted to Prince William of Gloucester Barracks, Grantham, as Chief of Staff, to establish a brand-new headquarters, working directly for a Brigadier, to oversee all training for TA units in the RCT, numbering at that time about 6,000 volunteers. For the first year, I spent the majority of my time setting up the headquarters, establishing procedures and issuing directives. It was very hard but worthwhile work. I lived in the Officers' Mess as the journey home of 80 miles was just too far to commute on a daily basis. But we settled into 'Clonmell' (named after my ancestral home in Ireland), and got to know the village and surrounding area. For a time, I was a member of the local golf club, but a combination of not enough time and playing with a group of farmers, with whose drinking habits I could not keep pace, decided me to leave.

The telephone rang in my office one morning and the caller introduced himself as Dr Paul Garner. He said that Angelika had miscarried overnight but she was now resting at home. I was completely taken aback as I had no idea that she was pregnant. I told the doctor, who subsequently became a very close friend, that I would be home later that day as I was in the middle of something important. Being what I now know as a plain-speaking Yorkshire man, Paul made it clear that I should drop everything and come home immediately: I did. Why Angelika never told me she was pregnant in the first place I never really understood. Happily, she recovered fully. During this period, Vivian was working hard towards her A Levels, while Juliet made her war towards O Levels – and Claire took to meeting the local lads in the bus shelter!

| Never a Dull Moment

John Walton looks at the new battlefield trainer aimed at putting the RCT's part-timers on the right road

LEARNING TO ROLL WITHOUT WHEELS

A BRAND NEW command and control trainer, in which the Territorial Army members of the Royal Corps of Transport can practise their war role of moving supplies without the expense and time of setting up a full weekend outdoor exercise, has opened at the RCT TA Headquarters at Grantham, Lincolnshire.

The new trainer, based on a formerly derelict building which had at one time been an RAF roller rink, will be available for use by the RCT's 13 TA regiments and ten non-regimented sub-units and Brigadier Ron Jenkins, Commander of the RCT TA, predicts that it will be in use for three weeks in every four. First bookings for 36-hour weekend exercises have already been made for the autumn.

Brigadier Jenkins declared: "We have felt for a long time that because the TA have so little time for training we needed to provide a stimulus so that in a short period of time they could simulate an exercise without taking troops on to the ground."

The trainer is based on the original concept already implemented at Sennelager and Bovington for teeth arms but it is the first time the principles have been applied by the British Army to logistics and Brigadier Jenkins believes it may be a world first.

Lieutenant-Colonel Ian Vaughan-Arbuckle, Chief of Staff at the HQ and WO 1 David Mycroft, the project officer, visited Bovington before starting the project. Their brief was to set up a facility to develop and practise in a realistic environment RCT battle drills and operational procedures for command control skills at regimental, squadron and troop level.

Some £50,000 was spent on the deserted building to create the control centre and communications room. The trainer also uses four old air raid shelters around the camp as command posts for squadron headquarters and three non-running vehicles as regimental headquarters and also as what is jocularly known as the 'sin bin'.

Lieutenant-Colonel Vaughan-Arbuckle explains this vehicle's role as being part of the realism of an exercise. "It will house people moving away from locations. For instance, if the CO calls an 'O' group and it's going to take half an hour for them to get from their notional locations

Pictures: Les Wiggs

battlefield procedures and field exercises are expensive and time consuming. Colonel Vaughan-Arbuckle believes that the trainer provides far more realistic training than command post exercises which also take a lot of preparation. "We aim to cut out the purely telephone battle" he says.

At present there is only one 36-hour exercise scenario. The large map in the centre of the control room covers an area stretching from Grantham in the south to beyond the Humber in the north. The exercising unit has to get supplies from the south to the infantry in the north. But other scenarios will follow for both UK and Rhine Army locations.
continued opposite

Will the call be put through? ▼

L/Cpl Maggie Day puts another vehicle load into play.

they will be in there for half an hour. Similarly, if the CO decides to move, he will go and sit in there for as long as he decides to be away."

Although the trainer is initially for the TA he believes it may have wider applications and the Regular Army might also benefit from it. But it is the TA who are most urgently in need.

"The TA have a vital role to play in defence plans. In the RCT, volunteers provide over 60 per cent of the mobilisation order of battle."

Key personnel need to be trained and practise their basic

SOME £400 worth of Lego has been used to make the vehicles and supplies which will be moved up and down the map during exercises. The man who thought of using Lego was the project officer, WO1 David Mycroft (above).

"I tried various firms to see if they made small scale vehicles of the British Forces and they didn't. Then one night my young niece and nephew, who were visiting, were playing with my boy's Lego. He's now 18 and we had fetched it down from the loft. It suddenly hit me. Lego is soldier proof and lasts for years and years."

Mr Mycroft leaves the Army at the end of July and says of the trainer: "It is my last fling. It does feel better than a normal job because I know it will be used not only by the officers and NCOs of today but those in the future and somewhere they will probably remember Mycroft having done this."

Command within the Territorial Army |

In discussion with the Brigadier, I came up with the idea of setting up an indoor trainer, using the principles employed by the RAF during the war to plot aircraft movements on a large table. As is often the case, the idea was latched upon by the Brigadier who gave me the go-ahead to progress the idea. The following article (overleaf) which appeared in *Soldier Magazine*, July 1983, tells the whole story.

It was in the summer of 1983, during a cricket match between the Officers and Senior NCOs, that I learnt that my next job was to be Commanding Officer of the Falkland Islands Logistic Battalion, about which I was pleased and excited. An operational command, something I had always dreamt of – particularly as, having been offered a vacancy on the RM Commando Course, my 'boss' said I could not be spared.

13: Falklands Aftermath

On 2nd April 1982, in an act of unprovoked aggression against British sovereign territory, Argentine forces invaded the Falkland Islands. These invasions were launched despite protracted efforts by various governments and the United Nations to persuade the Argentine Government to desist from military action. The invasion was immediately condemned by the UN Security Council in its Resolution 502. After all efforts failed to get the Argentina to withdraw its forces, it became clear that the islands would have to be retaken by force. A sizeable Task Force consisting of 28,000 men and 100 ships was despatched to the South Atlantic within seven weeks: a remarkable feat. After landing, British soldiers fought several pitched battles against an entrenched and well supplied enemy which at all times outnumbered our forces before they were brought to surrender within three and a half weeks.

The conflict resulted from the long-standing dispute over the sovereignty of the Falkland Islands and South Georgia, and the South Sandwich Islands. The most decisive factors in the land war were the high state of individual training and fitness of our soldiers, together with the leadership and initiative displayed by junior officers and NCOs. The campaign was also a triumph in logistical terms, having to be self-sufficient and at the end of an 8,000-mile line of communication from the UK. Overall, the Falklands Campaign confirmed that the British people had the will and resolve to resist aggression and the fortitude to withstand setbacks, lessons re-confirmed during subsequent campaigns, including Iraq and Afghanistan.

I described my trip to the Falklands in the Prologue. I arrived to take command of FILOG (Falkland Islands Logistic Battalion) about twenty months after the defeat and surrender of Argentine forces on the islands. What I found was a kind of vacuum, a militarily difficult situation with peace having been declared and yet a high state of readiness still invoked in case of a counter-attack by the Argentinians; we still carried arms and were subject to varying degrees of alert. British occupying forces were faced with immense logistical problems

| Never a Dull Moment

of having to ship everything from the UK to the South Atlantic. There was also the immediate task of clearing the debris of war which included, as a priority, identifying Argentinian minefields, and the rehousing of our own forces away from Stanley, capital of the Falklands. Bodies of Argentinian soldiers, together with loaded weapons, live ordnance and the detritus of war, were still being found all over the Falklands.

The role of FILOG was to provide co-ordinated logistical support to forces in the Falkland Islands, including the RN and RAF. To meet this role, the Battalion consisted of a headquarters, three squadrons, a workshop and other smaller components, a total of some 380 of all ranks, representing many corps and regiments of the British Army. In addition to its primary task, FILOG was required to be able to provide three ad hoc fighting units in the event of hostilities breaking out. This role was successfully put to the test in an exercise called, at short notice, during my time in command.

When I arrived, a part of 'my' unit was housed in Stanley, the seat of Government, and capital of the islands. Stanley had the only airfield link with the outside world although, towards the end of my tour, work had started on creating the new Mount Pleasant airfield. Stanley also possessed the only comparatively sheltered anchorage for shipping which brought down from the UK essential supplies and stores required by British forces to administer themselves. The problem was that the airfield could not accommodate large transport aircraft and the harbour had no quay suitable for ocean-going vessels.

| 256 |

Commanding Officer FILOG

Therefore, almost everything had to be lightered ashore using FILOG landing ships, wasteful in time, manpower and other resources. A plan to resolve this problem had been conceived by the time I arrived. This involved building a floating port and warehouse complex, called 'Flexiport', which provided a 'ship alongside off-loading capability'. Built in four sections by Harland & Wolff in Belfast, at a cost of £23 million, in less than two years, Flexiport was transported to the Falklands by heavy lift ships each carrying two barges across their beams. I was responsible for getting the facility 'up and running' and it was with a real sense of achievement that this revolutionary facility was opened for business by Sir Rex Hunt, the Governor, within a few weeks of arriving. The complex was estimated to have saved up to £15,000 per day through the release of chartered vessels retained for store-holding and refrigeration purposes, along with the associated military personnel, vehicles and landing craft. When I arrived, the MOD had no less than 25 merchant ships on charter to keep the forces supplied from Britain with fuel, food, supplies and stores of every description. Operating from the UK, I had to ensure we got our figures right, otherwise units would go short of the necessities of life. This was a huge responsibility which required everyone to work above and beyond the call of duty. We regularly worked a ten-hour day, seven days a week, although by the time I left all ranks had one day off per week.

| Never a Dull Moment

Falkland Islands Port & Storage System (FIPASS)

Another huge step forward was the introduction of two 'Coastels'. These were fully self-contained floating accommodation vessels designed for inshore waters and having a 'walk-on, walk-off' link to the shore. In reality, these were huge flat-topped barges carrying multi-storey accommodation of cabins for some 600 men, with washing facilities and lavatories, recreation and dining rooms and kitchens. Electric power, fresh water, heating and sewerage were on board. The one my unit occupied and which I controlled was named *Pursuivant* (5,500 tons). It was anchored in the harbour to the west of Stanley.

Meanwhile, the resident infantry units, during my tour, the Royal Scots and 7th Gurkha Rifles, were deployed throughout East and West Falkland, as were the missile and signal detachments and others. These locations required logistical support which meant I had a responsibility to visit them regularly to ensure re-supply arrangements were working smoothly. For this I had a helicopter tasked to me daily so that I could go anywhere at the drop of a hat. Some isolated two-men detachments, living under canvas over a trench on the far-flung extremities of the islands, where they spent up to six weeks at a time in charge of a Rapier missile, needed particular support to ensure they were getting what they needed – including their 'Blueys' (free aerogrammes) from home.

During my tour of duty, I worked for two Generals, each with very different styles of leadership. The first was General Keith Spacie, late of the Parachute Regiment, known for his tough, uncompromising style who made it his business to visit units without giving any prior notice. He was very much 'hands on' and fell out with the Governor, Sir Rex Hunt, when he found him visiting military units without authority. I experienced this at first hand when, one morning, Sir Rex appeared 'out of the blue' at my Workshop at Moody Brook on the outskirts of Stanley, to seek advice about his official car, a London taxi painted red, which had been playing up. The problem was solved but later, after he heard what had happened, General Spacie made it clear that he was to be called immediately if the Governor appeared alone in any of my locations. A potentially tricky situation which fortunately I never had to deal with.

Governor's official vehicle

A strict disciplinarian, General Spacie had no hesitation in sending home, in disgrace on the next plane, a junior officer he found sleeping when in command of a tactical location. He also authorised the immediate removal of a Major in my battalion whom I found asleep and hung over on board *MV Tor Caledonia*, which at the time was being used as a stores ship. The Major had been drinking – contrary to the very strict rules regarding alcohol in force at the time. General Spacie, who was a fitness fanatic, entered the Falkland Islands half-marathon and would have won had he not allowed a soldier to overtake him as they approached the finish! I also ran but never got near the General although I did subsequently race against him in the UK with more success.

General Peter de la Billière, late of the SAS, an inspiring leader whose exploits in modern times are legion, took over when I was about a third of the way into my tour. Quietly spoken but with a presence and force of personality which left no-one in doubt as to what he required, General de la B, as he was known, very soon made his mark. It wasn't long before he spent a whole day visiting FILOG. He displayed an understanding of the importance of logistics seldom seen in senior officers with an infantry background. Quick to make up his mind after listening to views, I remember explaining why large quantities of packed fuel were stored close to the petroleum depot on the Canache, the hinterland of a small bay outside Stanley. The General instructed me to relocate the packed fuel into an area well away from potential danger. This was an enormous task which, I estimated, would take about six days to complete. When I attended the General's daily orders group the following day, he asked me whether I had yet completed the move! After listening to my explanation why it would take much longer, he just said, "Get it done by close of play tomorrow, please." I did so by the skin of my teeth after diverting most of my available manpower, including myself, to the task. The General was pleased with the result. Unlike General Spacie, General de la B laid down that every man should have one day off a week and that, if possible, a programme of regular sport should be organised: it was!! One of his initiatives was to establish a successful and popular adventure training facility through which soldiers could be rotated. He also made a point of entertaining at his official residence, Britannia House – a large, prefabricated wooden villa, erected by the Argentinians, shortly before the war, to house the CEO of the Argentinian airline which was to have served the islands. The house was full of bullet holes through which water leaked. I went to dinner there soon after they arrived. He and his wife were generous hosts and it was nice to meet them in a social environment, even if we were dressed in combat fatigues!

Taking advantage of the new policy, I led a group of my soldiers on a five-day 'yomp' from Goose Green to Stanley, following the route taken by the Parachute Regiment, the difference being that we carried about twenty pounds of kit, whereas during the war, soldiers were carrying a minimum of sixty pounds, not including ammunition – a remarkable feat of strength and endurance. We took in Bluff Cove and Fitzroy where British Forces suffered severe casualties when Argentinian aircraft attacked and destroyed *RFA Sir Galahad* with the loss of 56 lives and 150 wounded. Our 'yomp' provided a welcome break as well as giving us the chance to see more of the islands, including where the proposed Mount Pleasant airfield was to be built and, within two years, was operational.

RAF Mount Pleasant – note the peat bog surrounding the airfield

Falklands Aftermath

Key personnel in the tri-Service organisation changed regularly so it was no surprise to see a new face at the General's daily orders group. On this particular occasion I caught a glimpse of a new naval officer. At the start of the meeting, the General introduced the naval officer as Captain George (aka Dod) Tullis, Commander of the Falkland Islands Task Group and Captain of *HMS Exeter*. I knew George and his wife Felicity from our Hong Kong days. They are mutual great friends of Richard and Sigrid Hutchings. George invited me to visit his ship, *HMS Exeter*, and was to arrange for the ship's helicopter to pick me up the next day. Alas! I was unable to accept Dod's invitation due, as far as I can recall, to some urgent matter requiring my attention and I never did visit his ship.

Back at home, Angelika kept the home fires burning brightly in Hilgay. The girls were still at school in Midhurst working towards their exams. We kept in touch with 'Blueys' – aerogrammes which I believe she still has to this day. Using the satellite telephone, we were also able to speak a couple of times. I started agitating to know where my next job was to be. I had been well reported on and had been told that, barring a catastrophe, I would be selected for promotion to Colonel in 1985. However, I was keen on obtaining a job involving practical soldiering rather than driving a desk. I had heard too many tales of those working in the MOD and other headquarters spending much of their time trying to deflect a decision to cut this or cut that; not the sort of thing I wanted to do even with promotion. As it transpired, I was selected to run the Army's recruiting organisation throughout the South of England from an office in Aldershot. To my mind, this was a 'non-job' and something I had no wish to do. I was desperately disappointed and made my feelings known to both General Peter de la B and the appropriate people in the UK. All to no avail, but I put my disappointment to the back of my mind until I had left the Falklands.

One of my 'extra' responsibilities was to brief important visitors who wanted to see for themselves what had happened during the battle for Goose Green and, in particular, the part played by 'H' Jones, the Commanding Officer of 2nd Bn The Parachute Regiment. I therefore made it my business to study the action by familiarising myself with the ground over which the battle took place. 'H' was an outspoken and somewhat controversial officer who led from the front. I witnessed his style at first hand when we attended the same Commanding Officer's course. The detail of Goose Green has been extensively written about so I have no intention of trying to do the same. Nevertheless, I wish to make my views clear on where I stand in the debate as to whether 'H' should have been where he was when he was killed.

2 Para's victory at Goose Green was outstanding. Goose Green was the first land battle of the war. It was also the longest, the hardest-fought, the most important to win, and the only one that hung in the balance for several hours. It established a physical and moral supremacy over the enemy and gave impetus to British forces to take the battle to the enemy. Subsequent victory over a determined enemy and without supporting fire was a vindication of the regiment's training, toughness, aggressive spirit and leadership at all levels. When the battalion came up against stiff resistance as they approached Goose Green, their advance faltered. Realising this, 'H' went forward to see for himself what the problem was. In an attempt to regain the momentum, 'H' urged another attempt to neutralise the machine gun position which was largely responsible for holding up the advance. This attempt also failed with a further four casualties including two Captains. Seeing this, 'H' decided to take matters into his own hands. He got up and shouted 'Follow me'. Carrying a sub-machine gun and wearing his steel helmet, he ran forward, accompanied by four or five others, towards the enemy machine gun position. What he had not seen was another enemy position on the opposite hill which had an unobstructed view of him. It was a shot from this position which brought him down and from which he died some fifteen minutes later.

Inspired by what they had seen, others got up and charged forward to neutralise both enemy positions. Ultimately, Goose Green was secured against a numerically superior enemy, thereby establishing a psychological ascendancy over the Argentinians which was never lost.

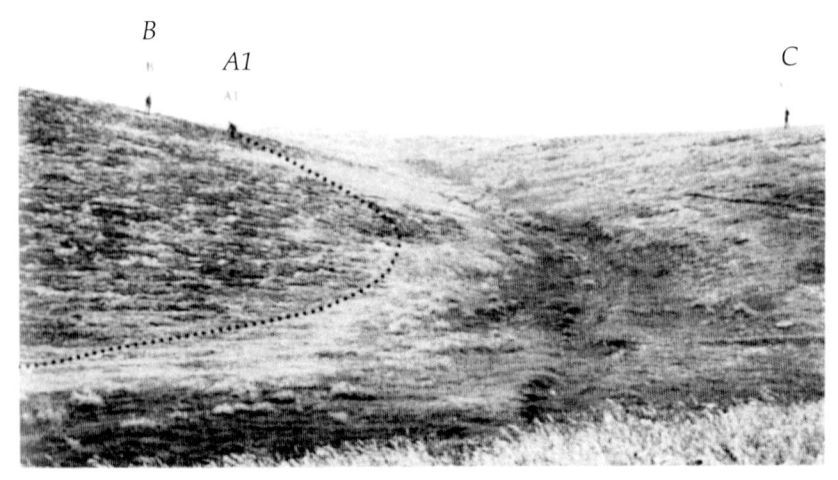

The photo shows the line of H's assault (A) against the position at B. He was shot from a trench at C when he reached A1

As to whether it was for the commanding officer to put his life at risk is a question which will remain talked about in military circles for generations of military circles to come. What is not in doubt is his leadership. He set high standards and led from the front. In the face of death, he continued to lead by example and that cannot be criticised. As to his award of the Victoria Cross, 'H' would surely have seen this as recognition of his battalion's outstanding performance, not just his own bravery. In Lord Moran's *The Anatomy of Courage*, he writes: *'It is not the number of soldiers, but their will to win which decides battles.'* This was assuredly the case at Goose Green. 'H' Jones was a leader in the best traditions of the British Army and I for one admired the way he led his men!

Jim Davidson is an English comedian. Despite early recognition and winning many awards throughout his long career, Davidson became known for his politically incorrect jokes in his stand-up act, which has made him a subject of negative media coverage and frequent criticism. Always supportive of the Services, he has made many visits to the Falkland Islands and other places where the Army have been on operations. He visited the Falklands when I was there and although I did not sponsor him, I was very much involved with the arrangements for his visit. During a week, he worked extremely hard to visit and put on a show, along with a troupe of dancing girls and folk singer Richard Digance, in all but a very few locations. As did his supporting acts, his brand of 'smutty' humour went down extremely well with the soldiers, particularly the girls! I was responsible for giving a lunch in his honour before he was due to give his final performance in Stanley. The lunch went on until after 4 pm at which point, through drink, he was almost incoherent. I finally persuaded him to retire in preparation for the evening show which was due to start a couple of hours later. Would he make it? was the question. With no more than forty minutes to curtain up, he was still being plied with copious quantities of black coffee. He briefly appeared to say a few words at the start of the show and then left the first thirty minutes to the girls and Richard Digance. Finally, Jim, made his entrance to thunderous applause and then proceeded to tell the lads what a great job they were doing (and they were), interspersed with 'taking the mickey' out of the senior officers sitting in the front row, of which I was one. He held the show together for the next two hours almost single-handedly – a truly staggering performance. At the time of writing, Jim is the Chairman of The British Forces Foundation charity, which aims to promote the well-being and esprit de corps of service personnel. For his work in support of Service charities, Jim Davidson was deservedly awarded the OBE. I have little doubt that, had he been less controversial, his official recognition would have been even greater.

With such a wide diversity of unique military activity, I thought it might be appropriate to commission an artist to visit and record aspects of daily life. I put this to the General and he agreed in principle to the idea. All I had to do now was to find a suitable and willing artist to rough it in the Falklands for a month or so. In discussion with a number of people, one likely candidate was David Bell whose work was known and valued. An ex-Merchant Navy officer, David's specialisation was marine subjects but he had also proved himself more than capable in other fields. Using the radio telephone, I called his number. His wife Jennifer answered and told me her husband was out at the time. I explained why I was calling. She seemed not to grasp the situation fully and enquired whether David could call me back! No, it would not be possible for him to do that but I would call again in a couple of hours. I did so and told him the outline of the task. His military flight to the Falklands, his accommodation and food would be free but there would be no fee. Instead, what he earned would be from his work. The flight would be leaving in about a week's time. I would see that he was kitted out with appropriate cold-weather clothing when he arrived. In answer to my question, David said that he was available and confirmed that he would accept the invitation. About a week later, I met a rather bemused David who, after a couple of days of settling in, started work. A delightful, understated and quiet man, David mixed well and became an honorary member of FILOG. During his month with us, David worked hard producing his own portfolio of watercolour paintings as well as completing a number of commissions for various units, including FILOG. His work was an unqualified success. Before leaving, he held an exhibition and sold all his work. I bought a painting of the wreck, *Jhelum*, located at the eastern end of Stanley harbour. The *Jhelum* was built in Liverpool by Joseph Steel & Son and launched on 24th May 1849. A wooden barque of 466 tons, she arrived in Stanley distressed and leaking, with a badly stored cargo of guano (excrement of seabirds used in the production of gunpowder), in August 1870 while sailing from Callao, Peru, to Dunkirk, and never left. The *Jhelum* finally lost her fight with the elements in October 2008.

David has since published two books illustrating his work, and together with Jennifer, in her own right a most successful painter of animals and birds, has a gallery in Lincoln. We have kept in touch over the years.

Living in a small cabin on the coastel *Pursuivant*, washing and eating alongside one's subordinates, meant that I had very little privacy; in fact, I was never off-duty. Many's the time when there was

Falklands Aftermath

Jhelum, by David Bell, with Mount Longdon in the background

a knock on my door at any hour of day or night with someone wanting a decision. I'm not complaining for it was my role to lead and to be available at all times, but it did mean that I had virtually no 'down' time when I could relax in my own thoughts. The only exception was on a Sunday when I made a point of attending Evensong at the Cathedral.

The weekly service, conducted by Harry Bagnall, a down-to-earth Yorkshireman with a keen sense of humour, who had remained with his flock throughout the Argentine occupation, gave me the opportunity of meeting Islanders. I also valued the chance to reflect and to thank God for blessing Angelika and me with three lovely daughters. In his book *Faith Under Fire*, Harry refers, in his dedication to me, to Psalm 23:4

Christ Church Cathedral, Stanley, in later times

– *'Even though I walk through the shadow of the valley of death, I will fear no evil; for you are with me; your rod and your staff, they comfort me'.* Ever since, I have taken comfort from these words at difficult points in my life. I am not a religious person but I have a faith and, against the odds, I have tried to lead a decent life. When asked about my religious beliefs, I reply that 'I am a vaguely practising Christian'. I have also developed an interest in Humanism and I am a member of the Armed Forces Humanist Society. Humanism is an ethics of fellowship. Among those who work and serve together, it is about loyalty, service, self-sacrifice and commitment. It is about the mutual trust that forges the strong and enduring bonds of comradeship that underlie our duty to one another and our community.

Not far from the cathedral was the one-and-only hotel on East Falkland, the Upland Goose, where I went a couple times, usually to entertain a visitor from the UK. Talking of geese leads nicely into the wildlife on the islands. Such was its importance, an army vet was present to minimise any danger or damage to the fantastic and unique wildlife on the Falklands. The vet also had to supervise the slaughter of sheep and cattle, and then certify them as fit fresh meat for the population to eat. To save transport costs in bringing meat down from the UK and to encourage trade with local farmers, I started to buy meat locally. In this I had to work closely with the Army vet. With very few trees able to survive the South Atlantic winds, birdlife was confined to small ground-nesting birds such as finches. Geese, waders and sea birds thrive there but it is the penguins and seals who are the 'stars'. Gentoos, King Penguins and Rockhoppers predominate in the penguin colonies, while elephant seal and sea lions are common sights.

'Up close and personal' is the description of the penguin and sea lion experience. It is as though the animals have no fear of humans. Living as they do on pure white sand and in crystal-blue water, the

Rockhoppers   *King Penguins*

wildlife provides magnificent photographic opportunities. One of my officers was a keen fisherman and at every opportunity, usually on a Sunday, he would venture out with his rod before returning, invariably with a huge catch of brown freshwater trout which we had for dinner the same night. He used to say that it was the easiest fishing he had ever experienced as the fish were so plentiful and not at all suspicious of humans.

There were many memorable incidents, two of which I particularly remember. The first involved a Chinook helicopter which was moving a fully 'stuffed' under-slung forty-foot metal container from ship to shore. This was a routine task completed successfully dozens of times a day. However, on this occasion, I watched the container starting to oscillate beneath the helicopter to such a degree that the pilot was fast losing control of his aircraft. As the helicopter lost height, the pilot jettisoned the container into the harbour before successfully landing on the shore. The only damage to the helicopter was to the rotor blades. This was a fine piece of airmanship which could have ended in loss of life and a valuable aircraft. The pilot rightly received an award for his outstanding airmanship.

Remains of the stricken Chinook

The other incident involved a Russian merchant seaman who was brought ashore by RAF helicopter to the military hospital after he had broken both his legs in an accident at sea. The trouble began when the man regained consciousness and realised, after seeing people in uniform, that he was in a military hospital! At this point, he got out of bed and made his way to the window of the first-floor ward, with the intention of escaping. But the window was locked. A military nurse tried unsuccessfully to restrain him and could not prevent the Russian diving through the glass window and landing on the ground below. When the nursing staff got to him, he was unconscious but without other serious injuries. For the next two weeks he had to be kept lightly sedated until he was fit enough to be taken back to his ship. Why did he react in this way? No-one knew for sure but the incident did wonders in stimulating Russian stories and jokes!

Coming to the end of my tour, I visited most if not all of the other units in theatre. I particularly remember having lunch with the Royal Scots at their base at Fox Bay when, at the end of the meal, the Commanding Officer, Lieutenant-Colonel Patrick Cardwell-Moore, presented me with a tune played on bagpipes in memory of our association, and the fact that my grandfather had been an officer in the regiment: A wonderful gesture which I very much appreciated.

I was scheduled to return home by air the whole way, the first stage by Hercules C-130 as far as Ascension Island, and then onward to the UK by RAF VC 10. The Hercules has pretty basic facilities for passengers: webbing seats close-packed side-by-side, touching those in the opposite row, slung the length of the cavernous cargo bay; the light is too poor to be able to read; the noise is so deafening as for one to need cotton wool in your ears; there are no washing facilities and only a screened-off Elsan toilet right up in the sloping tail of the aircraft. The flight to Ascension took, I think, twelve of the most uncomfortable hours I have ever spent in the air. Actually, we took off twice before making it the whole way to Ascension. The first time, the aircraft developed a fault after about two hours and we had to turn back. On the second occasion, we got about halfway when the weather deteriorated, so the necessary in-flight refuelling was not possible. When we had eventually travelled about halfway to Ascension, I was invited by the aircraft's captain onto the flight deck to watch our aircraft refuel from an RAF Victor aircraft. The rendezvous made a thrilling spectacle, as the pilot brought his Hercules close up under the tail of the tanker and slid his probe into the basket trailing on the end of the fuel hose, so that the two planes were linked by an umbilical pipe for fifteen minutes as 30,000 pounds of fuel were pumped across. The flight from Ascension to the UK was uneventful. Tom Ridgway, with whom I had served at Grantham, sent his car to meet me and take me home to Hilgay: a kind gesture.

So ended the busiest and most challenging appointment in my military career. Into seven or so months an incredible amount had been crammed. I learnt an awful lot and will always be grateful for the chance of putting my leadership to the test where what I did and the decisions I took were the difference between failure and success. The Falklands had been an unforgettable and unmissable experience. My report from General Peter de la B confirmed that I had had a successful tour and one that earned me an unqualified recommendation for promotion from one if not *the* most respected Generals in the Army (see opposite).

I subsequently wrote an article on FILOG for the *British Army Review* which was published in Number 79, dated April 1985.

of Superior Reporting Officers (SROs)

See MS Guide: para 6.06 for number of SROs needed; paras 6.07 – 6.08 for functions of SROs (including ading and assessment of potential); para 6.09 for filling in the form (including power to order changes); and paras 6.10 – 6.12 for notification of changes.

1st SRO's Report

a. How well do you know the officer? ~~VERY WELL~~ / QUITE WELL / ~~SLIGHTLY/NOT AT ALL~~

b. Do you agree the grading at 3f., any recommendation at 3c and all recommendations at 3g to j inclusive?   YES [X]   NO [ ]

c. Remarks

The Falklands environment has undoubtedly brought out the best in Lieutenant Colonel Vaughan-Arbuckle. His has been a diverse command, and a hectic command period which has included the commissioning of the new Port and Storage facility, and the move of every component of his battalion into new technical accommodation. He has shown tremendous energy and zeal, and considerable style, in carrying out his task; indeed he has probably been the best Commanding Officer the battalion has had in its existance.

I enthusiastically endorse the recommendation for promotion now.

Signature: [signed]   Rank and Name: MAJ GEN P de la C de la BILLIERE

Appointment: CBFFI   Date of Signature: 29/6/84   Officer's Initials (if necessary – para 6.12)

My 'End of tour' report from General Peter de la Billière

14: Out of Uniform

I duly returned to the UK for a well-earned spell of leave in Hilgay, during which family and friends were interested in my experiences 'down south'. One Sunday lunchtime, chatting with friends about the Falklands over a pint, an elderly man who was standing close by joined in the conversation. He made it clear that while he had every admiration for the way the Services had performed in the Falklands, actions of a similar size were being fought in hundreds of locations, every day, throughout the Second World War. How right he was and his astute observation put into context perfectly the Falklands campaign. I enjoyed my leave during which I was able to 'wind down' from the frantic pace of life of command in a semi-operational environment.

As the time to report for my next job in Aldershot drew closer, I started to think seriously about my future in the Army. Then, one day, an advertisement appeared in the Daily Telegraph for an 'Investigating Officer to work for the Army Security Vetting Unit (ASVU) in East Anglia'. Looking into the job more closely, it seemed that, together with my pension, I would be better off financially, I would be working from home and, most importantly, I would be working independently. The other great advantage, I thought, was that I would be able to spend more time at home giving the girls the support they deserved as they made the transition from school to work or further education. We had already made a circle of good friends in Hilgay, we liked Norfolk and the way of life suited us and, for the first time in my life, I felt that I truly belonged somewhere. Up to that point, I think I had lived in around 17 places.

Meanwhile however, I had to face my next posting. After reporting for duty and during the handover period, it was clear that the job would be a 'doddle' and provide none of the ingredients I had hoped for. Also, the thought of once again having to live in an Officers' Mess during the week filled me with dread. And then there was the weekly commute to and from Norfolk with which to contend. I therefore decided to submit an application for the vetting officer's job and within a month I was invited for an interview. The interview in London was straightforward and my confidence that I had done well was confirmed when I was offered the job. Angelika seemed supportive so I duly tendered my resignation from the Army. It took nearly six months for the procedures involved in retiring from the Army to be completed, including an interview with Lieutenant-General Sir Geoffrey Howlett whom I had met and played cricket with when he was serving with the Parachute Regiment in Hong Kong. A nice man for whom I had great respect, he tried hard to persuade me – over half an hour in his office – to think again, particularly as I was 'certain to be promoted to Colonel' later that year. I said that my mind was made up and the interview ended with a handshake and the General wishing me good luck.

A few days later, on 6th May 1985, I packed up my belongings, said goodbye to my staff and handed in my identity card, my final act as an army officer after 31 years' service. Hardly surprisingly, I had mixed emotions as I drove home. On the one hand I looked forward with anticipation and excitement to a new way of life and the challenge of a new job while, on the other, I was sad to be leaving an organisation which had been so good to and for me over a large part of my life. I would certainly miss the Army but the organisation I was joining meant I would still be involved but now 'out of uniform'. I counted myself fortunate to have spent so long doing what I loved and at which I had been reasonably successful. I had had a wonderful career, so full of reward, variety and, above all, comradeship. I had no regrets but was flattered to know that I had been selected for promotion. A few days later, I received a telephone call at home from a former colleague who thanked me for retiring as he had been told he was to fill the vacancy to Colonel I had created.

Once I had taken the decision to leave the Army, we looked for and found Rose Cottage, a classic Georgian-style house on the outskirts of Fincham, near King's Lynn, which we bought from an eccentric Pole named Bobby Hawreylak (sic). He had fought for the Allies during the war and had reached the rank of Lieutenant-Colonel. With this is common, he was easy to deal with over the purchase which at one time seemed as though it would founder – due to some skulduggery on the part of a local estate agent who spread the rumour that I had no money. Actually, for the first time in my life, I had some money. The house came with two acres of land and a stable which we later converted into a lucrative holiday home, before eventually selling it to Claire. The house and garden needed a great deal of work so we all had a turn at wielding a paintbrush while I got stuck into recovering the outer garden, once an orchard, restoring the paddock and cutting back the bramble hedges. My joy was the sit-on mower!

Clouds over Rose Cottage

After training at the headquarters of ASVU in what used to be the Royal Military Academy, Woolwich, I settled down to life as a vetting officer working in East Anglia. Although the investigatory work was interesting, it did take me some time to get used to working from home. I had always been used to an office with clerical support, whereas now I was required to type my own reports and submit them to my supervisor in Woolwich, a retired Commander in the Metropolitan Police. It was strange being at home permanently and this led to problems between Angelika and me. She had become used to doing things her way and, understandably, did not want interference from me. For my part, I felt awkward without a clearly defined role. Basically, I did not fit easily into the role of a house-husband. I hate 'fiddle' gardening, loathe housework and am quite useless when it comes to DIY. Not surprisingly therefore, Angelika was quite happy when I was away during the week.

After about 18 months, the Commander ASVU, retired Colonel Adrian Rouse, asked to see me. He had a job in Germany which he thought would suit me. I would be one of a team of five investigators working throughout West Germany in the British zone. The post he had in mind for me was in Fallingbostel, located in Lower Saxony on the Lüneburg Heath in northern Germany, a small garrison town part of the 4th Armoured Division area of responsibility. Angelika was all for it, but what about the girls? By this time, both Vivian and Juliet were settled in London in their own house while Claire was studying for A Levels at the Technical College in King's Lynn. Claire did not want to stay in the UK on her own so it was decided that she would drop A Levels and come to Germany with us. It was 1987, I think, when we went to Germany where we took over a large officers' married quarter and soon settled down to life in a garrison. It was a case of *déjà vu*. Claire got herself a job working in the legal branch of the divisional headquarters, at Verden, which involved a forty-minute drive. At the same time, it didn't take her long to establish a social network principally among the junior officers. She started to run and learnt to parachute through the British Army Parachute Club. It was certainly during this period that seeds were sown for the successful career she was to pursue in the Army. With her good looks, bubbly personality and adventurous spirit, she had her fair share of suitors. One was a young officer in the RCT to whom she became engaged for a short time. In my discussion with her, it was clear that Claire had no idea that, in agreeing to become engaged, she was essentially committing herself to marrying that person. The engagement didn't last long and the ring was returned.

Angelika's family in Bielefeld, two hour's drive south by *autobahn*, were far enough away for them not to pop in but we did see them every so often. Angelika was happy to be back in her homeland and generally life was very pleasant. Whisky, our West Highland terrier, was with us to keep us on our toes. We always knew when wild boars, prevalent in the area, were in the vicinity by the ferocity of his barking. Talking of wild boar, I remember waking up to look out of our bedroom window to see that the back garden had literally been dug up by a couple of boars hunting for food. Even a chain-link fence could not keep them out! I was into running at this time when one day out for a run on the heath I was confronted by a wild boar no more than a few yards in front of me. Our eyes met and, for a moment, I thought he was going to charge. As I moved my head to find an escape route, the boar snorted, turned and, much to my relief, ran off in the opposite direction.

During our time in Fallingbostel, Paul and Maggie (Garner) and their three children, Alastair, Isobel and Ann-Marie, came to stay. We had a wonderful holiday with them visiting places in Germany including Bavaria. Leaving our families to 'do their own thing', Paul and I climbed the Zugspitze (2962m), the highest peak in Germany, located in the Bavarian Alps, on a lovely day. I also recall sitting in the middle of an autobahn for around an hour when the traffic came to a standstill.

Bergen-Belsen (Belsen), a former Nazi concentration camp, was just the other side of the large training area only about ten miles from Fallingbostel. Originally established as a prisoner-of-war camp, it became a concentration camp. Between 1941 and 1945 some 20,000 Russian prisoners of war and a further 50,000 inmates died there, with up to 35,000 of them dying of typhus in the first few months of 1945, shortly before and after the liberation.

The camp was liberated on 15th April 1945 by our troops. They discovered around 53,000 prisoners inside, most of them half-starved and seriously ill, and another 13,000 corpses lying around the camp unburied. The horrors of the camp were described by David Dimbleby, war correspondent, who subsequently became a leading journalist with the BBC:

> *Here, over an acre of ground, laid dead and dying people. You could not see which was which ... The living lay with their heads against the corpses, and around them moved the awful, ghostly procession of emaciated, aimless people, with nothing to do and with no hope of life, unable to move out of your way, unable to look at the terrible sights around them ... Babies had been born here, tiny wizened things that could not live ... A mother, driven mad, screamed at a British sentry to give her milk for her child, and thrust the tiny mite into his arms, then ran off, crying terribly. He opened the bundle and found the baby had been dead for days. This day at Belsen was the most horrible of my life.*

Bergen Belsen: The burial mounds

Visiting Belsen all those years later was a harrowing experience. The birds were silent, the starkness of the place eerie while the huge mounds of earth, on which nothing grows, provide a permanent reminder of the mass graves. Built of grey stone, the visitor centre contains graphic images of the terrible atrocities that took place in Belsen. To their credit, the German authorities include a visit to Belsen for schoolchildren as part of their education. I was there during one such visit and heard the teacher explain to her children, who were silent and attentive, what had happened at this terrible place.

While we were in Germany, Rose Cottage was left empty. From time to time, Vivian and Juliet would visit, and we had a local man who kept an eye on the house and looked after the garden. It was during this time that we had the stable converted into a two-bedroom bungalow with the idea of letting it as holiday accommodation. We retained the features of a stable while installing all mod cons. It was ready by the time we returned to the UK and subsequently became a highly successful, popular and lucrative project which lasted about eight years under Angelika's careful management and hard work.

The Stable

One day we received a telephone call from an estate agent, saying he had a buyer for Rose Cottage who was offering us four times what we had paid for the house, and extra for the stable. I was very keen to cash in on an offer which would have secured us financially, but Angelika was adamant that it was her home and she was going nowhere! Thinking back, I still regret the decision although I have to concede that she was probably right in that Rose Cottage has been a wonderful family home, as well as providing a valuable income over the years as a successful B&B.

During a visit by Adrian Rouse, he offered me promotion if I would agree to working in Woolwich in a new post he had created for the management of all Field Investigating Officers. I realised this would be a case of living in London during the week, but it would be a further challenge and a considerable 'hike' in pay. With Angelika's agreement, I accepted the job.

The appointment as Investigating Officer Grade 1 (Co-ordinator) turned out to be interesting and demanding, and kept me more than a little challenged. Not only was I responsible for managing the workforce of forty investigators deployed all over the UK, in Germany and Cyprus, but I was often required to take on cases which had potentially serious security consequences. This involved me travelling to Hong Kong and Cyprus, as well as doing a stint in Northern Ireland, reviewing personnel who were involved in deep-cover operations against the IRA. I remember meeting one such Captain who arrived for our meeting with a beard, terrible body odour, long hair and an Irish accent. He had infiltrated the IRA, was leading the life of a lie, and in mortal danger of his life should his cover be blown. These 'guys' – and there were servicewomen in similar situations – were the 'brave of the brave' and deserving of the highest recognition. Another case I became involved with concerned a cabinet minister who had propositioned a young army officer on an overnight train to Scotland. Ultimately, no action was taken which affected the politician's security clearance, although every time I listened to him pronounce on some issue or other, I viewed him in a different light!

It was during this period that Peter Mears, with whom I had twice served, was leaving the Army. I was pleased when he contacted me to enquire about work as a vetting officer. Around the time that I was thinking about retiring from the Army, Peter had tried hard to persuade me to stay on the grounds that, like him, I would be promoted to Colonel. By that time however, my mind was made up even though I much appreciated his wise counsel. I told Peter how much I was enjoying the work, and so was delighted when he applied, and was accepted, for a position as a Grade 1 Investigating Officer in the ASVU. Peter and Ann became a very close friends and I have always valued their friendship and kind hospitality.

By this time, Claire was working in London for the solicitors, Boodle Hatfield, and had a flat in Streatham. She had joined the Territorial Army and was a private with the 4th Battalion, Royal Green Jackets, an infantry regiment. It was 1990. After a time, she was selected as an officer candidate and sent to Sandhurst. After successfully completing the two-week course, Claire was commissioned as a 2nd Lieutenant at the Passing Out Parade taken by a Brigadier. To my chagrin, as soon as I read the programme, the Brigadier in question was one I had investigated earlier that year and whose high-level clearance had been withdrawn, essentially because he had lied about an extra-marital affair. When we met at the post-parade reception, the Brigadier congratulated us on Claire's success without mentioning that we knew each other professionally.

On 2nd August 1990, Iraq launched the invasion of Kuwait by bombing Kuwait City, the capital. A series of UN Security Council resolutions and Arab League resolutions were passed regarding the invasion of Kuwait by Saddam Hussein's Iraq. One of the most important was Resolution 678, passed on 29th November 1990, which gave Iraq a withdrawal deadline of 15th January 1991, and authorised 'all necessary means to uphold and implement Resolution 660', and a diplomatic formulation authorising the use of force if Iraq failed to comply. In preparation for a series of covert actions and co-operation with American forces, high-level security clearance had to be expedited without delay. This involved the ASVU, like many other service and government departments in long hours of sustained work, so that by the time allied forces went to war in the Gulf in February 1991, they had all they needed. I remember driving back to Norfolk one Friday late afternoon feeling dog-tired, and found myself dropping asleep over the wheel on the M11. I pulled onto the hard shoulder to gather myself, and the next thing I remember was being woken up by a policeman knocking on the window. Did I realise it was an offence to stop on the motorway? he asked. Yes, I did but I explained why I had done so. Why had I not left at the last junction? Because I had not felt unduly sleepy at the time, I replied. He then asked whether I had been drinking. I assured him that I hadn't but he insisted on administering the 'blow into the tube' test, at the end of which I asked him for the result. He replied that I had passed. Yes, but had it showed any alcohol in my system? No, the policeman replied. He then said he was issuing me with an 'on-the-spot' fine which I refused to accept. He would see me in court, then – and with that I continued my journey thinking the policeman would probably come to his senses and let the matter drop.

No such luck, as some weeks later I received a summons to appear at Cambridge Magistrates Court, to answer the charge of contravening some piece of motorway legislation. After pleading 'Not guilty' to the charge, the magistrate asked the police prosecutor whether he was ready to proceed with his case. In replying that the constable was not present because it was 'unusual' for a plea of 'Not guilty' to be entered to such a charge, the magistrate replied that it was everyone's right to plead 'Not guilty' to any alleged offence. The case was duly postponed for three weeks with an apology to me for the inconvenience I had suffered.

The case was duly reconvened and, this time, I recognised the policeman who had questioned me. When asked who my defence council was, I replied that I would be defending myself. In giving his evidence, the policeman read from his notebook and clearly could not remember my case. I used this to full advantage, even to the point of getting him to admit that he couldn't really remember the circumstances, let alone what I had told him. When the bench retired to consider their verdict, the prosecutor said, "They'll definitely find you not guilty," which they duly did after deliberating for some twenty minutes. I was delighted that justice had been done and that the 'bully-boy' tactics of the police had been in vain. I was awarded a day's pay and expenses for my trouble.

Oh yes, the Gulf War effectively ended on 26th February 1991 when the Iraqi forces fled Kuwait City in total disarray. Pity that the coalition forces stopped short of going into Baghdad, thereby allowing Saddam Husain's tyrant regime to fight another day. But that's another story.

Then I received the letter inviting me for a job interview with the Foreign Office…

15: Travel – India, Pakistan and Nepal

There are some parts of the world that, once visited, get into your heart and won't go. For me, India is such a place. When I first visited, I was stunned by the richness of the land, by its lush beauty and exotic architecture, by its ability to overload the senses with the pure, concentrated intensity of its colours, smells, tastes, and sounds ... I had been seeing the world in black and white and, when brought face-to-face with India, experienced everything re-rendered in brilliant technicolour – Keith Bellows, National Geographic Society

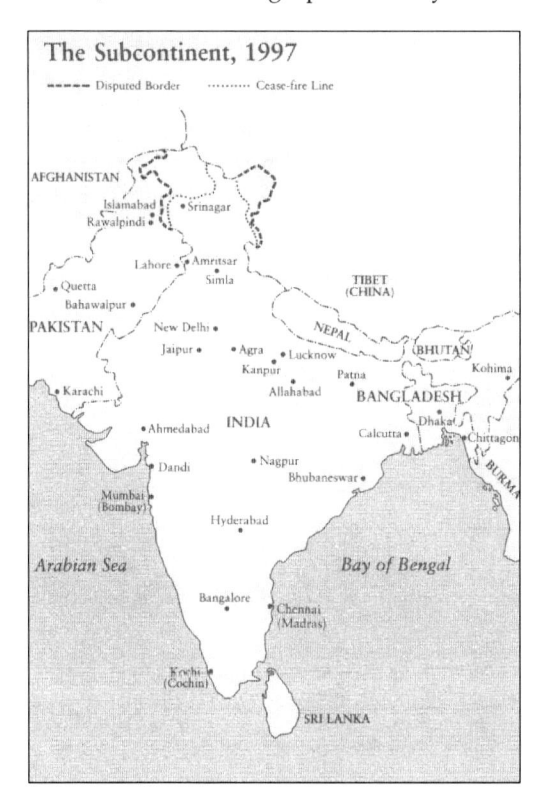

Ramblings Round India

India is a country made up of different cultures, languages, landscapes and people. It is a hugely diverse place, a country in the midst of fundamental change as it takes its place as one of the world's emerging economies. Apart from living there as a boy, I have returned to India a number of times in later life. Visiting India is an intense experience: there is so much to see that is beautiful, strange and touching. India is, for me, at its most beautiful and fascinating where it is still catching up and where remains of the British Raj can still be seen. Undoubtedly, the prettiest things are those that remind us of a simpler past, while the saddest are those that repeat mistakes that we in Europe have already made.

India is not a comfortable place, but it is an intriguing, captivating and thought-provoking one. Going there entails surprises, delights and shocks. Its landscapes, particularly in the Himalaya, are beautiful, its monuments and artistic treasures magnificent, and its people as fascinating as they are delightful. I particularly love the colour and excitement of India. The country is changing at a rapid rate and not always for the better. But for me it still holds a fascination born of the childhood I spent there with my parents, which I have described elsewhere.

Most visits to India start in Delhi, the capital city, which is a slightly schizophrenic place. The old city is everything you would expect: cacophonous, crowded, bursting with colour and bustle. Alongside it

India Gate

stands a very different city, a new one built by the British in the early 20th century, called New Delhi, which in 1911 replaced Calcutta as the capital. New Delhi is outlandishly grand and grandly colonial. Designed by Sir Edwin Lutyens, it houses the diplomatic, administrative and commercial centre of the country. I found this area most interesting for it is easy to see the legacy of empire playing an important part alongside modern India. For example, it is easy to imagine how a maharaja must have felt driving up the magnificent mile-long Raj Path, through India Gate, to the Viceroy's palace.

I got a real 'buzz' just walking 'the mile', in both directions, allowing my imagination to run riot, only disturbed by the interruptions of well-meaning locals enquiring, with the inevitable Indian shake-of-the-head, 'Your country'? I also recall watching a group of scruffy lads playing a game of knockabout cricket, pretending to be Sachin Tendulkar and the like, in the shadow of the imposing India Gate, which seemed to me to capture the essence of the country.

On all of my visits but one, I have stayed at the magnificent Imperial Hotel, a unique blend of the old and new. Built in 1911, to complement the development of New Delhi, its spacious high ceiling rooms, stunning chandeliers, sparkling marble floors, with an impressive collection of 18th-19th century art, attentive service and magnificent food, make the hotel world-class. The grandeur of the 24 king palms that lead up to the porch are an integral part of, and witness to, the creation of New Delhi. The status of the hotel is borne out by the fact that the Nehru family had a permanent suite there. Spending a night or two at The Imperial is an expensive luxury but a well worthwhile experience.

Imperial Hotel, Delhi

According to statistics, Delhi is one of the most dangerous cities in the world for road users. To observe, from another vehicle, drivers plunging into roundabouts and changing lanes without slowing or looking at conflicting traffic is as thrilling and nerve-racking as riding a big dipper at a fairground – and certainly more dangerous. To travel in a motor tri-shaw is to put your life on the line. Hand signals used by Indian drivers consist of flapping their arms out of the windows and these, together with a liberal use of the horn, seem to prevent many a catastrophe. Bicycles and scooters are often ridden against the flow of traffic. Carts are hauled the wrong way round roundabouts by hapless coolies. Buses and lorries race at high speed, with compressed-air horns screaming as if they were emergency vehicles answering a 999 call. But the most captivating sight is that of intrepid Indian women as they perch side-saddle on the pillions of scooters and motorcycles, a babe or two in their arms, with their colourful saris flowing in the slipstream.

Of all the places in Delhi open to the public, two favourites of mine are Mahatma Gandhi's house and Jawaharlal Nehru's palace. Both places provide an illuminating insight into the lives of these great men. The Gandhi Smriti is set away from the bustle of the town in peaceful gardens. This is the house where the Mahatma spent the last 144 days of his life, living in elegant simplicity. This moving memorial allows you to see where he prayed each day, where he slept each night, and where he was martyred on that fateful day in January 1948. A solemn path of footprints marks the last steps of his remarkable life. Like the man himself, this memorial eschews pomp and circumstance. In simple elegance, you share a connection with his life ... and his death. There is something very special about this place.

Harrow and Cambridge-educated Nehru was India's first Prime Minister from Independence in 1948 until his death in 1964. When he became Prime Minister, Nehru took over the residence of the British Commander-in-Chief, known as Flagstaff House. On his death, the residence was bequeathed to the nation to be used as a memorial. The imposing building, housed in magnificently maintained gardens, is faced in stone and stucco in a classical British style. Now named Teen Murti Bhawan, which literally means 'Three Soldiers Palace', it takes its name from the statue of three soldiers which stands proudly outside the gates. It is now the Nehru Museum. Some houses seem to retain the atmosphere generated by their former occupants – and I felt this strongly at Teen Murti House. Inside there is an interesting mix of public and private rooms. The study and bedroom have been left as they were in Nehru's lifetime, his wrist watch and a book on the bedside table. The living rooms are furnished comfortably but entirely without ostentation. Photographs of Nehru adorn most of the walls and give a revealing insight into the man, his life and interests. I, for one, had no idea how interested Nehru was in the mountains of India – a fact revealed by the pictures and the books in his library. As one might expect, a large part of the display is devoted to the growth and development of the Congress Party and the struggle for independence. The gardens at the back of the house, mostly grass and flowering trees, and well-kept with many rose bushes, Nehru's favourite flower, bordering the main lawn, are lovely. I spent an hour in the peace and quiet reflecting on what I had seen in the company of several peacocks who live there, while an aged cow was pulling a small roller, attended by three gardeners, across the grass. Typical of India with too many people employed doing too little! I very much enjoyed visiting this special house and gardens.

But, of course, no visit to the Indian capital would be complete without a visit to the Taj Mahal, considered to be one of the eight wonders of the world. Located some 150 miles from Delhi, the Taj Mahal is situated on the banks of the River Jumna. It is, without doubt, the most magnificent tomb ever erected. I have been there a few times but the splendour of the marble tomb, the general aura surrounding the complex, and seeing it in differing light, ensured that each visit provided a different experience. By far the best visit I made was the last when Lynn and I got up before dawn and saw the sun rise over the

The Taj Mahal

tomb from the riverside. The early morning emerging light ensured that we got a very special experience as a slight mist rose from the river to reveal a near-perfect reflection of the Taj. We then entered through the main gate to reveal the magnificent sight of the tomb changing colour every few minutes as the sun rose higher in the sky. We just stood there entranced, as the sun waxed and warmed in the morning light. No words can adequately describe the Taj: quite simply, it must be seen!

* * * * *

Mulligatawny Moments

I wrote the following article on my first visit to India, by myself, in 2003. It reflects my thoughts at the time.

It wasn't only my 65th birthday that served as a reminder that life was moving inexorably onward. There were other signposts on the road to rheumy-eyed discontent and wobbly decrepitude – memories for one. These were recalled by, I think, PG Wodehouse, as akin to mulligatawny soup: it's best not to stir it, but to stir it is a must.

"That's the highest place on earth. It's called Everest," my father explained as he painted a snow-capped mountain in the distance. It was 1947 and we were 'summering', like most Army families, in one of the hill stations to escape the oppressive heat of the Indian plains. That moment has stayed with me ever since, although I now know the mountain could not have been Everest. So, which was it and where were we at the time? Was it Ranikhet or Nainital, both favourites with my parents? I decided to find out as part of a need to give my memories of India a long overdue stir.

Like most capitals, Delhi has both grandeur and wealth, and poverty and squalor. I saw both while being driven around in Mr Singh's LPG powered-trishaw. Much has changed since the British departed in 1947. What has survived is the gridiron of wide avenues and public buildings. Rajpath, once Kingsway, ranks alongside The Mall and Champs Elysées, and the magnificent India Gate compares favourably with both Admiralty Arch and the Arc de Triomphe. All are a reminder of the immense contribution made by Sir Edwin Lutyens to the design of New Delhi.

Being rushed through Indira Gandhi's house was disappointing, and the Red Fort was shabbily maintained for a national monument. Jawaharlal Nehru's house, grand yet modestly furnished, was a joy: easy to walk around, well illustrated with narrative and pictures, in which the Himalaya was prominent. Mahatma Gandhi's house and memorial garden, where he was assassinated in 1948, I found a moving experience. Despite a foiled attempt to pick my pocket, I loved

Chandni Chowk in Old Delhi, particularly the spice market. But, for a no-frills look at the citizens of Delhi, Old Delhi station would be hard to better: it never sleeps. It was from here that I caught the night sleeper to Kalka to link with the famous 'Himalayan Queen' to Shimla (formerly Simla). Delhi station at 9 pm was a seething mass of humanity: people of all ages and strata of Indian society attempted to confirm their journey while self-important officials, mostly in uniform, perambulated seemingly with no purpose other than to blow a whistle now and again. Meanwhile, red-coated porters scurried around like worker ants hoping to earn a rupee.

The train on the narrow-gauge line – built 1898-1903 – to Shimla took six hours to cover the sixty miles from Kalka. Winding its way around a succession of hairpin bends, through 102 tunnels and over 800 bridges, the train chugged charmingly in search of the cool, buoyant air in the hills. I stayed at the Woodville Palace Hotel, magnificently set among deodar pines, about ten minutes' walk from The Mall (the town centre). Owned by a prince who spends most summers in residence, the hotel oozes history and is a splendid legacy of former times. Sipping an ice-cold drink, served by a waiter in traditional dress in the garden at dusk, was sheer Kipling-esque.

Woodville Palace Hotel Dining Room

Talking of which, Kipling was in love with Simla and the town features prominently in both *Plain Tales from the Hills* and *Kim*. Shimla was, and still is, an opiate from the pressures of life. Scandal Point, no longer infamous for the goings-on of be-whiskered gentlemen and bored ladies, remains the favourite evening rendezvous spot. The Mall, which seemed to be the centre of action, contains a bandstand and the neo-Gothic Christ Church that, built in the mid-19th century, is the second oldest church in north India. I attended communion there along with thirty pupils from a girls' local school and three fellow tourists. A combination of poor acoustics and the Indian vicar's lilt made it difficult to follow the service while a low-flying pigeon, which passed overhead from time to time, did not help reflection! Sadly, the Gaiety Theatre, built to resemble London's Garrick, although still used, is now a rather faded relic of the past.

After his brilliant achievements in the Sudan, Lord Kitchener (of 'Your country needs YOU' fame) was sent to India as Commander-in Chief where he lived in the magnificent Viceregal Lodge, Shimla, built by Lord Dufferin, Viceroy (1884-88), which had a staff of 850.

Lord Kitchener's former residence, Shimla

This house, now home to the Indian Institute of Advanced Study, has been chosen for many difficult negotiations, including the successful 1947 pre-Partition conference attended by Nehru, Jinnah and Mountbatten. The original small round table, used to ratify the Partition document, is still in situ and gives the place a tangible sense of history. Now called Rashtrapati Niwas (formerly 'The Viceregal Lodge'), with its magnificent panoramic views of the Himalaya, is a must.

The road to Rishikesh took me via Dehra Dun, home of the Indian Military Academy, where I arrived at about five in the afternoon. A smart, helpful and courteous Sergeant-Major explained that all the officers would be out until about 8 pm when they finished playing golf! I accepted his offer to watch the passing out parade rehearsal from out-

Travel – India, Pakistan and Nepal |

side the grounds as the senior cadets prepared for their 'big day'. Smart in their green gabardine uniforms and wearing the colourful headdress of their chosen regiment, they marched around to the strains of many a familiar tune, with the academy building, named after Field Marshal Sir Philip Chetwode, Commander-in-Chief India 1934, providing a splendid backdrop. Uniforms apart, I could have been watching a parade at our own Sandhurst.

Rishikesh, immortalised by the Beatles, who went there in the 1960s to see their *guru* Maharishi Yogi, was everything I had expected. Colourful, vibrant, crowded and yet radiating serenity, I found the ambiance of the town peaceful and relaxing. Rishikesh has long been a holy place of pilgrimage for Hindus, where they pay homage to Mother Ganga (River Ganges). The Ganges is believed to bring purity, wealth and fertility to those who bathe in it. No wonder therefore that Hindus make pilgrimages from all over India to submerge their bodies in the 'holy river'.

Ashrams (spiritual retreats) abound, which provide study in yoga,

Indian Military Academy

Bathing in the Ganges

Sadhu in Gangotri

meditation and spiritualism, and you can't walk many yards without seeing a *sadhu* (holy person) or a *guru* (teacher). I talked to a number of both and, in the main, found them to be educated, well informed and worth listening to. *Sadhus* are spiritual seekers who have renounced sedentary society and material comfort. They have severed themselves from home and family, and they move, with the seasons, from one festival to the next.

The town of Rishikesh is a photographer's dream. The ashram meeting I attended was based on maximum participation in prayer and song led by the *guru*. I was surprised to find the two sexes separated (voluntarily) but was told this was normal in Indian society.

Uttarkashi, a stopover on the way to my first trek, had little to commend it other than the Nehru Institute of Mountaineering. Located amongst the pines high above the chaotic and dirty town, the NIM provides mountaineering instruction at all levels. The Institute's most illustrious alumnus Bachendri Pal, was the first (and only?) Indian woman to conquer Everest. The campus is delightful and a visit to the museum and shop makes the small diversion worthwhile.

The 60-odd miles to Gangotri, starting point of my trek to the source of the Ganges, was exhilarating and potentially dangerous. In its final approach, the twisting road climbs steeply to present a potentially lethal trap for the unwary driver. The village of Gangotri was awash with pilgrims visiting this holy place. Hundreds of people jostled for a place to pray at the water's edge or to gain entrance to the Hindu temple to make *puja* (prayers and worship). The narrow main street is a resting place for dozens of mendicants seeking *baksheesh*: I stopped counting them when I reached sixty. It is, nonetheless, an extraordinary place where people-watching assumes an extra dimension.

The five-day trek to Gamukh (three up and two back) ranks as 'moderate', in degree of difficulty, although there are places where it becomes 'difficult'. The route follows the fast-flowing River Bhagirathi until, after merging with lesser waters, it eventually becomes the Ganges. The majority of the route has plenty of variety and an assortment of beautiful backdrops provided by snow-capped mountains, like Shivaling (21,640 feet), their stunning slopes translucent in the sunlight. The path is well used by a steady stream of supplicants on foot, on horseback, and even a few being carried on a *charpoy* (bed). On the trek I met one *sadhu* who had lost his wife so he was now devoting the rest of his life to 'God'. He had met his younger travelling companion on the road and, together, they intended visiting all five holy places in India on foot. These men never cut their hair, they usually go barefoot and rely on being given food and shelter on their journey. They often carry a *dekshi* (billy can) for their food and a wooden staff to ward off unfriendly dogs. Tangerine or yellow appear to be their preferred colours.

The final approach to Gamukh (13,800 feet), one of the holiest places in India, was barren and featureless. Then, suddenly, after a clamber over treacherous scree and large boulders, there it was, a black spot on the end wall of the glacier. The snout of the glacier gushed a torrent of muddy, turbulent water from the depths of it 'bowels'. At water-level, the immense power and accompanying noise of the torrent, as the green melting ice creaked and groaned, was awe-inspiring and not somewhere to dally. It is here that the great Ganges is born, a place with a powerful presence and not easily forgotten.

Gamukh

My experience of hotels was variable: most were rudimentary but comfortable while one or two were dirty and inhospitable. I arrived at one to find no power in my room. A call brought no action so I went in person to reception. "No problem," said the receptionist, with a characteristic sideways waggle of his head. Two hours later, after a meal, I still had no power. Back to reception: "No power? No problem," and with a flourish another man was despatched to correct the deficiency. Moments later, a man wearing a jacket and tie arrived. "Problem?" "Yes, but it's being seen to, thanks." "What problem?" "No power in room 106." "No problem. Give me key." Unwisely, I handed over the key and off he went. Moments later, the original man returned reporting that 106 now had power. The 'problem' was now mine as I had no key for my room. After some minutes, I decided to go to my room; it was locked! I went back down to reception where the original man, on seeing me, could not contain himself. "Other man he gone find you," he spluttered through a huge *betelnut*-stained grin! Typical of India!

I was looking forward to Ranikhet, as one of the places I remembered my parents talking about, and I was not disappointed. Situated in the Kumaon hills, this cantonment town is at a comfortable height of about 6,500 feet and has a pleasant temperature. I stayed at Holm Farm Heritage, originally a family bungalow, built by a British Army officer in circa 1869. Situated with a magnificent all-round view of the distant Himalayan mountains, the small hotel radiated peace and tranquillity. As I sat on the balcony sipping a cup of tea in the early evening, the only man-made sound I heard was a bugle call floating over the trees from the garrison some two miles away. Waking at dawn the following morning to the chirping of birds, the impact of seeing the hazy outline of the mountains behind the rising sun is a sight I shall never forget. Later that morning, driving around the area, I came across this traffic sign:

Maneesh, my excellent guide, needed no persuasion to take a walk in the hope of catching sight of this shy animal, which frequents those hills in significant numbers. Alas! no such luck but a lovely walk through pine forest, liberally sprinkled with rhododendron, was a joy. Ranikhet is home to the famous Kumaon Regiment whose busy soldiers, in their distinctive uniform, gave the place an extra dimension.

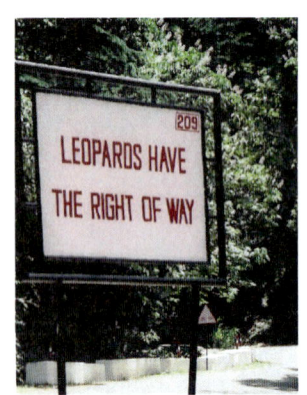

Kumaon Regiment soldiers

It was now time for my trek to Nanda Devi, at 25,645 feet, the highest mountain in India and the eighth highest in the world, conquered for the first time by an Anglo-American team in 1935. The literal meaning of Nanda Devi is 'bliss-giving goddess'. The starting point for the trek was Mansiari, an uninspiring place, but with a magnificent view of Panch Chuli (five peaks all over 20,000 feet). The route 'up' basically followed the river Gori Ganga through some testing terrain. On Day 3 we camped at Bugdiyar where an Indian Army post monitors all movement towards the Tibetan border. I duly presented myself to one of three scruffy soldiers cramped into a small smoked-filled room furnished with three beds and a table on which sat a radio which crackled into life from time to time. After a cursory examination of my passport, I completed the

Towards Devi

mandatory form, much of which duplicated information contained in my passport: the situation was reminiscent of *Midnight Express*. The fifty-kilometre route north towards the Devi was tough in places but generally straightforward with some wonderful views along the way.

We arrived at Ganagher (12,500 feet), a village uninhabitable during the harsh winter months, located at the point where the Panchu glacier meets the Gori Ganga. It is here that the route turns west towards the Devi. With a heightened expectation of, in the morning, moving to the Devi base camp, I went to bed happy only to be woken a couple of hours later unable to breath. Having twice before suffered from Cheyne Stokes syndrome, when in thin air the cardio-vascular system momentarily shuts down, I knew what was happening. The small tent only added to my sense of claustrophobia. Relief is often achieved by getting up so I left the tent to walk around in the cold night air. Feeling better, I went back to bed only to be woken again soon afterwards terrified that I was about to suffocate. Maneesh was terrific. Realising what was needed, he propped me up between our rucksacks and spent the rest of the night keeping me talking.

A call from Maneesh at dawn alerted me that something special awaited if I could summon the energy to get out of my 'bag'. He was right. There in the distance was the Devi, framed between two hills, bathed in orange sunlight as the sun began its climb upwards.

| Never a Dull Moment

Maneesh at our hotel!

Compared with any mountain I've seen, the Devi is scintillatingly beautiful – small surprise since she is a goddess to the people of Kumaon. As the sun rose, it was as though the mountain was aware of being watched by an admirer as she tried in vain to shake off the clouds which prevented her showing herself to best advantage. Considering my problems, there was no alternative to 'going down' so we set off without delay. Arriving at Railkot, for the second time in 24 hours, I decided to take a 'cat' nap. Disaster, as I was awoken by another struggle to get my breath. A further 'leg' of 14 kilometres, added to the 13 we had already done, resulted in us reaching Bugdiyar, completely shattered, in darkness six hours later. Much lower, I slept well that night.

The remaining distance back to Mansiari was completed without mishap. On the way, we passed thousands of goats and sheep making their way up to the rich summer pastures. I was also lucky to get reasonably close to a herd of notoriously shy *bharals*, commonly known as Himalayan blue sheep, whose coat changes depending on the angle of the sun. The male is a handsome animal with a powerful body and horns to match. Talking of fauna, the mountain chough was a constant and acrobatically adept companion on both treks. Surprisingly, I saw very few birds of prey. It was probably imagination but I had a distinct feeling I had travelled the mountain road to Nainital before. This sense of familiarity heightened when I saw the lake around which the town is built. And, after I took a ride to the highest point along what used to be the main bridleway, still frequented by numerous rhesus monkeys, very similar to a spot where previously I had been thrown off a horse and bitten, I was sure this was where my father had pointed to 'Everest'. Nainital (the Eye Lake) remains a popular summer retreat for families from the plains. The Boat Club, established in 1845, venue for my 'last supper' before returning to Delhi, has retained the décor, dress code and membership criteria almost certainly in place before the British left India.

My insatiable appetite to uncover legacies of the Raj took me to a forestry department bungalow near Nainital. Everything about the place was quaint and atavistic: the loo, the wooden floorboards, the plumbing and the high windows 'shouted' originality. After a small 'bribe' the *chowkidar*, who had been there for twenty years, agreed to show me around. The door creaked open to reveal a world that had long since passed. The smell was a mix of seasoned wood, damp plaster and musty carpets covered in a thin layer of dust. The place had a real charm set among a mixture of pines and deciduous trees that provided an ideal habitat for the dozens of rhesus monkeys who had made the area home. I enjoyed watching their sense of fun and mischief as they swung about in the trees. In this place I felt content and reassured that, fifty years on, places still existed intact as a reminder of former times.

The day after I arrived back in Delhi, I visited the Taj Mahal, hardly expecting the temperature to be a strength-sapping 48 degrees Celsius! Everyone in the world knows the profile of the Taj Mahal. But that does not diminish the impact when first seen. Built entirely of white marble, the tomb took 22 years to complete in 1653. The Taj is a symbol of Shah Jehan's love for his wife Mumtaz, who predeceased him. As one of the wonders of the world, the Taj Mahal is more beautiful than any words could ever convey.

During my thirty days there, during which I covered around 3,000 kilometres, I had no more than the merest glimpse of India. Its geography is vast, its history long, and it possesses a rich heritage. The Himalaya dominates the Indian subcontinent over several thousand miles. Despite several visits to Pakistan and one to Nepal, the first sight of the mountains in India filled me with awe. In an increasingly troubled world, in which the stresses and strains of everyday life take their toll, people are turning more to these mountains in the hope of finding the true meaning of life. That was certainly the case with Maneesh who had given up practising the law for the life of a guide. But that was not the reason why I went. On reflection, I suppose the answer in my case lay in my early life. Those boyhood images of snow-covered mountains glittering in the sun have remained vivid in my memory for the past fifty years. Also, the everyday sights, sounds and smells of India are unique and seldom forgotten.

So, has stirring the mulligatawny produced a good result? Most certainly is the short answer. India is a country of wondrous contrast, an experience around every corner where, if you take the trouble to meet people, you will be assured of a friendly welcome. This is particularly noticeable in Kumaon where the people possess charm and hospitality in the best traditions of Himalayan dwellers. But do not expect your visit to be without problems. Vehicles break down, punctuality is not generally a priority, trains are scruffy, hotels do not meet accepted European standards and, if you need to eat meat, do not stray from the main cities. But I felt comfortable, relaxed and at peace in India during an odyssey I shall never forget. In the words of Walter de la Mare, 'The journey is always worth making even though the end may not be in sight.' More mulligatawny? Any time!

* * * * *

'Trains and Tea, but no Tiger'

I wrote this piece on a subsequent visit to India in, I think, 2006-07.

India is a vast country, full of contrasts, complexities and contradictions. It is colourful, noisy, exotic and mystical, a land that demands the use of all five senses. It is a place where cows are sacred, monkeys roam unimpeded, pie dogs are tolerated and snakes are both reviled and revered. It is impossible to be unmoved by India. Flying into and out of Delhi, it was to the beautiful foothills of the snow-capped Himalayan mountains of India that I made my way in the autumn of 2004. Although discovered hundreds of years before, the Himalayas only truly entered the British psyche when Everest was first climbed in 1953.

Darjeeling, during British times a fashionable hill station, is now a thriving tourist resort for West Bengalis. But the town will forever be remembered as the home of Tenzing Norgay who, along with Ed Hillary, was the first to conquer Everest. The family house, aptly named after his father, is still occupied by Tenzing's son Jamling with whom I had the privilege of an 'audience' in the same room used by his father to receive guests.

Mount Trisul (7,120 metres) from Ranikhet

Soon after his epic climb of Everest, Tenzing was appointed chief instructor of the newly-founded Himalayan Mount-aineering Institute in Darjeeling, where he was laid to rest after his death in May 1986. The HMI is well worth a visit. The sight of Kangchenjunga ('five treasures of snow'), the third-highest peak in the world after Everest and K2, standing proud against a sky of deep blue on a plinth of foothills, is never-to-be-forgotten.

Since British days, Darjeeling has boasted a crop of excellent private schools, none better than St Paul's where I watched the sports day.

Such commitment, endeavour and sportsmanship I witnessed would grace any playing field in the world. Knowing that Margaret's Hope estate, about thirty kilometres from Darjeeling, produced tea for Buckingham Palace, I decided to take a chance and go there on spec: I was not disappointed.

Explaining that the estate still employed the principles on which it had been founded about 100 years ago, the manager Bijay emphasised that tea was a way of life. Family considerations were all important. Margaret's Hope employed over 1,000 which, together with families, effectively meant there were 3,000-plus living on the estate. The tradition of working on tea was passed down through generations. The estate provided schools, a hospital and a welfare service. Asked about the name, Bijay explained that in the 19th century it had changed due to a family bereavement. The owner's daughter, Margaret, loved the place so much that when she had to return to England to complete her education, it had been her fervent wish to return to the estate. Alas! on the boat home she fell ill and died. In her memory, her father had changed the name of the estate.

Train travel is and always has been a vital part of life in India. From the earliest days, Indians have taken the opportunity of riding anywhere on trains, including the roofs of packed

Jamling Norgay in his Darjeeling house

Kanchenjunga (8,598 metres)

Margaret's Hope tea estate near Darjeeling

| Never a Dull Moment

A control room on the Darjeeling Himalayan Railway

75 years 'young' at Darjeeling station

carriages. A long train journey is a must for anyone new to the country. The 'quill-pen' control systems are still as effective today as they where when first introduced by the British about 100 years ago.

If steam, smoke and soot are your passion, then northern India, home to two spectacular and historic steam railways, is a must. The Himalayan Queen and the Himalayan Railway to Darjeeling still provide a vital service today as they did when first introduced in 1903 and 1881 respectively. The route of the Himalayan Queen, the train which terminates at Shimla, from where the British Empire in India was run during the summer months, climbs 7,000 feet in sixty miles. After leaving the hot plains at Kalka, the line passes through some stunning scenery before reaching its destination some six hours later. As mentioned earlier, Shimla is a thriving town that has a wealth of history, and has managed successfully to retain the balance and charm of both the old and the modern. It is a 'must' for the discerning tourist. Over to the east, the award of World Heritage status to the Darjeeling Himalayan Railway is a tribute to an operation that has hardly changed since its opening in 1881.

Uninitiated train travellers would be wise not to become complacent even when in possession of a ticket. Armed with my ticket for the prestigious Rajdhani Express, from New Jalpaiguri to Delhi, a journey that would take 22 hours, I went to confirm my seat at the ticket office only to find that I was third on the waiting-list. "But do not worry, sir, as you will get a seat," I was assured. Checking again, about half an hour before the train was due to arrive, I was alarmed to discover that my situation had not changed; I was still on the waiting-list!! With a characteristic waggle of the head, I was advised to speak to the train manager once the train arrived. Great, but how would I recognise him? He would be wearing a blue coat and 'you have a 99% chance, so do not worry'. Indian railway stations are wonderful places for passing time, with the social divisions of caste, class and sex everywhere to be seen, but my mind was preoccupied by negative thoughts of what if? Picking out an official holding a clipboard, I was told that I could find the train manager at the far end of the train, some twenty carriages away. Accompanied by my porter, wearing his obligatory red turban, on which he balanced my bag, and his red waistcoat, I pushed my way through a crowd, all speaking at once, to see a man wearing a blue uniform and a peaked hat. After one feeble attempt to make myself heard, my 'Excuse me', delivered with a raised voice, had the desired effect. Stating my problem as succinctly as I could, he replied there were no seats available. What about if I paid extra? No reaction. In desperation, as he put his whistle to his mouth, "Can I upgrade?" With an incline of his head and a few words, my porter beckoned me to follow him into an air-conditioned sleeper compartment occupied by a man sitting crossed-legged on the seat opposite. Much relieved and breathing heavily, I settled into what was a fascinating and comfortable journey, in the company of the manager of a tea plantation and a lawyer.

After the hustle and bustle of bazaars and travel, it was nice to spend three days in the peace and tranquillity of the Corbett National Park where I hoped to see one of the hundred and fifty or so tigers whose habitat the park now is. The Corbett, cradled in the foothills of the Himalaya, is within easy reach of Delhi. Founded in 1936, it was renamed in 1955 after Jim Corbett, who hunted man-eating tigers and leopards and whose stirring tales, like *Man-Eaters of Kumaon,* are the essence of adventure in a bygone age.

Jim Corbett after shooting

Mounting the *howdah* (seating platform on top of an elephant) at around 5.30 am, we set off into the jungle comforted by the heat from the rising sun burning off the chilly morning mist. We were soon making our way silently through thick undergrowth the only sound coming from the elephant as she pushed aside saplings or broke off a branch to eat. As we made our way deeper into the jungle, I felt a frisson of fear run through my body as I imagined a tiger suddenly springing from the undergrowth to confront us: it was as though we were being watched. There was also the uncertainty of riding an elephant for the first time. I need not have worried, as the closest we got to a tiger were numerous examples of fresh pugmarks.

The *mahout* (elephant minder), apparently the most experienced in the park, ensured that we missed nothing by drawing attention to the abundance of other fauna including spotted deer, samba, jackal, langur and rhesus monkeys and wild boar, as well as demonstrating complete control of his elephant.

Later in the day, while on a jeep safari, I found myself in close proximity to a herd of wild elephants. Rounding a blind corner the herd, which included a youngster, was less than 100 metres ahead – an amazing sight. Then, as we edged forward, the naturalist told the driver to 'Stop!' in a tone that suggested all was not well. Moments later, no more than thirty metres ahead, a bull elephant crashed out of the undergrowth, stopped, and faced us with tail raised, a sure sign of agitation. Clearly, in the elephant's mind, we were not supposed to be there and, as the guard to the herd, he had to decide what action to take. Thankfully, deciding to rejoin the family group, he turned and trotted off. A scary moment for, if he had decided to charge, this huge creature would have been unstoppable.

The Mahout atop Jespi

Spotted deer

My second venture into the foothills of the great Himalayan range, mainly Uttaranchal, the newest Indian state, confirmed it as a place of rare beauty where great rivers are 'born', mountains dominate and the cults of Hinduism are perpetuated for all to see. Not seeing a tiger palls into insignificance when compared with other aspects of a trip I shall never forget, particularly the people whose friendliness, politeness and hospitality has left an indelible impression.

* * * * *

Highway to Nepal

(The EDP Magazine, 8 June 2002)

When intrepid traveller Ian Vaughan-Arbuckle trekked through the Himalayan foothills of Nepal he encountered Maoist guerillas and suffered the worst night of his life and yet wouldn't have missed any of it for the world.

Once the events of 11/9 put paid to my plans to explore Baluchistan, I decided instead to make the pilgrimage to Everest, or to give the mountain its Nepalese name, Chomolungma. As it was the International Year of the Mountains, to visit the greatest of them all seemed highly symbolic. My plan was to trek from Jiri to Everest Base Camp via Namche Bazaar, before retracing my steps to Lukla and flying back to Kathmandu. In all 21 days walking to a maximum height of 5,550 metres.

Kathmandu differs little from other Asian capital cities I have visited. Grid-locked with traffic, a seething mass of humanity goes about its business oblivious to the dangerous pall of smog that lurks menacingly overhead. Disappointingly to some, Buddhist values have given way to a fixation of achieving material progress.

None the less, the great stupa of Swayamburnath has survived intact. The steep climb to the stupa is well worth the effort to observe the supplicants and to watch the antics of the rhesus monkeys that have made the holy place their home.

Nepal is currently facing a political and constitutional crisis of Significant proportions. The tragic murder last June of King Birendra and Queen Aishwarya by their eldest son, Crown Prince Dipendra, who also killed seven other members of the royal family before turning the weapon on himself, has left the monarchy in a fragile and vulnerable position. To many citizens. the tragic massacre was a conspiracy prompted by India and executed on the orders of a prominent politician. Maoist rebels, meanwhile, are engaged in a terrorist campaign, which has seen attacks in both towns and rural areas.

Only the day before I left, 85 policemen were gunned down in their barracks in West Nepal. The Maoist threat has to be taken seriously despite government protestations that matters are under control. After

| Never a Dull Moment

only five days, we – Chabi my Sherpa guide and I – encountered the Maoist factor first hand.

In Junbesi, our 'landlady' told us that, the previous evening, a Maoist 'soldier', had held her up at gunpoint, demanding food and shelter. Then, the next day, we were confronted on a lonely stretch' of track by three smartly dressed, armed Maoist youths who demanded to know our personal details and proposed itinerary.

In the event, nothing untoward happened but these incidents served to prove the Maoist threat is alive and potentially dangerous. Walking against the grain, for the first seven days, was strenuous and provided ideal strength training and acclimatisation! In Nepal, it is all to do with how long rather than how far one walks. What really counts is the physical effort of negotiating demanding 'ups and downs' all day long. By the time we got to Namche Bazaar we had climbed almost exactly the height of Everest (8,848 metres) and the corresponding descents totalled the height of Ama Dablam (6,828 metres). In scenic terms, the

Travel – India, Pakistan and Nepal |

initial phase to Namche Bazaar is somewhat dull compared with what is to come. Much of the time is spent walking through small terraced fields of mainly rice and potatoes, patches of forest and rhododendron, across swing bridges spanning turbulent water and through hamlets of varying standard. We pressed on inexorably towards Everest, my appetite whetted by the occasional glimpse of giant snow-capped mountains.
The change, once we entered the Khumbu, was dramatic.
We approached Everest, up the wonderful Dudh Kosi (Milk River) until we crossed its tributary river the Bhote Kois on a rickety bridge. Here we were in the deep shadow of the gorge, which rose in a series of bare rock cliffs punctuated with patches of shaggy grass and bushes. It was here that I got a rare, close-up look at a herd of Himalayan tahr – wild goats – with a beard that looks like the devil.
Talking of animals and bridges, reminds me of the problems caused by yaks as they slip and slide their way across suspension bridges under

(Top) Mount Everest, left, from a distance of eight miles away.
(Left) Images of Nepal (l to r): cock and bull style on a hill farm, a temple in Kathmandu; a farstead at Piri, and the Tengboche monastery, with its outstanding views of the mountains beyond

their enormous loads. Although not inherently aggressive, the yak is an immensely strong animal and their horns tend to sweep around menacingly as they pass. I needed only once to be reminded not to stand on the exposed side of a path!

Somehow I sensed that day nine was to be special and I was not disappointed. About half way up a steep, relentless climb out of the valley, Chabi suddenly said "Everest" and there, sure enough, brilliantly framed through the trees was the highest of them all standing majestically with a wisp of spindrift blowing eastwards off the summit A never-to· be-forgotten moment! About an hour later, we were at the entrance to Namche Bazaar, the heart of the Khumbu region and homeland of the Sherpas.

Set in a small amphitheatre with rows of houses along the slopes, it reminded me of a Welsh mining village. Pandering to the 'needs' of the trekker, Namche is a thriving, vibrant place where virtually anything can be purchased from Tabasco sauce to freshly baked German bread. It now also boasts an Internet café, albeit served by a rather tenuous telephone link. It was here that I caught my first and only sight – Kathmandu apart – of the camera-shy Nepalese army.

The route, as we made our way north, was inexorably 'up'. After leaving Namche, heading towards Tengboche, we called in at the Everest View Hotel, built with Japanese money to cater for the rich tourist. Guests usually fly in by helicopter, stay a night. take advantage of the superb view of Everest [rom about 20 miles and then fly out. To facilitate instant acclimatisation, additional oxygen is provided in all rooms and there are two pressurised rooms for those needing extra help.

After a climb taking well over two hours, we reached the world famous monastery at Tengboche claimed, with some justification, to have the most beautiful situation in the world. Sighted strategically, with magnificent views, the monastery dominates the surrounding countryside and, so it is said, can be clearly seen [rom the summit of Everest. There is a real sense of tranquillity and peace about the place. On the day I was there, the younger monks, some wearing their saffron robes, were playing football against the local traders. Keenly contested, with Everest providing a stunning backdrop, the game was played with great enjoyment and enthusiasm, although I doubt the individual skills would have caught the eye of any lurking talent spotter.

The curse of pulmonary oedema – aka mountain or altitude sickness – which I had previously experienced in Pakistan, began to reveal itself at about 4,200 metres. To begin with the symptoms of a headache, lack of appetite and nausea were mild, but increased in severity as we went higher. By the time we reached Pangboche, I was struggling to get my breath and had a blinding headache so we headed for the Himalayan Mountain Sickness Clinic at Periche. Here, the resident female volunteer American doctor confirmed altitude sickness and told me to 'go down' if, after taking Diamox that night, my symptoms did not improve. That night turned out to be the worst of my life.

Lying in my room, unable to sleep, with a sickening headache and fighting for breath was simply terrifying. Many times during the night I thought I was going to die.

High-level soccer: monks at Tengboche

Cheyne Stokes respiration, which plagued me all night long, gradually increases the depth of breathing before rising, in short bursts, and then ceasing for a few seconds, causing extreme anxiety. Even re-zipping one's sleeping bag, after another inevitable visit to the toilet, was exhausting. The only way I found some relief was to dress and go outside where the icy air seemed to help regulate my breathing. But it was too cold to stay out there for long. My abiding memory of this dreadful night will be the clinking yak bells as the animals moved around on a tether outside my window! How I grew to hate that sound as I lay awake coming to terms with the inevitable conclusion that my ambition to visit Everest Base Camp was over.

We set off early the next morning and, after a strong day's walk, reached Punke Tenga, about 1,000 metres lower than Periche. Over dhal bhat that evening, I was alarmed to hear, from an emotional 'landlady', how she had found an American trekker dead in bed the following morning after complaining she felt unwell. But I slept well and awoke determined not to let my 'failure' get me down.

After a strenuous hike and an equally demanding verbal effort to get our flight changed, we boarded the twin-engined Otter of Yeti Airlines for the flight back to Kathmandu.

The runway at Lukla is built high on the side of a mountain with a difference of about 60 metres between each end. This helps planes both accelerate going out and slow down coming in to the short runway. There are no navigation aides at Lukla.

Strapped in to a rudimentary canvas seat with the intense vibration and noise made by the engines, reminded me of the many military operational flights I had previously taken. Views of great mountains including Cho Oyu, Makalu, Numbur and above them all,

Chomolungma, its triumphant pennant of snow blowing from the summit, made the 50 minute flight very special, if a touch nerve-racking.

Travel in the Khumbu region offers more than just superb mountain scenery. It provides an opportunity to meet people who have lived largely untainted by modern life. Here is evidence of community and happiness even though they lack amenities that we take for granted.

My abiding memory will be of the friendliness and hospitality of the Nepalese people, from whom Westerners could still learn some lessons for leading a peaceful and contented life.

* * * * *

The Karakoram Mountains: A Challenge Too High

Sitting in a snow hole alone on a 65° slope, 18,200 ft above sea level, with the incessant rumble of avalanches to remind him of the potential dangers of his situation Ian could perhaps be forgiven for allowing some negative thoughts to enter his mind…

After I decided to quit competitive running, about two years ago, I needed something to fill the void left by a sport which had dominated my life. Pakistan was a land I had longed to explore since childhood. My plan was to spend four weeks trekking with a group in the Karakoram (Western Himalayas) followed by a fifth week on my own travelling to places like the Khyber Pass, Quetta, Nowshera, Chitral and Gilgit.

First I needed to get fit. After a six month intensive training programme, I felt ready. But when I met the other five members of the group, I realised that, apart from the American, I was the eldest by at least 20 years and significantly less experienced in mountaineering terms. This gave me food for thought.

During some tough training exercises in the two weeks following our first meeting in Rawalpindi, we satisfied Pete, the leader, of our competence in mountaineering techniques. By this time, we had also completed a number of toughening-up walks through energy-sapping soft snow and at increasing altitude, all of which paled into insignificance with what lay ahead.

The four-day walk into Base Camp over difficult terrain, including moraine and glacier, and sometimes in heavy snow, had been demanding and yet spectacular, with glimpses of some superb mountains, including Masherbrum (25,600 ft), K6 and K7 (dubbed K by the military officer who first surveyed the Karakoram mountains).

Travel – India, Pakistan and Nepal |

After a further couple of days' acclimatisation in the vicinity of our base camp, we had decided to tackle Gondoro Peak (18,583 ft). We hoped to complete the estimated six-hour approach at night, to 'summit' the following morning when the snow was still crisp and stable and then get off the mountain as quickly as possible.

We assembled at 10.30 pm. Dressed and equipped for a technical climb and carrying a heavy pack, we set off in darkness, using head torches to find our way. After a pretty straightforward march along a valley, we donned crampons and roped-up at the point where we started to climb. Throughout the night we continued to move steadily upwards through snow storms, across moraine and over one extensive glacier. The poor snow conditions were by far the most difficult aspect of the trek. Every second step we were sinking up to our knees and, at one point, I fell into snow up to my waist and had to be physically lifted out by others. The march seemed interminable and the conditions strength sapping. Conversation had long since ceased, the only sounds being the heavy breathing as we struggled to get our breath, the crunch of crampons on the snow and the occasional expletive as someone lost their footing. Dawn broke at about 4.30 am, when we got our first glimpse of the mountain, a daunting sight standing proud and

Namika (20,746 ft) seen from our campsite. Note the glacier in the foreground.

View towards Saitcho with the Charakusa glacier in the foreground

defiant in the distance. It seemed quite close at that time, but how wrong that was to prove.

After about seven hours, one of our team, a TV journalist by profession, was being violently sick and decided to throw in the towel. He went back to base camp with one of the two high altitude porters who were accompanying us.

Progress seemed very slow. As the gradient got steeper, about nine hours into the walk, our Italian colleague also decided to call it a day. Everyone was digging deep into their reserves and having moments of self-doubt. I began to feel pretty wretched. I had a nasty high altitude headache and with each step I was fighting for breath. My heart felt as though it would burst out of my chest, my legs ached like never before and I was trying to be sick. When the landscape started to spin I had to ask for a rest. To make matters worse we were now following the ridge line with a sheer drop of thousands of feet to our right. Surprisingly, this did not affect me too much as I was almost beyond caring at this stage. Treacherous, steep, unconsolidated snow collapsed into the last step if you didn't lift your leg high enough. If you stepped too high your body refused to follow. With just over 200 feet left to the summit, I was forced to admit defeat. After some 10 hours of the hardest physical challenge I had ever faced, I had just run out of 'fuel'.

Pete told me to stay put while he and the three remaining members of the team went to the summit. He thought this would take about an hour.

As it turned out, however, I was alone for three hours in a snow hole as I waited for them to return. My relief can be imagined when the others reappeared above the overhang. By this time the sun had come out to turn the snow into dangerous slush so we made all haste to get off the mountain. In the end, we got back 'home' after nearly 18 hours of exhausting physical effort, without any hot food or drink.

Without doubt, Gondoro Peak presented me with a greater challenge than any other I have experienced. Although I shall never underestimate the effort required, for example, to run a decent marathon, I now realise there are more demanding challenges to be overcome. In future, I shall also have a far better understanding of and respect for those who climb mountains.

What next? At this time I'm not sure, but there's bound to be some challenge ahead for me, Inshallah – and with my wife's agreement!

The 'road' to Hushe

* * * * *

The Land of the Pure
Travels in Pakistan 2002

'Why you come Pakistan?' asked the tall, immaculately dressed customs officer as he thumbed through my well-travelled passport. Not again, I thought as I recalled the going over to which I had been subjected as I exited Islamabad two years previously. He set about my rucksack with an enthusiasm that would have done justice to a child

| Never a Dull Moment

with a bag of sweets. But none of this could spoil what had been another exhilarating holiday in this young country.

I had chosen to go to Pakistan with Jonny Bealby after reading For a Pagan Song (Heinemann 1998), an account of a journey he had made to the Hindu Kush. After drawing breath in Islamabad, we headed off to Peshawar, the capital of the North West Frontier Province, whose fortunes are inextricably linked to those of the Khyber Pass. Our itinerary included a visit to the Khyber Rifles, the famous regiment raised by the British, who still 'police' the border with Afghanistan – a role of ever-increasing importance. The influx of large numbers of Afghanis and their livestock is creating a potentially dangerous situation. Peshawar, with only 20% Pakistanis, is now the largest Afghan city outside Kabul. Any compassion felt by the Pakistanis for their Muslim brothers has been largely eroded as the Afghanis become ever more successful. Lunch in the Officer's Mess was preceded by a wonderfully athletic and evocative display of tribal dancing by Pathans and Chitralis, each of which would comfortably 'shade' the All Blacks' prematch Hakka.

That the NWFP attracted men of exceptional courage and leadership is axiomatic. To this day British soldiers are remembered with warmth and respect. During the drive north towards Chitral, via the Malakand Pass, the deeds of derring-do by our soldiers came to mind as we passed Churchill's Picket, which still dominates the surrounding countryside. In a despatch from here in 1897, Winston Churchill, a subaltern with the 4th Hussars, vividly described a bloody hand-to-hand action by British troops who found themselves outnumbered by at least four to one.

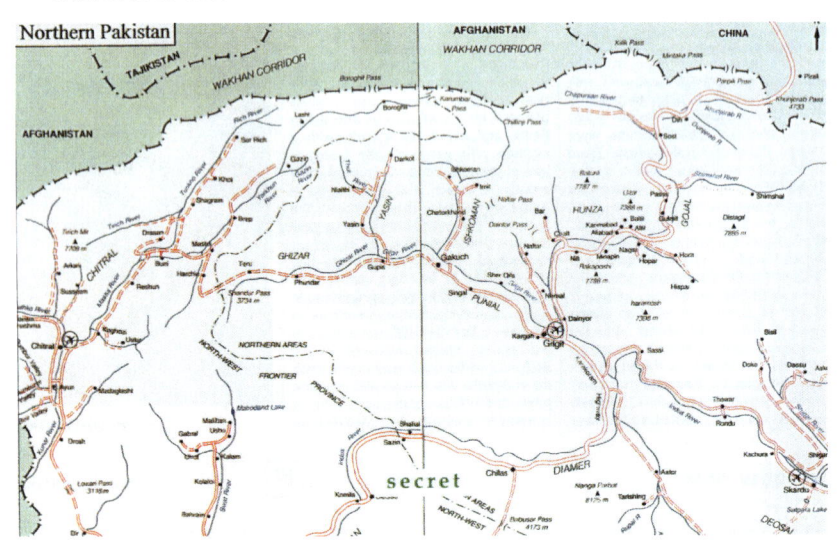

Travel – India, Pakistan and Nepal |

The Shaudur Pass

The view from the Lowari Pass (10,500 ft) of the valley below and the mountain slopes, with their patchwork of tall pines, was breathtaking. On the way down the road dropped away through regular switchbacks to the floor of the Chitral Valley more than a thousand feet below. Once down, the road to Chitral meandered through attractive green countryside mostly alongside the fast-flowing River Kunar.

Chitral lies in the heart of Marco Polo land, nestling between the rugged mountains of the Hindu Kush. Dominating all the others is Tirich Mir standing at an impressive 25,289 ft. Chitral is stunningly beautiful and steeped in British military history. The town is typically frontier; busy, basic and bustling. On the banks of the river stands Chitral Fort, formerly of some strategic importance but now rather run-down. It was here in 1895 that a British force found itself besieged. The much heralded Relief of Chitral was effected 48 days later by a force led by Colonel James Kelly who achieved the impossible by carrying two mountain guns 200 miles from Gilgit over the Shandur Pass (12,250 ft) through deep snow at the worst time of the year.

Polo is a religion in the NWFP. Played today (as it ever was) without rules, no quarter is asked or given by opposing teams. The field is a wide expanse of compacted dirt, set behind a low concrete wall, uneven and littered with loose stones. The Rajistan ponies, sturdily built on small frames, seem

Polo in Chitral

| Never a Dull Moment

High Street, Chitral

to relish the challenge of the game. With their horn-like ears pricked and nostrils flared, they respond fearlessly to the 'instructions' of their brilliant riders. The umpire's only obvious function is to throw the ball in at the start of each 25-minute chukka; thereafter anything seems to go!

Leaving Chitral, we headed for the area settled by the Kalash. From Ayun, we followed the fast flowing, colourful Rumbur river up the valley to the village of Balanguru. On both banks the valley floor was a patchwork of fields and dotted around with tall, stately walnut trees. A hospitable, peace-loving tribe, the Kalash are the only people in central Asia to have withstood the sweeping tide of Islam, despite offers of large sums of money to convert. They are subsistence farmers, living off the land, herding goats and sheep for meat and wool, and farming the valley slopes through an amazing network of irrigation channels that took centuries to create. Kalash men wear the traditional shalwar kameez (long shirt and baggy trousers) and Chitrali cap. Kalash women, on the other hand, wear traditional long black dresses embroidered at the neck, sleeves and hem and pinched in at the waist by a woven belt. From very young, women cover their head with a thick ribbon heavily decorated with cowry shells, beads, buttons and bells. Dozens of rows of beads are worn around the neck, the number denoting prestige and wealth. Thought to have links to the army of Alexander the Great, the Kalash are Kafirs (unbelievers) whose religion is complex and full of paradoxical beliefs.

Walking in the Kalash valleys is superb. A three hour walk, involving a climb of some 1,500 ft, took me to a summer pasture where I spent an unforgettable night with a Kalash family surrounded by mountains still home to wolves, bears and leopards, lit up by a full moon.

The next stage of our journey involved crossing the Shandur Pass, location of the highest polo field in the world and host to the legendary annual match between Chitral and Gilgit. Forget Oxford versus Cambridge or Liverpool against Manchester United – this is real rivalry, where these fierce competitors battle to bring honour to their town. The pass itself is stunning, with its crystal clear lakes and towering peaks on either side. After a night under canvas, which saw the thermometer drop to minus 10, I set off by myself on foot towards

Mastuj. Suddenly, there appeared from nowhere four scruffily-dressed, male youths, their features unmistakably Afghani. After exchanging the normal salaams, they were persistent in asking for 'Rupees'. Realising I was not about to give them any, one of them pushed me from behind causing me to stumble under the weight of my rucksack. Sensing danger, I raised my wooden staff. They retreated about 20 yards but then started hurling stones. Backing away, I was able to avoid the missiles and the danger eventually passed. A nasty moment, which served as a reminder of the potential dangers of travelling alone in this part of the world.

Two days later, after an overnight stay in Mastuj Fort, we reached Gilgit, a vibrant town based on one main road, and thronging with commerce. There's little

A Kalash girl

that cannot be bought in the shacks of Gilgit. Vendors are efficient, most speak English and they are willing to haggle. There is plenty of human noise, shouting above the constant din of engines and horns. It took me some time to figure out what was missing: the only women in evidence were the few dressed in a full black burqa. Tucked away towards the end of the bazaar, I found the resting place for twelve, long forgotten, Britons. These include George Hayward, the distinguished explorer, who was cruelly murdered in July 1870 on the orders of the Mir of Hunza, and Major Jimmy Mills and Captain Dick Jones who both perished on 18 July 1962, while climbing Khunyang Chish. I was appalled to learn that the current caretaker, Ghulam Ali and his father before him, had tended this Christian cemetery for over 50 years of their own volition and, visitor donations apart, without financial support. Despite a plethora of well-deserved complimentary remarks in the visitor's book, including one from a delegation from the House of Lords, it seems that Ghulam Ali has never received the support he surely deserves; my next project!

From Gilgit the road follows the brittle gorge of the Hunza River north towards Karimabad (formerly Hunza). Landslides and rock falls are common. The first glimpse of Rakaposhi (25,550 ft) is unforgettable. Rounding a corner, the mountain is revealed in all its glory: snow-covered summit, glacier receding far up under the base of the mountain and green wilderness pouring down to the road. Further up the road, the bare mountains give way to fertile valleys. As we approached Karimabad, the 600 year old Baltit Fort dominated the valley, a blaze of reds, greens and yellows provided by the trees in their Autumn 'plumage'.

Having previously experienced the 14 hour, bone-shaking journey along the Karakoram Highway, news that the Fokker Friendship would fly to Islamabad was most welcome (even if the aircraft was 40 years old). More often than not the flight has to be cancelled because of poor visibility. I now know why! Soon after takeoff, Nanga Parbat came into view at 26,656 ft; dwarfing all other mountains, including Haramosh, she soars to her immense height in majestic isolation. To the spirit hungry for exploration, adventure and a sense of history, Pakistan calls. Until my plans to explore Baluchistan become a reality, I shall have to content myself with these memories of 'The Land of the Pure'.

Hunza Valley

* * * * *

Journey to the Khyber

Danger is an ever-present feature of life in the North-West Frontier Province (NWFP) of Pakistan. Murder, intrigue and lawlessness abound in an area which, to this day, is controlled by war lords, not the Pakistani government. The landscape is harsh and the people, mostly Pathans, cold, hard and fierce; and yet they live by a clearly defined, understood and accepted code of conduct. Because of its geographical position, the NWFP has always been a strategic and natural target for the collection of intelligence, these days mostly concerned with drug-trafficking and terrorism.

After Arthur Connolly, a lieutenant in the Bengal lancers, and a colleague were beheaded in 1842 for being caught red-handed making maps, the British government decided to use native travellers to survey these sensitive and dangerous areas. Since even suspicion would have resulted in death, their existence and activities were a closely-guarded secret. The techniques they used were ingenious. They were taught to count the number of paces during a day's march, they used Buddhist rosary beads to keep track of distances and had false pockets to conceal maps and other objects. It was these brave men – the pioneers who established the infrastructure and the soldiers who garrisoned British India – to whom my thoughts turned as I stood at the Western end of

Travel – India, Pakistan and Nepal |

the Khyber Pass, looking towards Afghanistan, on a sweltering day in July 1998.

To live in a place, to yearn for it after leaving and then finally to return is exciting. As a boy, I had lived with my parents in Landi Kotal, the capital of the Khyber region, where my father commanded an Indian Army training unit. My memories were of starched uniforms, colourful accoutrements, whitewashed walls, bugle calls and trains. It seems that not much has changed in the intervening 50 years.

My first night was spent in Peshawar, capital city of the NWFP, where the contents of the bazaar are as diverse as the people within it. Alongside colourful secret rugs, woollen Balti hats, spices and fresh vegetables, is the contraband smuggled in via the Khyber Pass from Europe. Poverty and affluence co-exist in an atmosphere of free trade. A tug at my sleeve and 'Chai?' prompted me to follow an urchin boy with a cheeky grin into a rather dingy shop, where I drank a cup of piping hot, sweet brew under the gaze of what seemed like several dozen people, keen to witness the 'event'. After a further couple of hours exploring the alleyways and watching the comings and goings, I returned to the hotel excited and stimulated by what I had seen.

My initial plan to travel to the Khyber by rail was dashed when I discovered, during a visit to the cantonment station, that the train now ran only once a month. Seeing how disappointed I was, the helpful station master arranged for me to see the two remaining steam locomotives, built in Glasgow in c. 1920, and rolling stock 'parked' in

*Pakistani 'truck art':
Bus up the Khyber*

a nearby siding. Now decrepit and yet still standing proud, they evoked strong images of better days when the engines daily puffed the 30 or 50 miles up severe gradients towards the railhead at Landi Kotal. Rumbling over 92 bridges, thundering through 34 tunnels and zigzagging through the mountains, the train was always a magnificent sight and a constant tribute to Victor Bayley's engineering skills in building one of the world's most remarkable railway lines.

I was now left with travelling by road as the only alternative way of reaching the Khyber Pass, for which I would need to obtain the obligatory permit to travel. Early the next morning, I made my way to the Office of the Political Agent where I was granted an entry permit and allocated my Khussador (Tribal Guard) who would ensure my safety in the tribal area of the Khyber Pass. Permit in hand and accompanied by Masif Mohammed, a Pathan armed with a Kalashnikov and four full magazines, we set off on the crowded road from Peshawar. The heat was punishing and the road bumpy, in an ancient Morris, on the way to the gateway to the Khyber at Jamrud. Here my permit was checked by men of the Khyber Rifles who were wearing the same brown uniform and pugree (headdress) as they had done when they were part of the British Army. In the background behind the gate stood Jamrud Fort, now proudly flying the Pakistani flag, which had previously housed so many famous British regiments. A sign on the other side of the gateway reminded travellers to 'Seek help from Almighty God'!

The Khyber now lay ahead. Thirty miles of menacing, winding road where danger lurked hidden from the unsuspecting traveller. It was over this hostile, inhospitable terrain that British soldiers fought many a bloody battle against the Pathans, who have only ever been defeated by Alexander the Great. Regimental badges fashioned in concrete and located at points along the only road provided another reminder of former days. I found myself imagining soldiers marching in columns to fife and drum towards another fight against a deadly foe. The bravery and courage shown by our soldiers, as adversaries, is largely responsible for the respect shown by the Pakistanis towards the British which is found in the region today. Most wanted to know where I was

Travel – India, Pakistan and Nepal |

I can if you can!

from – which invariably resulted in an animated Gateway to the Khyber at Jamrud undeclared conversation and the offer of a chai.

The ultimate status symbol in this part of the world is the personal weapon. Crossed bandoleers hang over men's shoulders and daggers are de rigueur. Violence is a way of life. Cold eyes, set in sunken sockets, survey all before them from behind full black beards, giving the men a fearsome aura. The shops in the Landi Kotal bazaar openly stock assault rifles, machine guns, pistols, grenades and ammunition. At one such shop the proprietor offered me a pen pistol and seemed offended when I explained that to attempt to take such a thing into the UK would land me in jail!

Landi Kotal is awash with narcotics so it should not have surprised me when a young local offered me a 'smoke'. In excellent English he said, 'It's a special smoke, Sahib', and seemed very disappointed when I refused. Mohammed, my minder, had no such inhibitions! Being a border town and free of customs, a huge smuggling trade passes through Landi Kotal. After journeying from all over the world to Kabul, goods are transferred to lorries and taken to near the Pakistani border where they are cross-loaded onto pack-mules or camels. Convoys of contraband are a common sight and I particularly enjoyed seeing camels struggling into the town loaded with lorry tyres. No duty is paid at any stage.

Gateway to the Khyber at Jamrud

Violence pervades every aspect of life in Pakistan and yet, ever since my early days in what was then India, I have never felt at risk. On the contrary, my experience is of genuine affection and respect for the British. A dangerous place it may be for the unwary, but for me the NWFP of Pakistan is a place that has thrilled, excited and daunted me.

16: An Invitation from the Secret Intelligence Service

If this part of my story seems a little vague and thin on detail, it has to be because I am still subject to the Official Secrets Act.

I took a cursory glance at the brown envelope on my desk in the MOD. It was like most others except that, unusually, it was addressed to me by name whereas most were directed to my official designation. The first thing I saw on opening the letter was that it came from the Foreign Office. 'Dear Mr Vaughan-Arbuckle … your name has been passed to us as someone who might be interested in an appointment for which we have a vacancy.' The letter went on to say that if I was interested I should phone a number to make an appointment to discuss matters further. No-one else in the office seemed to have any idea of what or who was behind the letter. All manner of thoughts ran through my mind for the rest of that day. Was it because I had been turned down for promotion in favour of a senior retired Commander from Scotland Yard because 'I was too young' or, perhaps, it was something to do with the fact that I had let it be known that I wanted to return to investigatory work rather than be stuck in an office in the former Royal Military Academy, Woolwich?

The number was answered by a cultured female voice that impressed me by knowing exactly who I was. Without delay, an appointment was made for me to see a Mr 'R'. The promised confirmatory letter followed with exact instructions. I was to report to a house in Carlton Gardens, bringing my passport, about two weeks later.

As I made my way by train into central London, my mind churned over the possibilities of what this was all about. I came to no conclusions except that it must surely be connected to my work as a vetting officer, at which I had done well within the MOD. After making sure I knew exactly where I was going, I circled around Horse Guards, wasting time, before knocking on the shiny black door at precisely 2 pm. The door was opened by a security guard who asked me to sign in and invited me to take a seat in the foyer. The house was impressive with high ceilings, oak doors with brass furniture, oil paintings hanging on most walls, and a winding, carpeted staircase leading away from the reception area. No sooner had I sat down, than a young woman introduced herself by her first name and said that 'Derek' was ready to see me.

After a few pleasantries, Derek opened the proceedings by asking me 'whether I knew where I was?' Funny question, I thought as I replied, "The Foreign Office, Carlton Gardens." "It's not quite like that," he replied, as he went on to explain that he was a recruitment officer for SIS (Secret Intelligence Service) or MI6 as it is sometimes inaccurately called. I tried not to show my surprise and excitement at this unexpected revelation. The chat-like, yet probing interview, during which it became obvious I was being considered for an appointment in the vetting section, lasted about an hour. At the end, Derek thanked me for taking the time to attend and for being such an interesting interlocutor! I would be hearing from him within fourteen days. Under no circumstances was I to say anything to anybody, including my wife, about the job or the interview.

Sure enough, another envelope appeared on my desk within two weeks saying 'they' would like to take matters further by inviting me to a final interview to be held at Carlton Gardens. On the appointed day, I arrived to find the same procedures in place, except that this time I was offered a cup of tea. On entering the room, there were three men sitting behind a table with a single chair in front of them. Derek was sitting to one side and a secretary on the other. The three introduced themselves: the chairman was from the security department, with a member each from personnel department and the vetting section. The general line of questioning was unexceptional and mostly to do with my life, aspirations, likes and dislikes, social life and particularly my military career and vetting work within the MOD. Then, out of the blue, one of the Board – the chairman, I think – said, "There is a strain running through your military reports which suggests that you can be impetuous at times. If you were vetting a female undergraduate at Cambridge for a job with us, who was reluctant to answer the more personal questions, how would you handle the situation?" Surprised by the question, I replied instinctively, "Well, I certainly wouldn't be impetuous." My answer made them laugh and, if there was any ice to be broken, this did it. The rest of the interview passed without incident. I was thanked for attending and informed that I would receive the result within two weeks: I still could not say anything about the process through which I was going.

Meanwhile, the MOD had sent me on a project management course at the Civil Service College. One evening towards the end of the week, the telephone rang in my room. It was my very old, close chum Richard H who, after leaving the Army, had joined SIS and was at home on leave from South America. Learning that I was awaiting the outcome of my Board, he said that he would find out how I had got on. About an hour later he phoned back to say that I had passed and would be getting my 'offer letter' shortly. I did and it contained all I needed to know about the terms of service for me to make a quick decision to accept the offer and resign from the MOD. But my offer was dependent upon the successful conclusion of the security vetting process. My vetting review, for I already had high-level security clearance, was carried out at my home in Norfolk by an investigating officer who, throughout the two-hour interview, took no notes as he perched on a chair in the sitting room which I was in the midst of decorating. As an experienced 'vetter' myself, I found this approach intriguing. The interview must have revealed no adverse matters as I was subsequently deemed suitable and granted enhanced high-level security clearance.

I joined on the same day as a group of others who had been recruited by SIS to fill all manner of jobs. We had all reported to an anonymous multi-storey tower block south of the Thames, called Century House, whose existence as an SIS building was never supposed to be made public. Straightaway we were briefed that whenever coming to this building we should approach with discretion, taking appropriate action not to draw attention to ourselves. However, as I subsequently found out, travelling on London buses, conductors approaching the area would invariably announce with more than a degree of mischief, "Lambeth tube station; all spies alight 'ere!"

For the next week, we were taught the way things were done in the office, some of which were distinctly idiosyncratic. The rabbit warren of Century House, with its peeling lino and Formica tables had a forlorn air and hardly provided accommodation in keeping with the headquarters of SIS. On the following Monday, I reported to the building where I was to be based. This was on the south side of the Thames next to what is now the Globe Theatre. 'I've arrived,' I thought, as I took in the unobstructed view from my new office directly opposite St Paul's across the Thames. My new boss, Alf C, was a white-haired gentleman who sat jacketless, displaying a pair of red braces holding up his baggy trousers, wearing a bow tie to match his braces, and with a pair of bifocals perched on the end of his nose – very much a professorial figure, who invariably had a transistor radio playing classical music. After a few perfunctory questions about my background in vetting, he pointed to a large pile of files on the floor beside his desk, invited me to read them and then be prepared to come back and discuss each case. "Oh yes, and please get into the habit of not knocking before entering an office. All to do with ensuring that no-one can get up to mischief," he explained. I retreated to my office weighed down by the files. About an hour later, Alf came in to enquire how I was getting on! Admitting that I had barely digested the first file, he sat down and, over the next three hours, proceeded to explain each case in detail without referring to either the file or to any notes, pausing after each to seek my views! A masterful performance of recall and perspicacity, the like of which I had never previously experienced nor have I since!

Within the next few days, I was allocated a couple of cases, both of which involved a considerable amount of travel, very efficiently arranged by my personal secretary. When I presented these cases completed, written up and fully documented, a couple or so weeks later, Alf called me in to discuss them. He was entirely satisfied with the work but invited me to 'slow down a bit' otherwise I would get a reputation for being over-zealous! What a change from the 'quantity before quality' approach which had prevailed in the MOD.

Vetting has been around for as long as one person has had to decide whether or not they could trust another. In former times, this was done informally by asking questions, followed by a snap judgement, and confirmed by a shake of the hand. Security vetting as we know it today was originally introduced by Prime Minister Attlee in 1948 at the onset of the Cold War to prevent the leak of information to the Soviet Union and its communist allies. Over the years, usually in the wake of a major spy scandal, the system has been refined and amended. Vetting was seen in the SIS as the first line of defence in ensuring against infiltration by a hostile country, and to provide periodic checks of those in the Service to ensure that they remained honest, reliable and trustworthy. Latterly, emphasis turned more towards vetting against a member of the Press or terrorist sympathisers getting into the Service. The issue of vetting those from a foreign background, whose mother tongue would be useful, was brought into sharp focus as the Service attempted to recruit those who could speak Arabic, Pashtu and Urdu to help in the fight against Al-Qaida.

When I first joined, SIS lived beneath the shroud of secrecy within which no-one could admit to working in the Service. That was all to change soon after the move to Vauxhall Cross when legislation to put SIS on a statutory footing was piloted through the House of Commons by the then Foreign Secretary, Robin Cook. There was a definite fear that avowal would strip the service of its mystique, built up largely by fictional characters like James Bond. This had been perpetuated through secrecy since no-one had any way of judging whether the fictional portrayal was on the mark or not. There were definitely those who were furious that the Service had 'come in from the cold' – in the main, the older element – while others welcomed the new way of things.

History has provided numerous cases, from Blake to Prime and, more recently, Ames to Nicholson, of those who have chosen to betray their country. The main weakness of any vetting system is that clearance is only good for the day on which it is granted. Thereafter, great reliance is placed on those with responsibility to flag up worries about individuals in their care. Too often, significant indicators that all might not be well with someone having been ignored, sometimes with potentially catastrophic consequences. Take, for example, the bachelor SIS station clerk working in the Middle East who was regularly drinking over 140 units of alcohol per week in sleazy bars and nightclubs, running up significant levels of debt and conducting extra-marital affairs. This state of affairs only came to light during a routine interview of a friend of his who said he was worried about him. I was subsequently sent to investigate the matter, only to find the head of station defensive and unco-operative in case the matter should reflect badly upon him personally! After my report had been considered, both the head of station and the clerk concerned were called back to the UK, the latter for treatment and rehabilitation, and the former to be reprimanded for his unprofessional conduct.

As might be expected, the majority of people, particularly those in SIS, are responsible and law-abiding. Part of the vetting process is to provide after-care to those whose lives have got into difficulty. It is hardly surprising that, being a microcosm of society, potential recruits and those serving in SIS are vulnerable to the weaknesses of flesh and mind, as are members of the wider public. In the case of the individual in the Middle East, after two years of being kept under review and receiving treatment for alcoholism, he had his clearance restored and continued to complete a full career. A vetting officer's job requires dedication, compassion and an understanding of human behaviour and weaknesses. During a talk to SIS staff by John Le Carré (aka David Cornwell), he recalled that probably the most interesting, satisfying and personally challenging job he had while working within the Intelligence Services was as a vetting officer. The work of a vetting officer is seldom without interest, incident or surprise and, like any job, it does have its lighter moments. Take the occasion when the family dog took a fancy to my leg, just as I was about to probe the question of sexuality! I also well remember the occasion when a piece of paper fluttered down from an interviewee's wallet. Seeing that, he went bright red, and picking it up, I was surprised to read, 'I fancy you like mad and would like to go to bed with you. If you agree, smile and I'll know. If not, please return this card as I am rather short of them!'

During my twelve years' working as a vetting officer for SIS, I had many difficult cases. There was, for example, the attractive, talented and capable young woman who had worked in the MOD who was a Reserve officer in the RAF. She was trying to join SIS with the help of a couple of 'inside' contacts. After passing the recruitment process with flying colours, her file was passed to me to confirm the high-level security clearance she had already been granted. After examining her CV and other associated documents, which noted that she had studied in Russia where she had married 'for convenience', and a number of other potentially adverse indicators, I decided to carry out a full investigation of her background – an unusual decision, given that she already held a valid security clearance. I did so because her previous clearance had been rather superficial and had not fully answered questions which came to mind in reading her papers. After carrying out extensive background enquiries, I called her in for a whole-life Subject Interview. So complex was the case, it took two days to complete. Because of the potentially complex and controversial nature of the case, I asked the technical department to provide a hidden camera to record the interview verbatim. To the great embarrassment of those who had set it up, the camera failed and I was left writing up the interview from the notes I had taken. My conclusion, which was supported 'up the line', was that 'Kate' was, in all probability, a Russian 'sleeper' with the long-term aim of infiltrating SIS. Despite her undoubted linguistic talents, she was not granted clearance.

Then there was the very clever young man of Chinese origin who had been privately educated at an English public school at the expense of his father, a Hong Kong policeman of modest rank. No-one, including the candidate, could explain how his father had managed to find a total of around £100K to fund his son's education. What was not in doubt was that the candidate's father had strong connections with the Triad communities in Hong Kong and, through this, to Triad members in the UK. During my protracted investigation, many facts emerged to cast doubt upon his background and family and, therefore, the suitability of 'Chan We Sun' for high-level clearance. He was denied clearance and failed his candidature. Vetting failures were not always popular with either the recruiting staff or the sponsoring section which sometimes led to heated round-table discussions with a senior officer in the chair. Most realised, however, that where there was any doubt, the benefit had to be given to a non-recommendation – for experience proved that to overturn a vetting recommendation could, in the long term, have catastrophic consequences.

A high-profile example of a flawed vetting case concerned a disaffected officer named Richard Tomlinson who, having been sacked, decided to 'sell' his knowledge of the Service. Tomlinson had joined as a potential high-flyer from *The Times* where he had worked as a journalist. He had also been a soldier in the SAS TA unit. His vetting investigation had not been entirely straightforward, with a couple of his referees casting doubt on his suitability for high-level clearance and there had been a failure to take up some of his references. He was nevertheless granted clearance and soon proved to be an eager and enthusiastic SIS officer, perhaps a touch *too* eager to please, some thought. He was also seen as a loner. After being 'sacked' by SIS for 'inefficiency', Tomlinson wrote a book exposing the 'ins and outs' of his time in the Service. A massive effort was mounted to keep the damage limitation to a minimum. As in all cases where there appears to have been a failing in the vetting process, I was tasked to review certain aspects of his case. Part of this was to interview his superior officer in the SAS who confirmed that, had he been asked, he would not have recommended Tomlinson for an appointment in SIS!

One of the most 'colourful' members of the Service whose clearance I reviewed was 'Barry'. Despite being a married man, 'Barry' had the reputation of having a twinkle in his eye, particularly when overseas on a 'job', something which, if true, could have made him vulnerable to blackmail. During my interview with him, 'Barry' freely admitted that, if a single female member of staff in the embassy showed an interest in him, he found it difficult to pass up the opportunity for casual sex. "You see, what I do is exciting, and this seems to rub off on others! After a successful operation, we tend to celebrate and quite often one thing leads to another," he explained. "Does your wife know about your dalliances, and if not, what would you do if someone attempted to pressure you by threatening to tell her?" I asked. Looking me straight in the eye and without any hesitation, 'Barry' said he would have no hesitation in telling his wife. After all, both parties agreed and no false promises were made. He was not in any way proud of his behaviour. It was just that it seemed to go with the territory after a high-pressure, successful operation, sometimes within a hostile environment. My assessment was that he did not constitute a risk and, on my recommendation, his clearance was renewed.

In addition to investigatory work, as one of three team leaders responsible for the allocation and assessment of cases to six or so investigators, I also inherited the section training role. This involved a number of duties which included arranging a two-day training seminar. One year, I arranged for a team from the CIA (Central Intelligence Agency) to come and discuss the case of Aldrich Ames.

Ames and his wife had been arrested by the FBI in February 1994 for providing highly classified information to the Soviet KGB and its successor organisation, the Russian Foreign Intelligence Service. Later, in 1994, Ames was found guilty of espionage and sentenced to life imprisonment: his wife received a five-year prison sentence for conspiracy to commit espionage and tax evasion. Ames received a total of $4.6 million for his spying, making him the highest-paid spy in American history. I arranged to meet the three-man contingent from the CIA under the clock at Waterloo Station and to accompany them to where the seminar was being held. My boss at the time was a formidable woman who wanted to know how I was intending to link up with the team from America. Knowing that she sometimes lacked a sense of humour, I said that I was going to go up to anyone hanging around in the vicinity of the clock at Waterloo Station who looked vaguely American and ask them if they were from the CIA. Her immediate reaction, until she realised I was 'having her on', was one of absolute horror! In the event, I hung around watching people until I was sure (and that was easy, given their trench coats turned up at the collar) they were the right people before introducing myself. The seminar went well, as did the session in the bar that evening, so I feel sure they returned to the USA in good heart, if with slightly sore heads!

The majority of my time in SIS was spent working close to the post-modernist building in Vauxhall Cross on the Thames. Staff dubbed Sir Terry Farrell's vast cream and green-coloured ziggurat 'Legoland'. It was also known as Babylon-on-Thames, for there are sixty terraces, as well as cameras surveying spiked railings from every angle. Staff entered and left as inconspicuously as possible through electronically-controlled gates.

SIS Headquarters, Vauxhall

From time to time, a small group of retired officers from the three Services would go out for a lunchtime 'pint'. Just as we were leaving one Friday, our female 'boss' caught sight of us and enquired where we were going. I replied that we were just off for a haircut. Thereafter, Friday excursions were known as 'Going for a haircut'. Our regular group, christened 'The Musketeers' included Alan Y (retired RN Commander), Trevor G (retired RAF Group Captain), Derek F (retired Colonial Policeman and former member of the Security Service), Jim M and Jeff D (both fellow retired army officers). Together with others, we still continue to meet twice a year in London for an extended 'haircut and lunch', always a pleasant gathering among old friends.

During the week, I lodged with various landladies in London. The two I remember were the daughter of Prince Alexander Obolenski who scored two tries on his debut game for England against the 1936 All Blacks: I lodged with her in Clapham for about eighteen months, and also with June Whitfield who lived in Hurlingham Gardens. From here I used to have my daily run along the Thames towpath, past Fulham football ground and then back along the other side to Putney Bridge – about three miles. Another of the advantages of working in London was having regular contact with the girls. Quite often we met in the evening and one Christmas we had breakfast at The Ritz.

I was in the office when the 9/11 attack on the Twin Towers in New York took place and, along with others, watched the TV pictures beamed to the UK. It was clear that this attack would have a fundamental and lasting effect on the work of the Service. It would now concentrate its work against the real threat of international terrorism. For my part, I was sent to the Service's technical branch near Milton Keynes as the resident vetting officer. Prior to 9/11 the

Breakfast at the Ritz

establishment had been visited by vetting officers whenever there was a need. Once my presence was accepted, the staff embraced the concept on having a vetting officer on site, which led to a number of difficult and controversial cases.

I enjoyed my time working with the technocrats of SIS. It was from here that the rituals of retirement loomed large as I approached the fiftieth anniversary of the 10th May 1954, the day I had joined the Army. In a gesture that I shall never forget, my ex-military colleagues presented me with a framed silver medal inscribed 'For General Service' in recognition of my fifty years' public service and, I suspect, in lieu of the official recognition they perhaps thought that I should have received. After a thoroughly enjoyable social occasion with old chums, I had to attend Head Office where there was to be a gathering of the 'great and good' of the Security Directorate. In my final report, Alastair D, who initially had been my minder and subsequently my superior, wrote:

> Ian comes to the end of fifty years' public service with another characteristically excellent year. Ian is simply the most experienced vetting officer in this, and probably any other, Service. His dedication and enthusiasm for the work of the section is an example to all. His overall contribution to the vetting work of the Service over the years has been immense. HMG, and SIS in particular, has much to thank Ian for – this Service is undoubtedly a more secure place because of his diligent and perceptive vetting work. Well done, Ian, and many thanks for your outstanding contribution.

I was very proud to receive such a glowing testimonial. Earlier that day, I had hosted my own farewell gathering in 'Legoland', attended by Claire, my youngest daughter, who was allowed to enter the building as she too held high-level security clearance from the Army.

That I was no longer a member of SIS was brought home to me when I had to hand in my pass. But there were no tears. During my second career, I had had the privilege of meeting and interviewing some eminent people, including Douglas Hurd, the Foreign Secretary of the day, Professor Christopher Andrew, the Cambridge don, author and leading expert in intelligence matters, and many of the wonderfully gifted senior officers in SIS, including three 'Cs' (Heads of SIS), David Spedding, Richard Dearlove and John Scarlett, latterly of 'Dodgy Dossier' fame, and Harold (Shergy) Shergold, who had been personally involved in the case of the spies George Blake and Oleg Penkovsky. My work took me to many countries, including Jordan,

An Invitation from the Secret Intelligence Service

Italy, Nigeria, Germany, Norway, Sweden, Hong Kong, Bosnia, Pakistan, Spain, Croatia and the Irish Republic.

During a trip to Rome, my colleague Alan Y met the naval attaché in the British Embassy. This chance encounter led to us meeting up that evening for a night out in Rome – and what an evening that turned out to be! I thought army officers could drink until the experience I had in the company of these two seafarers! Before eating, we consumed a 'couple' of beers, followed by copious quantities of red wine over the meal in a restaurant close to the Coliseum. After eating, we continued to drink until I reached the point where I could take no more. My refusal to partake in another round prompted the comment from the naval attaché, "Doesn't your brown job friend drink?" to my colleague, Alan!

I feel privileged to have been part of an organisation which, for so long, has upheld the best traditions of our country in a changing and challenging world. So that, for the first time since I entered the Army aged 16 all those years before, I was no longer employed. What now, as I made my way home with a carload of pictures, books and memorabilia which I had always kept at work? Actually, as subsequent chapters will show, there's really been no such thing as retirement. That I would be a newcomer to the outside world would be a challenge but one which I felt able to face and embrace.

17: Travel – Tigers, New Zealand, Yemen and China

Twenty years from now, you will be more disappointed by the things you didn't do than by the ones you did. So throw off the bowlines, sail away from the safe harbour. Catch the trade winds in your sails: Explore; Dream; Discover – Mark Twain

Ever since I was a boy, exploring on my bicycle or walking in the countryside, I have always loved the adventure of travel – the unknown, something different, something new. This feeling of exploring has remained with me throughout my life. I have been extremely lucky to be able to feed my passion for travel – funnily enough, more so since I left the Army. Travel broadens your mind. You meet new people and share new experiences. I love the freedom of travel and the 'getting away from it all' feeling, while the sensation of having to fend for yourself is extremely powerful.

I have been very fortunate to have been able to travel extensively in my life. Spending some of my formative years in India, that country and the Indian subcontinent generally holds a special place in my heart. What I have decided is to reprint here, and in chapter 15, are a few of the pieces I have written about places I have visited and people I have met. These are reproduced in no particular order.

* * * * *

Tiger! Tiger! (with apologies to Rudyard Kipling)
The Bengal tiger *(panthera tigris tigris)* is a solitary, essentially nocturnal animal, so to see one in the wild is something of a lottery. Despite numerous visits to various national parks in India, including Corbett National Park, named after the famous English tiger hunter-turned-conservationist Jim Corbett, I had failed to catch even a glimpse of the charismatic giant of the cat family. So it was with only a glimmer of hope that I decided to include a visit to Ranthambore National Park during a holiday to Rajasthan, India, in February 2010.

My long-held interest in the tiger was first awakened when, as a small boy, I lived with my parents in India and overheard grown-ups

| Never a Dull Moment

telling tales of their encounters with India's most famous animal. In those days tigers roamed freely, in considerable numbers, throughout the Indian countryside. Then there was Rudyard Kipling's *Tiger! Tiger!* – a tale of the man-eater that was ignominiously trampled in his lair by a herd of buffaloes, and the related poem by William Blake which starts *Tyger! Tyger! burning bright, in the forests of the night* ... which further developed my fascination with the tiger.

Ranthambore is one of India's largest and most famous national parks. It is about 180 km east of Jaipur. Ranthambore was established in 1955. It is currently thought to be home to around forty tigers. The park lies at the edge of a plateau, includes part of the Aravalli Hills, and is bounded to the north and south by rivers. Covering an area of 392 km², the park is made up of dense tropical dry forest, open bush and rocky terrain interspersed with lakes and stream. Other than the tiger, the park is home to leopard, nilgai, wild boar, sambar deer, hyena, monkeys, sloth bear and chital. It has a wide variety of trees, plants, birds, reptiles and a large number of crocodiles.

The day started at around 4.45 am with a cup of *chai* (tea). I was already excited about the possibility of meeting with the most charismatic of all mammals, the Bengal tiger. We entered the park just as dawn was about to break. A mist hung around and there was a real chill in the air, but nothing could quell the anticipation of seeing a tiger. As the sun broke through, it revealed the splendour of the park with its huge escarpments, towering banyan trees and the leafy trails which tourist vehicles are required to follow. I was in the front of the Canter, a 15-seater, open 'spotter' vehicle, painted camouflage green, as it bumped its way over the rough ground. As dawn was breaking, green parrots screeched their way from one tree to another, peacocks foraged for food, spotted deer and nilgai (the largest antelope in India) continued to graze unconcernedly as we passed, and langur monkeys swung noisily through the canopy as we drove around: but no sign of a tiger even though dawn is the time most favoured by the tiger for hunting.

We had been on the go for about an hour and I was beginning to think the worst, when, all of a sudden, the guide raised his hand to bring the vehicle to a halt. His finger, raised to his lips, indicated that he wanted, and got, complete silence. Not too far away, the distinctive alarm call of the langurs was unmistakable. Then the bark of a chital seemed to provide confirmation that a tiger was in the area. With a wave of the guide's hand, accompanied by *Challo!* (Go!), the driver sped off in the direction of the cries of alarm. After travelling a couple of hundred yards, the vehicle slowed and, sensing that we might be in the vicinity of a tiger, everyone's attention was on the undergrowth. The anticipation was palpable.

Suddenly our guide uttered the word we had all been waiting to hear – 'tiger!' – pointing to the undergrowth. There, no more than twenty or so feet away, was a young male tiger. It was a moment of awe. The hairs on the back of my neck were standing up, I felt excitement but not fear, for the tiger seemed completely unconcerned by our presence. You could hear a pin drop as the realisation dawned that this was a very special moment. As the tiger continued on his path through the undergrowth, seemingly oblivious to our presence, I came to my senses and began to snap away in the hope of capturing images of this magnificent creature in the warm light of dawn..

As he got closer and took stock of the situation, I noticed the tiger's topaz eyes, which are both arrogant and dismissive. He had decided that we were of little consequence. He turned to regard us with a look of infinite and bored indifference. It was as though he was used to seeing vehicles, although I suspect it might have been different if we had been on foot! And then, as if relenting, he reached up the tree to claw the bark to reveal his full majesty, I felt the power of his presence and the strength in his body: small wonder that the tiger is a much feared predator. Crossing directly in front of our vehicle, he moved gracefully and deliberately into the undergrowth, on the other side of the path, before disappearing out of sight. He was gone as suddenly as the moment when he first came into sight.

'My' tiger

| Never a Dull Moment

It had been a perfect couple of minutes watching this imperious cat. I felt privileged to have seen one of the last remaining Bengal tigers in the world. The Bengal tiger is the symbol of India's wilderness. Its savage beauty and might, and its ability to melt into the forest like a phantom, makes the tiger an animal of legend and awe. The sense of achievement and good fortune of seeing a tiger in the wild was uplifting and an experience I shall never forget.

Although Project Tiger is making progress to protect the tiger in India, every day that passes sees a further diminution of its habitat. That the skin and bones of the tiger are still in huge demand in China, particularly as 2010 was 'The Year of the Tiger', gives additional cause for concern. Consequently, the pressure of survival in the modern world threatens the very existence of this magnificent creature. My hope is that man will make an even greater effort to protect animals like the Bengal tiger, so that future generations can enjoy the thrill of seeing them in the wild and not behind bars in a zoo.

*****

The Spirit that is New Zealand

As part of our six-week adventure in New Zealand, in January-February 2008, my partner Lynn and I chose to walk the little-known Kaikoura Coast Track (KCT), in addition to a number of New Zealand's better-known 'tramps' like the Tongariro Crossing, Abel Tasman and Queen Charlotte's Track. We were not disappointed.

The KCT starts a mere 1½ hours' easy drive north from Christchurch, the 'capital' of the South Island, and is en route to the town of Kaikoura, known best for its famous dolphin and whale trips, making it a perfect way to explore the east coast. The walk is about 40 km long, an easy three days, and well within the capability of the less experienced, particularly as packs can be ferried ahead by hosts.

A warm welcome awaited us on arrival at the Staging Post, part of the original Hawkswood Estate, owned by the legendary 87-year-old JD Macfarlane whose vision created, along with two other farming families, the KCT in 1994.

After settling into our bunkhouse accommodation, we were granted an 'audience' by JD who, over a glass of wine, explained that the two murals I had spotted on the walls of an adjacent building were depictions of the two actions in the Second World War for which Charles Upham had won his two Victoria Crosses (the highest decoration for 'Valour').

After discovering that Charlie Upham, a Boy's Own hero and Colditz escapee, had farmed locally after the war, the walk assumed a far greater significance for me. The chance of learning more about this remarkable soldier-legend was an opportunity not to be missed.

With JD Macfarlane

Linda, JD's daughter-in-law, with whom we had had convivial supper the night before, took us to the start of the walk. The first part of the track was a fairly gently uphill, which to begin with criss-crossed a stream, through a light forest of regenerated native trees including Black Beech and Tree Fern, to reach the crest of the Hawkswood Range, 50,000 acres of which have been farmed by the Macfarlanes since 1872. The silence was broken only by the cacophony of sound created by crickets while fantails

One of the Upham murals

flitted from branch to branch around us as if to say 'Photograph us if you can'. Ahead was Skull Peak (490 metres) standing proud, which required some scrambling to reach the top in a strong wind. From here, there was a magnificent all-round view of mountains, grazing land and the Pacific Ocean as far as the eye could see. It was now about lunchtime so we headed for the purpose-built hut a short walk away along a good track. The panorama from here was stupendous. The after-lunch walk was more or less downhill through grazing land and meadow bordered with eucalyptus trees to Ngaroma Homestead and that night's charming attic accommodation. That evening the Kaikoura Mountains, in the distance, revealed their tops covered in snow, lit by the orange glow of the setting sun, a magnificent view as we compared the day's walk with two Kiwis who were also tackling the KCT.

Kaikoura Mountains

The second day started with a stimulating three-mile walk along a black-sand beach with the sound of crashing waves from the Pacific, a constant reminder of our vulnerability. The rain was tippling down but this did not detract from the stark beauty of the wilderness where we saw a single pied shag but no other human as we battled against the elements for a couple of hours in the shadow of eroding cliffs while the relics of 800-year-old tree stumps which – rising, Phoenix-like, from the sands – seemed totally out of place.

After leaving the beach, an ancient Maori campsite provided much-needed respite from the incessant driving rain we had endured for the past few hours. It was here that I found a rhododendron stick, which I brought back to the UK and still use. Now, heading inland, we paused at the cliff top to look back along the deserted beach we had negotiated, before crossing acres of grazing land, home to hundreds of ewes, heads down, nibbling the lush grass. Then, somewhat unexpectedly, the track entered a deep gully for an hour's walk through close bush and under a thick canopy of native trees. During this 'phase' we crossed the Medina Stream about ten times. This part of the walk has been covenanted as a conservation area of environmental importance by the Queen Elizabeth Trust. Finally, emerging from the gully, we reached another hilltop pasture and, after descending a 'steepish' hill, rounded an attractive man-made lake before walking uphill in to Medina. It was still raining. The Garden Cottage, our accomm-odation for the night, delightfully situated in the middle of a paddock, provided a snug haven from the elements as we dried our sodden clothes after a testing day's walk. Early

The Kaikoura Coast

Seventieth birthday location and guests

that evening, we were visited by Selina, the farm owner's daughter, who, having heard it was my big 70, had baked me a birthday cake – candles and all. A wonderful gesture and typical of the Kiwis we met throughout our trip.

Next morning, collected in a 4 x 4 by David Handyside, we visited the farm owned by Charles Upham until he died aged 84 in 1994. Before the war, Upham had spent some time working with David's father (Miles Handyside), on his land at Ngaroma, farming sheep, a period he had much enjoyed. So, when Miles Handyside decided to split his farm, he offered Charles Upham the opportunity to buy some land and establish his own farm, a chance he accepted with alacrity. Now owned by an absentee landlord, the farmhouse is situated on a terrace overlooking the sweeps of the coast in one direction and the upsurge of the Kaikoura Mountains in the other. An idyllic location much loved by Upham, his wife Molly and their three children. David Macfarlane, who knew Charles Upham as a close friend and fellow farmer, answered our questions about the great man with patience and obvious candour. In discussing his heroism, David explained that Charles wasn't the only the World War II hero in the area. In fact, the Hawkswood Valley had become known locally as 'Gong Alley' in recognition of the fact that, in addition to Charles Upham's two VCs, David's father had won a DSO and another farming neighbour a DFC and Bar! Some record! Charles Upham's remarkable life story is told in *Mark of the Lion* by Kenneth Sandford (Penguin).

The last day of our walk was to provide probably the sternest challenge. Dropping down to cross a creek, the path then climbed steadily through paddocks of grazing sheep to reach gorse-covered hillsides and eventually, after a stiff climb, to 'summit' Mount Wilson (647 metres). From here the 180° vista was stunning including, tantalisingly, a glimpse of the Staging Post, our final destination, in a distant valley. After descending the Humpy Hills to cross Chilly Stream, a final steep ascent, through sycamores and oaks, brought us back to where we had begun three days previously.

This had not been a particularly challenging 'tramp' but it had most definitely been an enriching and enchanting experience. The track was well maintained, clearly marked and thoughtfully routed through spectacular and varied countryside, and along a ruggedly beautiful coastline. But more than anything it provided an opportunity to meet a cross-section of warm, hospitable and generous Kiwis who host this privately owned track. The Kaikoura Coast Track in all its varied aspects epitomised for us the spirit that is New Zealand.

* * * * *

Why Yemen?

'Why on earth would you want to go there?' was perhaps the understandable reaction of our friends, given the political problems and perceived security risks, to the news that we were going to Yemen on a two-week holiday. I suppose it was a combination of the mysterious, its inaccessibility and the ancient history of the country, the reputed home of the Queen of Sheba, which drew us to Yemen. Also, I had visited Aden during the period when Britain had been engaged fighting the left-leaning insurgency, and I wanted to go back for 'old times' sake'.

The modern Republic of Yemen was born in 1990 when traditionalist North Yemen and Marxist South Yemen merged after years of border wars and skirmishes. But peace broke down in 1994 before a short civil war ended in defeat for separatist southerners and the survival of the unified Yemen. Since then, Yemen has been modernising and opening up to the world, but it still maintains much of its tribal character and old ways. Many people still wear traditional dress, although the tradition of carrying firearms has all but disappeared. Yemen has also gained a reputation as a haven for Islamic militants, including Al-Qaida, which has been an adverse factor in the country's effort to attract tourists.

Our tour started in the capital Sana'a, one of the oldest cities in the world, where the houses are made of mud and brick, are painted with broad white lines, and have a gingerbread look to them. Men walk around in flowing Yemeni-Arab robes with a *jambiya* (a curved dagger) stuck through an embroidered belt, and wearing a *keffiyeh* (traditional Arab headdress fashioned from a square scarf) while using mobile phones. Yemeni women are hardly seen on the streets but when they are, they hurry around in the all-black *burqa* with only their eyes revealed. So it was with some surprise that we came across shops selling lacy, colourful, transparent lingerie which even liberated western women might find too risqué! Being conventional Muslims, most women do not work outside their homes, where they are fully occupied often looking after a large number of children. Photographing Yemeni women is strictly forbidden.

After lunch, Yemen virtually grinds to a halt, when most men can be seen with a bulge in their cheeks, a give-away sign that they are chewing Qat (pronounced 'cat'). Qat is a green leafy plant, the effects of which are something like amphetamine sulphate (Speed). Qat challenges convention. It is legal and illegal, safe and unsafe, and addictive and non-addictive. It depends where you are. In the USA it is illegal, while in the UK it is tolerated. Most men in Sana'a seem to use Qat, while on the island of Socotra we saw very few with the tell-tale sign of a bulging cheek. The taste of Qat is bitter and I thought resembled privet. It did nothing for me! Walking through the *souk* in Sana'a, the somnolent vigil of the Qat-chewers was there for all to see. Unlike most of the rest of the Arabian Peninsula, which is barren, Yemen resembles a green paradise. Yemenis are so inclined to spend a large chunk of their paltry incomes on Qat that farmers generally favour the popular evergreen with its year-round profit. One late afternoon, as I went to the post office in Sana'a, a large number of older men were lying on mats with padded backrests and elbow supports chewing their Qat, while a heated discussion ensued – almost certainly about the prevailing political unrest.

Qat users

One of our early visits in Sana'a was to the Al Saleh Mosque. Built on the instructions of, and supposedly financed by, President Ali Abdullah Saleh, the mosque is characterised by its six distinctive minarets, each reaching a height of 100 metres. Most materials used in the construction were sourced locally. The main hall has a capacity of 13,000 worshippers and has a smaller prayer hall for women. The mosque combines traditional Islamic elements and Yemeni architectural features. The stained glass windows are stunning. Despite rumblings among the populace, including our driver Khalid, that the $60 million used for the construction could have been better spent on hospitals and the like, the mosque is hugely impressive and a place of great beauty.

After a day in Sana'a, we took a flight to Socotra. Located some 200 miles off the southern coast of Yemen, in the Indian Ocean, Socotra and its little archipelago is home to flora and fauna found nowhere else on earth.

Al Saleh Mosque, Sana'a

The Socotra archipelago is one of the most remote places on earth, but with the introduction of two flights a week, the islands are slowly opening up to the world. After landing, we made straight for the capital Hadibo, located beneath the granite peaks of the Haggeher Mountains. Hadibo is a functional town which provides a meeting-place for Socotran society, including the many distinctive Negroes descended from slaves brought to the island from Africa.

Dragon's Blood trees

Leaving Hadibo, we headed up into the mountains for two days' trekking. Rising to over 1,500 metres, the Haggehers dominate the skyline throughout the island. Moving along the Diksam Plateau, we walked freely among the iconic Dragon's Blood trees. The trees are almost surreal. They look like an umbrella stuck in the ground as they grow in profusion on the hillsides.

The famous red resin that gives it its name is exuded from the bark after wounding. The medicinal and colouring property of this resin was recorded by the ancient civilisations of Greece and Rome. It continues to be used in medicine, dyes, varnish and incense. Our first day's walking took us deep into the mountains. As we climbed, the vegetation varied between nondescript bushes and fabled trees including Frankincense, Desert Rose and the Cucumber Tree. Some of the scenery was stunning with huge granite peaks rising from deep valleys cut through the mountains by rivers swollen during the monsoon.

Our camp on the second night was close to a settlement of cave-dwellers who were quick to seize on the opportunity of selling us a goat for supper. The Yemenis have an unsentimental affection for their animals. Having agreed a price, the goat was blessed and then despatched by having its throat cut. I did however find it somewhat incongruous that the 'farmer' lovingly cradled the goat in his arms when he was about to butcher the animal.

Egyptian Vultures

That said, the animal was quickly killed. Goats are to Yemen as cows are to India: ubiquitous and free-roaming – but not sacred! No sooner had the goat been killed than Egyptian vultures could be seen circling above, before swooping down in numbers to compete for the intestines. Socotra has, apparently, one of the world's largest colonies of this large bird, with its yellow face and considerable wing-span.

After leaving the mountains, we camped on the beautiful white sands at Amaq on the south coast, lulled to sleep by the sound of the surf. Next day, we drove through the fertile Wadi Dirhur, where we spent a pleasant couple of hours lunching, and swimming in one of the many natural pools in the area. We next visited Hoq Cave. Ascending 350 metres on foot through scrubland, we reached the cave after about an hour. From an unspectacular entrance, the cave stretches for about three kilometres into the rock to reveal a magical world of huge stalagmites and stalactites dating back thousands of years. And there is still more to come, for the cave is only partially explored. This is a 'not to be missed' place.

On our way to Ditwah, we passed a number of abandoned Russian tanks, relics of the military aid given to South Yemen in its battle with the North. When asked what the Russians had contributed to life on Socotra, an islander was heard to say, "Tanks and alcohol was all they gave us!" The protected area of Ditwah, adjacent to a shallow lagoon, was where we spent an idyllic night sleeping under the stars so bright you could almost read by them. Walking around the lagoon, we met up with a local fisherman who volunteered to reveal some of the fish resident in the lagoon. Using his hands and a small stick, he located and picked up an octopus, a Moray eel, two balloon fish, a sea urchin, a starfish and sea cucumber. We spent a wonderful hour in his company which he willingly gave us without thought of payment.

The next morning we boarded a brightly painted *sambuq* at Qalansiya, a picturesque fishing village, for our trip to Socotra's westernmost point.

Powered by a Japanese outboard engine, our Sambuq cut its way through the swell with consummate ease. We

Qalansiya

waited for a while watching the black cormorants nest in the cliffs and sooty gulls enjoying the early morning sun. Then the dolphins turned up, leaping from the turquoise water, catapulting themselves into corkscrews and flopping on their sides as if to say, "Are you watching?" We spent the remainder of the morning on a deserted white-sand beach squinting into the shimmering crystal-clear, sapphire-blue water on the lookout for stingrays which are said to lurk in the shifting sands below the breakers. Suddenly we caught sight of one as it twisted and turned through the shallows into deep water and was gone.

Then it was back to Hadibo for our last night in the modern comfort of the Summerland Hotel. Before leaving to catch the plane back to the mainland, I decided to take a last walk. In doing so, I came across a demonstration in support of regime change. After asking a policeman for permission, I took a couple of photos before returning to the hotel. One or two of my fellow travellers also took photos. As we assembled in the foyer, the local Tourist Inspector of Police asked us to delete any photos we might have taken of the demonstration. As you can see, I did not!

Unrest on Socotra

Because unrest had spread while we were on Socotra, our scheduled programme had to be altered to take out planned visits to Aden, Taez and Ibb. Instead, we returned to Sana'a and next day ventured out to visit Wadi Dahr. Gazing over several miles of cultivated land a thousand feet below, in an amphitheatre setting surrounded by ancient watch-towers, the view was breathtaking. The focal point of this surreal landscape was the former Imam's Palace like a plug of sandstone rising vertically, with a traditional Yemeni mansion on the top. This astonishing building is one of the iconic images of Yemen. It was formerly the residence of Imam Yahya but until recently, when it was restored and reopened to the public, it had languished unoccupied for many years.

On the route to and from Sana'a we passed through at least four check-points of varying size, manned by either the army or the police. One or two consisted of a couple of soldiers with sub-machine guns slung across their bodies while the others were manned by far more soldiers supported by menacing armoured vehicles, mounted with heavy machine guns, parked for all to see. Soldiers of the Yemeni Army do not inspire confidence. They look a 'rag, tag and bobtail' outfit wearing scruffy

Imam's Palace

uniforms, boots unlaced, unshaven and, worst of all, obviously chewing Qat! That they have opened fire indiscriminately on protestors is not in the least surprising! Political unrest in Yemen is due to a significant number of Yemenis wanting President Ali Abdullah Saleh to stand aside after 32 years in power. The situation is exacerbated by a sense of exclusion felt by those in the south of the country.

Kindness, a keen sense of humour and generous hospitality are the heart of Yemeni life. Yemen has a wealth of natural resources to develop as a major tourist destination. But the news that the security forces are now regularly opening fire on demonstrators and further destabilising the country is sad and does not augur well for tourism. I was glad to see Yemen when I did and, *Inshalla*, I hope the country overcomes its travails to return to a way of life free of bloodshed and strife, for it would then become available for all to visit.

I visited Yemen, during the period 27th February to 10th March 2011.

* * * * *

Wild Swans and Chopsticks

My journey began in Hong Kong where, seeing a PLA sentry standing underneath the Chinese flag at the entrance to the Prince of Wales Building, formerly HQ British Forces, provided a stark reminder that the former colony had been handed back to the Chinese on 30th June 1997. Otherwise not much seemed to have changed in recent times. The green and white Star Ferry vessels, that I first used in 1949, were still plying between Hong Kong and Kowloon; Sam the Tailor, an institution, still made shirts for the world's celebrities and shopping for

Former Prince of Wales Building

a bargain remained the preoccupation for most residents.

Next, after a comfortable flight with China Airlines, I was been met by a diminutive official of China Travel who took me to my hotel in central Shanghai. She knew nothing of my request to visit a farm and she seemed flustered when I declined her offer to show me around the following day. She would have to check with Head Office (or was that the PSB (Chinese police?) Next morning, I set off on foot to explore the narrow, densely packed lanes of this unique Asian city, home to 15 million. It is a place where old and new has evolved and now happily co-exists. Of the 'old', the former residence of Doctor Sun Yat-Sen, hailed as 'Father of the Chinese Republic' created the most profound impression. Beautifully maintained, the house had a tangible sense of history about it. Even the façade in the library provided historical evidence of the purge of all books, ordered by Mao Tse-Tung, as part of the Cultural Revolution. Elsewhere, the new is epitomised by Asia's tallest building, the Oriental Pearl TV Tower, a fascinating contrast to the stately colonial waterfront on the opposite side of the busy Huangpu River. The remarkable urban generation of the Pudong, which was paddy fields until 10 years ago, is proof that Shanghai is a city on the move.

The following morning, my 'minder' announced that she had been given permission to take me to a farm, but before that we would visit the Bund (formerly the commercial centre of Shanghai). I thought it best not to tell her that I had spent most of the previous day soaking up the sights and sounds of that area. The only landmark I remember her pointing out, which I had not previously seen, was the sign in the

The Bund, Shanghai

former French Concession that read 'Chinese and Dogs Keep Out'! We then took a hair-raising ride, in an 'office' car, to the farm. This turned out to be a huge area of greenhouses employing intensive hydro-cultivation methods first developed in Scandinavia!

The next morning, at Shanghai's rambling main railway station I was confronted by a maelstrom of swirling colour, movement and noise.

People scurried around like ants under attack trying to find an escape, burdened with an assortment of luggage, making it impossible for them to change direction without bumping into each other. And, always in the background, security staff in their olive green uniforms.

Being unable to read, or for that matter speak, any Chinese it was a matter of considerable luck that I found myself at the correct platform. I knew this since, after examining my soft-sleeper ticket (there were hard-sleepers) to Guangzhou (formerly Canton), the railway official waved me through the barrier. At the train was pandemonium. Bodies were crammed in like sardines. Every carriage was packed to the doors, with passengers desperately fighting their way onto the train, even though there were still 20 minutes to departure. A friendly-faced young female in uniform saw my pathetic plight, came over and, with a smile guaranteed to lift morale, pointed to my carriage. After depositing my rucksack on the lower berth (knowing that my ticket was for the upper one) I did not have long to wait before my companions for the 26-hour journey 'revealed' themselves.

Dr Sun Yat-Sen's house

Having boarded the train at Shanghai station, I didn't have to wait long before my travelling companions arrived. First a middle aged couple, followed by a single man, who, after twice looking at his ticket, and me, decided to cut his losses and accept the upper bunk. Meanwhile, the couple, having sorted out an assortment of plastic bags, proceeded to partially undress before donning flannel pyjamas. About an hour after leaving

A busker, Chinese style

Shanghai, the older man suddenly asked me what I was reading. To my relief, he seemed unaware that Yung Chang's *Wild Swans* was at one time banned in his country. It transpired that he was a professor of mathematics, who had studied at London University in the 1980s, on his way to deliver a 'paper' at Guangzhou University.

Looking out of the train window in the Yangzi Basin was like watching a repetitive programme on farming. Field followed field; men in black, mostly carrying umbrellas, stood around watching bullocks grazing; submerged ploughs prepared rice fields for planting and vast tracts of reddish soil were interspersed with shanty villages. Conversation with the professor ensured that I was never bored nor left wondering about some aspect of life in his country. As twilight descended, the smell of the professor's wife preparing their evening meal of noodles in the carriage made me hungry. With the aid of a short lesson in Cantonese from the professor, I set off to find some food. 'Mei fei son', I spluttered. The very fat waiter, who was smoking a foul smelling cigarette, ignored me. This prompted a soldier, who was lolling in the seat opposite, to say something that made the waiter return to our table. Another official-looking fat man, who had the most enormous bunch of keys dangling from his belt, joined us and a heated discussion ensued. Just as matters seemed to be getting out of control, my guardian angel, the professor, arrived and, after a few words from him, it was smiles all round. My bowl of vegetables and rice was delicious and well worth the trouble of trying to use chopsticks.

When I returned to the carriage my three companions were locked in discussion. This was the first time I had heard the young man say anything. 'Our friend heart surgeon' the professor revealed during a lull in their conversation. Thereafter, the journey took on a different perspective! The ensuing question and answer session was fascinating.

Sunrise over the Pearl River

What was I writing? A travelogue. What was my work? A civil servant. "Xisi" (spy) retorted the professor with a smirk. At that moment, the carriage door opened to reveal a young woman in a blue uniform. I produced my passport as requested, which she took an age to thumb through. Oh yes, she knew exactly what she was looking for, the professor confirmed after the young woman had left.

My travelling companions

After a fitful nights sleep I woke to the sound of the brakes being applied as we arrived at Changsha, a major rail terminus. The professor announced that he too was awake with a burp, a f..t and a cough! Alighting to stretch my legs, the concrete structure, without any of the adornments usually found on railway stations in the UK, made a depressing sight. But there was no shortage of manpower, with at least two attendants and a policeman for each of the twenty carriages, and a large team of cleaners, wearing bright yellow jackets, sweeping the platform! The professor's wife produced a tasty breakfast of noodles for us all as we continued our journey. River after river, into and out of tunnels, including the longest in China of 14 kilometres guarded at all times by the PLA, and eventually some hills and trees to break the monotony. After travelling some 1100 miles we arrived, on time at Guangzhou: eat your heart out British train operating companies.

A seething mass was trying to get out of the station: eventually I made it through but no sign of my guide. I hung around for 30 minutes before deciding to find a hotel. Just as I'm about to hail a taxi, I see a young woman, smartly dressed, obviously looking for someone. When we got to the hotel and I saw myself in the hotel lobby mirror, I understood why she had chosen to ignore my presence at the station! Next morning, I opened the curtains to a magnificent sunrise over the Pearl River, twinkling with an irresistible beauty, which will be hard to forget. After a trip around the town, with very little to commend it, I caught the hydrofoil back to Hong Kong. So ended a week's adventure to a country, steeped in history and culture which will continue to perplex, fascinate and concern the rest of the world.

18: Family Matters

Knowing that this chapter was going to be difficult to write, I have left it to last. If what I have to say causes anyone hurt, then I am truly sorry. But if I were to skate over certain issues, my story would be incomplete and my family would know that I had taken the easy way out. I am, of course, referring to my unfaithfulness which ultimately led to the irrevocable breakdown of my marriage to Angelika when, in December 2005, she asked me to leave. To put matters into perspective, she had previously threatened me with expulsion but had relented on an assurance that I would not stray again. So, what happened? I think it is necessary to turn the clock back to the circumstances in which we had first met. Angelika was a beautiful young woman and I quickly fell for her even though we were worlds apart in background, culture and, of course, nationality. But this did not seem to matter: love is blind and all that. We became engaged quite quickly and married within six months. It was an exciting time and I was in love with being in love. My parents liked her and were supportive of our plans to marry, even though my commanding officer had sounded alarm bells by saying that he thought she was unsuitable. I think this made me more determined to go ahead. Angelika's friends and family also had misgivings and it was her sister, Ingrid, I think, who said she would be back home within six months.

In fact, Angelika survived a very difficult time when we returned to England to live in a small semi-detached house in Salisbury during which time Vivian was born. Angelika spoke very little English; she had no friends and our social life was non-existent. We also struggled for money. It is greatly to her credit that she 'got on with it' and, in doing so, allowed me to work without worrying, which is something she did throughout our 42 years together. She was a marvellous wife and mother, and made a significant contribution to any success I may have had in life. So, what went wrong? Basically, I was unfaithful. Why I strayed is a more difficult question to answer. This is no place to try and analyse the reasons, but the fact is that I was attracted to others and weak enough to accept a couple of opportunities to stray which came my way. I'm not proud of what I did nor can I make any excuses. But, to use a rather overused cliché, I do think 'we grew apart'. I still had a zest for life: sport and physical fitness were important to me; I was selfish and perhaps self-absorbed, whereas Angelika was happy in her home and enjoyed running her very successful Bed and Breakfast business. I could go on but this would serve little or no purpose. I had a couple of affairs: she found out and for her that was, justifiably, the final straw and she asked me to leave.

During the summer of 1976, my last season of Army cricket, the team were invited to a party where I met a young woman, Lynn Francis, who worked at the animal research laboratory at Porton Down. There was an immediate and very strong mutual attraction. She was single and had her own house in a nearby village. I started an affair with her which carried on until I was posted to Germany, although we continued to keep in touch. She eventually got married, had two children and ran a business with her husband, Bill, not far from Newbury. I had no contact with her until, out of the blue, she wrote in 2002 saying that she had completed the 125-mile Devizes to Westminster Canoe Race which she knew would be of interest to me. We subsequently met for dinner when I was working at Hanslope Park, and I knew the chemistry between us was still there after all those years. She then came with me on a walking holiday in Ireland and our affair was rekindled. Angelika found out and told me to pack

With Lynn in New Zealand, 2008

my bags. I did and moved into a small town house in Downham Market which Lynn visited as often as she could. She then decided to leave Bill her husband, but not until her two daughters Clare and Amy had finished their exams. It was in June 2007 that we set up home in Wantage, chosen to be near enough for Amy and Clare to retain their social life.

Wantage, within the M4 corridor, was never our preferred area so, once Amy had finished at Cambridge and gone to work in Canada and Clare had started teaching, we moved to Langton Matravers. We now live in an idyllic location with views across the Isle of Purbeck to Nine Barrow Down and east over Swanage, a traditional seaside town, to the Isle of Wight: hence Island View, the name of the house.

Vivian left school in 1982 after taking and passing her A Levels. The school had put her forward for a place at Newham College, Oxford. She found the interview a traumatic experience and was judged not to possess the qualities to be offered a place. She was then presented with her Duke of Edinburgh's Gold Award at Buckingham Palace by The Duke of Edinburgh. Vivian made some close friends at St Margaret's, two of whom she still sees today. Not sure what she was going to do, Vivian spent six months as an *au pair* with an aristocratic German family outside Munich – with the aim of improving her spoken German. This was not a particularly pleasant or productive time as the family treated her like a servant. Returning to the UK, she got a job working at Barclays Bank, Downham Market, before transferring to the Cavendish Square branch in London in 1984. With basic banking experience 'under her belt', she got a job with Nomura, a Japanese multinational conglomerate of financial services, as an assistant in the Money Market team.

By this time Juliet had moved to London and soon after the girls bought their first flat in Harbut Road, Clapham, together. After spending seven years in the banking sector, Vivian decided to change direction and trained as a Montessori teacher. Montessori education is characterised by an emphasis on independence, freedom within limits, and respect for a child's natural psychological development, whilst bearing in mind technological advancements in society. Around the same time, she started a relationship with Rob and decided to go to Tokyo with him. Once there, she taught Montessori and told me that living in Japan had a 'profound positive impact on her self-confidence'. Sadly, the relationship did not work out and Vivian returned to England, but not before she was able to see me compete in the 1993 Veteran World Championships in Miyasaki. It was lovely to see her there and I shall never forget our post-race evening together.

Vivian and I at the World Veterans' Championship

Vivian and David 31st May 1997

Soon after returning to England, Vivian got a job working abroad for the wife of the Sheikh of Ras al-Khaimah, one of the emirates of the United Arab Emirates, in the east of the Persian Gulf. I visited her during the year she was there, without managing to meet the Portuguese engineer with whom she was involved at the time! Returning home, Vivian again worked at a Montessori School in London before meeting and starting a relationship with David Lloyd-Seed, at Juliet's wedding, which was to turn out to be 'the real thing' as they were married from home nearly two years later, on 31st May 1997. The wedding was such an emotional roller-coaster that I was unable to stop a tear as I said goodbye to the newly-married couple at the end of a truly memorable day.

Vivian and David have two lovely children, Megan and Alec, and live in a large detached house in Worplesdon, not far from Guildford. Both children are doing very well.

Alec and Megan taken 2012

At the time of writing, David works for Dixons Retail plc, one of the largest consumer electronics retailers in Europe, as their Corporate Affairs Director.

Juliet and Vivian both started at St Margaret's in 1975, when Juliet was 9 and Vivian 11. Being younger, Juliet left school two years after Vivian in 1984. Juliet took her A Levels but did not do as well as was expected and started a 'crammer' at King's Lynn Technical College with a view to achieving better grades. Juliet became unsettled and just wanted to start work, so she left college and got a job as a Grade 10 civil servant working in the Falkland Islands Department in the Foreign and

Commonwealth Office. She lived in their hostel in Queen's Gate but never really settled and found the salary barely enough to live on. Consequently, she resigned after a year, came home and started a secretarial course at Cambridge, from which she successfully graduated after nine months' hard work. She went back to London and in a succession of jobs worked for Bosch, Westminster Estates and Jackson the estate agents. Juliet then got a job with Charterhouse Tilney Securities with whom, over a period of eight years, she had a series of appointments including Director's Secretary, Chairman's Personal Assistant, Corporate Entertainment Manager and Corporate Finance Executive, which she found too pressurised so stepped down to become Office Manager. It was during this time that she met, and subsequently married, Jonathan Page, who was working in the City. They were married from Rose Cottage, on 8th July 1995, an occasion unlikely to be forgotten by anyone who was there. It was a great celebration.

For a time after she got married, Juliet continued to work for Le Club Tricolore, a London-based learning centre in French with a variety of activities for children and adults alike. It was during this time that Juliet designed and supervised work on a house they bought in Clapham. So successful was this project that, over time, they purchased three flats before reinstating the property into a large London house in Nightingale Square. This was a highly successful and

Juliet and Jonathan 8th July 1995

profitable project which was all due to Juliet's vision and management skills.

In 1999, by which time Juliet had given birth to Hugo, Jonathan got a job in Hong Kong. They had a house in Chung Hom Kok, very close to Repulse Bay where we had all lived in the 1960s. Another coincidence was that Juliet had her second son Oliver at the Matilda Hospital where she herself had been born in 1966 when it was the Army maternity hospital, BMH Mount Kellett. In November 2002, an outbreak of what was believed to be severe acute respiratory syndrome (SARS) began in the Guangdong province of China, which borders on Hong Kong. By early 2003, SARS had spread to Hong Kong, at which point Juliet, who was pregnant with Theo, came home. Juliet took a rented house in Winchester for just under a year, during which time Theo was born.

Returning to Hong Kong with three boys, the family moved into a house overlooking the sea in the same complex where they had previously lived. Jonathan was now working for a firm of stockbrokers, successfully selling Asian equities in the Benelux countries and Australia. In 2005, Theo was diagnosed with autism, confirmed by a world-renowned specialist whom Juliet visited in Australia. The confirmed diagnosis was of a mild form of autism and one which, all things being equal, would allow him to lead a reasonably normal life. Since then, Theo has received a massive amount of one-to-one therapy and is now able to take his place at school without personal supervision. It is to be hoped that he continues to develop positively throughout his secondary education and, in time, enable him to lead a normal life.

In addition to having to contend with the extra care Theo required, Jonathan announced in January 2006 that he was having an affair. Juliet stayed in Hong Kong for a year, hoping to save her marriage before eventually giving up and coming home in April 2007. By this time Jonathan had bought a partially converted barn near Truro, the full renovation of which Juliet supervised over 18 or so months from a small house they rented in a neighbouring village. Tredinnick Barn, when finished, provided a marvellous home but this had to be sold when Juliet decided she could take no more, after Jonathan became a father to the other woman's child. Juliet ultimately divorced Jonathan in 2011 and now lives with her three sons Hugo, Oliver and Theo, in Truro. All three boys are doing well. Hugo and Oliver who started at Truro School in 2011 are now making their mark as good all-rounders. Great credit is due to Juliet for the way she has nurtured the boys through a difficult period to give them the best opportunity of making a success in life.

Hugo, Theo and Ollie 2012

    Juliet has just started work again doing house design which she loves and at which she is very talented.

    A part of Claire's life, including her considerable athletic prowess, has already been featured, so I will take up her story after we returned from Fallingbostel. Claire got a job with Bendal Roberts, solicitors in Ely, before moving to Cambridge to work for Few & Kester, also solicitors. In, I think 1990, she moved to London and got a job with Boodle Hatfield, a highly successful law firm which has been in business since 1722. But such was her success in the TA, Claire decided to apply for a regular commission. Passing the Regular Commissions Board, she went to the Royal Military Academy in early 1992 and was commissioned into the Adjutant-General's Corps later that year.

'Rambo' VA at Sandhurst

Family Matters |

I was immensely proud to attend Claire's passing out parade at Sandhurst.

In becoming an army officer, she became the sixth consecutive generation of Vaughan-Arbuckles to do so. We bought Claire a Westie, which she named Campbell, as a Christmas present and he too turned out to be a wonderful companion .

Since then her postings have included Northern Ireland and Kosovo, where she was awarded a commendation for excellence by the commanding General. As a result of consistently high-grade reports, Claire was promoted before her time and, at the time of writing is a Major.

Proud day at Sandhurst

In 2006 Claire met Jim Hudson, an outgoing sort, who was into cycling and gliding, and married him on 21st June 2008.

Claire and Jim 21st June 2008

| Never a Dull Moment

Unlike Vivian and Juliet, Claire and Jim chose to organise their own wedding, using a hotel in Winchester. It was a wonderful occasion, blessed by good weather and a nice mix of solemnity and informality. They have been blessed with two lovely children, Tom and Emily.

Jim and Tom, Claire and Emily September 2012

Pooling their resources they bought a house backing onto the Royal Winchester Golf Club which they redesigned and refurbished. It is from here that Jim runs his own successful audio-visual design business. It seems likely that Claire will leave the Army sooner or later to concentrate on family affairs.

Juliet's engagement celebration, 1994

Family Matters

Family in 1998

Claire, Juliet and Vivian circa 2009

The 'gang' including Campbell circa 2006

| Never a Dull Moment

My 70th

Epilogue

The Moving Finger writes; and having writ,
Moves on: nor all thy Piety nor Wit
Shall lure it back to cancel half a Line,
Nor all thy Tears wash out a word of it.
Omar Khayyam

As I come to the end of my ramblings, what, I ask myself, does the future hold for people of my age and older who find themselves in areas of our country almost entirely populated by those from foreign countries? Our kith and kin are mostly decent, friendly folk – but where for them is the multicultural experience dreamt of by Tony Blair and perpetuated by his successors? To my mind, this policy, which was supposed to be good for the country, has had the opposite effect so that the welfare system is in crisis, the roads are congested and badly maintained, our streets are filthy, the police are struggling to cope with violent crime mostly committed by young black men, the NHS is falling apart, schools are overcrowded, the standard of our secondary education is overrated, our magnificent Armed Forces are being dangerously reduced – and we have no money. And then there's the Royal Mail which was, until a few years ago, the most reliable postal service in the world and is now totally unreliable, inefficient and costly. Worst of all, free speech is a thing of the past. Whoever coined the term 'Politically Correct' did our society a massive disservice. Can we still call ourselves a real democracy when people are terrified of saying what they really think for fear of being reported as being a racist! And, what about the insipid celebrity culture which is consuming our sensibilities? I'm not an angry old man or a racist, but I am concerned at the way our country is heading towards mediocrity because of weak and ineffectual leadership, and I fear things have gone too far to reverse the ill-considered policies which have brought us to this point.

The Army is a brotherhood of which I am proud to have been a part. I have often reflected on the fact that, by dint of circumstances beyond my control, I have never seen action under fire. On one hand, I'm grateful but, on the other, it is something that makes me feel cheated for not having done so. It is easy to be brave from a distance but, faced with live combat, how would I have coped? There remains, therefore, an unanswered question of 'How would I have reacted to real danger?'

The Army gave me the most comprehensive and far-reaching training and experience one could wish for. For this I owe the Army an enormous debt of gratitude. Any success I might have had after, largely, wasting my time at school, I got from my time in the Army. The qualities of commitment, loyalty and determination, inculcated by the Army, have stood me in good stead. What young people need in today's Britain is a good dose of these basic qualities. If role models are needed, there are plenty on our television screens returning home from Afghanistan, particularly those with horrific injuries, who just get on with their lives without complaining. They have every reason to give up, but they don't.

A large part of the problem of unfitness and being overweight is that our children spend too much time in front of screens rather than enjoying the benefits of playing outside. I can remember a time when it was possible to roam unsupervised all day: I did and no serious harm ever befell me. This enabled me to develop the confidence and skills of being self-sufficient. Significantly, there were no daft 'Health & Safety' regulations to restrict me when I was growing up! Getting outdoors and closer to nature has all sorts of benefits for children. It keeps them fit, they can learn about the world around them: it's fun and, most of all, it costs nothing.

Whether my life has been a success is for others to decide. What I do know is that I have enjoyed my time and I hope this continues to the end. Getting the balance in life between family, career and society was never easy. I count myself fortunate to have lived when I have, and to have experienced the final years of the British Empire. Some people will run down our record as colonisers but, during my travels, I have heard little negativity. On the contrary, particularly in India, people look back on the days of the Raj with fond memories.

I have had a good run, I have no major regrets although, looking back, I might have handled a few personal situations differently. People have said that I suffer from being impetuous and impulsive: I agree, but I would be rather this than being labelled dithering and indecisive. I consider myself a positive person. Accepting that you can't perform at the level you once did and managing one's own expectations, is hard as you grow older. The poem *If* by Rudyard Kipling (1865-1936) contains mottos and maxims for life, and the poem is also a blueprint for personal integrity, behaviour and self-development. I reproduce it here as an easy reference, and commend it to anyone who might need some inspirational words from time to time:

IF you can keep your head when all about you
Are losing theirs and blaming it on you,
If you can trust yourself when all men doubt you,
But make allowance for their doubting too;
If you can wait and not be tired by waiting,
Or being lied about, don't deal in lies,
Or being hated, don't give way to hating,
And yet don't look too good, nor talk too wise:

If you can dream - and not make dreams your master;
If you can think - and not make thoughts your aim;
If you can meet with Triumph and Disaster
And treat those two impostors just the same;
If you can bear to hear the truth you've spoken
Twisted by knaves to make a trap for fools,
Or watch the things you gave your life to, broken,
And stoop and build 'em up with worn-out tools:

If you can make one heap of all your winnings
And risk it on one turn of pitch-and-toss,
And lose, and start again at your beginnings
And never breathe a word about your loss;
If you can force your heart and nerve and sinew
To serve your turn long after they are gone,
And so hold on when there is nothing in you
Except the Will which says to them: 'Hold on!'

If you can talk with crowds and keep your virtue,
' Or walk with Kings - nor lose the common touch,
if neither foes nor loving friends can hurt you,
If all men count with you, but none too much;
If you can fill the unforgiving minute
With sixty seconds' worth of distance run,
Yours is the Earth and everything that's in it,
And - which is more – you'll be a Man, my son!

I am grateful for the experience of having served with so many fine soldiers in an army career spanning 31 years, and to have, subsequently, worked with and for some fine people in SIS was a great privilege. Throughout my working life I cannot remember waking with a negative thought that I had to go to work, nor do I recall there being a period when life was routine: in fact, I cannot recall a dull moment. I like to have my glass half-full, not half-empty. I have thoroughly enjoyed my travels and the variety of experiences these have brought me, particularly in the Indian subcontinent where I have crossed paths with people from many diverse backgrounds.

If I were to be asked whether I would do it all over again, my answer would be an unhesitating 'Yes'. I have written this book to record my life, for I believe that everyone has a tale to tell, and to chart the history of the Vaughan-Arbuckle family before the name 'dies' at the end of this generation. Writing these memoirs has been an adventure because, in writing them, I have been discovering myself and reliving times I had forgotten. There is also an acute sense of relief that, after so long thinking about it, the book is shortly to be published.

I want to thank my family for the unwavering support and love they have given me as I made my way in life. I could not have done it without them. I am an extremely proud of the way Vivian, Juliet and Claire have conducted their lives and brought up their children. I wish my grandchildren – Hugo, Megan, Oliver, Alec, Theo, Tom and Emily – happy, successful and healthy lives. Finally, I wish to record my love, affection and admiration for two ladies, Angelika and Lynn, who have both, in different ways, played such an important part in my life.

GLOSSARY

Ranks in the British Army

Non-Commissioned Ranks (Soldiers)
Private
Lance-Corporal
Corporal
Sergeant
Staff Sergeant
Company Sergeant-Major (Warrant Officer Class II)
Regimental Sergeant-Major (Warrant Officer Class I)

Commissioned Ranks (Officers)
Second Lieutenant
Lieutenant
Captain
Major
Lieutenant-Colonel
Colonel
Brigadier
Major-General
Lieutenant-General
General
Field-Marshal

Note: The above are in ascending order

RASC – Royal Army Service Corps
Blighty – American slang for England
Yomp – Royal Marines slang describing a long-distance march carrying full kit
FILOG – Falkland Islands Logistic Battalion
RCT – Royal Corps of Transport
Dal baht – boiled yellow lentils

Chapatis – unleavened bread baked in a clay oven
Pugree – turban-like headdress usually adorned with a regimental head band
HQ – Headquarters
BOAC – British Overseas Airways Corporation
DSO – Distinguished Service Order
DFC – Distinguished Flying Cross
CMG – Companion of the Order of St Michael and St George
Chawkidar – guard
NATO – North Atlantic Treaty Organisation

Never a Dull Moment – Timeline

1938	– Born Cairo, Egypt
1939-45	– Wartime in England
1945-47	– India
1947-48	– Hong Kong
1948-50	– St Margaret's School, Walton-on-Thames
1950-54	– The King's School, Peterborough
1954	– Joined the Army
1958-59	– Pakistan
1960	– Commissioned and UK
1962-64	– West Germany and married Angelika
1964-66	– UK: Vivian born
1966-71	– Hong Kong: Juliet and Claire born. Promoted Major
1971-76	– UK: captain of Army cricket
1976-78	– West Germany
1978-79	– Turkey
1979-84	– UK: promoted Lieutenant-Colonel and command of TA regiment
1984	– Falkland Islands
1984-85	– UK: retired from Army
1985-88	– UK and West Germany with Army Security Vetting Unit
1989-2004	– UK: Secret Intelligence Service
2004	– Retired to Norfolk
2005	– Separated
2007 ff	– Living with Lynn Francis